The Methodology of Comparative Research

The Methodology of Comparative Research

Edited by

ROBERT T. HOLT
AND JOHN E. TURNER

*A Symposium from the Center for Comparative Studies
in Technological Development and Social Change and the
Department of Political Science, University of Minnesota*

THE FREE PRESS, NEW YORK
Collier-Macmillan Limited, London

*The Free Press
A Division of the Macmillan Company
866 Third Avenue, New York, New York 10022*

Collier-Macmillan Canada Ltd., Toronto, Ontario

Library of Congress Catalog Card Number: 70–80471

Printed in the United States of America

PRINTING NUMBER
1 2 3 4 5 6 7 8 9 10

*To the challenging future
in Comparative Research*

Contents

Preface

THIS volume grew out of the seminar in comparative methodology, which is an important ingredient in the graduate curriculum in political science at the University of Minnesota. In the spring of 1966, the seminar members were privileged to have distinguished scholars in the field of comparative politics and methodology discuss significant research problems with them. The seminar, however, was not conducted in the usual way. Minnesota scholars in other social sciences, as well as the political science comparativists, attended many of the sessions. The format was this: each invited scholar prepared a written essay especially for the occasion, and these were duplicated and distributed among all seminar participants well in advance of the discussion meetings. On the basis of the seminar critiques, the authors then revised their essays and prepared them for publication. Needless to say, a seminar conducted in this way is a highly beneficial enterprise.

The editors of this work have enjoyed the task of getting it ready for the bookshops. The various authors have been most cooperative in taking time from their busy schedules to revise their essays in accordance with the suggestions that were sent to them. We want to take this opportunity to thank them not only for helping us to meet the publication deadlines, but also for sharing their wisdom with our graduate students.

Appreciation must also be expressed to the Department of Political Science at the University of Minnesota, and especially to its former chairman, Professor Charles H. McLaughlin, for making funds available for the seminar.

A publication of this sort necessarily involves administrative, typing, and editorial chores which are often dull but always important. For helping us to meet our responsibilities, we extend our sincere thanks to Mrs. Patricia Hayman-Chaffey, Mrs. Diana Rigelman, and Miss Diane Johnson.

Robert T. Holt
John E. Turner

ix

CHAPTER 1

The Methodology of
Comparative Research

ROBERT T. HOLT

and JOHN E. TURNER
University of Minnesota

SINCE THE early 1950s, *methodology* has been a key word in the rhetoric of political science. Much confusion has arisen, however, over just what the term means; in the parlance of the discipline, both its denotative and its connotative meanings have been ambiguous. Some scholars have used the term almost synonymously with *political behavior* to denote a body of empirical theory and the research designs and research techniques associated with it. For others, methodology refers much more narrowly to the research techniques and analytical routines employed in the analysis of data, especially quantitative data. Whereas the denotation of the term has reflected ambiguity, its connotation—to be more accurate—has been conflicting. For many of the younger members of the profession during the 1950s and early 1960s, methodology connoted all that was worthwhile in political science, and behind this shield they stormed the barricades of tradition in the discipline. For others, it was a term of derision, connoting a substantively empty neo-scholasticism that diverted the attention of scholars from the crucial issues of a value-sensitive political science.

In light of this confusion, it is essential, at the beginning of a book on the methodology of comparative research, that we indicate what we mean by the

1

term. The goal of any science is to develop a valid, precise, and verified general theory. The methodology of any science involves its *rules of interpretation* and *criteria for admissible explanation*, as well as the research designs, data-collecting techniques, and data-processing routines that have been developed from these *rules* and *criteria*. Because the expressions *rules of interpretation* and *criteria for admissible explanation* are not commonly used in the literature of political science (or in other social sciences, for that matter), some elaboration is needed.

How does one verify a general theory or a specific theoretical proposition? "The key to verification of theories," John Kemeny has stated, "is that you never verify them. What you do verify are logical consequences of the theory. Verification is the process of seeing whether something predicted is really so. Since we can only observe particular facts, we must verify particular consequences of a theory, not the general theory itself."[1] But what facts do we observe, and how do we understand the theoretical implications of empirical observations? The rules of interpretation provide the answer to this basic question. They tell us "which of the statements in our [theoretical] language describe observable phenomena, and just what observations will establish whether the predictions of a given theory are right or wrong."[2] These rules of interpretation are not found in a textbook under an appropriate and identifiable subheading. They are to be found more or less implicitly in the commitments of the practitioners of a science to certain types of instrumentation and to preferred kinds of data processing. According to the distinction we are making, survey research, content analysis, certain types of case studies, and some kinds of comparative research are all *instrumentations*, whereas such routines as the product-moment correlation coefficient, regression analysis, and factor analysis are kinds of data processing.

To illustrate how rules of interpretation are involved in any research in which empirical observations are to be given theoretically relevant interpretation, let us suppose that the researcher wants to test a hypothesis derived from a theory of voting behavior, and he conducts a survey of a random sample of eligible voters. The very use of the survey research instrument involves a set of assumptions concerning the relationship between what people say about how they will vote (or how they have voted) and how they actually cast their ballots in the secrecy of the voting booth. We are not questioning whether such assumptions are valid. We are merely pointing out that the use of the survey research instrument in this case involves a specific rule of interpretation, which carries the researcher from the "facts" he observes to the different "facts" that are involved in checking the predictions of a given theory. In other words, the commitment to the instrument necessarily carries with it a commitment to the rule of interpretation.

Let us suppose, too, that the researcher calculates from his survey results a correlation coefficient between voting behavior and certain measured psychological characteristics of eligible voters. From the analysis of the responses in his sample, he wants to infer characteristics about the relationship between these variables in the population from which the sample was drawn. Such an inference is based partly upon assumed congruence between certain characteristics of the empirical system under study and the mathematical formulation from which the statistical formula was derived. This assumption is also a rule of interpretation that must be taken into account if the particular theory is to be checked empirically.

Closely related to the rules of interpretation are what we have called the *criteria for admissible explanation*. Explanation is one of the basic goals of any scientific enterprise, but what do we mean by it? Let us return for a moment to our expert in voting behavior. He may run a multiple regression analysis between voting behavior as a *dependent* variable and four other *independent* variables. After completing his statistical runs, he finds that he can account for nine-tenths of the variation of his dependent variable in terms of his independent variables, and he then claims that he has *explained* voting behavior. What does he mean by *explanation*? He means that he can, with certain confidence, predict values of the dependent variable from a knowledge of the value of his independent variables. Is this an acceptable explanation? It depends entirely upon what one means by explanation, or, in other words, what one accepts as an admissible explanation. The criteria for admissible explanation exist independently of any data-processing routine. But the commitment to any particular routine, if it is being used for anything more than mere description, involves the issue of admissible explanation. If, for example, the analyst is seeking *generative* explanations, he must demonstrate in his explanation how the behavior in question is generated. With respect to voting behavior, Simon has enunciated a set of criteria for admissible explanation that are very close to a generative explanation:

> I submit that we would regard the phenonema as "explained" if we could state a relatively simple set of invariant rules or "laws" that would enable us to predict the answers to all the questions on the polls at time *t* on the basis of our knowledge of the answers to the questions on the polls prior to time *t*, and correspondingly, predict the actual voting, communication, or other political behavior of the respondents at time *t* on the basis of the information gathered prior to time *t*.[3]

If by invariant rules or "laws" Simon is referring to rules of behavior that, if followed by individuals, would lead to the observed outcome, and if there is strong evidence that this set of rules is being followed by the observed individuals, then we would have a generative explanation. Note that a regression analysis (or any other statistical routine) cannot by itself provide a generative explanation. Note also that if the researcher accepts these kinds of criteria for admissible explanation, he must select an instrumentation and

3

data-processing routines that will enable him to demonstrate how he meets the criteria for admissible explanation.

In summary, then, the methodology of any science deals not only with the proper use of its preferred instrumentation and data-processing techniques, but more basically with its rules of interpretation and the criteria for admissible explanation that exist independently of these instrumentations and routines. If this view is accepted, it naturally follows that methodology is extricably linked with theory, because the rules of interpretation and the criteria for admissible explanation are partially derived from the theory. All are a part of what Kuhn has referred to as a scientific *paradigm*.[4]

This close link between theory and methodology has some interesting consequences in the developmental history of a scientific field. In a field where there is a consensually accepted paradigm and a rigorous theory with great deductive power, methodology is seldom considered to be a subject of separate concern. The reason is that the rules of interpretation and the criteria for admissible explanation are so obviously derived from a basic theory, which is widely accepted, that methodology does not need to be given special consideration, except for the learning of research techniques. In political science, however, there are competing paradigms, none of which is widely accepted, and none of them has a deductively powerful theoretical element. Rules of interpretation and criteria for admissible explanation are unclear; hence, there is much room for discussion and debate on methodological issues, and it is impossible to determine which instrumentation and which analytical routines are the most useful to practitioners in the field. This is the reason why so much attention is given to special courses in methodology and why the discipline has even developed specialization in methods. But if our view of methodology is correct, methodological issues can never be resolved unless theory and methodology are closely articulated. Unfortunately, however, the separate concern for methodology at the present time seems to be an institutional block to such articulation. In other words, the situation in political science that prompts separate treatment of methodology tends to inhibit the kind of development necessary for the resolution of the important methodological issues.

This view of methodology obviously raises nasty questions about the legitimacy of a book on the Methodology of Comparative Research. The enterprise may seem even more questionable when we look briefly at the field of comparative politics.

What Is Comparative Politics?

Political scientists like to trace the field of study known as *comparative* back to Aristotle's comparative analysis of the constitutions of Greek city states, and Comparative Government and Politics has occupied a conspicuous place in the curriculum of political science since its emergence as a separate discipline. The subject matter of "comparative politics," however, has always been ambiguous. Before the behavioral revolution in political science, comparative government in American universities tended to be nothing more than the study of discrete foreign governments. Given the concepts in vogue at that time, greater stress was placed upon uniqueness than upon elements of commonality; any comparisons that were drawn were largely for pedagogical or rhetorical reasons.

If we examine the writings of the major scholars in comparative politics since the early 1950s, especially those that have had the greatest impact on the discipline, an interesting development becomes noticeable. Although the Almonds, Apters, Riggs, Eksteins, LaPalombaras, and Pyes have used foreign political systems as the main foci of their research, their most influential writings have dealt with empirical political theory. In a discipline where the term *theory* has traditionally referred to political philosophy, experts in the comparative field have tended to emerge as the dominant macrotheorists. They are *comparativists* largely in the sense that their theories are applied to more than one political system.

In anthropology and in at least a part of the sociological tradition, the term *comparative* refers not to a substantive field, but to a method of research and analysis. But in political science few studies in comparative politics have employed the comparative method, as envisaged and used, for example, by Durkheim, Nadel, and Murdock.[5] Nor have political scientists produced any writing on the method of comparative analysis that even approaches the methodological work done by the sociologists and anthropologists. This is somewhat surprising because the common-sense meaning of the term *comparative*, unadorned by any scholarly tradition, generally refers to a method of study and not to a body of substantive knowledge. In light of our conclusion that specific methodological concerns taken independently of a scientific paradigm, and particularly of its theoretical element, is a weakness, the failure of comparativists to focus solely on the comparative method has perhaps been a blessing. But now that scholars in comparative politics are so deeply involved in empirical theory, the field would be improved if they devoted attention to the development of some rigorous guidelines for the use of the comparative method.

Comparative Method

If political scientists are to generate a body of theory and concentrate their efforts on making the theory more general and valid, comparative cross-cultural research is absolutely essential. Political scientists can hardly take issue with Murdock's conclusion that "there can never be any generally valid science of man which is not specifically adapted to, and *tested with reference to* the diverse manifestations of human behavior encountered in the thousands of human societies differing from our own . . . "[6] Because scholars were interested in developing and testing theories that would be applicable beyond the boundaries of a single society, the comparative method came into use in the social sciences. It is in carefully designed comparative research that the social scientist, especially if he is concerned with macrosocial phenomena, finds something comparable to the controlled laboratory experiment of the natural scientist. In the chemistry laboratory it is possible for the researcher to add one substance to another in a test tube, to heat to a specific temperature, and to observe and measure the reaction. But it is impossible for the social scientist to add or to remove a social class from a society for a fifty-year period in order to examine the effect of this class upon political change. In other words, the social scientist is rarely able to manipulate the variables directly. With the use of the comparative method and through the careful selection and/or sampling of research sites, however, he can manipulate the experimental variables indirectly. Max Weber did this in his comparative studies of religion, which analyzed the relationship between the *Wirtschaftsethik* in various religions and the rise of capitalism.

In principle, there is no difference between comparative cross-cultural research and research conducted within a single society. The differences lie, rather, in the magnitude of certain types of problems that have to be faced. For example, the scholar who studies political parties in ten states in the United States will encounter differences in dialect in different sections of the country, and he will have to take these into consideration in interpreting the results of his interviews. For the reasonably sensitive researcher who has grown up in the United States, this should present no formidable problem. But the scholar who studies political parties in ten countries, each with a different language (to say nothing of parochial dialects within each country), confronts enormous problems of linguistic comparability which must be solved if the results of the interviews are to be properly analyzed. Before identifying the problems that are of particular consequence in cross-cultural research, it will be instructive to look at the general problem of preparing any research design.

Ideally, scientific research in its simplest form involves, first, the deduction of a hypothesis from a set of theoretical propositions, and, second, investigations to determine whether the facts of relationships predicted by the hypothesis manifest themselves empirically. Typically, the hypothesis involves a predicted relationship between at least two variables and takes the general form of, "If A, then B." Little research in political science, however, follows this ideal. The major reason for this is obvious, and has already been indicated. The theoretical structure in political science is not deductively powerful, and hence the rigorous deduction of hypotheses is, with few exceptions, impossible. Most hypotheses that are tested by political scientists are either the loose implications of a rather amorphous theory or are simply the researchers' hunches about a reasonable outcome of empirical research. Indeed, much of the research in the field is not oriented toward hypothesis-testing at all, but is exploratory in nature and is undertaken to aid in the development of hypotheses. But, regardless of how the research questions have been arrived at, a major purpose of much of the research is to identify the relationships among variables. A discussion of the problems of verifying the "If A, then B" type of hypothesis is thus relevant to any research that attempts to establish with confidence the relationship among two or more variables.

Nadel has stated a central problem clearly:

> The basic formula, "If A, then B," at which all experimental methods aim, will emerge from co-variations of two different kinds. In the first, the presence or absence of one social fact will determine the presence or absence of the other, so that we can extract a straight or parallel correlation; in the second, the presence of one fact will determine the absence of the other, so that the correlation is inverse ... Schematically expressed, in "all or none" form, we obtain these two formulae (the index^0 meaning the absence of the fact in question):
>
> A ... with (XYZ) ... with B $\qquad$ A ... with (XYZ) ... with B^0
> A^0 ... with (XYZ) ... with B^0 $\qquad$ A^0 ... with (XYZ) ... with B
>
> These correlations are over-simplified, not only because they operate with two co-variants only, but because they leave undefined the "setting," the surrounding circumstances, in which the co-variants occur. The main difficulty involved in our experimental technique lies precisely in defining these surrounding circumstances and their bearing on the correlations we extract. In the simplest case the surrounding circumstances will be identical ... Instead of
>
> $$Z \ldots \text{ with } (XYZ) \ldots \text{ with } B$$
>
> we shall then specify
>
> $$A \ldots \text{ with } (PQR) \ldots \text{ with } B$$
>
> Here, then, we have a clear-cut distinction between "background features" (which remain unchanged) and the relevant factors (the "co-variants"). But let me stress again that it is we who produce the identical setting for the sake of convenience, so that our initial hypothesis may be verified with relative ease, and perhaps so that some such hypothesis may readily suggest itself. We cannot assume that the "background features" are in fact irrelevant for our correlation; we can only choose our conditions so that these additional features can be disregarded. This is the familiar condition of *ceteris paribus* which, though it simplifies analysis, may also hide unsuspected co-variants, and thus limit the validity of our correlations.[7]

Nadel clearly recognizes the problem, but his treatment of it is somewhat confusing. In order to aid in the explication of the relevant issues, we offer a stereotypical example. Suppose that an expert in comparative politics is interested in the association between types of election systems and types of political party systems, and he gathers data on democratic elections in the United Kingdom, France, Germany, and the United States during the twentieth century. He observes that where a single-member, plurality-type of election system exists, he finds a two-party system; and where he finds proportional representation or a single-member district, majority-type system, he also finds a multi-party system. Can he conclude that the relationship between a single-member district, plurality system and a two-party system is not spurious? The problem with such a conclusion arises from the possible influence of what Nadel calls "background features." How can the scholar be sure that there is not some other variable (or variables) operating in the United Kingdom and the United States that gives rise to the two-party system, or that there is no variable operating in France and Germany that inhibits the rise of a two-party system? If we were to pursue the matter, we could probably list other conditions that might account for the same observed facts. A good research design has to control for other possible variables so that the scholar can be confident that the observed relationships are genuine.

Basically, three ways of doing this are open to the researcher. The background variables can be controlled for by randomization, by specification, or by some combination of these two.

Control of Background Factors by Randomization

The problem we have just identified is raised in one form or another in every introductory statistics textbook, along with a suggested solution. The solution is clearly presented by R. A. Fisher:

> ... the uncontrolled causes which may influence the results [of an experiment] are always strictly innumerable. When any such cause is named, it is usually perceived that, by increased labour and expense, it could be largely eliminated. Too frequently it is assumed that such refinements constitute improvements to the experiment ... [W]hatever degree of care and experimental skill is expended in equalizing the conditions, other than the one under test, which are liable to affect the result, this equalization must always be to a greater or less extent incomplete, and in many important practical cases will certainly be grossly defective ... [T]he simple precaution of randomization will suffice to guarantee the validity of the test of significance, by which the result of the experiment is to be judged.[8]

Although this volume is not intended to be a book on statistics or the logic of research design, several comments are in order.

First, randomization as a technique to equalize the conditions (other than those under test) that might influence the result makes it possible for the researcher to employ many powerful statistical routines to aid in the interpretation of the data. The application of these routines, however, depends upon the correspondence between the theory that underlies the statistical routine being used and the operations called for by the research design. Although this point is made, usually with elaboration, in any textbook on statistics and experimental design, it appears to have had little impact upon many contemporary political scientists. The statement of William Hays should be plainly displayed in every room where political scientists are working on the statistical analysis of data:

> It is a sad fact that if one knows nothing about the probability of occurrence for particular samples of units for observation, he can use very little of the machinery of statistical inference. This is why the assumption of random sampling is not to be taken lightly . . . In practical situations, the experimenter may be hard put to show that a given sample is "truly" random, but he must realize that he is acting *as if* this were a random sample from some well-defined population when he applies the methods of statistical inference. Unless this assumption is at least reasonable, the results of inferential methods mean very little, and these methods might as well be omitted. Data that are not the product of random sampling may yield extremely valuable conclusions in their own right, but there is usually little to be gained from the application of inferential methods to such data. *Certainly, the application of some statistical method does not somehow magically make a sample random, and the conclusions therefore valid. Inferential methods apply to random samples, and there is no guarantee of their validity in other circumstances.*[9]

Second, whereas the "precaution of randomization" might be simple in experimental research, as Fisher indicates in the passage cited, it is often a very complex matter for most social scientists, and may indeed be impossible in much cross-cultural comparative research. Let us examine briefly some situations in which randomization is either a difficult or impossible device to use in controlling for background factors.

The hypotheses a researcher is interested in testing may be derived from a theory that is applicable to an autonomous political system (nation-state, city-state, empire, and so on), and the formulations may have to be tested at that level. Although he might be able to draw an acceptable sample of autonomous political systems (including contemporary and historical cases), much of the data he needs for the testing of the hypotheses may not be available and may never be available. What, for example, does the scholar do if Sung China, the Roman Republic in the first century, B.C., the nineteenth-century Zulu kingdom, and the Egyptian Empire at the time of Ramses III show up in a sample randomly drawn? If, in the test of the hypotheses, he needs data on specified types of governmental expenditures as a percentage of Gross National Product, he will probably be unable to gather all of the necessary information.

Or, to take an even more difficult problem, let us suppose that the researcher is interested in testing some hypotheses dealing with politics in modern industrial societies. These societies can be defined fairly precisely in terms of such indicators as per capita income, the proportion of the labor

9

force engaged in agriculture, and the availability of energy from non-animate energy sources. But, on the basis of any of the commonly employed definitions, there are only about eight to twelve modern industrial societies in the world today. The scholar could use these few societies to examine the relationship between some aspect of economic organization and political behavior, in contrast with a study of the same relationship in a sample of nonindustrial societies. Assume that the results clearly demonstrate that the relationship is different in the two samples. Although the investigator will be able to make a statement about this relationship in the eight or twelve present-day societies, what could he say about the relationship in the fifty or so modern industrial societies that will probably exist in the year 2000? He can use the eight or twelve as a sample of the fifty only if he knows the probability of the occurrence of his sample. In principle, however, there is no way to determine this. In this case, inferential statistics are useless, and if the researcher applies them, the results will be misleading. This does not mean that he must throw up his hands in despair; it means, rather, that he must approach the problem by a different route, which will be suggested later in our discussion.[10]

We turn now to a final point about the use of randomization to control for background factors. Some research problems cannot be solved by drawing a random sample of some real world population, even though this may be feasible or even simple. The rules of interpretation underlying the use of randomization in nonexperimental research usually assume that the predictions from a theory can be checked against a real world population. In the history of the development of the natural sciences, this assumption has not always been reasonable. Consider, for example, the problem faced by Galileo when he was studying the phenomenon of falling objects. He could have selected a random sample of falling objects and measured the acceleration of descent, the time it took them to fall specified distances, and many of their physical characteristics, such as weight, density, and so on. If he had had access to a high-speed computer, he might have been able to make some sense out of the data collected—he might even have tried factor analysis! But if he had taken such an approach, there is little reason to believe that he would ever have formulated a law of gravity. The law he formulated applies to objects falling in a vacuum, and, obviously, no real world objects on this earth fall under such conditions. Ideally, his empirical studies could best be conducted with objects of a high density, a low surface area to volume ratio, and a shape that would offer minimal air resistance. In other words, he needed a sample of a hypothetical population of objects falling in a vacuum. A most atypical object, however, is the best sample of this hypothetical population. The most common falling objects on earth (in terms of frequency) are the microscopic particles of dust and air pollutants. Leaves falling from trees also have a high frequency. If Galileo had studied a random sample of falling objects in which dust particles and leaves were properly represented, it is difficult to imagine what sort of a generalization he might have formulated.

In the social sciences today, great benefits might be derived from the development of laws that apply under specific but rare situations. Empirical studies could perhaps then be undertaken on very rare events because they best approximate a sample of some important hypothetical population. Random sampling of some real world population is often no way to control for background factors in the test of hypotheses that apply to an ideal situation. Yet such hypotheses and the theories from which they are derived may be the most significant.

Control of Background Factors by Specification

A second way to control ideally for the effect of background factors is by identifying and holding constant every relevant background factor in such a way that each has identical values in both the control and the experimental groups. In nonexperimental research that is not trivial, the ideal may be approximated but never achieved.

This approach, or what we call *specification*, is essentially what Max Weber attempted in his classic studies on the relationship between the "Protestant Ethic" and the rise of capitalism.[11] Weber realized that to demonstrate the causal relationship he hypothesized without comparative studies would be impossible. He found it necessary to demonstrate that capitalism did not develop in the absence of the *Wirtschaftsethik* of Protestantism, even though the "material factors" considered in alternative hypotheses to be important in the development of capitalism were in fact present. In his research design, he had to indicate specifically that certain variables in the societies he chose to study were equal, and that capitalism developed only in those societies that had previously developed a *Wirtschafts* under the influence of certain branches of Protestantism. Parsons sums up Weber's approach as follows:

> A variable cannot, of course, be isolated unless other possibly important variables can, within a relevant range of variation, either be held constant or their independence demonstrated. Weber attempted to deal with this problem by showing that, in the different societies he treated, *before* the development of the religious ideas in which he is interested, the state of the material factors and their prospective autonomous trends of development was, in the relevant respects, essentially similar. That is, for instance, in his three best worked out cases, those of China, India and Western Europe, he attempted to estimate the relative favorableness or unfavorableness of the economic situation, the "conditions of production," to capitalistic development. The outcome of his studies in this respect was the judgment that there is a high degree of similarity in all three variables in this respect, with, if anything, a balance of favorableness in favor of India and China.[12]

11

Robert T. Holt and John E. Turner

Weber could clearly demonstrate that the beliefs he defined as the *Wirtschaftsethik* of Protestantism did not exist in the religions of India and China, whereas the *material factors* that might "cause" capitalism to develop were present not only in Western Europe, but also in India and China. But, given the nature of his study, he could not demonstrate that other factors existed in a proper combination to produce capitalism in Western Europe but did not exist in India and China, and that these unrecognized factors were the most crucial to the development of capitalism. In other words, Weber controlled only for the variation of the material factors, and he "experimentally" manipulated the *Wirtschaftsethik* of capitalism through the selection of research sites.[13]

The key to the use of specification for the control of background factors rests in the proper selection of research sites. We can illustrate the importance of this by reviewing briefly one of S. F. Nadel's studies, which illustrates a degree of specification rarely possible in cross-cultural research. In his field work in Africa, Nadel came upon several pairs of societies which had many characteristics in common. Nupe and Gwari made up one of these pairs. They are alike in virtually every respect:

> The two societies are neighbors in an identical environment and also maintain frequent contacts. They speak closely related languages and have an identical kinship system, based on patrilineal succession, patrilocal residence, and localized extended families. Political organization and the regulation of male adolescence are closely similar in both tribes; so is their economy, though marketing and trade are on a much larger scale in Nupe. The religion of Nupe and Gwari is again closely similar (ignoring here the more recent spread of Islam), and the conceptions of life and death, of a body possessed of a double soul ("shadow-" and "life-soul"), and of the reincarnation of ancestral souls, are identical even as regards nomenclature.[14]

The witchcraft beliefs are also virtually identical, with one notable exception: in Nupe, witches are believed to be female, in Gwari they may be of either sex. This is an ideal research site for studying the causes of specific sex identification in witchcraft beliefs. Any factors identical in the two societies cannot be a cause of the phenomenon under study. With so many similarities in the two societies, a large number of background factors are controlled.

Nadel discovered that one of the few differences between the two societies is in the economic position of the women. In Gwari, women are in an economically dependent position, but in Nupe the wives, because they are itinerant traders, are often much better off economically than their husbands. Frequently the Nupe men are in debt to their wives who, in accordance with ideal norms, should occupy subordinate and dependent roles. Nadel concludes:

12

> In practice, then, the men must submit to the domineering and independent leanings of women; they resent their own helplessness, and definitely blame the "immorality" of the womenfolk. The wish to see the situation reversed is expressed in nostalgic talk about "the good old days" when all this was unheard of (and which are disproved by all genealogies and concrete records of the past). Equally, it can be argued, the hostility between men and women *plus* this wish-fulfillment are projected into the witchcraft beliefs with their ambivalent expression of sex-antagonism, in which men are the "real" victims but the "utopian" master of evil women. A final item of evidence . . . lies in the identification of the head of the witches with the official head of the women traders.[15]

Nadel argues that the relationship between man and wife in Nupe is the source of great stress and strain, and that the female sex identification of witches is conspicuously related to these stresses and strains.

It is difficult to imagine a study in which more factors are controlled by specification, but the price Nadel pays for this elegance is exorbitant. He did not select a research site in order to control and manipulate specified variables; rather, his hypothesis was dictated by the research site. This procedure may be of some utility in the early stages of theory development, but it makes little contribution to the testing of important propositions derived from a developing body of theory.

Nonculture-Bound Concepts and Operational Definitions

In dealing briefly in the previous section with two different types of research design that may be used by comparativists, we made several references to the source of the hypotheses to be tested. Our preference is for the rigorous use of the deductive method as a means of deriving hypotheses from theoretical propositions, or what is sometimes called the *postulational technique*. Although in its most exacting form this approach is so rare as to be almost absent in the literature of political science, it nevertheless represents an ideal to be relentlessly pursued. The postulational technique is one of the pillars of the scientific method.

Another buttress in the scientific enterprise is *operationalism*. Although the rules governing the development of acceptable definitions and the operationalization of concepts are no different for cross-cultural comparative studies than for studies in a single culture, they are far more difficult to apply, largely for practical and technical reasons.

The concepts that are used in the hypotheses to be tested in a research design must be nonculture-bound, at least as the concepts are applicable to the cultures included in the empirical research and to those cultures that will be embraced by the generalizations which grow out of the findings. The development of new conceptual frameworks which adorn present-day

13

literature in comparative politics stems from the explicit recognition that the old political science was concerned primarily with Western democratic systems—a parochialism that was reflected in the concepts employed. Such concepts—parliaments, political parties, interest groups, formal courts, and so on—proved to be inadequate for an understanding of the new despotisms that sprang up during the interwar period, and they were even less appropriate for studies of the new nations that appeared on the world scene after World War II had ended. When scholars like Gabriel Almond shift the attention of comparativists from parties to *interest aggregation* and from legislatures to *rule-making*, and when they begin to deal with *political socialization* and *recruitment* as major concepts in a conceptual framework, they are reacting against the culture-bound character of political science concepts, that were in vogue when the discipline was preoccupied with Western institutions. But it is hardly surprising that political scientists would seek to develop new concepts as they pushed their research interests beyond the boundaries of Europe and North America. When scholars in other social science disciplines have made large-scale use of the comparative method, they too have had to wrestle with the problem of nonculture-bound categories.[16]

In this introductory chapter, we shall do no more than mention the problem of nonculture-bound categories. Later chapters by Riggs, LaPalombara, and Apter deal in large part with nonculture-bound categories and the appropriate levels of analysis for comparative politics. The problem of operationalizing nonculture-bound concepts, however, deserves particular attention at this point.

This problem has moved into sharper focus in recent years as political scientists have sought to operationalize such concepts as *political culture*, *political socialization*, and *political development*. The last-mentioned concept, which has its roots in the conceptual schemes of the economists, has been particularly troublesome, and scholars have attempted to operationalize it in a variety of ways.[17] Some have focused attention upon one or more types of governmental structures; others have concerned themselves with socio-psychological attitudes held by certain groups within the population. In some instances, development has been linked with democracy—a mix that raises special difficulties of its own, since even the attempts to operationalize democracy have resulted in separate sets of indicators which are not highly correlated.

But let us confine our discussion to those concepts that have passed the initial hurdles and now appear as variables in a theory or in a hypothesis. Empirical research requires that each variable be measured and its value be ascertained in the different cultures. In its simplest form, this means that the researcher has to develop some index that will indicate the values of the variables, and the index is, in effect, the operationalization of the concept. Such an index, however, can be greatly affected by differences in the cultures being examined. To be valid, an index has to measure what it purports to measure, and the comparativist has to be alert for local peculiarities which, undetected, can blunt the research instrument and lead to spurious findings.

Suppose, for example, that the researcher is interested in using crime rates as an index of social disorganization. When we see the difficulties that criminologists and other sociologists have faced in trying to standardize statistics on crime in the United States, we immediately become aware of the hazards that are encountered when scholars attempt to refine such data for use on a cross-national basis. Impediments to valid comparison of crime rates inevitably arise out of national differences in judicial structures and procedures, the efficiency of criminal detection, and cultural norms that may sanction violations of formal law (such as the falsification of tax returns in France). In some countries, serious crimes committed within certain sub-cultures—say, *within* an oppressed minority group—may go unreported or be overlooked by the police. Even more difficult is the problem of trying to standardize for intersocietal use the definitions and classifications of crime. In the United States, it may be illegal to engage in some types of segrega-tionist activity, but in South Africa individuals who violate the segregation laws are subject to arrest. Given these cross-national complexities, increased crime rates may stem from a variety of factors, and an index constructed from them may not be a valid indicator of social disorganization.

In some societies, a high incidence of divorce may reflect a breakdown in the family system, but in other settings the divorce rate is a meaningless indicator of family instability. Although the frequency of divorce is influenced by such obvious factors as the grounds for divorce permitted by statute and the access of impecunious groups to legal assistance, cultural differences operate even more to distort an intersocietal index. Some countries under the influence of Islam, for example, have traditionally had few legal or religious barriers to divorce, and marriages could easily be dissolved by mere pronouncement of the husband or his family. By contrast, divorce is virtually impossible in some societies—Italy is a good illustration—where both the government and the church take strong stands against it. Until recently, divorce was impossible for members of the upper class in India, and, although divorce was possible among lower-class groups by custom, the purchase of brides tended to place an economic restraint upon it.

Within the more common orbit of political science, let us assume that the comparativist is interested in developing a cross-cultural index of party competition or voter concern with issues, and he toys with the idea of using statistics on voter turnout for this purpose. Obviously, this would not be a valid index in totalitarian systems where the voters are exposed to inten-sive pressures to go to the polls. But even in a democratic state the construc-tion of such an indicator presents difficulties. In some countries—as, for example, the United States—idiosyncratic registration and election laws set up obstacles to an accurate calculation of the number of eligible voters.

In other societies, such as Australia and Belgium, the system of compulsory voting would inject imperfections into the index.

Let us look at voter turnout statistics from a slightly different perspective. In examining the low degree of electoral participation in local (as compared with national) contests in Britain and the United States, scholars have suggested that this is a reflection of national politics impinging upon the local arenas. What would happen if we decided to use figures on voter turnout in constructing an index for measuring the impact of national politics upon the local scene? Such an indicator would certainly be distorted in the case of Japan, where more than 90 per cent of the eligible voters in rural areas troop to the polling stations in local elections—a higher proportion than in national elections—largely as a result of pressures being exerted by locally influential leaders.

These examples are so obvious that the reader may be tempted to think that we are just setting up a straw man; no mature scholar makes the kinds of errors we have drawn attention to. The hazards, however, can be subtle but serious when one is using indices that require cross-cultural validity. To illustrate one of these hazards, let us examine briefly Professor Samuel Beer's discussion of "party cohesion" in his excellent, perceptive study of the British political system. He looks at this phenomenon at several places throughout the book, and he seems to reach the following conclusion:

> ... these mass parties had managed in a remarkable degree to "speak with one voice." To an Attlee harassed by Bevanite rebels on the backbenches, in the constituencies, and among the unions, or to a Macmillan assaulted by Suez rebels under the leadership of a Cecil, this assertion may seem painfully laughable. It is when we look at the situation in the light of what once prevailed—or what prevails in other parties such as those of the United States—that we properly appreciate the degree of cohesion achieved. The rise of party unity in parliamentary divisions is the most striking exhibit. From the mid-nineteenth century, when it had fallen to American levels, party cohesion in Britain had steadily risen until in recent decades *it was so close to 100 per cent that there was no longer any point in measuring it.*[18]

Note at the outset that, even without the reference to "American levels," this statement loses some of its thrust unless it is viewed comparatively. But how we view it comparatively depends largely on the way in which the variable "party cohesion" has been measured. Professor Beer measures it by examining the frequency of votes against the party leadership. In seeking to illustrate the unity of the Parliamentary Labour Party in quantitative terms, he drew a sample of division lists (about which we shall have something to say shortly) during the first parliamentary session of the Attlee regime, 1945–1946. From this sample, he detected only one division in which members of the Labour Party voted against the Government, and on that vote only four M.P.s from the majority party walked into the opposition lobby. This is certainly close to 100 per cent cohesion when compared with the frequency of votes against the party leadership in the American Congress. Or is it? To answer this question we need to look at the setting in which votes against party leaders occur in the House of Commons and in the American Congress to see whether the index is a cross-culturally valid one.

Three points should be made about votes against party leadership as an index of party cohesion in the British system: (1) The sanctions that the party leaders can impose upon those who jump the whip are extremely severe, and are certainly of a different order of magnitude from those that operate in the American Congress. For this reason, negative votes against the leadership constitute a far more serious act. (2) In addition to the normal sanctions that support the maintenance of party discipline, a special sanction can be employed against members of the Ministry who vote against their government; they will almost automatically lose their jobs, an outcome that very few of them are willing to risk. Since about 25 per cent of the M.P.s in the government party (including the whips) are in this category, the government is, in effect, guaranteed a large bloc of votes on any issue. To include these people in the analysis tends to distort the index; some measure of the voting patterns of just the backbenchers, who have a wider range of options, would probably be a more sensitive indicator of party cohesion. (3) An index that takes account only of those who actually vote against the government necessarily treats abstainers as government supporters for the purpose of measuring party cohesion. Because negative votes against the government may have serious consequences for an individual M.P., some dissidents express their disagreements with the leadership by willfully abstaining. In the House of Commons, a three-line whip issued by a party usually requires that its members be in the division lobbies except under out-of-the-ordinary circumstances. This means that many abstentions are likely to be willful, and it would be more appropriate to treat them as indicators of diminished cohesion.

To see how abstentions might be taken into consideration, let us examine the situation at the time of the vote on the Bretton Woods Agreement—the one division in the 1945–1946 parliament in which Professor Beer noted four votes against the Attlee Government. This vote was taken on the evening of December 13, 1945. Just a few minutes before this vote, the House was divided on the issue of the American Loan. On this division, which was conducted under a three-line whip, twenty-three Labour backbenchers voted against the Government, and at least three others were known to have willfully abstained. Then, within a matter of minutes, the Labour backbenchers, again under three-line discipline, were called upon to support the Bretton Woods Agreement, which was closely related to the issue of the American Loan. On this vote only four backbenchers marched into the opposition lobby. But these four rebels did not represent all of the dissidence by any means. Twenty-three Labour M.P.s who were in the lobbies to vote in favor of the American Loan (some of them reluctantly) did *not* record

17

their votes on Bretton Woods a few moments later. In addition, eighteen rebels who were in the House to register their opposition to the American Loan did *not* vote on the Bretton Woods measure. It is highly probable that these forty-one people willfully abstained on this second vote, which was on an unpopular measure. The patterns of *backbencher* voting of the two issues were as follows:

	Number of Backbenchers*	Yes Votes	No Votes	Probable and Known Abstainers	Unknown
American Loan	311	(258) 83.0%	(23) 7.4%	(3) 1.0%	(27) 8.7%
Bretton Woods	311	(238) 76.5%	(4) 1.3%	(42) 13.5%	(27) 8.7%

* Five backbenchers were known to have been sick or abroad and hence unable to participate in the voting. These are not included among the number of backbenchers in this listing. Some commentators have indicated that approximately 44 backbenchers abstained on the American Loan. This, however, is hardly a plausible figure. The total number of backbenchers voting "yes" and "no" was 281, leaving only a total of 36 remaining backbench members—a number that includes those who were sick or abroad.

The importance of these points becomes even clearer if we look briefly at the meanings that are attached to voting against the leadership in the American Congress. In the undisciplined Congressional party, the individual legislator is relatively freer to vote against his leaders. His opposing votes may be prompted by one or more of several factors: ideological outlook, personal frustration, antagonism toward the political style of the leadership, constituency interests, and national pressure groups to which he is vulnerable. On a given issue, he may have told his party chieftains that he is willing to vote "Yes" if it will "make a difference," and then vote "No" with the acquiescence of the party leaders because his support was not needed or because the cause was already lost.[19] In this freewheeling system, negative votes may be used as measures of ideological position, personal loyalties, blocs influencing each other, and the impact of national pressure groups and/or constituency pressures. With relatively few sanctions at the disposal of the party leaders to keep their members in line, the researcher has a rich data base when he uses negative votes as an indication of any or several of these factors.

The British M.P., by contrast, is much more constrained by party discipline, and a vote against his leaders is a much more serious matter and is more likely to be based upon fundamental differences with his party leaders. For him, constituency interests are less influential in his voting decisions, and pressure groups are less operative upon him as an individual.

It is apparent, then, that votes against the leadership mean quite different things in the British and the American legislative chambers. For this reason they cannot be used as an index of the same thing. Professor Beer's analysis may indicate that there is more party discipline in Britain than in the United States. But whether, on the face of it, it indicates greater party cohesion is another matter.

The Problem of Comparability of Sampling

Closely related to the problem of operationalizing definitions in a manner that achieves cross-cultural comparability is the problem of comparable samples. The use of the same sampling technique in different cultures does not insure comparability, and it may even distort interpretations made from the sample. We can raise the points that need consideration by looking further at Professor Beer's method of sampling party votes in the study just mentioned.

In measuring party cohesion in the British parliament, Beer bases his index of party voting and his coefficient of cohesion upon an examination of one voting division in every ten. Although he appropriately points out that that the Labour Party was torn with dissension in the years following 1946, he indicates that throughout "the life of Attlee's Governments, party cohesion in the division lobbies continued to be virtually perfect."[20] However, he supplies quantitative data only for the period from 1945 to 1946, using a division sample of one in ten.[21]

Some care must be exercised in making inferences that are supposed to be generally valid from a sample drawn from a one-year period at the *beginning* of a regime. At the time of the 1945–1946 session, the Labour Party had just emerged from a long spell in the political wilderness, assuming majority control of parliament for the first time in its history. As Beer points out, the major core of its legislative program had been hammered out during the years when it was out of office, and by 1945 the organization had achieved a high level of consensus on the essential features of its program. Intoxicated with the exuberance of victory, the Labour backbenchers had little reason to oppose their leaders in the early stage of the Attlee regime. But as the new Government was forced to make compromises as a result of international crises and internal economic problems, rebellious spirits within the party grew much more vocal in their opposition to certain Government policies, and in later parliamentary sessions the incidence of whip-jumping rose, both in terms of negative votes and willful abstentions.

Typicality of time periods is not a difficulty that is directly linked with the problem of comparative research. It does suggest, however, that the researcher interested in making comparisons among national legislatures might be better off to choose time periods that are not comparable in calendrical terms, but in terms of some other factor, such as the number of years since a general election, or the size of the government's majority.

An even more important point should be made about sampling procedure. Whereas a systematic sampling of one voting division in every ten may be completely appropriate in the American Congress, it distorts the results when applied to the division lists in the House of Commons. Opposition to party leaders represented by negative votes and willful abstentions is

19

associated with specific issues. When one of these issues arises, several votes on aspects of the problem may be taken in a short period of time. Furthermore, party leaders may try, whenever possible, to space parliamentary action on controversial issues so that they are taken up at intervals rather than in quick succession. This means, in technical terms, that there may be a certain amount of periodicity in the occurrence of votes in which significant opposition will be registered. Where such periodicity is likely to exist, systematic sampling is not appropriate.[22] Depending upon the starting point and the interval, the incidence of opposition may either be badly overrepresented or badly underrepresented in the sample, and in either case the result is likely to be a poor basis for generalization.

The kind of periodicity that occurs in House of Commons voting is probably much less common in the American Congress, and a systematic sampling of votes in Congress may be entirely appropriate. The point is that identical sampling procedures in two different cultural settings may not lead to comparable results. The comparative analyst must be alert to these kinds of problems and sensitive to the basic dimensions on which he seeks comparability.

In this discussion of indices and sampling problems, we do not mean to concentrate criticism on this small portion of Professor Beer's first-class study. It is just that, by focusing upon a specific example, it is easier for us to make the general point that identical procedures for developing indicators and drawing samples in two different cultural settings may not lead to comparable results. The types of problems we have identified are commonly found in the literature on comparative politics.

Summary

Although it cannot be questioned that cross-cultural comparative research is indispensable to a developing science of politics, the problems that comparative specialists encounter are formidable. These range from the highly technical problems of indexing and sampling, to the more general problems of developing nonculture-bound categories, to the even more basic issues revolving around the rules of interpretation and the criteria for admissible explanation. The more technical questions cannot be resolved satisfactorily until scholars focus more explicitly on the rules of interpretation and the criteria for admissible explanation. When this is done, they will have a more solid intellectual base for developing more sophisticated conceptual schemes and more appropriate data-processing routines. Methodology ties into more theoretical issues at this point, and for this reason we must turn to an examination of the state of theory in comparative politics.

CHAPTER 2

Competing Paradigms
in Comparative Politics

ROBERT T. HOLT

and JOHN M. RICHARDSON, Jr.

A discussion of the state of theory in the field of comparative politics is a necessary backdrop for a treatment of some of the major methodological problems of comparative research. Drs. Holt and Richardson have undertaken this task by looking at some major theoretical formulations in political science from the point of view of a scientific paradigm as this concept has been developed by Thomas Kuhn. Although Kuhn's ideas developed largely from an examination of the historical development of theory in the natural sciences, they provide an interesting and useful perspective from which one can look at theories in the social sciences.

A number of contributors to this volume have developed major theoretical systems for the analysis of comparative politics, but it did not seem appropriate to include a critique of their works in this chapter. They have an opportunity to speak for themselves in the remaining chapters.

Dr. John M. Richardson, Jr., was a SSRC postdoctoral fellow in 1968–69 and spent the academic year working on mathematical models and formal theories in the Center for Comparative Studies in Technological Development and Social Change. He holds an A.B. in history from Dartmouth College and a Ph.D. in political science from the University of Minnesota. He is the author of Partners in Development: An Analysis of AID-University Relations, 1950–1965.

I N THE PREVIOUS chapter, this observation was made: "Methodological issues can never be resolved unless there is a close articulation between theory building and methodology. . . ." It is appropriate, therefore, to have a chapter early in the book on the methodology of comparative research which examines major theoretical issues in comparative politics.

In a jargon more current in the profession a decade ago, this chapter would have been referred to as a *stock-taking* effort. It is not the first such effort; indeed, in the 1950s and 1960s a considerable body of literature has been built up, which has assessed in one way or another the field of comparative politics and made recommendations on how it could be improved.[1] One cannot assess a field of endeavor and compare the various approaches to theory construction and empirical research unless he has a set of categories in terms of which he can assess and compare. We propose to examine the field of comparative politics in terms of what Thomas Kuhn has called a scientific *paradigm*.[2] In order to do this, however, it is necessary to examine in detail what is meant by a paradigm.

The Nature and Function of Paradigms

In its simplest terms, a paradigm is just a pattern or framework that gives organization and direction to a given area of scientific investigation.[3] But to use paradigmatic concept to examine various approaches to comparative politics, it is necessary to identify explicitly the various elements of a paradigm.

The first might be called a *conceptual* element. The paradigm contains the concepts that are used in the theoretical propositions and which, directly or indirectly, provide a focus for empirical investigation. In other words, the conceptual element of a paradigm provides an answer to the question: "Of what is reality composed?" The conceptual element of a paradigm is illustrated by Kuhn, using an example drawn from seventeenth- and eighteenth-century physics.

> After about 1630 . . . and particularly after the appearance of Descartes' immensely influential scientific writings, most physical scientists assumed that the universe was composed of microscopic corpuscles and that all natural phenomena could be explained in terms of corpuscular shape, size, motion and interaction. That nest of commitments . . . told scientists what sorts of entities the universe did and did not contain; there was only shaped matter in motion.[4]

Two points should be made regarding the conceptual element of a paradigm. First, although the basic substantive concepts must have an

23

empirical referent, there may be no technically feasible way to observe directly the reality that is identified by them. We must remember that for several centuries after Descartes no instrumentation was available that allowed scientists to determine directly if there were, in fact, any microscopic corpuscles that were assumed in the paradigm. The second point follows directly—an essential arbitrariness is involved in the development of the basic concepts. In the example just given, it is quite clear that the microscopic corpuscles were not in any sense discovered through empirical research. Rather they were developed as an intellectual enterprise and justified, not by asking whether they were true or false, but by demonstrating their utility in empirical investigation and in the development of theory. In the words of the mathematician, John Kemeny, concepts are nothing more than the "free creations of the human mind which have proved useful for the formation of theories about experience."[5] Kemeny illustrates the point with reference to Newton's definition of the concept of force, $F = ma$ (force equals the product of mass and acceleration).

> Instead of using the concepts of mass and acceleration (m and a) we could invent the new terms meleration (M, standing for $m - a$) and accelass (A, standing for $a - m$). Then using the same concept of force, the force is no longer the product of mass and acceleration, but $\frac{1}{4}$ the difference between the squares of the meleration and the accelass; that is, $F = \frac{1}{4}(M^2 - A^2)$. Objects *have* melerations and accelasses just as much as they have masses and accelerations, but the new concepts make our theories much more complex.[6]

Our discussion up to this point can be summarized in a single sentence, *Concepts are judged not by their truth or falsity, but by their theoretical utility.* In our discussion of various competing paradigms in the field of comparative politics, we shall waste no time arguing, for example, whether or not there *are* such things as *demands, supports,* and *functional requisites.* We are concerned only with how useful the concepts are in a particular paradigm.

We shall call the second element of a paradigm its *theoretical* element. Because the term *theory* has a variety of uses in the social sciences, it will be helpful to define what we mean by this term. A theory is a deductively connected set of propositions, which are, depending on their logical position with respect to one another, either axioms or theorems. The axioms of a theory are a limited number of independent and consistent propositions that are logically prior to a much larger set of propositions, the theorems. In a sense we might say that the axioms are empirical laws whose truth is taken for granted (at least temporarily).[7] Theorems are deducted from the axioms and as the theorems are verified, the axioms tend to be confirmed.

Unlike the conceptual element, the theoretical element of a paradigm can be subjected to empirical verification. The propositions are either true or false. As we are concerned with the examination of a field in which there is no consensually accepted paradigm, a brief comment regarding verification is in order. To repeat Kemeny's statement quoted in the first chapter: "the key to verification of theories is that you never verify them. Verification is the process of seeing whether something predicted is really so. Since we can only observe particular facts, we must verify particular consequences of a theory, not the general theory itself."[8] Furthermore, the implications of a given scientific theory can be compared with nature often in only a relatively few areas. For example, no more than three such areas are even yet accessible to Einstein's general theory of relativity.[9] Indeed, one of the major enterprises of what Kuhn calls *normal science* (research within the confines of a consensually accepted paradigm) is the analysis of the theoretical element of the paradigm to discover ways in which discriminating tests can be made of the predicted consequences of certain laws.[10]

In order to understand the theoretical implications of empirical observations, it is necessary to have *rules of interpretation* that "tell us which of the statements in our language describe observable phenomena and just what observations will establish whether the predictions of a given theory are right or wrong."[11] These rules are the third element of a paradigm. For the practitioners of normal science, commitment to particular rules of interpretation involves, among other things, "a multitude of commitments to preferred types of instrumentation and to ways in which accepted instruments may legitimately be employed."[12] In the social sciences, much of the methodological literature on, for example, survey research falls within this general area.

The intimate relationship between this element of a paradigm and the theoretical and conceptual elements should be emphasized. Even in the social sciences a close association exists between certain instruments, such as projective techniques and survey research, and certain fairly explicit theoretical postures. The use of a particular set of instruments depends very much upon how reality is perceived and upon accepted theoretical propositions. A striking example of the way that perception is constrained by the paradigm, which in turn affects the rules of interpretation, is presented by Kuhn:

> An investigator who hoped to learn something about what scientists took the atomic theory to be asked a distinguished physicist and an eminent chemist whether a single atom of helium was or was not an atom. Both answered without hesitation, but their answers were not the same. For the chemist, the atom of helium was a molecule because it behaved like one with respect to the kinetic theory of gases. For the physicist, on the other hand, the helium atom was not a molecule because it displayed no molecular spectrum. Presumably both men were talking of the same particle but they were viewing it through their own research training and practices ... Undoubtedly, their experiences had had much in common, but they did not, in this case, tell the two specialists the same thing.[13]

Note that in this example there could be no empirical resolution to the disagreement unless there was first a basic agreement on definitions. Because they were derived from different paradigms, the physicist's and chemist's conception of a molecule differed fundamentally.

A fourth element of a paradigm is that which identifies the *puzzles* which the members of the scientific community who accept the paradigm deem to be worth solving. They are worth solving because their solution will lead to a greater articulation, precision, and confirmation of the basic paradigm itself. The use of the term *puzzle* illuminates a particularly important characteristic of paradigm-delimited research. Puzzles are generally defined as "that special category of problems that can serve to test ingenuity and skill in solution." A criterion of a puzzle, therefore, is the *assurance that a solution exists*. This assurance derives from the confidence of the practitioner in the conceptual and theoretical elements of the paradigm.[14]

The assured existence of a solution is a characteristic of a normal research problem, but the solution itself may be of no intrinsic interest. The *way* in which the puzzle is solved or irrefutable proof that there is no solution are the interesting findings. The latter, of course, will tend to destroy the paradigm.

Another aspect of the puzzle-identifying element of a paradigm is of particular consequence to the social sciences. The puzzles identified by the paradigm are the only problems the scientific community deems worth solving. Thus the scholars are to a considerable degree insulated from a whole host of problems that may be generally related to their field and of great social importance, but which are either far too problematic, too scientifically trivial, or have only an applied (as contrasted with a scientific) interest. "Such problems," Kuhn points out, "can be a distraction, a lesson brilliantly illustrated by several facets of seventeenth century Baconianism and by some of the contemporary social sciences. One of the reasons why normal science seems to progress so rapidly is that its practitioners concentrate on problems that only their own ingenuity should keep them from solving."[15]

Political scientists should be reminded that "peace with honor" in Vietnam and "preventing the decay of cities" may not be puzzles at all. Indeed, it would be rare that any problem stemming largely from ethical concerns could be of interest to the political scientist *qua* scientist.

In addition to delimiting a set of puzzles that become the major foci for research, the paradigm must also define the criteria that determine admissible puzzle solutions.[16] These criteria emerge from the deductive elaboration of the theoretical element and from the rules of interpretation. The question that must be posed to the scholar who has formulated a particular "solution" is not simply, can this formulation be derived from *some* set of general premises and rules of interpretation, but rather can it be derived from that set of general premises and rules of interpretation that are defined by the paradigm. For example, the explanation of a variable in terms of other variables in a multiple linear regression equation is not a solution unless the scholar can demonstrate the position of all variables in a theoretical framework and can show that the assumption of the regression model is consistent with the criteria of admissible explanation from the paradigm. If journal editors accepted this as a "criterion of printability," there might be a recession in the printing industry.

A final element of a paradigm we have labeled, a bit ostentatiously, the *ontologic-predictive* element. Perhaps we use a big word because this element is less explicit and less uniquely subject to differentiation. In brief, the ontologic-predictive element suggests what the conceptual and theoretical elements would look like if the paradigm were fully articulated. It defines, albeit roughly, the boundaries of the set of potentially solvable puzzles even though the set is not partitioned into its minimal elements, and it suggests what a full blown set of laws would be.

Paradigms and the State of Theory in Comparative Politics

As we pointed out at the very beginning, we defined our task as one of comparing and evaluating the various competing paradigms in the field of comparative politics. The conceptual and theoretical elements, the rules of interpretation, the puzzle-defining aspects, the criteria of admissibility, and the ontologic-predictive element provide a set of dimensions on the basis of which various paradigms can be compared. In order to evaluate, however, we need a set of evaluative criteria.

Some of these criteria follow directly from the foregoing discussion, or from the more general logical and methodological constraints that are operative for all scientific enterprises.[17] For example, a competitor that includes logically sound propositions which interrelate at least some of the major concepts and have been subjected to verification through research and the application of explicit rules of interpretation would be more promising than a paradigm that was little more than a body of concepts. In fact, as our readers are no doubt aware, unfortunately many alleged theories of political phenomena are really nothing more than a specialized vocabulary for description.

Clearly the science of comparative politics is presently in a preparadigmatic stage. It is intriguing to note that Kuhn describes this stage of the development of a science as one characterized by much "random fact-gathering," which "in the absence of a reason for seeking some particular form of recondite information . . . is usually restricted to the wealth of data that lie readily at hand."[18] He goes on to say:

> If a body of belief is not already implicit in the collection of facts—in which case more than "mere facts" are at hand—it must be externally supplied, perhaps by a current metaphysic, or another science, or perhaps by personal and historical accident. No wonder, then, that in the early stages of the development of any science, different men confronting the same range of phenomena, but not usually all the same particular phenomena, describe and interpret them in a different way.[19]

If this appears to have been written specifically about political science over the past twenty years, we must remember that the characterization applies also to the study of mechanics before Newton, of heat before Black, and of chemistry before Boyle and Boerhaave.

We may well ask this question: How does a science move from this period of confusion into a stage where a paradigm is consensually accepted and most of the activity becomes normal research? When the adherents of a particular competing paradigm can demonstrate that their approach is more successful in solving a few problems that a wider group of practitioners in the field recognize as significant, that paradigm should gain in status. But what seems to be more important than the results of a particular application or series of applications is a growing consensus on the greater promise of a particular paradigm. The boundaries of and the partitioning of theoretical space by the conceptual and ontologic-predictive elements are particularly important in this regard. Agreement about these two elements leads to a consensually accepted vocabulary and a delimited set of operational objectives. Thus scientists are free from the constant need to reiterate fundamentals and can begin to undertake more precise and focused empirical and theoretical work that is far more additive than the diffuse explorations which preceded it.

An approach to the problem of evaluation can be inferred from this discussion. It suggests that the potential range of future applications of partially articulated schema may be far more important than the range and even the precision of present applications. The potential deductive power and richness of the theoretical element should receive particular attention.

The task of evaluation and comparison is not an easy one. Clearly it would be difficult to survey the entire field of comparative politics in a book-length monograph, let alone a short essay. Furthermore, we are faced with serious problems of organization, as there is no way to partition neatly the set of proposed theories into disjoint subsets. In the following discussion we partitioned the field into five major approaches—structural-functionalism, general systems analysis, psychological approaches, rational formal models, and atheoretical approaches—each of which seems to have certain distinctive characteristics although sharing certain features. In each of these areas, we tried to select one or two representative works to analyze in some detail, rather than attempting a broader survey. However, we do not claim that these are the only works that might have been selected or that the boundaries between approaches or schools of thought can be specified completely. Indeed, the lack of such boundaries is a characteristic of an area of investigation in its preparadigmatic stages.

Schools of Thought in Comparative Politics

Structural-Functional Analysis

It should come as no surprise that we begin our stock-taking by examining structural-functional formulations in comparative politics. A fair number of scholars in the field have adopted some form or another of structural-functional analysis, and one of the authors of this essay works within this paradigm.[20] Indeed, it would be useful to take his approach simply to illustrate how one can analyze a certain school of thought by systematically identifying how each of the five elements of a paradigm is treated.

Holt has a very explicit answer to the paradigmatic question, "Of what is reality composed?"

> . . . we take the position that structural-functional analysis is a distinguishable approach primarily because of the selective aspects of social reality that it seeks to describe, explain and predict. It describes social reality largely in terms of structure, processes, mechanisms and functions.[21]

Other concepts are also important—role, social system, cultural system, functional requisites, and so on—but their number is very limited. Ideally, all of the propositions, both logical and empirical, should contain no scientific terms other than those that have been defined within the paradigm. We shall return to this point later with some specific illustrations.

Holt's paradigm is very weak in its theoretical element—in its general empirical propositions, laws, and hypotheses—but even as prejudiced observers, we do not think that he is atypical in this respect. His formulation does contain some specific hypotheses concerning, for example, the increase of the functions of government in primitive societies, and the political factors that are preconditions of early industrialization. But in a well-articulated paradigm, those propositions would have to be deduced from some more general ones, and nowhere in his writings can one find a statement of these more general propositions. But although these propositions are absent, there is a clear indication of the general form that they should take.

> [Propositions] that would be of explanatory and predictive importance would be based on the fundamental proposition that the state of the system at any time t_1 is determined by its state at some other time t_0 and by all the events which occur on the boundary during the time interval $t_0 - t_1$. The state of the system is described in terms of the determinate sequence of structure-mechanism and process-functions.[22]

29

A general statement is presented identifying the major puzzles:

> The phenomena of structural alternatives—that different structures in different types of systems may contribute to the satisfaction of the same functional requisites—is fundamental to this whole framework. It is this phenomenon that is of explanatory and predictive interest. The problem [puzzle] is to explain why a certain structure rather than another contributes to the satisfaction of a given requisite or requisites in a given social system at a given time and to predict what specific structure or structures will contribute to the satisfaction of a given function at some specific time.[23]

Such a general statement of a puzzle is not much of a guide to empirical research, but it is possible to look at a specific empirical problem and to interpret it within the confines of this kind of structural-functional framework. This is what Holt and Turner did in their analysis of the political basis of economic development. They noted that England and Japan industrialized very rapidly after the introduction of an industrial technology, while France and China moved very slowly. Their analysis suggested that the difference in these two sets of cases at time t_1 (several decades after the technology of industrialization became available in each of the four countries) could not be accounted for by events on the boundary of the social system in the time interval $t_0 - t_1$ (where t_0 is some time several centuries before the knowledge of an industrial technology became available in each of the four countries). If this assumption were correct, then the differences in outcome between the two sets of cases would have to be accounted for by differences in the state of the system in the time interval t_0 to t_1. The state of the system, in turn, would have to be described in terms of the different patterns of structures that contributed to the satisfaction of the four functional requisites of any society and by the different ways (procedures) by which a given structure contributed to the satisfaction of a given requisite. (The introduction of this latter consideration of *procedures* represents a further articulation of the paradigm.)

Holt and Turner were largely interested in government, in the alternatives to this structure that were obvious from a consideration of just these four societies, and in the procedures of governing. In other words, they asked two questions: Are there certain functional requisites to which government must contribute and others to which government must not contribute in the time period t_0 if a society is to industrialize rapidly after knowledge of the necessary technology is available? Are there certain ways (procedures) in which government must (and must not) contribute to certain functional requisites in the time period t_0 if a society is to industrialize rapidly after the knowledge of the necessary technology is available? The answer to these questions was a set of empirical propositions about functions of government and procedures of governing. For example, they hypothesized that if the state of the system in time t_0 includes a government that contributes significantly to the satisfaction of the adaptive functional requisite, there will not be a rapid industrialization in time t_1.[24] This proposition referred to a function of government. The following is a proposition that dealt with the way in which procedures were relevant. *A government that contributes to the satisfaction of the integrative functional requisite by severely restricting mobility from merchant and entrepreneurial groups into the traditional aristocracy in time t_0 enhances the probability of rapid industrialization in time t_1; and a government that contributes to the satisfaction of the integrative functional requisite by facilitating mobility from commercial and entrepreneurial groups into the traditional aristocracy in time t_0 prevents rapid industrialization in time t_1.*[25]

Let us review briefly what we have done in the past few paragraphs. First, we examined a structural-functional paradigm identified as a general puzzle. Second, we observed an interesting contrast in the industrialization experiences of Japan and England as compared with France and China. Third, we defined this particular empirical situation in terms of our general puzzle. Finally, we came up with a set of propositions that account for the difference in outcome. Note that we were careful to keep all of these propositions in a form that conforms to the rules established by the paradigm. The difference between the state of the system in the two sets of cases at time t_1 has been accounted for by differences in the state of the system in t_0 (there were no significant differentiating events on the boundary during the time interval) and the state of the system was described in terms of structures, functions, and procedures. (Unfortunately, the prose one is forced to adopt is far from graceful, but we have not yet discovered a way in which we could both conform to the rules of the paradigm and have graceful and eloquent prose.)

The next question we must ask is whether or not Holt and Turner solved the puzzle. The answer is "no," but as the two works on structural-functional analysis referred to earlier give no rules governing what solutions to the puzzle are admissible, we must elaborate in some detail. The empirical proposition on the political basis of economic growth asserts that differences in the state of the system at time t_0 "determines the differences at time t_1." But they do little more than state an association between two variables, one of which is temporally prior to the other. In order to solve the puzzle the authors must do much more than that. They must show (1) that there is a set of rules of behavior that, if followed by a large number of individuals, will have the aggregate consequences we observed, and (2) that a large number of individuals in fact made decisions according to these rules.

Let us look at these requirements in relationship to the hypothesis (stated earlier) on the role of the government in controlling social mobility in preindustrial societies. Holt and Turner argued that at the time the technology of industrialization becomes available there must be a significant proportion of the population with a relatively high propensity to save and that there must be some high concentrations of capital available for investment in new physical capital.[26] In all four countries, they held, the economically active elements of the population sought both wealth and prestige, but that the utility schedules were such that the marginal utility of an additional unit of prestige exceeded that of an additional unit of wealth at fairly low levels of wealth. Beyond some threshold, therefore, propensities to consume would remain about constant, or perhaps even rise slightly if individuals followed their own preferences unrestricted by any parametric conditions. This was essentially the case in France and China where government policy made it easy for individuals to opt for prestige. In England and Japan, by contrast, such choices were effectively blocked by the government, and as individual income increased, the propensity to save increased. This led to significant (although small) rates of economic growth in a preindustrial period and (when combined with other mechanisms) to concentrations of wealth available for investment in the new physical capital required by an industrializing society. (It should be pointed out that these rules can be stated symbolically with great precision and take the form of a context sensitive transformational grammar.)

We can demonstrate that these rules of behavior, if followed, would lead to the observed outcomes. This, however, is not sufficient. We must demonstrate that this set of rules, rather than some other set that would lead to the same result, was the one being followed. It taxes our ingenuity beyond the breaking point to figure out a way in which we can demonstrate in a convincing manner that people who lived in four different countries several centuries ago were in fact following these rules. To solve our puzzle, we must turn to another research site.

The requirements for this site are in basic outline simple. It is necessary to find an area with two separate preindustrial populations that have the following characteristics: (1) they are well insulated from one another; (2) they are identical in every regard except that in one there are legal restrictions on movement from the commercial and entrepreneurial groups into the traditionally most prestigious classes; (3) they are experiencing significant economic inputs that would lead to identical increases in income.

To find a site that would conform exactly to these requirements is, of course, impossible. However, a close approximation is the northeast corner of the kingdom of Morocco. In that area of the country, distinct groups of Berbers and Arabs live in close proximity but remain relatively well insulated from one another largely because of topographic features. The Berbers and Arabs in this area have many features in common. They profess the same religious faith, live in similar physical environments, have similar educational levels, and use a similar productive technology. According to the literature, however, the social systems of the Berbers and Arabs have important structural differences, particularly in social stratification and social mobility. The Arabs are described as having a rigid stratification system with sharply differentiated classes which may take the form of endogamous castes. The Berbers, by contrast, have social differences that are less well defined partly because of the openness of the system. Apparently no formally ascribed characteristics are requisite for achieving positions of prestige and power in the traditional social system. The differences between Berbers and Arabs in kinship patterns seem to be closely related to this difference in mobility.

In northeastern Morocco a large dam that has just been completed will supply water for an irrigation system which will cover over 300,000 acres within about 25 years. Berbers and Arabs are equally affected and will be able to shift from a high-risk, small grain agriculture with low productivity into highly productive citrus fruit cultivation. Income levels should rise rapidly, but we would predict that Berbers would spend more for purchasing prestige than would the Arabs and would have significantly lower propensities to save. This research site can determine whether or not individuals are following the rules of behavior Holt and Turner have hypothesized and, if so, whether or not they lead in the aggregate to the predicted results. If the hypotheses are confirmed, we can say that we have solved this one little puzzle.

All of the elements of a paradigm outlined in the introduction to this chapter have been reviewed in this example. Evaluation is another matter, however, and we shall have some comments on this later. Let us look first at another, quite different functional approach.

The most widely heralded and best known structural-functional paradigm in political science is that developed by Gabriel A. Almond.[27] The extent to which Almond's framework has penetrated the discipline in just a few years is remarkable. A decade ago terms like *interest aggregation* and *interest articulation* were unknown in the profession; today it would be a foolish graduate student indeed who would walk into an oral examination without knowing their meaning. One cannot examine the state of theory in comparative politics without devoting considerable attention to analyzing Almond's point of view.

On two of the five aspects of a paradigm outlined earlier, Almond is very explicit. First, he has provided a rich and relatively exhaustive set of concepts in terms of which one can describe the political system. With the possible exception of certain problems that have captured the attention of students of the totalitarian systems, there seem to be few phenomena of interest to contemporary political scientists that could not be described in terms of Almond's framework. *Political system, political structure, political functions, political culture, political socialization, capability,* and many other terms provide a rich conceptual basis for his paradigm.

Second, Almond has explicitly addressed himself to the problem of what

33

a theory stated in his terms would look like. In his earlier writings he stated:

> The functional theory of the polity which we have elaborated above does specify the element of the polity in such a way as may ultimately make possible statistical and perhaps mathematical formulation. What we have done is to separate political function from political structure. In other words, we have specified the elements of the two sets, one of functions and the other of structures, and have suggested that political systems may be compared in the terms of the probabilities of the performance of the specified functions by the specified structures. In addition, we have specified styles of performance of function by structure which makes it possible for us at least to think of a state of knowledge of political systems in which we could make precise comparisons relating the elements of the three acts—functions, structures and styles—in the form of a series of probability statements.[28]

Although his later writings clearly indicate that this formulation should be expanded (for example, they include statements about the variation in the capability of different political systems), the probability relationship between structures and functions remains of central concern.

> . . . All political systems can be compared in terms of the relationship between functions and structures. That is, in a particular political system at a particular interval of time, (sic) there is a given probability that function A will be performed by structure X (e.g., that political demands will be made by associational interest groups). This proposition assumes that all the political functions can, *in some sense*, be found in all political systems, and that all political systems, including the simplest ones, have political structure.[29]

A probabilistic theory of the polity containing theoretical propositions linking structures and functions is a highly commendable goal. The future of theorizing in political science would be rosier if more political scientists would conceive of the direction in which they are heading with the same degree of explicitness. However, considerable refinements will have to be made in the formulation before this laudable goal can be achieved. The major problems are the lack of rigorous definition of *structure* and *function* in general and the absence of rigorous definitions of many of the political structures in particular. Let us take the latter problem first. Almond does not explicitly define many of the structures like *interest group* and *political party* that are crucial in his analysis. There is a tendency to define structures in terms of their functions. Interest groups are groups that articulate interest; political parties are structures that aggregate interests. As long as structures are defined this way, there can be no probabilistic theory of the polity in the form Almond proposes. The propositions linking structure and function will be logical propositions devoid of any empirical content. The probabilities in statements linking structure and function will all be 1.0, and cannot be tested empirically because they will be true by definition.[30]

34

Correcting this shortcoming will be no easy matter, largely because of the imprecision in the basic definition of structure and function. Almond defines structure as a related set of roles.[31] Role is referred to as the "observable behavior of individuals,"[32] but no clear definition is presented. One does not know, for example, if "role expectations" are included in the definition of role or if they are determinates of role. Lack of clarity on definitional matters like this will make it difficult to develop a definition of a particular political structure that is independent of a particular function.

The kinds of propositions in which Almond uses the term *role* may also be confusing. For example, he speaks of "intermittent structures and roles." ("The citizen of the modern democracy is an intermittent politician . . . ") This raises the question of whether or not the role exists independent of a particular time when the behavior was directly observable. Is there a role of voter in the United States on a day in which no election is being held? If the role itself is intermittent, the answer to this question must be no. But this formulation tends to confuse the concept *actor* with the concept *role*, which in turn makes it difficult to define a structure.

Similar problems crop up in Almond's definition of *function*. Let us look briefly at some of the statements in which he uses this term. "Interest articulation is particularly important because it marks the boundary between the society and the political system."[33] Interest articulation is a function and therefore can *mark a boundary*. We find it difficult to understand the meaning of the concept *function* when used in this manner. In another place Almond states: "Political socialization is the process by which political cultures are maintained and changed."[34] As political socialization is a function in the basic formulation, we must conclude that a *function* can be a *process* at least under some conditions. But what these conditions are and what the general relationships between function and process are is left to the reader's imagination.

The lack of clarity in the definition of basic concepts and a certain confusion in their logical interrelationships make it very difficult to determine the theoretical aspects of Almond's paradigm. That is, we cannot identify clearly which propositions are theoretical, and thus are empirically testable, and which are logical and true by definition. Let us look at some statements that illustrate the problem. A scholar working with the Almond framework could easily advance the following proposition:

> The greater the structural differentiation, cultural secularization, and subsystem autonomy, the more democratic the system.

But is this proposition true because of the way in which basic items like *democratic system* and *subsystem autonomy* are defined (and therefore a tautology), or is it a proposition that could be proved false through empirical research?

35

We do not know the answer because parts of Almond's writings imply one answer and other parts another answer.

The same kind of problem emerges if one examines propositions that relate to political development. The following statement seems to us to be derivable directly from Almond's writings:

> The more specialized the roles for extraction of resources, the more efficient the extraction of resources (or the greater the performance potential).

We cannot find, however, a clear definition of *efficiency* (let alone an operational definition), nor can we determine any way in which Almond would define "roles for extraction of resources" independently of "extraction of resources." Indeed, sections of his writings suggest that *increased specialization of roles* for extractive purposes is measured by greater efficiency.

We will not belabor the point by listing a half dozen statements that contain similar ambiguities. The point is that because we cannot distinguish with any clarity between logical and empirical propositions, we cannot examine the theoretical aspect of Almond's paradigm.

As the puzzles emerge largely from the way in which clearly separable logical and empirical propositions are interrelated, we cannot identify any puzzles in Almond's paradigm. In other words, we cannot find a good researchable problem whose solution would aid in the further articulation of the paradigm. There is, however, a passage in which Almond states his interest in problems of generalization and prediction, and to this we take exception.

> The problem of generalization and prediction . . . is of particular concern for two reasons. First, we are ethically concerned with the problems of political development and political change in the contemporary world. The prospects for democracy and human welfare in many parts of the contemporary world are unclear and troubling. We regard the confusion and often threatening events of the last twenty years, and the search for solutions to the problems of instability and internal warfare as challenges to us as citizens and as political scientists. They are a part of the challenge to all the social sciences to help men describe, explain, and predict the events of social life in order that they may grapple with their problems in a rational manner.[35]

This statement is indicative of the deep and laudable humanistic concerns that pervade Almond's writings. But such concerns, when they are identified with the role of the political scientist as well as with the role of the citizen, may be the source of an insidious weakness which greatly inhibits scientific advance. We pointed out earlier how Kuhn emphasizes the importance of a paradigm in helping to insulate the scholarly community from a whole host of ethically and socially pressing problems, and how he partially attributes the enormous progress that science has made to the effect of this insulation. If in the foregoing passage Almond is suggesting that effort be devoted by political scientists *qua* scientists to solving problems such as political instability and internal warfare *because* of their social importance, we take a strong exception. Exactly such concerns may delay the development and articulation of a paradigm that contains the knowledge that will make these problems soluable in the long run. If they are not puzzles that are identified as puzzles by a paradigm in its present stage, attention to them is likely to delay rather than facilitate scientific progress. Our humanism at present is better expressed as citizens than as scientists.

We can conclude that the conceptual element in Almond's paradigm is rich, but logically confused. This confusion makes it virtually impossible to identify the theoretical element, the puzzles and rules of interpretation, and the criteria of admissibility.

Systems Analysis

We have categorized a second group of paradigmatic competitors under the heading of "Systems Analysis." Within this group, we include the works of those scholars whose intellectual debts to the pioneering approach of cyberneticians such as Norbert Weiner[36] and to the more recent work of members of the Society for the Study of General Systems,[37] are relatively self-conscious and explicit.[38]

Excluded are the structural-functional approaches and a large number of works in which political system is used simply as a substitute for conventional terms such as *government, state,* or *nation* with no significant change in meaning or explicit system-theoretic orientation.

We shall examine in some detail the contributions of David Easton, whose name is most frequently associated with the term *systems analysis* in political science[39] and Karl Deutsch who is concerned more explicitly with applications of the concepts of cybernetics to political phenomena.[40] Before proceeding with this examination, a few general comments on what we perceive to be the general system theoretic paradigm upon which these contributions are based are in order.

The reality of the systems theorist comprises behavioral patterns that can be represented as a set of determinate or stochastic mapping functions or transformations.[41] In the most general terms a system is simply a "set of objects, together with relationships between the objects and between their attributes."[42] To say that a system exists, however, one must be able to specify a set of elements (objects) and a set of relationships between the elements that are essentially invariant (or vary only within explicitly defined limits). In other words, the boundaries between the system and its environment must be defined. The task of the system theorist, then, may be characterized as a search for rules of interpretation which enable him to establish correspondence between some aspect of nature and the structure of his model. If and when such correspondence is established, a very large number of interesting puzzles relating to the maintenance, control, regulation, and decline or breakdown of the defined system are posed for solution. Furthermore, an elaborate set of concepts and theorems can be brought to bear on the puzzle-solving enterprise.[43]

Two characteristics of this approach seem to render it particularly attractive for social scientists in general and for students of comparative politics in particular. First, it is equally applicable to all aspects of nature, regardless of the substantive context in which patterned behavior occurs. As Ashby emphasizes:

> Cybernetics deals with all forms of behavior in so far as they are regular, determinate or reproducible. The truths of cybernetics are not conditional on their being derived from some other branch of science. Cybernetics has its own foundations.[44]

Second, the properties of homomorphism or isomorphism between systems hold out the possibility that the progress in paradigm elaboration in an area where problems of observation and experimentation are solvable can contribute to progress in areas where these problems seem insurmountable. Furthermore, adoption of the general systems paradigm can facilitate interdisciplinary communication by providing a set of basic concepts and even theorems that are equally relevant (and have the same meaning) for all practitioners.

It would seem, then, that the general systems approach holds out considerable promise for the field of comparative politics. However, before turning to the specific attempts at application which we wish to consider, we must sound a note of warning. The most fruitful applications of systems analysis in other disciplines—for example, biology, economics, and physics—have required a degree of methodological sophistication not generally found among political scientists. The discovery of rules of interpretation that permit the reduction to puzzle form, in terms of this paradigm, of the extremely complex phenomena with which political scientists are concerned would seem to require *at least* a comparable degree of sophistication. This competence gap between the requirements of the paradigm and the capabilities of most students of comparative politics has not, we believe, been sufficiently emphasized in the works about to be considered. Consequently, the claims that are made for this type of approach tend to be presented in an oversimplified form, which does not adequately reflect the coherence and power of the paradigm itself.

38

The Nerves of Government: A Cybernetic Approach to the Analysis of Political Phenomena

In *The Nerves of Government*, Deutsch claims to be presenting no more than a "point of view" and a "body of ideas and suggestions." Thus it is perhaps unfair to evaluate his approach as if it purported to be a fully developed paradigm. Yet if we exclude criteria of admissibility and accept a set of insightful but intuitive propositions in lieu of a rigorously defined theoretical element, all of the essential components of a paradigm are at least partially articulated.

Deutsch is particularly explicit in his definition of a set of basic concepts in terms of which reality is to be perceived. *Cybernetics* is defined as "the science of communication and control." Its focus is "the systematic study of communication and control in organizations of all kinds . . . The viewpoint of cybernetics suggests that all organizations are alike in certain fundamental characteristics and that every organization is held together by communication." Because "governments" are organizations, we should, according to Deutsch, be sensitized to the crucial importance of those concepts in terms of which information processes can be represented.[45]

Although not all of Deutsch's concepts can be discussed in detail, it will be helpful to consider some of the most important. We have already noted that organizations are viewed, in general, as information-processing systems. Information is a patterned relationship between events. Communication is the transfer of such patterned relationships. Channels are the paths or associative trails through which information is transferred.

These three concepts—information, communication, and channel—assume the status of theoretical primitives in terms of which further definitions are constructed. Before looking at them, however, it will be necessary to examine Deutsch's general model of an information processing system, i.e., the propositions in terms of which the behavior of such systems is described.

The mechanism chosen for a model is one that is particularly common in complex weapons control and guidance systems, the error controlled regulator. It is not, we should emphasize, the only mechanism he might have chosen, though Deutsch devotes little attention to considering other possible alternatives. This mechanism may be described in general terms as follows: the system has information, either internally or externally imposed, about a set of states of goals to be attained. These goals may refer either to the maintenance of the system itself (i.e., the restriction of internal variables within specified limits) or to more purposive objectives. The latter may also be defined as the attainment of a set of states, but in this case not directly related to the maintenance of the system.[46]

When the system is in a state that differs from a particular goal, an error signal is generated. In Deutsch's system (but not all error controlled regulators), internal mechanisms compare the error signal with "memory," which includes information about the state of the system and, to the degree that the system has this capacity, previous learned behavior. Out of this process of comparison, initial corrective action is initiated. This brings us to the important concept of *feedback*. The feedback network in the system carries information about the effects of previous increments of corrective action. Thus information affects the generation of new corrective increments in a continuous dynamic process until the goal is attained.

A more rigorous specification of the model could conceivably lead to a set of testable propositions, some of which would be, in principle at least, verifiable. It is apparent, however, that this is not Deutsch's intention. Instead, his ambitious goal is to propose suggestive guidelines for research by explicating the traditional concerns not only of political science, but also of political philosophy and normative political theory in terms of cybernetic or quasi-cybernetic terminology.

Readers familiar with *The Nerves of Government* will probably concur with our conclusion that Deutsch has been remarkably successful in attaining this goal. A wealth of suggestive insights and avenues for research are offered that are relevant to the stability, adaptability, and efficiency of governmental and, for that matter, nongovernmental organization. Furthermore, many of the compelling normative issues that have concerned students of politics such as the relationship between politics and evil[47] and between love, cosmopolitanism, and nationalism[48] are the subject of prescriptive as well as analytical statements and/or hypotheses.

It is not the attainment of the objective of presenting a cybernetic "point of view" with regard to a multitude of varied and compelling concerns which we wish to question, but the objective itself. For despite its breadth and eclecticism (or perhaps because of it), Deutsch's formulation can hardly be regarded as a serious attempt at paradigm articulation. It is only possible to progress from the theoretical primitives—information, communication, and channel—to the partially articulated theoretical model, to the descriptive, prescriptive, and analytical statements about government and political life by intuitive leaps. Certainly the prospective puzzle solver is alerted to the fact that communication processes are of crucial importance for the functioning of organizations, political and otherwise, but beyond that point he is faced with an enormously complicated problem. In order to begin an enterprise resembling normal research, either theory articulation or empirical investigation, he must choose from a myriad of alternatives, all of which seem equally attractive intuitively but none of which is reducible to puzzle form.

Also a second problem to a considerable degree devolves from the breadth and eclecticism of Deutsch's concerns—the disarming simplicity in terms of which applications of the basic cybernetic model are suggested. Deutsch seems to imply, at least by the general tone of his discussion, that political phenomena can be interpreted using such a model in a relatively simple and straightforward fashion. However, we can assert on the basis of personal experience that for all but the most exceptional students of comparative politics, a serious attempt to work within this theoretical frame of reference will require a long and often discouraging task of methodological retooling, the payoffs of which are by no means assured.[49] Yet a lesser commitment will lead to nothing more than a type of theoretical dilettantism already too prevalent in political science. We believe, as does Deutsch, that cybernetics suggests intriguing possibilities for the rigorous analysis of political phenomena. Furthermore, quite possibly the theorems derived from such a paradigm may ultimately take a form that is somewhat similar to the intuitive insights he has presented. Given the evidence presently available, however, it is also possible that this approach may be of little or no value, and that the paradigm for comparative politics may take an entirely different form. Unfortunately, the crucial questions which a paradigm must begin to resolve in order to gain acceptance have not been seriously considered by Deutsch's insightful prolegomena.

The Eastonian Paradigm: "A Systems Analysis of Political Life"

No discussion of *systems theory* in comparative politics could be complete without some reference to the work of David Easton. However, given the fact that the name Easton and the term *systems analysis* are almost inextricably linked, it is somewhat startling to discover that Easton's paradigm differs significantly from the other formulations usually associated with the label. Although Easton is obviously familiar with the formal theory of general systems discussed earlier, he proposes in his two most recent works a fundamentally different approach to the study of political phenomena.[50]

As we shall see, the use of the term *system* or *political system* is the crux of this difference and the source of apparently insolvable theoretical and methodological problems in Easton's formulation. Before addressing ourselves to these points, however, it will be useful to examine some of the other elements of the Eastonian paradigm.

The form which the laws derived from the paradigm will take is discussed quite explicitly in one of Easton's earlier works:

> The fruitfulness of the approach is suggested by its implications for the comparative study of political institutions. Given the discovery of similar or identical tasks in every political system, contemporary or historical, it would then be possible to examine comparatively the way in which these institutions

41

fulfill the same tasks under differing conditions in each political system. Political science would then be in a position to draw generalizations that pass beyond the experience of any one political system or of the systems in any one culture or civilization.[51]

How is this potential fruitfulness to be attained? As is the case with the other paradigms which we have examined, Easton has some rather specific ideas about the way in which reality should be perceived and which specific research tasks should be undertaken. "Political interactions in a society," he asserts, "constitute a *system of behavior* which is analytically separable from the total social system."[52] Thus it is possible to discriminate between the "essential variables" within the system (the allocation of values and the relative frequency of compliance), the environmental variables that influence the system, and the outputs of the system. Certain properties of systems are also discussed. First, it is assumed that they may be adaptive. Regarding this point, Easton observes:

> "they" (systems) must have the capacity to respond to disturbances and thereby to adapt to the conditions under which they find themselves. Once we are willing to assume that political systems may be adaptive, and need not just react passively to their environmental influences, we shall be able to cut a new path through the complexities of theoretical analysis.[53]

Second, they may be subjected to stress, that is, the "danger that the essential variables will be pushed beyond what we may designate as their critical range ... "[54] Third, they have empirically discoverable "life processes," that is, "those fundamental functions without which no system could endure, together with the typical modes of response through which systems manage to maintain them."[55] Fourth, they have *elements* or *units*, that is, "political actions."[56] And, fifth, they have *members*. Presumably, although Easton does not say, the concept of members of the system refers to some specifiable set of individuals who perform political actions. However, he does tell us that we should be primarily concerned with a subset of this membership, the authorities. It will be helpful to quote from Easton's discussion to clarify this point:

> When we speak of the system acting, we must be careful not to reify the system itself. We must bear in mind that all systems, to make collective action possible, have those who usually speak in the name of or in behalf of the system. We may designate these as the authorities.[57]

This brings us to the final property of systems, *political outputs*. "These are the decisions and actions of the authorities ... "[58] Elsewhere the political outputs are defined as "authoritative allocations of values."[59]

Earlier, we referred briefly to the environmental influences and disturbances that impinge upon the boundaries of the system. Obviously the variety and complexity of environmental variation pose a serious analytical problem. However, Easton observes that "we can greatly simplify the task of analyzing the impact of the environment if we restrict our attention to certain kinds of inputs that can be used as indicators to sum up the most important effects, in terms of their contributions to stress, that cross the boundary from the parametric to the political systems. In this way we could free ourselves from the need to deal with and trace out separately the consequences of each environmental event."[60] He elaborates as follows:

> As the theoretical tool for this purpose, it is helpful to view the major environmental influences as focusing on two major inputs: demands and support. Through them, a wide range of activities in the environment can be channeled, mirrored, summarized and brought to bear upon political life. Hence they are key indicators of the way in which environmental influences and conditions modify and shape the operations of the political system.[61]

It may seem to our readers that what has been presented corresponds to what we have called a theoretical element of a paradigm, i.e., a formal model from which empirical propositions corresponding to reality can be deduced. Indeed, Easton reinforces this presumption by referring to his formulation as a "flow model of the political system." However, it is quite clear that in reality something quite different from a formal model has been presented.

Easton asserts that "if the idea system is used with the rigor it permits and with all its currently inherent implications, it provides a starting point which is already heavily freighted with consequences for analysis." He is thus making explicitly a point that should already be obvious to our readers, namely, that the concept *system* is of crucial importance in his formulation. Clearly the assertion that "political interactions in a society constitute a system of behavior" has significant meaning only if (1) the concept, system of behavior, has been clearly defined, and (2) sets of political interactions exist in societies that conform to this definition. Furthermore, if such a concept has "inherent implications" and is "heavily freighted" with consequences for analysis, it seems reasonable to presume that such implications and consequences are the *deductive* implications and *logical* consequences of a well-developed body of theory. Indeed, it would not be unreasonable to presume that it is the general systems approach which Easton is talking about. However, he seems to reject this approach explicitly. For he asserts that "we may define a system as *any set of variables, regardless of the degree of interrelationship between them.*"[62] Thus we are left in a curious theoretical limbo, for it does not seem on the face of it that the concept "any set of variables regardless of the degree of interrelationship between them" is freighted with any consequences or implications. Easton's justification of this definition does little to clarify matters. He asserts that:

> The reason for preferring this definition is that it frees us from the need to argue about whether or not a political system is really a system. The only question of importance about a set selected as a system to be analyzed is whether this constitutes an interesting system. Does it help us to understand some aspect of human behavior of concern to us?[63]

This statement, we submit, can only be interpreted to mean that the Eastonian form of *systems analysis* directs our attention to the study of "any set of variables, regardless of the interrelationship between them" that "helps us to understand some aspects of human behavior of concern to us."

Before any sort of theoretical elaboration or empirical investigation relevant to political life can be undertaken further definitions are necessary. At a later point, Easton provides us with one. "The political system," he states, "can be designated as those interactions through which values are authoritatively allocated for a society."[64] This definition, however, leads to a question that seems critical to the presumption that the set of propositions constituting the core of Easton's "framework" can be used as a model, namely, what is the nature of the relationship between the system as defined and the statements purporting to describe its attributes? We know of no rules of inference that permit us to make unambiguous statements about the elements, members, boundaries, or environment of a "system" that has been defined in this way. By opting for a definition of "the system" that is so general as to include practically anything, Easton has presented us with an emasculated paradigm virtually devoid of a theoretical element. To be sure, such a definition "frees us from the need to argue about whether a political system is really a system." But if Easton's paradigm is to be anything more than an interesting collection of descriptive categories and intuitive generalizations, that is exactly what we should be arguing about.

It should now be quite clear why we have suggested that Easton's approach is fundamentally different from that of the other general systems theorists. Although he employs some of the language of more conventional forms of systems analysis, the propositions that are presented as a model and as guides to further research are nothing more than a set of interesting but *ad hoc* statements about governments. To clarify this point, it will be helpful to refer again to the discussion of stress. Easton offers the following concrete examples of stressful conditions:

> What this means is that something may be happening in the environment—the system suffers total defeat at the hands of an enemy or a severe economic crisis arouses widespread disorganization in and disaffection from the system. Let us assume that, as a result, either the authorities are consistently unable to

44

make decisions or the decisions they do make are no longer legally accepted as binding. Under these conditions, authoritative allocations of values are no longer possible, and the society collapses for want of a system of behavior to fulfill one of its final functions.[65]

It is extremely difficult, we contend, to think about a "set of interactions" being subjected to total defeat at the hands of the enemy or to severe economic crises. Nor is it usual for such "sets" to be the object of widespread disaffection. If the term *government* is substituted for systems, however, these statements become at least plausible. But to say that these statements and the other statements in terms of which the Eastonian framework is presented can be given a plausible interpretation is not to say that they can be expressed in puzzle form. Given the absence of a meaningful definition of the term *system*, it is difficult to see how this could be done. Indeed, if our assessment is correct, Easton's framework does not meet the basic requirements of a paradigm at all. By discarding the formal model of the general systems theorists, Easton has also discarded the "inherent implications" and "consequences for a whole pattern of analysis" with which it is freighted.

Psychological Approaches

The approaches discussed thus far are macrotheoretical, and the explanations of political development phenomena tend to be *emergent* rather than *reductive*.[66] Although this kind of paradigm is the most common in contemporary political science, a number of students of comparative politics place a great deal of weight on personality variables and attempt to explain important political system characteristics in terms of the personality characteristics of the actors in the political system. This emphasis is not new in political science. Harold Lasswell's works in the early 1930s—particularly *Psychopathology and Politics*[67] —attempted to bring theoretical work in individual psychology to bear on problems of political analysis. Nor is the approach limited to political science. The works of David McClelland and Everett Hagan (to mention only two scholars) provide an explanation of economic development in terms of dominant individual personality characteristics.[68]

In the field of comparative politics, Lucian Pye has developed some of the most interesting and comprehensive psychological approaches. His explanation of the rigidity and formalism in the Burmese bureaucracy provides a typical example of how he uses psychological concepts as explanatory variables.

> The urge to withhold confidence in subordinates permeates almost all hierarchical relationships within the present-day Burmese bureaucracy. Thus barriers are established to casual, relaxed, and informal relationships, creating a situation especially disturbing to men who initially learned that government

45

service could and should offer warm, close, and exciting personal associations. Now all relationships seem to be cold and indifferent. There is an increased need to emphasize status considerations in order to insure one's security in the hierarchy. The result is an enveloping sense of isolation and loneliness. In addition to feeling that they have been under constant attack from politicians on the outside, the senior administrators feel themselves about to be waylaid and criticized by people within their establishments.

The feelings of isolation and insecurity of course breed further distrust and the belief that discipline should be more strongly enforced, which, when combined with the basic Burmese desire for status but fear of decision and choice, tend to choke off the flow of communication within the administrative service. Superiors cannot share their problems with subordinates, and subordinates feel it necessary to adhere rigidly to correct form and procedure in all their dealings with their superiors. There is thus a profound psychological reason why it is impossible to hold staff meetings within the Burmese bureaucracy, and why superiors and subordinates cannot explore operational problems together. Trial and error and free discussion might only prove that superiors are fallible. And here we find the basic psychological reason why the Burmese administrative class clings so tenaciously to formal procedure. Confronted with a pervasive sense of insecurity, everyone must fall back on the safest course of action; everyone must adhere strictly to form, to procedure, to ritual.[69]

By quoting these two paragraphs, we do not mean to create the impression that Pye limits his concern to an explanation of a certain kind of behavior in a governmental bureaucracy. He goes much further than this and uses his psychological approach to account for the failure of certain systems to modernize.

As Pye's book on Burma is a case study rather than a general theoretical work like those of Almond, Deutsch, and Easton, it is understandable that he has not provided the same degree of conceptual elaboration. The conceptual element of his paradigm employs a technical vocabulary with explicit definitions for dealing with personality characteristics; however, when dealing with the characteristics of the bureaucracy he operates with more general terms. Thus terms like *identity crisis* and *associational sentiments* are carefully defined and discussed at some length, whereas *formalism* and *rigidity* when used to refer to the bureaucracy are not.

Although the conceptual element of his paradigm is not well articulated, (and again let us state that this is not inappropriate for this type of case study), it is a tribute to the clarity of his presentation that one can abstract a set of propositions that represents the basic core of the theoretical element of his paradigm as it is applied to explaining slow progress towards nation-building.

1. Large, complex, effective, and thus flexible organizational forms are a crucial feature of a modern society.

46

2. Large, complex organizations cannot be flexible and effective unless, in addition to their formal structures, there exist significant informal structures, especially informal channels of communication.
3. Only individuals who have developed *associational sentiments* can form and effectively participate in these informal structures.
4. Individuals who are insecure and distrustful cannot manifest associational sentiments.

Therefore:

5. Organizations in which a significant proportion of the members are insecure and distrustful cannot have effective informal structures.

Therefore:

6. A modern society (which, by definition, has large, complex, effective, and hence flexible organizations) cannot develop when the crucial large-scale organizations have a disproportionate number of insecure and distrustful individuals.[70]

Propositions 3, 4, and 5 are particularly central in Pye's argument, and are based upon assumptions that are central to the theoretical element in most paradigms that fall under the general rubric of "psychological approaches."

The typical psychological approach identifies certain personality characteristics, which in turn give rise to certain individual needs. The attempts of numerous individuals to satisfy these needs result in patterns of behavior that characterize the macrosystem under consideration. Thus Pye finds the Burmese bureaucrat manifesting feelings of insecurity, which give rise to needs such as the "urge to withhold confidence," the "desire for status," and the need to "adhere rigidly to correct form and procedure." The behavior involved in satisfying these needs inhibits the development of informal structures and thus the development of flexible and effective organizational forms.

The leap from personality characteristics and needs, on the one hand, to behavior patterns, on the other, is far more problematic than the scholars who advocate psychological explanations seem willing to admit. Research in individual psychology indicates how complex and hazardous it may be. Political scientists who employ psychological approaches tend to use words like *insecurity, distrust,* and *aggression.* Few psychologists would move from concepts at this level of precision and generality to an analysis of behavior. The concept of *defense mechanisms* is usually introduced. Thus an individual who has pervasive feelings of insecurity may rely on the defense mechanisms of *regression, rationalization,* and/or *repression.* An individual who has feelings of aggression may rely on *projection* and/or *reaction formation.* To know that an individual has feelings of insecurity is not to know what defense mechanisms he employs in what situations. And to know what defense mechanisms he

47

employs is not to know what kind of behavior he engages in, because the behavioral manifestations of different defense mechanisms may be different in different people. For example, the person who relies heavily on projection to cope with feelings of aggression may be retiring and indecisive or he may show great intolerance of ambiguity and be decisive and driving. In a bureaucratic organization, he may rely rigidly on formal relationships that conform to the letter of organizational rules, or he may build up a clique of close friends at different positions in the hierarchy and use this network to bypass and even to undercut the normal bureaucratic channels. Simply to know that he has feelings of aggression and that he relies on projection does not form much of a basis for predicting how he will behave in the bureaucratic setting.[71]

It seems clear that the behavior of individuals with similar personality characteristics who employ similar defense mechanisms is heavily determined by their cultural and social structural setting. The setting varies significantly not only between societies but also within a given society. However, the way in which this cultural and social structural setting channels behavior and thus sets limits on the range of options that an individudal may choose to help to satisfy certain needs is largely ignored by those who favor psychological approaches. This is not to say that they ignore culture and social structure, but they use these variables to account for the development of common personality characteristics and values rather than for explaining how behavior is channeled by these factors. In other words, they are greatly concerned with the process of socialization, and one cannot understand the theoretical element of their paradigm unless one examines their approach to the process of socialization. This is certainly true of the works of Lucian Pye.[72]

We have several questions about the way in which the process of socialization is conceptualized by those who employ psychological approaches, and these questions cast some doubt on its utility. Pye relies heavily on the psychoanalytical tradition of psychology as evidenced by his acknowledgement of the theories of Eric H. Erikson. The early work done in socialization by those influenced by the psychoanalytic tradition was carried out in simple, relatively homogeneous societies, and the results of this early empirical research remain as a significant residue in contemporary theories. Modern societies like the United States, or developing societies like Burma, however, have a range of class, ethnic, and regional diversity that must be accounted for in any theory of socialization. In other words, modal values are not most significant, because nobody "comes into contact" with cultural values writ large. Rather, the kind of values institutionalized in the social structures most crucial in the socialization process are most relevant. Values institutionalized in families in different social classes, ethnic groups, and regions may vary considerably in different directions from the societal

48

mode. Therefore, to identify modal values and modal socialization practices, and to argue that these are most important in producing individuals of similar personality types and with similar values does not seem appropriate.

An even more significant problem of conceptualizing the socialization process is rarely recognized and never adequately dealt with. The differences in the structures in which socialization takes place may affect the manner in which similar values are incorporated into the personality structure in such a way that the behavioral manifestation of the same values are different in different individuals. A number of years ago, Vera French reported that philosophic-religious values may be incorporated as part of the "super-ego" structure or as part of the "ego" structure. Although individuals who displayed these different types of personality structure could not be distinguished on the basis of the content of their philosophic-religious beliefs, the behavioral manifestations of their beliefs were different.[73] Few clues in her work or in other psychological literature indicate how similar values come to be incorporated in different aspects of the personality structure, but we would hypothesize that it has much to do with the type of structure in which socialization takes place. If this is a reasonable hypothesis, then students of socialization must look beyond the content of values expressed by individuals into their personality structures and into the effect that the different socialization structures have on the relationships between individual values and personality structure. This would seem to be particularly important with respect to politically relevant beliefs and values.

We must make a third point, even though it takes us far beyond what students of political socialization have considered to be relevant. Recent studies indicate that there may be important genetic determinates of value proclivities.[74] These references do not suggest that political scientists must undertake work in genetics; they simply indicate that one must recognize the possible importance of genetic factors so that any differences in values and personality structure resulting from genetic differences are not attributed to socialization processes. Students of comparative politics must be particularly aware of the problem because of the different gene pools of widely separated societies.

Although we have these questions about the way in which the socialization process is conceptualized, they are not the most important part of our critique of psychological approaches to comparative politics. Psychological explanations are reductive explanations in the sense that they attempt to explain the behavior of a macrosystem in terms of some microsystem. For example, Pye tries to account for failures of "nation-building" in terms of individual personality characteristics. No one can doubt the power and desirability of reductive explanations, but in order for them to be understandable, there must a specification of the composition laws by which one moves from the micro to the macro level. Indeed, a conceptualization like

Pye's involves the more difficult methodological problems of moving from the cultural and societal level, to the individual (in the analysis of the socialization process), and then from the individual level back to the societal level to account for failures in nation-building. This is a formidable task, and one cannot be critical of those who fail in a given effort to master it. It seems to us, however, that the very approach taken to the problem precludes a solution. The psychoanalytic approach to socialization, while providing great insights, seems particularly unable to cope with the methodological problems of composition and decomposition. Anthony F. C. Wallace has identified the two major fallacies very well:

> The progress of research in culture-and-personality is, at times, hampered by the common use of fallacious metaphors and by faddish enthusiasms for particular jargons and techniques. But it is important to distinguish between fad and fallacy, on the one hand, and legitimate specialization, on the other.
> Conspicuous examples of the fallacious metaphor are the frequently mishandled words "internalization," "impact," and "mold." Thus, it is sometimes said that personality *is* (ontologically) culture "internalized" in the individual; that culture change has an "impact" on the individual; that culture "molds" the individual. Such expressions, and theoretical formulations based on them, are meaningless in any literal sense. As Radcliffe-Brown once remarked, "To say of culture patterns that they act upon an individual . . . is as absurd as to hold a quadratic equation capable of committing a murder." As we observed in connection with systems analysis, culture and personality are constructs of different "logical type," in Russell's sense; that is to say, the concept of a culture is a set of propositions about some of the same propositions which are included within the concept of one or more of the personalities within the society. Thus, to use transitive metaphors like "internalize," "impact," "mold," and so on, to describe the relation between culture and personality, is precisely comparable to claiming that a circle has an "impact on," or "molds," the points which constitute it, or that the points are "internalizations" (or "expressions," or "phrasings," or "transforms") of the equation describing the circle.
> The obverse of the "internalization" fallacy is the "statistical fallacy," which offers an enumeration of the properties of individual persons as if it were a description of a social or cultural system, without any demonstration that a non-random relationship obtains among the dimensions considered. Such statistical "structures" are mere archival materials unless a systematic relationship among the dimensions can be demonstrated.[75]

It is perhaps not too much of a generalization to state that most of the psychological approaches to comparative politics involve either the internalization or the statistical fallacy, and some, unfortunately, involve both.

This, of course, is a serious problem because the interesting puzzles that emerge from a psychological paradigm like Pye's should focus on the relationship between the personality as the micro-unit and some larger macro-unit like an organizational bureaucracy or a society. But there can be no significant puzzles until the composition laws are made explicit. Wallace is justified in using the term *fallacy* to apply to the internalization and statistical approaches to the relationship between personality and some larger unit because the composition laws implied by these approaches are logically nonsensical for the reasons he advances. Empirical research in psychology indicating that personality characteristics by themselves are not good predictors of behavior cast doubt on the possibility that there are any logically acceptable composition laws which will enable one to relate personality characteristics to larger group phenomena. Additional research and more sophisticated theoretical formulations may force us to modify this statement. Our evaluation of psychological approaches, however, will always concentrate on the composition laws advanced. These laws must not only be logically acceptable; they must also at least imply the rules of interpretation and the criteria of admissible explanation necessary to provide meaningful and challenging puzzles.

In conclusion, we should emphasize the point that our pessimism about the future of psychological approaches is not based upon a pessimism concerning the feasibility of reductive explanations. It derives from conceiving of the personality as the micro-unit in reductive theories. The conceptualization of the micro-unit as the *role* or as the *decision unit* would seem to us to be a more hopeful, but certainly not an easy, line of inquiry.

The Rationalistic Paradigm in Comparative Politics

Methodological individualism (and the reductionist explanations associated with it) is a cornerstone in some social science theories that are not derived from the tradition of individual psychology. Theory in the field of economics, which has one of the most fully articulated paradigms in the social sciences, is the prime example. We use the term *rationalistic* to characterize this paradigm because a set of assumptions about the rational behavior of economic man provides the axiomatic foundations upon which such towering theoretical edifices as Keynes' *General Theory of Employment, Interest, and Money*[76] and Von Neumann and Morganstern's *Theory of Games and Economic Behavior*[77] have been erected. The present state of the art in economic theory provides ample justification for the claim that economics has progressed much further along the road to normal science[78] than other social science disciplines. Thus, it is not surprising that both economists and political scientists have in recent years turned their attention to applications of the rationalistic paradigm which are outside the traditional concerns of economics. Some of the most rigorous and creative work in the areas of voting behavior,[79] group theory,[80] conflict,[81] and the design of political systems[82] has resulted from these efforts. Indeed, this relatively delimited body of literature provides such evidence as exists for the argument that a positive science of politics[83] is possible not only in principle but also in fact.

51

Robert T. Holt and John M. Richardson, Jr.

Although we are concerned with the relevance of rationalistic approaches in general, we shall focus explicitly on a contribution that seems especially germane to the concerns of comparative politics—Riker's *Theory of Political Coalitions*.[84] In many respects this creative and pioneering study remains a classic, although several scholars (including Riker himself) have gone beyond it in developing mathematically elegant, theoretical models of social behavior.

Scholars who use the rationalistic approach fully recognize that a commitment to the scientific method involves a commitment to a positive science and thus to deductive theory. Riker's position on this point is stated explicitly in an introductory chapter, "The Prospect of a Science of Politics,"[85] which mirrors many of the concerns that have been expressed in this essay.[86] "The essential feature of this [scientific] method," he observes, "is the creation of a theoretical construct that is a somewhat simplified version of what the real world to be described is believed to be like." He elaborates as follows:

> This simplified version or model is a set of axioms (more or less justifiable intuitively) from which nonobvious general sentences can be deduced. These deduced propositions, when verified, become both an addition to the model and a description of nature. As more and more sentences are deduced and verified, greater and greater confidence in the validity of the axioms is felt to be justified. Conversely, the deduction of false or inconsistent sentences tends to discredit the axioms.[87]

This discussion paves the way for a detailed elaboration of the conceptual and theoretical elements of Riker's paradigm.

In our introductory discussion we observed that the conceptual element of a paradigm provides an answer to the question: Of what is reality composed? Riker's position is quite clear. Following Easton,[88] he defines "distinctively political" action (or politics) as the "authoritative allocation of values,"[89] where "allocation refers not to a physical process, but to the social process of deciding how a physical process shall be carried out."[90] Riker argues that decision-making processes involving authoritative allocations have two important characteristics in common. First, they are almost invariably group decisions. Second, "if groups are more than two persons, the process of making [decisions] is invariably the same. It is a process of making coalitions."[91] He elaborates on this second point:

> Typically some part of the authority-possessing group comes together in an alliance to render a decision binding on the group as a whole and on all who recognize its authority. This decisive "part" may be more or less than one-half; indeed it may be two persons or the whole group itself. But regardless of the number of persons conventionally believed to be decisive, the process of reaching a decision in a group is a process of forming a subgroup which, by the

rules accepted by all members, can decide for the whole. This subgroup is a coalition.[92]

The conclusion that "much the greater part of the study of the authoritative allocation of values is reduced to the study of coalitions" provides the basis for a theoretical element based on the theory of *n*-person games. The axioms of this "model" are (a) the condition of rationality, and (b) the zero sum condition. Both assumptions are supported by arguments of intuitive plausibility as well as theoretical usefulness.[93]

Obviously, axioms of rational behavior are an essential element of any rationalistic approach. However, one of the major difficulties encountered in applications of the rationalistic paradigm to noneconomic decision-making is the development of rules of interpretation for the concept of "utility," which is an essential element of the rationality condition. In economics isomorphism between a utility scale and some monetary unit has often been assumed.[94] However, such a rule of interpretation allows for the possibility of irrational behavior in violation of the axioms of the theory. Thus, a second school of thought has assumed that *any* decision is rational.[95] Obviously this approach solves the problem of irrational behavior (which is impossible by definition) but makes interpretation of the concept of subjective utility virtually impossible.[96] Riker attacks this problem with characteristic directness. "How," he asks, "can the rationality condition be stated in such a way that it is more than a tautology but not subject to the criticism implied in those experiments which show that the scale of individual utility is not the same as a scale of money?"[97] The key to a politically relevant definition lies in the concept of "winning." "Politically rational man," according to Riker, "is the man who would rather win than lose, regardless of the stakes." It is reasonable to assume that in the market, election systems, warfare, and so on "a premium" is placed on rational or winning behavior.[98] This assumption leads to an alternative definition of rationality which, the author argues, is "defensible" and "non-tautological."[99] This definition is the following:

> Given social situations within certain kinds of decision-making institutions (of which parlor games, the market, elections, and warfare are notable examples) and in which exist two alternative courses of action with differing outcomes in money or power, or success, some participants will choose the alternative leading to the larger payoff. Such choice is rational behavior and it will be accepted as definitive, while the behavior of participants who do not so choose will not necessarily be so accepted.[100]

The reader will note that the theoretical element suggested by Riker's definition does not differ significantly from the approach that assumes that utiles and monetary units are isomorphic. Instead he has merely suggested different rules of interpretation so that utility can be measured in money, power, or success. Concomitantly, the set of admissible puzzles has been necessarily broadened to include any social situations (within certain kinds of decision-making institutions) where any of these values is authoritatively allocated. Apparently, the cost of broadening the puzzle-defining element of the paradigm in this way is to incorporate some of the less desirable features of both the approaches mentioned earlier. Thus the problem of irrational behavior (in violation of the axiom of rationality) still exists, whether or not it is accepted. In addition, the problem of unambiguously interpreting scales of power and success or of assigning ordinal positions to alternatives involving differing combinations of money, power, and/or success is introduced. However, as Riker emphasizes, "this revised form of the rationality condition can be verified in only one way; that is by showing that a model using it permits the deduction of nonobvious hypotheses which can themselves be verified by experiment, observation, and prediction."[101] Thus before considering the problem of interpretation and the means by which Riker proposes to resolve it, we should discuss his second assumption along with the nonobvious hypotheses (theorems) that are derived for verification.[102]

As we have noted, the second assumption of Riker's proposed paradigm is the zero sum condition. Because this assumption is less characteristic of rationalistic approaches in general, we will not dwell upon it here. We should note, however, that Riker's justification for it provides an interesting example of the interrelationship between the conceptual, theoretical, and puzzle-defining elements of a paradigm. He argues that (a) the processes of political decision-making can be interpreted in such a way as to satisfy the zero sum condition, and that (b) it is very useful for methodological reasons to do so.[103] ". . . Whether or not one should use the zero sum model *depends entirely on the way one's subject is commonly perceived.*"[104] It follows by implication that no phenomena that cannot be perceived in this way are admissible as puzzles, and that all nonzero sum aspects of those phenomena which are admissible are of no concern to practitioners who use this paradigm. Indeed, given the logical structure of the theoretical element, it is impossible to take such aspects into consideration.[105]

Using the assumptions already discussed and the theory of *n*-person games, Riker derives "three main propositions about political coalitions." These are summarized as follows.[106]

(1) *The size principle:* "In *n*-person, zero sum games, where side-payments are permitted, where players are rational, and where they have perfect information, only minimum winning coalitions occur."[107]

(2) *The strategic principle:* ". . . In systems or bodies in which the size principle is operative, participants in the final stages of coalition formation should and do move toward a minimal winning coalition.[108]

(3) *The disequilibrium principle:* "In systems or bodies where the size and

strategic principles are operative, the systems or bodies are themselves unstable. That is, they contain forces leading toward decision regardless of stakes and hence toward the elimination of participants."[109]

Assuming that no errors in logic have been made (and we believe this is a legitimate assumption),[110] verification of these theorems should provide support for the entire paradigm. Since proposition (1) is logically prior to propositions (2) and (3), an examination of the way in which this theorem is verified will provide an indication of some of the strengths and weaknesses of Riker's formulation. In addition, this examination will point towards some more generally relevant conclusions regarding the usefulness of rationalistic approaches to comparative politics.

In order to verify the size principle, Riker first formulates an "analogous statement about the real world":

> In social situations similar to *n*-person, zero-sum games with side-payments, participants create coalitions just as large as they believe will ensure winning and no larger.[111]

He then provides verifying examples from American, Indian, and world politics. The discussion of "Overwhelming Majorities in World Politics" is typical.[112]

First, the author notes that "the development in the sixteenth century of the system of European nation states and the fairly recent extension of this system of the whole world created a pattern of international politics which is very like an *n*-person game." Where "total war" occurs the operation of the system is analogous to the zero sum game.[113] Having interpreted the central concepts of his model in this way, Riker suggests the following conclusion:

> If one side actually wins [in a total war]. . . , then victory, by removing the losers, transforms a (probably minimal) winning coalition into a grand coalition. And, if we accept characteristic function theory, grand coalitions are worthless. Assuming, as I shall, that winners in total war retain for some time after victory the zero-sum habits of thought engendered by their very participation in it, then they will reject a coalition of the whole and begin to squabble among themselves. Presumably they will seek to substitute for it something that approaches a minimal winning coalition. If, in fact, they actually do so, their action constitutes further verification of the size principle.[114]

To verify the proposition which he has derived, Riker examines the "three instances of total war in the modern state system: the Napoleonic wars and the first and second world wars."[115] In each instance, the grand coalition that emerged victorious at the end of the conflict quickly divided into opposing factions. Thus, the Concert of Europe was divided over the territorial aspirations of Russia and Prussia (which were opposed by England and

55

Austria). After World War I, the Germany that "England had sought to revive effectively broke the Allied coalition by flirting . . . with the dreaded Bolsheviks of the USSR," and within a year after World War II, "the United States and the USSR were scrambling about the world to gain the allegiance of the uncommitted nations to one of the two hostile coalitions they were forming."[116] The author summarizes his analysis of these three empirical cases in the following way:

> From these three instances of the end product of total war one can readily conclude: the winning coalitions of total war do not long survive victory. Both in the model and in actuality they have become valueless. They die because victory renders them nugatory. To win something of value in the next phase following total war, the size of the winning coalition must be reduced. From the evidence of total war also, the size principle is thus additionally verified.[117]

In order to assess the validity of this, we must look again at the proposition which Riker was attempting to verify and its axiomatic base. Following the conventions of the rationalistic paradigm, Riker began by specifying that the *basic behavioral unit* in his formulation was the individual. The *decision-making rule* which this individual followed was to select those alternatives which produced "winning" outcomes, rather than losing ones. It was specified, furthermore, that this individual was highly competent in making these choices, i.e., he was in possession of "perfect information." Finally it was specified that the only empirical instances that would be admissible were those that met the zero sum assumption. If we are correct in stating the set of assumptions from which the size principle was derived, this raises serious questions about the rules of interpretation that connect the descriptive terms in the formal model to real world empirical phenomena. The basic difficulties with the examples cited are that the basic behavioral units in the empirical cases are not individuals but nations, and that the emergent coalitions being examined are not minimal but simply less than maximal. We have no rule of interpretation that indicates what attributes would denote a minimal winning coalition in world politics.

From the standpoint of comparative politics, the problem of the relationship between individual behavior and the behavior of institutions is particularly crucial. Are we to assume that because all individuals behave rationally, any social unit in a zero sum decision-making situation must conform to the model of rational man with respect to decision-making *and* competence? In the theory of pure competition in economics, where it is assumed that there are no institutional mechanisms of coordination or integration, this assumption has been very useful. However, it does not seem justifiable for political institutions, especially such complex ones as nations. Certainly Riker has provided us with no theorems or rules of interpretation that connect the rational behavior of individuals and the behavior of nations. The concept of a nation's behavior is in itself a very difficult one which certainly requires more elaboration than has been provided here.

This objection does not negate the rationalistic paradigm entirely. It merely suggests that the linkages between the rational behavior of individuals and the rational behavior of social institutions are somewhat more complex than Riker seems willing to admit. However, a more fundamental objection seems applicable to most uses of the rationalistic paradigm. We do not believe that the general usefulness of the competence assumption about rational man has been convincingly demonstrated. Although the model has been fruitfully applied in a few limited areas, it seems likely that a set of axioms that conform more closely to our intuitive notions about behavior may provide a more appropriate basis for a generally relevant paradigm. In this regard, Herbert Simon's critique of more than twenty years ago still seems valid:

> Real behavior, even that which is ordinarily thought of as "rational" possesses many elements of disconnectedness not present in this idealized picture [of the rationalistic paradigm]. If behavior is viewed over a stretch of time, it exhibits a mosiac character. Each piece of the pattern is integrated with others by their orientation to a common purpose, but these purposes shift from time to time with shifts in knowledge and attention, and are held together in only slight measure by any conception of an overall criterion of choice. It might be said that behavior reveals "segments" of rationality—that behavior shows rational organization within each segment, but the segments themselves have no very strong interconnections.
>
> Actual behavior falls short, in at least three ways, of objective rationality. . . :
>
> (1) Rationality requires a complete knowledge and anticipation of the consequences that will follow on each choice. In fact, knowledge of consequences is always fragmentary.
> (2) Since these consequences lie in the future, imagination must supply the lack of experienced feeling in attaching value to them. But values can be only imperfectly anticipated.
> (3) Rationality requires a choice among all possible alternative behaviors. In actual behavior, only a very few of all of these possible alternatives ever come to mind.[118]

We should make it clear that we are not proposing that the axiomatically defined behavior of a basic behavioral unit—whether it is an individual, group, political system, or such—should necessarily conform to our intuitive notions about such behavior. But it does seem that the burden of proof for the usefulness of axioms that differ from our intuitive notions as radically as do the axioms of rationality should rest upon the practitioners who use this paradigm. Despite the mathematical elegance of rationalistic models, we do not believe that their broad applicability has been convincingly demonstrated.[119]

Riker's formulation provides an example of this point which is by no means atypical. He asserts that assumptions of his model are applicable to a very broad range of political phenomena, indeed to virtually all of political life. Yet the empirical cases which he examines are very carefully selected and even these require a stretching of the basic assumptions. Other examples of this problem can be found in recent works of Downs[120] and Tullock.[121] Although these authors state their commitment to the rationalistic paradigm very explicitly, they have been forced to deviate from it to a very significant degree in order to examine phenomena which they found intrinsically interesting. It should also be pointed out that this observation does not apply only to noneconomic areas of investigation such as politics. In the areas of developmental economics and the study of nonmarket economies such as the Soviet Union, the rationalistic paradigm has been found to have only limited applications.[122]

Earlier we noted that "when the adherents of a particular competing paradigm can demonstrate that their approach is more successful in solving a few problems that a wider group of practitioners in the field recognize as significant, then that paradigm should gain in status." The advocates of the rationalistic paradigm have obviously gone much further in developing a complete paradigm than many practitioners, but they have not as yet provided such a demonstration. We do not believe that a commitment to a positive theory of comparative politics necessarily implies a commitment to a rationalistic model of man. Other sets of axioms, such as those formulated by Herbert Simon, should receive greater attention from advocates of positive theory.[123] Nevertheless, even if the paradigm for comparative politics ultimately takes a very different form, we would claim that the contribution of rationalistic approaches to the development of systematic analysis based on deductive theory has been very significant.

Atheoretic Approaches to Theory Development

That there are difficulties with the various competing paradigms in comparative politics should be obvious from the critique thus far presented. This is no novel conclusion. Virtually all of the various stock-taking efforts referred to in the introduction to this essay have a critical tone and have proposed new approaches as well as refinement in old approaches.

Some scholars have reacted to the inadequacy of paradigms by turning to a form of twentieth-century Baconianism. The emphasis has been placed upon gathering the "facts" and submitting them to various analytical routines to determine their interrelationships. The volume by Banks and Textor and the work of the Yale Political Data Program, especially its notable *Handbook* by Russett and others, are the best examples.[124]

It is perhaps unfair to label these efforts as unadulterated Baconianism.

The Yale Political Data Program was stimulated by Karl Deutsch and reflects his opinion that contemporary political science is theory rich and data poor,[125] and that we have an abundance of hypotheses but a poverty of data and analytical routines by which we can test them. While not concurring with Deutsch's observation that the discipline is theory rich, we can nevertheless agree that it is data poor. Our basic concern with the massive efforts devoted to fact gathering relates to some fundamental questions about what criteria should be used to identify the facts that should be collected. Let us look briefly at the volume by Russett and others in relationship to this basic question.

The handbook contains aggregate data by "countries" on 75 different variables, ranging from such things as area and population, to GNP per capita and daily newspaper circulation, to Roman Catholics as a percentage of the total population. Anyone familiar with the data in the book may be surprised to be reminded why data on these particular 75 variables were selected. The preface (if one can take a preface without the proverbial grain of salt) is explicit on the matter. It opens with a selection from the Universal Declaration of Human Rights and then goes on to imply that the data were collected to facilitate comparison of nations "as to their relative implementation of the asserted rights."[126]

We have already indicated that ethical problems present a very bad focus for research if one is primarily concerned with developing scientific theory. We would extend this comment to include simple measurement. There seems to be no obvious reason why data designed to measure the achievement of certain ethical ends should be appropriate for the development and testing of scientific theory. We should hasten to add that the preface also points out that the handbook stems from some long-term interests— including scientific as well as ethical concerns—of Deutsch and Lasswell.

An examination of the data included suggests, however, that many if not all of the variables were included largely because the relevant data were available in a convenient form.

No political scientist who is remotely interested in theory development and testing can possibly be interested in the 75 variables simply as data. They are important only as measures of variables that are in turn important in certain theories. The authors of the handbook appear to recognize this point, and in the introductory paragraphs preceding the presentation of related variables suggest the way in which they can be used as measures. For example, before presenting the data dealing with mail flow, they make the following comments:

> These figures are useful for the examination of a number of problems. Obviously the domestic mail per capita data form another measure of complex internal communication and interaction; they also provide an excellent check

on official statistics of literacy. The foreign mail per capita series can test a number of hypotheses about the involvement of a state in international affairs.[127]

It is legitimate to ask, however, whether or not the scholar interested in "complex internal communication and interaction" and/or in the "involvement of a state in international affairs" would want these data rather than others. If our position—that there may be only a few areas in which a theory can be confronted with reality and that rules of interpretation are crucial in this confrontation—is correct, then it is most unlikely that data collected to assess the relative achievement of human rights or simply because they are handy would be of any use whatsoever.

The most interesting section of the handbook is Part B entitled, "The Analysis of Trends and Patterns." This section begins with twenty-three pages of tabulations showing the product-moment correlations among the 75 variables. In the introduction to these tables, the authors state:

> The product-moment correlation coefficient is an adequate measure of the relationship between two variables when this relationship is approximately a linear one and when the data are distributed in an approximately "normal" (bell-shaped) fashion . . . As is clear from the graphs at the top of each table in Part A, many social, economic, and political national attributes are not "normally" distributed, with most cases near some mean and fewer and fewer cases on either side the further away from the mean one looks. To improve the chances of detecting relationships with the product-moment coefficient, those variables found from their graphs to have highly skewed distributions have been subjected to a logarithmic transformation before being correlated.[128]

Conceivably some scholar may be interested in a description of the way in which all or some of the 75 variables are interrelated, but, as the authors point out, no inferential use can be made of the correlation coefficients. They describe the relationship only among the countries on which data were available and say nothing intelligible about relationships among other countries, past, present, or future, in regard to the same variables. It should also be pointed out that there may be relationships among the variables that do not show up in the tables. Whereas the authors state that they have transformed variables when the graphs indicate that they are not normally distributed, they have, in fact, only transformed those with a "j-curve" distribution. Let us look at the distribution of two variables on page 61.[129]

Clearly these variables are not normally distributed and yet they have not been transformed. If the joint distribution of two variables is bivariate normal, then the regression of one variable on the other is linear and the product-moment r is an appropriate measure of association. If the joint distribution is not bivariate normal, the regression of one variable on the other may or may not be linear. If the regression is linear, r is an appropriate

60

descriptive measure of association regardless of the distribution.[130] If, however, the regression is curvilinear, *r* is not useful because it may be very small when there is a high degree of association. Thus it seems meaningless to compute automatically all of the *r*'s without first checking for the linearity of regression by means of a scattergram.

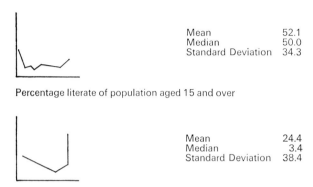

Mean	52.1
Median	50.0
Standard Deviation	34.3

Percentage literate of population aged 15 and over

Mean	24.4
Median	3.4
Standard Deviation	38.4

Votes for Communist Party as percentage of total vote

Because the intercorrelation matrics are not a particularly important part of the volume, perhaps we should not be too critical. The computer can print out all of the tables relatively cheaply, and thus it may be reasonable to include them. This leads us to wonder, however, if the computer is altogether an unmixed blessing.

Of much greater concern to us is the section dealing with *Multifactor Explanations of Social Change*. In this section, Russett and Alker use multiple regression analysis to "explain" the variation in one variable in terms of several others. Before starting our major objection to this approach, we should perhaps raise one which is, if only by comparison, somewhat less consequential. This has to do with the assumptions that underlie the use of the multiple regression model. The first assumption is obviously that the regression is linear, as already discussed. Linearity of regression is guaranteed only if the joint list of independent and dependent variables is normal. Thus if the distribution is not multivariate normal, lack of linear relationships does not imply that a relationship does not exist. It will be helpful to illustrate this point with an example drawn from the explanation of birth rates by Russett and Alker. Regarding the influences of "percentage Catholic" on this variable, they observe:

> . . . we find also a small positive relationship between percentage Catholic and fertility, with other variables controlled. A 1% increase in the Catholic population seems to cause a .01 addition to the birth rate. These coefficients

61

must now be revised to β—weights, to allow for the great variation in the ranges and standard deviations of the variables.

β—Coefficients of for BRTH	Log_2 GNPC	LIT	GPCH	MARG	CATH
	$-.34$	$-.54$	$-.43$	$-.19$	.05

We now see that the major effect (always with the other variables controlled) is produced by variations in literacy but that each of the other variables except percentage Catholic bears an important relation to birth rates. But rather surprisingly, with this group of countries Catholicism makes very little difference to the birth rate.[131]

In order to make our point explicit, it is necessary to look at the actual distributions of the variables with which Russett and Alker are concerned. These are presented here:

Explaining crude birth rates

Mean	35.7
Median	40.7
Modal Decile	IV
Range	45.5
Standard Deviation	12.6

Live births per 1,000 population

Mean	9,454
Median	1,063
Modal Decile	X
Range	443,240
Standard Deviation	42,235

Gross National Product, 1957, $U.S. (L)

Mean	52.1
Median	50.0
Modal Decile	I
Range	97.5
Standard Deviation	34.3

Percentage literate of population aged 15 and over

Mean	68.0
Median	2.99
Modal Decile	VI
Range	2.55
Standard Deviation	9.8

Annual growth of GNP per capita

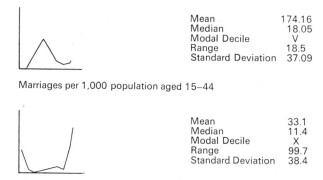

Mean	174.16
Median	18.05
Modal Decile	V
Range	18.5
Standard Deviation	37.09

Marriages per 1,000 population aged 15–44

Mean	33.1
Median	11.4
Modal Decile	X
Range	99.7
Standard Deviation	38.4

Roman Catholics as percentage of total population, 1958

Since the nonnormal marginals show that the point distribution is not multivariate normal, the relationship between the independent variables—"percentage literate population aged fifteen and over" and "Roman Catholics as a percentage of total population"—and the dependent variable—"live births per 1,000 population"—may not be linear. Alker and Russett are surprised at the low beta weight (.05), which suggests a slight relationship between fertility and Roman Catholicism. The low coefficient implies that the percentage of Roman Catholics in the total population is of little use in predicting crude birth rates in a *linear* regression, but does not imply that a relationship does not exist between these two variables. Perhaps even more surprising, however, is the fact that this analysis is used as the basis for asserting that "the major *effect* [on fertility] is produced by variations in literacy." Does this imply that couples who read books in bed do not have offspring?

As this is only our minor objection, we will not belabor the point any further. Of greater consequence is the interpretation that is made of the findings. *Multifactor Explanations of Social Change* is the title of the section (emphasis added). The authors have now left the realm of purely descriptive statistics and are making inferences about some population other than the one on which they have data. The inferential step is particularly hazardous when one is explaining social change from a cross-sectional sample. It is perfectly acceptable, for example, to state that countries in their sample which have differences in growth rates of 1 per cent have differences in birth rates of 2.12 per 1,000. But there is no reasonable basis whatsoever for maintaining that "an increase of 1 per cent in the growth rate (is) associated with 2.12 births per 1,000," if one is to interpret this statement to be saying anything about social change. Some very crucial taxonomic assumptions must be made in order to generalize from a cross-sectional sample to social change over time. The authors do not deal with these assumptions.

If this were the only major problem, we could discuss the kinds of assumptions that are involved. This, however, is not worth the effort, because we object to the very concept of *explanation* that is being employed even if we grant the legitimacy of the inferential leap. What does the term *explanation* mean when used in the context of a linear multiple regression? It means simply that the values of some dependent variable can be predicted from a knowledge of the values of several independent variables. If one starts from the data themselves and not from some theoretical proposition to be tested, it means nothing more than this. We could imagine other variables that might do just as well if not better in explaining crude birth rates. If, for example, one had data on the percentage of the population between ages 13 and 15, 15 and 17, and so on that was married and data on expenditures for birth control devices divided by the total number of women of child-bearing age, one might account for 3/5 or 4/5 of the variation in births per 1,000 population. Let us assume that we had these data and that the regression equation supported the conclusion. There is absolutely no way in which one could choose between these equally acceptable explanations. Thus, to use the term *explanation* in the way in which it is used by Alker and Russett is to adopt the conventions of statistics as one's rules governing the admissibility of explanations.[132]

The most fundamental question remains to be raised. Why would anyone want to formulate an explanation of crude birth rates? The only answer we would accept to this question is that the phenomenon of crude birth rates is an area where a theory can confront reality and that by explaining crude birth rates one is testing at least a part of a theory. The atheoretic approaches to theory construction avoid this question altogether. At the very best a series of statistical explanations of certain specific variables might tend to confirm a theory if a theory could be found in which the variables employed were crucial concepts. But the very strategy of this approach tends to make it difficult, if not impossible, to provide a tight refutation of such a theory *modus tollens* by a falsified prediction. Paul Meehl has an excellent statement of the logical difference between research designed to confirm a theory and that designed to refute it.

> Inadequate appreciation of the extreme weakness of the test to which a substantive theory T is subjected by merely predicting a directional statistical difference $d>0$ is then compounded by a truly remarkable failure to recognize the logical asymmetry between, on the one hand, (formally invalid) "confirmation" of a theory via affirming the consequent in an argument of form: [$T > H_1$, H_2, infer T], and on the other hand the deductively tight *refutation* of the theory *modus tollens* by a falsified prediction, the logical form being: [$T > H_1, \sim H_1, \text{infer} \sim T$].[133]

In Meehl's criticism of research in psychology, he likens the researcher who tends to provide *ad hoc* explanation for *ad hoc* findings to "a potent but sterile intellectual rake, who leaves in his merry path a long train of ravished

64

maidens but no viable scientific offspring."[134] Perhaps the reader less myopic than ourselves can find the viable scientific offspring in the *Handbook*.

Factor Analysis

Perhaps the most sophisticated form of what we have called "twentieth-century Baconianism" to emerge as a consequence of the trend toward fact collection and the availability of high speed computers is factor analysis. The very broad claims advanced by social science practitioners[135] who employ this technique are summarized by R. J. Rummel in a recent article:

> Factor analysis can be applied in order to explore a content area, structure a domain, map unknown concepts, classify or reduce data, illuminate casual (sic) nexuses, screen or transform data, define relationships, test hypotheses, formulate theories, control variables, or make inferences.[136]

> ... Since factor analysis incorporates analytic possibilities as a theory and empirical techniques for connecting the theory to social phenomena, its potentiality promises much theoretical development for the social sciences. Looking ahead for a century, I suggest that factor analysis and the complementary multiple regression model are initiating a scientific revolution in the social sciences as profound and far-reaching as that initiated by the development of the calculus in physics.[137]

As the reader might surmise, we view this methodological tool somewhat differently, especially when it is applied to "masses of qualitative and quantitative variables"[138] to develop the conceptual and even the theoretical elements of a paradigm.[139] The issues which we wish to raise regarding the use of factor analysis to "discover" regularities in data or to "structure the analytic framework or theory" do not differ substantially from those which have been raised with regard to atheoretic approaches in general. However, the orientation of factor analytic practitioners toward the types of theoretical and methodological concerns expressed in this paper differ so fundamentally from our own that we feel compelled to spell out our objections in some detail. It will be helpful to begin our discussion with a very brief overview of some of the research that has used this approach.[140]

The use of the "R" technique to uncover underlying dimensions of nations or national behavior has been the most common application. For example, Cattel, in a pioneering work, derived twelve "cultural dimensions of syntality" from a 72 variable, 69 nation matrix.[141] More recently, Banks and Gregg have derived seven "dimensions of political systems" from a 68 variable, 115 nation matrix using data drawn mostly (but not entirely) from Banks' and Textor's monumental *Cross-Polity Survey*.[142] Rummel and Tanter have undertaken several essentially similar studies, using different data, to identify dimensions of conflict behavior within and between nations.[143]

A second approach has involved the use of the "Q" technique to group social units with respect to attributes.[144] For example, Banks and Gregg factored a matrix of 68 variables for 115 nations to identify five categories that "appear[ed] to delineate significant components of difference among major political groupings of the world."[145]

A third approach has been used by two economists, Cynthia Morris and Irma Adelman, as an alternative to multiple regression analysis to explain the variance in levels of economic development and fertility among "seventy-four less developed countries"[146] in terms of social and political structure.

In our discussion we shall focus on the first type of approach, drawing upon Rummel's 1963 study of "Dimensions of Conflict Behavior Within and Between Nations" for illustrative examples; however, our comments are for the most part intended to apply to the entire body of factor analytic literature in comparative politics.

The basic elements of a typical factor analytic study may be summarized as follows.[147] First, a set of variables is selected for analysis according to various criteria. In the past, U.S. statistics, *Facts on File, Keesings Archives,* and other compendia of a similar nature have been consulted. However, we expect that with the increasing availability of large banks of data from enterprises such as the Yale Political Data Program, the Dimensionality of Nations Project, and the Minnesota Historical Data Archive, these latter sources will be used exclusively. Second, each variable is intercorrelated with every other variable to form the matrix that is to be factor analyzed. Problems arising from the different types of scales (nominal, ordinal, interval, and ratio) in terms of which the different variables may be expressed can be resolved in a variety of ways. For example, point bi-serial correlations can be used to combine nominal and interval data, various rank-order correlation techniques can be used for ordinal data and so forth. Another alternative is to develop an arbitrary interval scale and express all variables in terms of it, thus permitting the use of product moment correlations throughout.[148] Unfortunately the reasons for opting for one solution to this problem rather than another are rarely made explicit in published studies. Indeed, frequently this problem is not even mentioned.[149] The matrix of intercorrelations is simply presented as a "given." The next step is to factor analyze the intercorrelation matrix. The major alternatives which may be utilized at this stage include the Bi-Factor, Principal Factor (Principal Components), Multiple Group, and Multiple Factor techniques. Each of the possible solutions has distinguishing mathematical and theoretical characteristics.[150] Given the factor solution, it is then possible to rotate a selected number of factors in order to arrive at a more desirable solution, according to various criteria. A large number of solutions—both orthagonal or oblique—are possible, and students of factor analysis have devoted con-

66

siderable attention to developing criteria for distinguishing those solutions which are theoretically or mathematically interesting.[151]

The final step, which is uniquely associated with factor analytic approaches, involves the naming of each factor that has been identified. In psychology, this process has been guided by rather specifically articulated paradigms. For example, Thurstone has observed that "the derived variables are of scientific interest only insofar as they represent processes or parameters that involve the fundamental concepts of the science involved."[152] In comparative politics, however, where the principal use of factor analysis has been to define the conceptual elements of a paradigm, the process of labeling has been more arbitrary and *ad hoc*.[153] When the practitioner has labeled the factors, an additional step, the formulation of explanatory propositions, is also possible. Such propositions can take a variety of forms and are not unambiguously derivable from the analysis itself.

We have presented a rather lengthy discussion of a typical factor analytic study in order to emphasize the large number of points at which the assumptions underlying a statistical model, or judgmental criteria being applied, may affect the final outcome. We now wish to address ourselves to these points more explicitly.

The first point, obviously, is the selection of a particular area of investigation and the choice of relevant data. Rummel's comments with respect to these issues are, we believe, quite typical.

> This study has been undertaken with the conviction that to understand war and other forms of violent international behavior is the first step to avoiding them, and with the belief that the road to understanding such conflict is through systematic scientific research.[154]

Clearly, "conflict behavior" was chosen as an area of investigation because of its social relevance, not its theoretical relevance. Rummel makes this point even more explicit in his discussion of the criteria in terms of which data were selected:

> The measures used here were chosen on definitional, practical, and statistical criteria. *Theoretical relevance within the context of conflict theory was not made a criterion.* (Emphasis added.) Possibly, if such were done, the over-all results would be more theoretically relevant, and would help to choose between competing theories of conflict. Such a criterion is not used here, however, because of my belief that such comprehensive theories of conflict *capable of test* do not exist.[155]

We are in agreement with Rummel on one point, i.e., that theories of conflict capable of test do not exist. Indeed, as we have noted, the establishment of correspondence between theory and reality is often one of the most difficult tasks of paradigm elaboration. However, we find it difficult to see how the application of an analytical routine, however elegant, to data selected on the basis of explicitly nontheoretical considerations can contribute significantly to its accomplishment.

Furthermore, fundamental questions must be raised regarding the character of the data often used in factor analytic studies. As we have noted, these data are often expressed in the form of a product moment correlation through a variety of *ad hoc* techniques. If variables such as "presence or absence of guerilla warfare"[156] are to be used, this often means that nominal, ordinal, and ratio scale measures are combined in a single matrix. We have no basis for assuming that the cells of such a matrix can be interpreted unambiguously, let alone subjected to a technique which assumes that all correlations are product moment.

Let us suppose, however, that all of the problems raised earlier have been or can be resolved satisfactorily. The crucial judgmental considerations underlying the choice of one method of analysis or another, the selection between rotated and unrotated solutions, the selection between oblique and orthogonal solutions, and, if one opts for a rotation of a particular type, the choice of a particular solution must yet be considered. In comparative politics the principal factor (or principal component) method of analysis is used almost universally. Rummel's explanation for the choice of this method is typical:

> The technique chosen here is called principal components (or principal factor) and is chosen from among competing techniques because it yields a mathematically unique solution and because the first factor extracts the maximum of variance from the original data while each succeeding factor extracts the maximum of remaining variance.[157]

What must be emphasized is that this explanation is hardly an adequate justification for the use of the principal components approach. The passage quoted simply defines, in general terms, certain statistical characteristics of the technique itself; it says nothing about whether or not we should reasonably expect that a theory of conflict behavior (or dimensions of political systems) would take this form. Indeed, in psychology the bi-factor, multiple group, and multiple factor solutions, which lead to "level" contributions of each factor to the total variance, are considered preferable.[158]

Thurstone's criterion of "simple structure" is most frequently used as the basis for choosing from among possible rotated solutions. Again, Rummel's comments on this point are typical:

> There are several possible criteria for orthagonal rotation which could be used. The one chosen here is an analytic criterion that has gained wide recognition for yielding a meaningful and invariant solution—Thurstone's simple structure criterion as determined by Kaiser's varimax analytic solution.[159]

What is generally not made clear is the paradigmatic basis for this "invariant" and "meaningful" solution. Thurstone's justification seems quite explicit.

> Just as we take it for granted that the individual differences in visual acuity are not involved in pitch discrimination, so we assume that in intellectual tasks, some mental or cortical functions are not involved in every task. This is the principle of "simple structure" or "simple configuration" in the underlying order for any given set of attributes.[160]

Are we to assume then that *this* criterion of "simple structure" provides a theoretical basis for identifying dimensions of conflict behavior? If so, it seems to us that the meaningful character of solutions that are derived from the application of this criterion requires further examination.

Factor analysis has been presented as a systematic alternative to the more tedious methods of paradigm construction that are suggested in this paper. However, it is the judgment of the practitioner, not some magical property of the technique itself, that determines not only the way in which the emergent factors will be interpreted but also the form of the factors themselves. Thus, in order for the factors to be meaningful, these judgmental criteria must be made quite explicit. We claim that the only possible basis for formulating such criteria is a paradigm.

A similar observation was recently made by J. Scott Armstrong. In an article in *The American Statistician,* whimsically subtitled, "Tom Swift and His Electric Factor Analysis Machine,[161] Armstrong concluded:

> The cost of doing factor analytic studies has dropped substantially in recent years. In contrast with earlier times, it is now much easier to perform the factor analysis than to decide what you want to factor analyze. It is not clear that the resulting proliferation of the literature will lead us to the development of better theories.

> Factor analysis may provide a means of evaluating theory or of suggesting revisions in theory. This requires, however, that the theory be explicitly specified prior to the analysis of the data. Otherwise, there will be insufficient criteria for the evaluation of the results. If principal components is used for generating hypotheses without an explicit *a priori* analysis, the world will soon be overrun by hypotheses.[162]

If this view is correct, the claim that factor analysis can be used to discover the theoretical and conceptual elements of a paradigm cannot be supported.

Conclusions: The State of Theory in Comparative Politics

There are a number of competing paradigms in the field of comparative politics, ranging from those that are conceptually rich but tend to be devoid

69

of puzzles and criteria of admissibility, to those that concentrate largely on data and data analysis and are conceptually quite empty. All of the different types, however, suffer from a major shortcoming—they have virtually no deductive power; that is, there is no set of propositions from which one can deduce in a logically tight manner a wide range of additional propositions, some of which can be empirically verified.

The grand paradigms of Almond, Deutsch, Easton (and for that matter, Holt and Turner) are little more than heuristic schema. They present an interesting way of looking at political phenomena, but do little more. What is needed is clear. First, a small group of theoretical primitives must be established. Second, additional concepts must be defined, using *only* these theoretical primitives and some specifically identified logical (or mathematical) operations. Third, a set of axioms must be developed using only the concepts and operations defined. Fourth, a set of propositions must be deduced from these axioms for empirical testing. Fifth, criteria of admissibility and rules of interpretation must be developed.

None of these steps except the first can be taken satisfactorily without the use of some body of rules that establish the principles for deduction. Our suggestion is that political scientists must turn to mathematics for these rules of logic and that until this is done, the grand schemata will remain essentially heuristic. We do not make this suggestion lightly. Political scientists are not known for their mathematical skills or interests, but we can see no other way to introduce the necessary deductive power into a paradigm.

Furthermore, the problem may be more difficult than that of simply learning certain bodies of existing mathematics. Newton's theoretical formulation required an invention of a new mathematics, the calculus. Progress in mathematical economics was blocked at the end of the nineteenth century because there was no mathematical way known of solving the equations that had been formulated. Not until further advances had been made in pure mathematics was the way cleared for real progress. It is not unlikely that the mathematics that presently exists is unsuitable for handling our problems, in which case the development of theory in comparative politics may depend upon innovative work in pure mathematics.

The kind of commitment to mathematical sophistication cannot be made easily in political science. It is not only the formidability of mathematics that is a roadblock. The kind of paradigm of which we conceive is a "pure scientific" paradigm. Its only purpose is to improve the description, explanation, and prediction of political phenomena. The puzzles in this paradigm are important only for scientific reasons. A science that is heavily committed to dealing with socially and morally relevant problems finds little use for this kind of paradigm or for the commitment to mathematics that it requires. For political science to advance, it must shed this professional commitment to solving social and moral problems. This does not mean that the political scientists have to become amoral monsters. It does mean that their role as scientists must be clearly separated from their role as policy consultants and community activists. For the socially concerned, we may speculate that efforts devoted to making political science more of a pure science now may well hasten the day when the body of knowledge in political science can serve directly the needs of society by providing a reliable base for the political scientist *qua* engineer who devotes his time to applying science to curing the ills of humanity.

The reader may well wonder why we have concluded with an appeal for mathematics in a paper in which we were so critical of those approaches in comparative politics that seem to be the most mathematically sophisticated. The answer to the paradox is contained in the word *seem*. In making an appeal for more mathematics, we are not talking about statistics. It is not that we have any objection to statistical analysis in principle, when it is used properly. Indeed, many of the interesting puzzles that will probably emerge in an acceptable paradigm require statistical data processing for their solution. But statistics provides a science with a basis for rigorous *induction*. Our critique suggests that the crying need in comparative politics is for more rigorous deduction and this is where mathematics, not statistics, is relevant.

There are in political science, of course, certain areas where the kind of mathematical analysis we are suggesting is applied. The rationalistic approaches are perhaps the best example. The problem with the rationalistic paradigm, in our opinion, is that it is so limited in the range of political phenomena that it can deal with that it can never be an acceptable paradigm for comparative politics. Confronted with the choice between a rigorous, deductively powerful, narrowly based paradigm with some successful application and a broad deductively weak paradigm, we might be inclined to put our money on the latter. But the models that are presently being employed seem to have inherent limitations that restrict future elaboration.

Although the problems of theory in comparative politics will not be solved even if we get a deductively powerful and conceptually rich paradigm, there are a whole host of basic technical and methodological problems involving cross-cultural comparative research that will have to be dealt with before we are in a position to solve any interesting puzzles. A number of these methodological problems are treated in the following chapters.

CHAPTER 3

The Comparison of
Whole Political Systems

F R E D   W .   R I G G S

University of Hawaii

Since the mid-1950s, a number of scholars have turned their attention to macropolitical theory. This, of course, is no new concern for political scientists; it dates back at least to Aristotle. But as the horizon of political scientists has expanded significantly beyond the Western-type nation state, the old holistic categories for comparative analysis, which had progressed little beyond Aristotle, proved to be inadequate. A new conceptual basis was required both for the development of theories that applied at the level of the political system generally and as an aid in the development of comparative research designs.

In Chapter 3, Professor Riggs addresses himself directly to the problems of comparing whole political systems. After an introductory section in which he treats some general methodological and theoretical points and sources of confusion, he turns his attention to the development of a taxonomy of politics. No one can question the central importance of a classification scheme for the more general problems of comparing whole systems and for the more specific problems of selecting research sites and interpreting empirical findings. Riggs tackles this problem with typical ingenuity and imagination. As with any pioneering venture, a number of objections will be raised to his formulation, but anyone who challenges the classification scheme cannot take the task lightly.

Fred W. Riggs, Professor of Political Science at the University of Hawaii, is no stranger to the field of comparative politics. The products of his prolific pen have been well known in the profession for over a decade. His recent books, Administration in Developing Countries; *and* Thailand: The Modernization of a Bureaucratic Polity, *are major contributions to the field. As the central figure in the Comparative Administration Group, he has been responsible for stimulating much creative research and writing in the field of comparative administration.*

IME WAS WHEN a political scientist would have felt no diffidence about the analysis and comparison of whole political systems.* Indeed, he would have felt quite at home in dealing with such categories as republics and monarchies, federal and unitary states, parliamentary and presidential systems, or democracies and autocracies. The description and analysis of political systems in these terms is as old as Aristotle and, with the weight of tradition behind it, would have perplexed no one.

But in recent years, notably since World War II, a revolution has occurred in the perspectives of political scientists. Among the reciprocally reinforcing causes of this revolution: an emphasis on functionalism based on cultural anthropology and Parsonian sociology; the influence of behavioralism and psychological perspectives; the emergence of ex-colonial countries as numerous and strange objects of conscious inquiry. The traditional holistic categories for comparative government seemed not to apply—or to apply only as a Procrustean bed—to the realities of these unfamiliar polities. On closer analysis it became apparent that they lacked many institutions taken for granted in conventional theory, and those they had behaved quite differently.

Both functionalism and behavioralism seemed to offer an escape from the trap of ethnocentric institutionalism. Functionalism, by speaking of the "functional requisites of any society," led many of us—including myself—to an examination of new analytic categories that were presumably applicable to all political systems. These included the "input-output" categories presented by Gabriel Almond, with their associated functional rubrics of political communication, socialization, articulation, aggregation, rule-making, rule-application, and rule-adjudication. Other schemes, such as Parsons' system problems of pattern-maintenance, integration, adaptation, and goal-attainment, were also widely utilized for the comparative study of political and administrative systems. The influence of Parsons' pattern

* This essay was first written in 1966, while the author was Carnegie Visiting Professor at MIT. Subsequent revisions were made during 1967 when he was a Fellow at the Center for Advanced Study in the Behavioral Sciences, Stanford. Since then he has modified his views on some key points in the essay, but it has not been possible to incorporate these changes in the present text. They may be found, however, in: "The Structures of Government and Administrative Reform," Ralph Braibanti and Associates, *Political and Administrative Development* (Durham, North Carolina: Duke University Press, in press); "System Theory: Structures of Government and the Dialectics of Development," in Michael Haas and Henry Kariel, eds. *Approaches to the Study of Political Science* (Chandler Publishing Co., in press); "The Dialectics of Developmental Conflict," *Comparative Political Studies*, Vol. I, No. 2 (July 1968) pp. 197–226; and "Bureaucratic Politics in Comparative Perspective," *Journal of Comparative Administration*, Vol. I, No. 1 (May 1969) pp. 5–38.

variables—universalism-particularism; achievement-ascription; specificity-diffuseness; emotional-rational—was particularly notable, reinforcing as it did the earlier development schemes of Toennies, Durkheim, Maine, Weber, Cooley, Becker, and others. These concepts seemed to be particularly helpful in the analysis of political change, and I used them myself in formulating the prismatic model as an intermediate kind of social system with many apparent relevancies to the study, not only of politics, but also of economic and social problems in the developing countries.

The baffling phenomena of the Third World, the expanding world of the new and modernizing states, also reinforced the interest of political scientists in behavioralism, by which I understand not only the attempt to utilize quantitative methods more systematically for the study of social phenomena, but also a tendency to view politics from the perspective of the individual voter or actor. I hesitate to call this approach *reductionist* because of the bad connotations of the word, but in a real sense behavioralism was often accompanied by the assumption that if one could discover the motivations, perspectives, and roles of individuals in the political process, then one would somehow also understand the system as a whole in which these actors were engaged.

Difficult as it was to discover how the leaders and the masses felt and acted in the Third World, it was perhaps possible to conduct village surveys, to utilize biographic data for elite studies, and with the aid of that modern genie, the computer, to process one's data and discover new clues to the perplexing problems of political development. Except for some diehard traditionalists who continued to think and work in a Europe-centered field called *Comparative Government,* the avant-garde happily ventured forward to the new frontiers of Comparative Politics and Comparative Public Administration.

I fear that we have been gulled by our own ingenuity. In discarding the older categories for describing political systems as wholes, we have weakened our capacity to see the Gestalt of politics, not only in the careening parade of societies in transition, but also in the more stable landscapes of the Western world. To contrast democracies and totalitarian regimes, to say that England is a monarchy and France a republic, that the United States is presidential and Italy parliamentary, seems so obvious as to be unimportant. But have we anything more concrete to offer in place of such banalities? We can, it is true, describe how interest groups operate in countries that have not yet formally recognized either the existence or the legitimacy of the lobbies, but although this adds detail to our image of how democratic polities behave, it does not give us a new or effective handle for securing a usable purchase on so obdurate a subject as whole political systems.

Perhaps the difficulty with the traditional approach was not intrinsic to it, but stemmed rather from a premature ossification of the older framework.

It may not have been the principle of institutional analysis that was at fault, but rather the way in which it was used. The institutionalists, convinced of their own erudition and the truth of what they knew, reacted to the functionalists and behaviorists as impostors and intruders. Thus alienated, the young turks of political science blithely rejected institutional synthesis as they pursued their own exciting ventures into the unknown. Perhaps reciprocally, the onslaughts of the iconoclasts also tended to block efforts by the institutionalists to expand their established frame of reference so as not only to accommodate any valid insights generated by functionalism and behavioralism, but also to revitalize their own stock in trade and thus make it more relevant, not only to the emergent non-Western world but also to the familiar terrain of the West.

At least, it now seems to me that we do need institutional analysis. Functionalism has led us unwittingly to a precipice where we can almost think that all institutions which perform equivalent functions are essentially the same, that any pattern of change which achieves developmental goals is equal to any other on grounds of cultural relativism, and that the significance of institutions can be discovered exclusively in their social or economic consequences, not in their intrinsic characteristics. The worst crimes are attributed to institutionalists: ethnocentric bias and value loading. To avoid such accusations, have we not rushed pell mell into obscurantism?

The truth, I believe, is that institutions, social structures, patterns of action do indeed matter, not only for their social and economic consequences, but also because of their essential interest, because there are only a limited number of ways in which certain important goals can be attained, and the way that is chosen therefore does make a difference. In a sense, comparative government involves study of the relatively few political and administrative technologies which human beings have so far had the wit to devise. Our goal should be not only to study the varied consequences of diverse technologies, but also to understand each technology in its own terms, to discover what brings it into existence, how it works, what alternative choices it presents for subsequent modification, and how it compares with other technologies as to costs and benefits.

In this chapter, I shall attempt to outline, in a preliminary and speculative way, some ideas about what the major governmental institutions and systems are, what their relevance may be for comparative politics, and how they relate to some important functional and behavioral variables. This is not to say that we should reject functionalism and behavioralism as important modes of analysis, or even as a way of trying to understand governmental institutions better. Rather, it is suggested that some important advantages may accrue to us if we occasionally look on patterns of government as independent variables, treating other aspects of social and political systems as dependent variables.

Fred W. Riggs

Let us begin first by discussing our key term, *whole political system,* proceed then to a heuristic typology of whole political systems, and conclude with some suggestions concerning possible hypotheses and research strategies.

The Whole Political System

What do we mean by a *whole political system?* The answer is more complicated than it seems at first to be. Let us begin with some illustrations. Nation states, such as the United States, France, Japan, Mexico, Thailand: these can be regarded as whole political systems. So can city states such as the ancient republics of Greece, and imperial regimes such as Sung China, the Byzantine Empire, Czarist Russia. Feudal principalities and primitive tribes can also be treated as whole political systems.

Provisionally, let us use the word *polity* as a convenient synonym for *whole political system.* A bureaucracy, political party, legislature, court, voting system, and other functional subsystems of polities may be referred to as partial political systems, or as *components* of polities. Territorial units within a polity, such as provinces, states, municipalities, districts, may be treated as *subpolities,* but if they are sufficiently autonomous, as in a feudal society, then the distinction between polities and subpolities becomes blurred. Similarly, a set of polities linked in an international system may be treated as a macropolity. However, if the bonds between the component polities become sufficiently strong, as in the transition from a confederation to a federation, or after the establishment of an international government, then the boundary between macropolities and polities also becomes blurred.

Perhaps we can best approach the problem of identifying *whole political systems* indirectly, not by way of a formal definition but through a discussion of some theoretical and methodological problems that have thrown obstacles in the way of clear thinking on this subject. By this means we may hope to clarify, if not overcome, some of the difficulties that stand in our way.

I shall attempt to deal with five sources of confusion: the fallacy of projection or transference, the abuse of functionalism, the impact of reductionism, the phobia against neologisms, and the confusion of extrinsic for intrinsic criteria.

The Fallacy of Projection

Difficulties in our analysis of unfamiliar systems often arise because we are unable to imagine something quite different from what we are familiar with. If there are living creatures on Mars, we can imagine them only in forms similar to those of Earth creatures, and the cartoonist's image of a robot is of a tin man, not of a computer. The anthropologists have a good word for this, *ethnocentrism*, but its relevance is primarily to the projection of our cultural values on to peoples whose norms and cognitions may be quite different from our own.

Many efforts have been made to overcome this perceptual bias in the study of politics in primitive societies and non-Western countries, but with only partial success. No doubt it is difficult to empathize with others who are unknown, whether one is a Turkish peasant or an American political scientist. And it is no solution to declare that the proposed subject of study is inscrutable, irrational, or just uniquely different. Our problem is to discover wherein lies the difference, and then to create a theoretical model that will identify the dimensions of variation and hopefully provide measures for them.

Among the more important models which have been used with this end in view is the input-output model of a political system devised by Gabriel Almond on the basis of functional requisite analysis. Because this framework did indeed provoke a creative breakthrough in the analysis of Western polities by helping us overcome some of the rigidities that institutional and structural conceptualizations had incurred, and because it also spoke of universal requisites, presumably applicable to any society, this model came to be widely accepted as a useful tool for the study of politics in traditional and non-Western societies.

In my opinion, however, the model is not universally relevant, and has in fact led many of us to project into other societies conceptions that are quite irrelevant to them. Perhaps the easiest way to see this is first to recognize that an implicit assumption in the input-output model is the existence of an organization in the sense of a formal organization or a complex organization. According to Caplow, "an organization is a *social system* that has an *unequivocal collective identity*, an *exact roster* of members, a *program* of activity, and procedures for replacing *members*."[1]

In any *organization*, then, members are committed in advance to comply with policies adopted in an authoritative fashion by the organization, and procedures exist for establishing what the legitimate goals, rules, and policies of the organization will be. For such an entity, the input-output model is highly relevant. Clearly procedures must exist for socializing participants if the organization is to recruit and replace its members. Channels must be provided for them to articulate their interests insofar as they are affected by the organization, for arriving at a consensus through processes of aggregation, for translating these agreements into formally prescribed rules, and then for implementing and testing these rules in various administrative processes.

The input-output model, in other words, applies not only to the American nation-state as a territorial organization, but also to a host of local governments, private associations, corporations, trade unions, and churches.

It is clearly relevant to apply the term *politics* to the decision-making processes of all these organizations and to apply the Almondian model to an analysis of these processes. In this sense, it is quite valid to study the *private politics* of nongovernmental organizations as well as the *public politics* of organized states. One can also make a clear distinction, in these terms, between the role of an interest group as an actor in the system of organized American politics, and the structure of *private politics* in the processes by which such an interest group decides what it should do.

It is clear, however, that many social systems in the United States do not meet the criteria of an organization. To mention an obvious example, the market is one. A large number of outcomes (let us not use the word *decisions* here) are determined through the market as a result of the aggregative impact of innumerable private decisions. Clearly the price of steel or the wages of auto workers may be raised or lowered by collective decision of the state, enforced through its bureaucracy, or by the operation of market forces. Consequences (functions?) may be similar, but the causal mechanisms involved are quite dissimilar. If one turns to non-Western countries and folk societies, one is struck by the fact that social outcomes are determined much less by collective decisions reached through organizations, including the organized state, than by other social systems. If, then, through selective perception, one is able to see only those behaviors which fit the model of organized collective action, one is certain to miss most of the processes by which social outcomes are determined. In this respect, political scientists face a problem similar to that faced by economists. For economics, despite numerous disclaimers, a service is an economic good only if it is sold—one buys domestic help, which therefore becomes part of the GNP, but one does not buy the house work of his wife, which therefore cannot enter the GNP. Yet what is the substantive difference? Consequently the economist tends to see only those transactions which can in some manner be quantified, notably by attaching prices to them, and in similar fashion the organizational model leads political scientists to see only those operations that are processed through collective input-output institutions.

Almond adds a second criterion, however, to restrict the application of the model by ruling *private politics* out of consideration. The test of legitimate exercise of violence as a last resort is imposed to determine whether or not an organization is governmental, and therefore validly *political*. This draws a neat line in Western contexts between *public politics* as a subject of interest to political science, and *private politics* as a subject up for grabs, presumably for sociologists interested in theories of organization to look at, although I find little in their writings on this topic. A self-defeating limitation this is, as I shall try to show.

80

The Comparison of Whole Political Systems

Let us construct a simple two-by-two matrix, shown in Figure 3-1. On one axis we shall put "society," and on the other "organization." On the first axis, a plus means treatment of society as a whole, a minus means treatment only of subsystems within a society. On the second axis, a plus means the presence of "organization" in Caplow's sense; a minus means absence of organization, though of course not absence of other kinds of social system.

We can see that Almond's input-output model combined with the criterion of ultimate legitimate use of violence fits only box A, in which we are dealing with an organized whole society. The input-output model, as already indicated, also fits box B, which includes organized private politics, but the legitimate violence criterion excludes this box from Almond's idea of a political system.

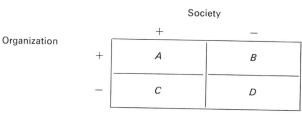

Figure 3-1.

If we look now at box C, we are directed to think of systems that embrace a whole society but are not organizations in the formal sense. All traditional societies fall under this heading. Much, if not most, of what I consider to be politics in transitional societies also falls in box C, although we can also discover there, in embryonic form, behaviors that fit the Almond model of box A. However, if we limit our perceptions to the A-type phenomena—which is like the economist seeing only market-oriented activities in a predominantly subsistence economy—then we shall see only the exposed portion of the gigantic iceberg of politics in these countries. In other words, my conception of a *whole political system* includes C as well as A.

We may refer to the content of both A and B as any organized political system, and the contents of box A alone as any organized whole political system. In this terminology C refers to any nonorganized whole political system. (The words *disorganized* and *unorganized* are too negative in connotation for use here—actually an *organized* system may also be *disorganized!*)

To keep the symmetry of our matrix, let us refer to any social system at the subsocietal level as a partial system, in contrast to whole systems which apply only at the societal level. Then B and D refer to partial systems, B to organized partial systems, and D to nonorganized partial systems. There are, of course, many D systems in every society, including our own: the family, crowds, communities, audiences, shrines. The political scientist may well say that such matters are outside his disciplinary interests, gladly leaving them to sociologists and anthropologists to study. But if one wants, as a political scientist, to understand the politics of transitional, to say nothing of traditional, societies, then he should at least be aware that to a considerable degree the functions which, in a developed political system, are performed by institutions in box *A*, are in these societies carried out by social systems which fit in box D.[2]

To summarize, let us set up a table to go with the matrix:

Table 1.   Types of Political Systems

A	organized whole political systems—Almond model
B	organized partial political systems—for sociology?
C	nonorganized whole political systems
D	nonorganized partial political systems
A & C	*whole political systems*—the subject of this essay
A & B	organized political systems—the input-output model
B & D	partial political systems—(an academic "no-man's land")
C & D	nonorganized political systems

It is, of course, open to anyone to guess what politics may have been like in primitive human groupings that have left no archaeological, to say nothing of historical, records. Nor can the evidence of contemporary ethnography help us much to reconstruct the social structure of peoples far more primitive, presumably, than our most primitive contemporaries. Yet it seems likely that the earliest social systems must have been those we would put in box *D*, i.e., nonorganized partial political systems. Among primitive food gatherers, indeed, one could scarcely demarcate the nuclear family as a *society*, but one might not be able to identify any larger social entity as a society either.

The emergence of a nonorganized whole political system may well have come—thousands of years later than the evolution of man—when first some common authority figure was recognized by members of more than one family. Such a figure (an individual, a totem, god, or collectivity) could scarcely have exercised much coherent power, and yet we might date the appearance of a polity from some such episode. The minimal whole political system, then, is a *null* system in which no concrete structure for the exercise of authority over a suprafamilial collectivity exists.

From the first appearance of a collective authority figure, and hence the emergence of a *polity*, to the crystallization of an "organized whole political system" is a long distance, both historically and structurally. Box *C*, if we wanted to do it, could be subdivided into many layers celebrating a long evolutionary process. A few landmarks might be noted. Authority by itself does not necessarily involve influence, the capacity to shape the behaviors of others by deliberate design. With the gradual appearance of influential authorities at the societal level, we might speak of the formation of *powers*, a more developed kind of polity.

But the existence of a power by no means requires the concept of membership. It is only with the emergence of the idea of membership that we can speak of the *state*. By now we are moving into relatively recent times, in terms of the life of man. The Greek city states are among the earliest known instances. But even here, the members, the citizens, constitute only a small part of the total population in the power. We might distinguish the Athenian state as a subsystem of the Athenian power. It is only at a much later stage that the idea begins to prevail of a state whose members include all the permanent residents of a territory. With the acceptance of this idea, the *nation state* appears, and now we are talking about only the last hundred years, more or less, for the idea appeared some time before the practice.

The Almond model and box *A* apply with particular force to the nation state. It may be stretched to include any state, even if not a nation state. But the comparison of whole political systems contemplated in this essay embraces polities and powers that are not states, and thus includes nonorganized as well as organized whole political systems.

The Abuse of Functionalism

Whereas the Almond model is too restrictive in some ways, by excluding nonorganized whole systems, it is too open in another. This difficulty arises because the model relies on functional or analytic categories where structural concepts are needed, and because the unit of analysis is not clearly specified. If one were studying American politics, for example, one could interpret the model in a narrow sense to include only behaviors relevant to the operations of the American state as an organized whole political system. However, one might also have in mind America as a society. If the latter unit of analysis is taken, and I think this is frequently done, then any performance of an input function in America is drawn into the concept of a political system. Let us take socialization as an example. Every American is socialized not only to perform roles as a citizen of the nation state, but also to take part in many other organizations, and in nonorganized social systems, such as the market, driving in city streets, playing games. To include all of these activities under the heading of politics is to bring together a vast assortment of unrelated items and to confuse hopelessly the problem of political analysis.

One reason for this difficulty is precisely the failure of the model to make clear that the input-output concept applies to organizations, but not to other kinds of social systems. If this distinction had been made clear, then one might have seen that the concept of socialization could have been given a more delimited reference by using it only for the socialization of members to take part in an organization. Because the concrete wholeness of socialization for any individual involves preparing him to take part in many organizations, one would have to include, in studying a particular political system such as the American state, only that aspect of socialization which involved preparation for participation in the life of the state. To apply this distinction would be difficult, of course, but it would at least clarify the matter. No action would be regarded intrinsically as one of socialization, but any action could involve socialization for a role in X organization, provided the organizational relevance could be demonstrated.

The same remarks apply to the other items in the input-output model: communication, articulation, aggregation, rule-making, and so on. By defining the concept of a *political system* to include all instances of the performance of these functions, almost every kind of social action that occurs in a society is included, and hence the boundaries of the political system disappear. Yet for purposes of comparison, we need criteria that will enable us to exclude as well as to include. Otherwise theory becomes nonoperational and hypothesis formation impossible.

Perhaps one reason why this rubbery approach to functionalism has been so popular is that it seemed to provide an escape mechanism for the inherent limitations of the organized political system model. If one could not find organized political systems in traditional societies, and only to a limited degree in transitional societies, then one could at least find these political functions. Since no distinction was made between socialization (1) as a generic process, and socialization (2) for participation in an organization, it was possible to discover socialization (1) (the generic process) everywhere, and ignore the fact that it may not have included socialization (2) (for organized action). The point is that participants have to be socialized for their roles in nonorganized and partial social systems, as well as for organized whole political systems. Thus at the same time that the political system model was tightly drawn (box A only), the related analytic functions were loosely drawn (to fit boxes B, C, and D as well as A). If, in other countries, one failed to find concrete political systems that could fit box A, then one could easily fall back on the study of functions (even though they related only to concrete systems in boxes B, C, or D). Unfortunately this approach served only to confuse the issue of what a *political system* is and how it can be profitably studied.

Perhaps an underlying reason for this confusion has been the tendency, typical of all common sense thinking, to mix structural and functional criteria in definitions. Let me illustrate by a homely example. A *coat* might be defined functionally in terms of how it is worn, or structurally in terms of its shape. However, a coat may be used for abnormal purposes, as something to be thrown over the body, like a blanket, for example. Moreover, blankets may be worn the way a coat is, as some American Indians are imagined to do. A strict structural definition would specify the shape of coats, including the possession of sleeves, and the shape of blankets, as flat and sleeveless. Hypotheses, not definitions, could then assert that coats are normally worn and blankets used as bed coverings, leaving open for further explanation the exceptional circumstances in which coats are thrown over sleeping persons and blankets used to drape walking men.

Science has faced and solved similar problems. Traditional grammar, for example, confusingly defined parts of speech, such as nouns and verbs, in terms of the uses (functions) to which they are normally put, but in practice it accepted as nouns only words with specifiable structural characteristics. Thus, structurally speaking, a common noun can fit in the expression "a—," such as "a coat," "a blanket," and verbs in the expression "to—," such as "to wear," "to sleep." Linguistics was able to move forward analytically when it could define parts of speech independently of the uses to which they were put, and then make hypotheses about their normal meanings. The gain arose not only in precision of thought but in a greatly increased ability to operationalize such terms as *nouns* and *verbs*.

This approach, let us note, placed emphasis on the meaning of concepts as taking priority over the definition of words. Linguistics, unlike traditional grammar, does not start by trying to define such words as nouns and verbs, but rather by trying to establish useful categories. What classes of items are found in speech? Having identified the classes that seemed important, linguists could assign names to them. If a word like *noun* seemed appropriate, it was appropriated. But if not, new words had to be coined. Such unfamilar expressions as *phoneme* and *morpheme* had to be invented and were widely accepted precisely because they made it easier to refer to useful ideas than did reliance on familiar words with different meanings. Needless to say, the same problem arises in political science. In what follows I propose to define politics structurally, and if familiar words are not available to use as labels for the key concepts, then I shall not hesitate to use unfamiliar words or even to coin new ones.

The approach proposed here does not reject functionalism, but seeks to combine functional and structural categories in a fruitful manner. In other words, political structures must be defined and identified by structural, not functional, criteria. Similarly, functions must be identified, not in terms of intrinsic behavioral criteria, but in terms of system relevancies. A function is defined by the effects of behaviors in one system on another system, typically by a subsystem on a larger system to which it belongs. Understanding will come to the degree that we can show what effects identifiable structures have on other systems (making *structures* the independent variable) and, alternatively, if we can show how particular effects on a system are accomplished by different structures (making *functions* the independent variable).

Fred W. Riggs

The Impact of Reductionism

Perhaps the term *illegitimate reductionism* should be used here, for admittedly much is to be gained if one can show that particular kinds of phenomena can be explained as a special case of some more general pattern of behavior. This kind of legitimate reductionism, however, is very difficult to accomplish. More frequently we are tempted to hope that a solution to a complex problem can be found if we can solve a simple problem thought to be similar to the more complex one. In the foregoing discussion, for example, it may have seemed to some writers that, if one could describe the way in which certain political functions were performed—socialization, communication, aggregation, and so on—in unfamiliar societies, then one might understand how the political system worked in these settings. Actually, as I have tried to show, this effort could not be illuminating insofar as the characteristics of (nonorganized) political systems were different from those presupposed in the system model for which the functions were identified as relevant.

A different kind of reductionism has had a major impact on the study of comparative politics, namely, the attempt to derive political system characteristics from the traits of concrete components of the system, or from features of its environment. This tendency is closely related to the phenomenon of behavioralism, which focuses attention on the attitudes and conduct of individual actors in social systems, often at the expense of studying the system in which they act. It is as though one were trying to understand what was going on at a football game without any knowledge of the rules of the game. If it seemed too difficult to learn what these rules were, one might seek understanding by interviewing each player to learn about his background, attitudes, motivations, and other traits. Interesting and quantifiable as the findings of such research might be, they would not necessarily give much insight into the nature of the game. Nor would aggregative statistics about the players necessarily help one understand what was going on.

There has been an increasing tendency in comparative politics to look to aggregate statistics about societies and political systems as a basis for comparison. If we consider that polities vary in terms of the number of citizens who constitute them, we can use demographic statistics to establish a rank order of states in terms of population size. Yet clearly such figures tell us little about the intrinsic characteristics of the polities enumerated. Similarly, one may compare polities in terms of average per capita income, the number of radio sets per thousand, calorie consumption levels, infant mortality rates, suicide rates, the incidence of violence, and so on.[3]

Yet one must wonder whether such comparisons tell us much about political system characteristics. For the most part, these statistics give us information about environmental variables. Their usefulness arises in the context of explanation, not of comparison as such. Once we have identified, by structural criteria, a variety of types of political system, we can then compile statistics about the number of each kind. Having done that, we might then use environmental statistics to test hypotheses about relationships between various kinds of political systems and, let us say, level of economic growth, population size, incidence of violence, and so on. The statistics will be useful for such purposes only after we have first established the relevant attributes of political systems as such. If we have information only about characteristics that are not those of polities, we will never learn much about whole political systems. There is no reductionist short-cut, in other words, to the comparison of polities. But once we have learned to identify, classify, and describe polities, we can then use information about other things, including data about components and environmental conditions, to help us test hypotheses explaining the causes and consequences of polity behaviors and transformations.

Reference ought to be made in passing to a fallacy that is, logically, the opposite of reductionism, although we seem to lack a word for it—perhaps *inductionism* would serve the purpose. Academically this is the conventional logic of area studies. It involves the conception that every system is unique, that we cannot understand any political system as an example of a more general rule, but must view it as a whole, as distinctively different from every other polity. Thailand, it is said, can no more be compared with England than apples with oranges. This statement is, of course, as absurd as the cliché that "an exception proves the rule," if taken in the vulgar sense that an exception validates a rule. Any thing can be compared with anything else if one can establish categories to which they both belong, or to which one belongs but the other does not. Let us make a definition for a *widget* and then look at S and T. If we find that both S and T are widgets, or that S is a widget but T not, then we have compared S and T. If you establish a category of fruit and show both apples and oranges to be types of a fruit, then they have been compared. If you establish a subcategory of fruit belonging to the family Citrus, then you can show that an orange belongs to this family but an apple, belonging to the family Malus, does not. You can also then show that lemons belong to the same family as oranges, and pears to the same family as apples. If you can establish a quantifiable variable, like price or calory content, applicable to both apples and oranges, then they can be compared in terms of numbers also.

In this chapter, I shall attempt to establish a basis for comparing political systems in the same way that fruit can be compared in terms of family. If we find that the English and American states belong to a family of whole political systems included in box A in Figure 3–1, but that Thailand and the Siamese kingdoms of old cannot be classified in box A, but can be classified in box C, then they have been compared. If I can also show that both Thailand and England belong to a category of whole political systems that includes boxes *A* and *C*, but not boxes *B* and *D*, then I have also compared them. My endeavor in this essay, therefore, will be to discover what kinds of political structures fit into boxes *A* and *C*, so that I can separate polities from nonpolities, and then to construct a set of smaller boxes within this larger box so that all polities can be sorted into one of the subtypes. It is by no means easy to formulate criteria for these smaller boxes, however, and it is almost as difficult to find appropriate labels for the boxes once they have been demarcated.

The Phobia against Neologisms

Mention has already been made of such well-established terms for the comparison of polities as *monarchy, republic, parliamentary, federal,* and so on. But clearly these words have limited utility since they force us to put in the same categories such varied republics as classical Athens, the United States, and the Soviet Union, or in the category of monarchy polities such as the France of Louis XIV, the England of Queen Elizabeth II, the Siam of Chulalongkorn, and Byzantium under Julian. Confusion, in this instance, has arisen from the anachronistic transfer of concepts that were meaningful in Aristotle's time for distinguishing between monarchies, aristocracies, and democracies, but have lost their significance when applied to nation states today.

In the contemporary literature such terms as *democracy, dictatorship,* and *totalitarian* have become popular, but they do not refer to institutional or concrete structural characteristics of polities. They are, rather, functional characterizations in terms of the distribution and modes of allocating power. Moreover, they refer primarily to characteristics of political systems in the industrially advanced Western countries. It is, again, anachronistic to use these terms for political systems in preindustrial societies where their relevance is limited. Let me illustrate by a simple example. We can distinguish quite a variety of organized groups, ranging from clans and tribes as found in folk societies to associations and corporations as found in contemporary mass societies. Let us suppose now that we come across Robin Hood's band of outlaws and ask what kind of group it is. It seems, on the one hand, to have some of the particularistic traits of a tribe, and some of the universalistic traits of an association, yet it does not fit very easily under either heading. Facing this difficulty, we might decide to call Robin Hood's band a *band*, and point out that bands are distinctively different in several respects both from tribes and associations.

Similarly, the characteristic types of political system to be found in premodern and modernizing polities do not clearly fit either the ancient categories formulated by Aristotle or the modern categories formulated by texts in Comparative Government. We may not be able to find words as simple as *band* to use for them, but we shall have to search for words that at least avoid the connotations of the standard terminology used in the ancient and the modern literature. Moreover, because these ancient and modern words tend to overlap, because we find *republics* and *monarchies* in both, it seems necessary to throw these words out, at least for the time being, as likely to create confusion. We need new words like *Citrus* and *Malus* to use instead of oranges and apples. Once we have a precise set of terms, we can perhaps then reintroduce words like *monarchy* with qualifying adjectives to indicate the different usages of the term. Because of a widespread and, within limits, justifiable repugnance to neologisms, many political scientists shun novel expressions even when exclusive dependence on the established lexicon obscures distinctions needed for clear thinking in a field that has become increasingly complex and subtle. If we are to advance the comparative analysis of political systems, we must overcome this crippling phobia against neologisms.

The Confusion of Extrinsic with Intrinsic Criteria

Types of political system are often distinguished by extrinsic rather than intrinsic characteristics. For example, when we use such words as *modern, traditional, ancient, primitive, premodern,* we are essentially using temporal or historical categories rather than terms that designate system characteristics. Similarly, if we speak of Western, non-Western, African, Asian, Russian, American, and so on, we are using spatial or geographical concepts. As soon as we formulate a hypothesis to justify this usage, we can recognize the underlying fallacy. To speak of "modern political systems" is to imply that "all modern societies have significantly similar political systems," and "the characteristics of polities in modern societies are known." Unless both propositions are true, the term *modern polity* is a semantic blank. Similar propositions are implied for traditional polities, African polities, non-Western polities, and so on.

Extrinsic categories used for the classification of political systems are not limited to temporal and spatial criteria. We find, for example, that terms suggesting different stages of economic growth are sometimes extended to political systems. A *developed polity*, for example, may mean "the political system of an industrialized society," carrying the implicit assumption of a direct correlation between the political and economic system characteristics of different societies. An interesting example of this usage is contained in a recent book entitled *Stages of Political Development*, which treats, rather, the characteristics of political systems at different stages of economic development.[4] Imaginative and stimulating as this work is, it is not really a comparison of whole political systems. Rather, it compares the

89

performance of governments in meeting a set of economic problems that are regarded as developmental in the sense that one set of these problems must be solved before the next can be handled. It shows how varying economic and social conditions affect polities without distinguishing sharply between the various types of political system.

To dramatize the implicit assumptions behind such extrinsic classifications, let us imagine that political systems were thought to be closely correlated with racial features, justifying a typology of Caucasian, Mongolian, and Negroid polities, or that polities varied directly with population size, leading us to distinguish between tiny, medium, large, and super polities, using population figures of one million, ten million, 100 million, and 1,000 million as critical dividers. One aim of our exercise should, of course, be to make possible the testing of hypotheses about relationships between different kinds of political systems and other variables such as space, time, economic growth, race and population size, but not to take these criteria for granted as the basis for a classification of polities. This argument, incidentally, forces us to reject such extrinsic categories as modern, Western, developed, traditional, and transitional as criteria for comparing whole political systems.

A Taxonomy of Polities

Having rejected extrinsic, functional, and anachronistic classifications of polities, we are now compelled to ask whether we can discover or devise a taxonomy that is *intrinsic, structural,* and *orthochronistic* in the sense that the terms used refer to the appropriate time period or stage of development. Let us start by looking again at the standard concepts used in conventional comparative government. Here we find a major distinction being made between parliamentary and presidential systems. Whatever other limitations may be charged against these terms, they patently do refer to structural characteristics, a polity in which the chief executive is selected through legislative vote as contrasted with one where he is chosen by popular vote.

This distinction is clearly important. Difficulties arise only when it is used where it is not appropriate. For example, if there is no legislature, and if voting is not practiced, then the distinction is clearly irrelevant. Another major distinction is made in the standard texts between two-party, multiparty, and one-party systems. Again this is surely a basic distinction, but it cannot be aptly applied to polities in which there are no parties, to countries, like India, which have a single dominant party plus many secondary parties, or to Thailand, which sometimes has and sometimes does not have political parties.

The solution to our problem is not to reject these established categories, but to provide a broader structural framework within which they can be shown to be special cases. If, for example, we distinguish between polities having legislatures and those that do not, then the parliamentary-presidential system dichotomy clearly applies only to polities with legislatures. Similarly we might distinguish between polities with party systems and those without. This provides a clue to the solution of our problem. Let us enumerate the most important kinds of governmental institutions or organs of government, and then let us ask how they are typically combined in different polities. This may give us a basis for establishing the kind of taxonomy we are looking for.

The next question which arises is, of course, what organs to treat as decisive. We might start with a random list including such items as: kings, elections, legislatures, courts, bureaucracies, armies, cabinets, presidents, political parties, interest groups, mass media, schools. Actually, such a list would not be very long, but it is already longer than we need. We can eliminate some items, like schools and mass media, considering them environmental constraints on government, not intrinsic parts of a polity; and we can drop others as examples of a larger category: for example, kings, cabinets, and presidents might all be lumped together under the more general heading of executives. Executives chosen by hereditary principle are kings; by popular vote, presidents; by legislative vote, prime ministers. Executives may be individuals or collectivities, such as cabinets or boards. Armies may be included under the heading of bureaucracies, for they have the same structural characteristics, being composed of a hierarchy of positions established to serve the state.

We find courts in all kinds of polities, from the most primitive to the most developed. Although they frequently play an important role in government, I am not prepared to assign them the same degree of decisiveness as did Montesquieu. Interest groups, as formally organized associations, are important only in polities that also have political parties, but as groups in a more general Bentleyan sense, can be found in every kind of polity. At any rate, it seems unnecessary for this provisional analysis to include either courts or interest groups. Similar remarks might be made about elections.

Four Basic Institutions

We are left, then, with four basic kinds of institutions: *executives, bureaucracies, legislatures,* and *parties.* A provisional taxonomy of polities can be constructed by combining these structures in various ways. Arbitrary names will be assigned to the various combinations in order to escape the connotations of the familiar words now in general use. After the taxonomy has been created, it will be possible to establish identities between some of the peculiarly labeled systems in the taxonomy and familiar words. In this sense, the new terminology is a kind of scaffolding, which can be torn down after a building is finished, but which must be erected first in order to make the more solid construction possible. It may also turn out, of course, that some of the novel words in the taxonomy have no equivalent term in the familiar vocabulary. We might want to keep them, or hunt for some other new word or phrase which would be both unambiguous and easy to remember. The reader is advised not to worry too much about trying at this stage to remember the neologisms which I shall soon introduce because they may later be rejected or revised. A quick glance at a chart will enable one to keep the different concepts in mind. It is primarily to help us differentiate between quite a few meanings that this rather eccentric device is introduced.

When we look carefully at these four key institutions, we will find that some of them serve as prerequisites for others, at least historically. There may be exceptions, but I shall treat the normal sequential pattern as valid for a first approximation, leaving for later modification the treatment of any deviant cases. In other words, I shall suppose that *there is no polity with a bureaucracy that does not have an executive, no polity with a legislature that lacks a bureaucracy, and no polity with political parties that lacks a legislature.* The last in this series is the most shaky, as I can think of some cases in which political parties exist without legislatures, but even in these instances the idea of a legislature is known and the government is probably committed to the proposition that one should be established at some future time.

Before going further, let us define these institutions a bit more carefully. An *executive* will be defined as the head of a polity, usually an individual, such as a king, president, or prime minister, but often also a collectivity such as a council of elders, a senate, an assembly, or a board. If there is a bureaucracy, the executive heads it. If there is a party system, the executive is normally, though not always, the head of it, although he may be a member and may be selected by it. The executive may be selected in many ways, ranging from highly ascriptive inheritance of office to highly universalistic recruitment by popular elections.

A *bureaucracy* is defined as a hierarchy of nonhereditary positions subject to the authority of the executive. Thus the executive is not considered a member of the bureaucracy. But the bureaucracy does include military, religious, and judicial officers if they hold their appointments under the authority of the executive. There may, of course, be autonomous military, religious, and judicial organizations not part of the bureaucracy, just as there may be civil authorities, local governments, private associations, and corporations that are not a part of the bureaucracy. Any of these autonomous organizations within a polity may have its own bureaucracy, but they will not be included in the term *a bureaucracy* or *the bureaucracy* unless clearly indicated by the context. Thus if the word is used in the plural, as the bureaucracies in a polity, or with a qualifying adjective, such as *private bureaucracies*, then the reference will be to both the state bureaucracy and other bureaucracies in a given polity. Offices that are hereditary in character may be subject to the nominal authority of the executive, but are also not included as part of a bureaucracy. However, if the office is in principle subject to appointment by the executive, even though in practice it may tend to become hereditary, then it would be considered a part of the bureaucracy.

A *legislature* will be defined as an assembly of individuals holding office by election and making decisions in polyarchic fashion, by majority votes. As with the concept of bureaucracy, there may be many legislatures in a polity, serving as organs of local governments, corporations, and associations. But if I speak of *a legislature* or *the legislature*, reference will be to the salient legislative body of a polity. The legislature in this sense, however, may consist of a set of sublegislatures, as in a bicameral or multicameral congress. Although the leading function of a legislature may be rule-making, it is important to limit our definition to structural characteristics, leaving us free to specify by hypotheses the extent to which a legislature is or is not a rule-making body. The election of members is an important criterion for it enables us to distinguish between nonelective assemblies, such as a town meeting of all citizens and legislatures. A senate is an assembly of elders, or of heads of a set of smaller polities united in a confederacy. Therefore, a senate is not a legislature, although particular legislatures may be given this name, such as the U.S. Senate. It is important to remember that the name given to a particular institution may not at all conform to the general meanings assigned to the same word as a label for a concept, i.e., for a category of similar items.[5]

A *political party* will be defined as a membership association that has as its formally stated purpose the nomination of public office holders whose selection is determined by electoral means. An organization which secures the appointment of its candidates by nonelectoral means may be a faction, but not a party. A group that promotes selected ideologies, programs, or issues but does not nominate candidates is an interest group but not a political party. However, political parties may also advocate programs and ideologies. They may or may not succeed in securing the election of their candidates. They may be created and managed by politicians who are already in office, with the ostensible aim of nominating candidates at future elections. Parties, in other words, may be used for purposes quite different from those specified in their charters. Members may have little to do with the nomination of candidates, even though the charter calls for their participation. It is the structural form of the political party that identifies it for our purposes, not its actual functions, which, as with legislatures, will be specified in hypotheses, not in the definition.

Let us now, using these definitions and recalling the hypotheses stated earlier about institutional prerequisites, set up a simple table of basic types of polity, as follows:

Table 2. Institutional Combinations

Presence of:	P	L	B	E	N
Executive	+	+	+	+	—
Bureaucracy	+	+	+	—	—
Legislature	+	+	—	—	—
Political Party	+	—	—	—	—

The letters at the head of each column can be used as a temporary shorthand referring to five basic types of polity. *N* stands for *null*, meaning no executive, bureaucracy, legislature, or political party. We can think of stateless polities in which the family or kin-system serves all the functions of government, and no executive is recognized as having authority over individuals not identified with a kin group. Ethnographers have given us descriptions of some primitive societies having these characteristics.

The letter *E* stands for a polity with an *executive*, but no bureaucracy, legislature, or political party. The classic polities described by Aristotle seem to meet this condition. The executive may have been a king or tyrant, an aristocratic council or an assembly of all citizens. There may have been public offices, but they were not formally organized in a hierarchy so they would not meet the definition of a bureaucracy. Members of the assembly were not elected, so they were not legislatures. Political cliques and cabals can be found, but they do not meet the definition of a political party. Confederations with councils composed of heads of clans or cities can also be found among these polities, but they fail to meet the criteria set for legislatures. Indeed, the oldest terms for types of polities—*republics, aristocracies, monarchies*—can be found within this *E*-type category. This illustrates well, I think, the dangers of extending these terms to apply to polities of the remaining *B*, *L*, and *P* types, which, as we shall see, are structurally quite different.

B, in this typology, stands for a polity having a *bureaucracy* and an executive, but no legislature or political party. Traditional bureaucratic empires, of the type described by Wittfogel and Eisenstadt, clearly meet this criterion. But so do feudal polities such as we find in medieval Europe and premodern Japan.[6]

L-type polities, then, include all political systems having executives, bureaucracies, and *legislatures,* but no political parties. Empirically the *L*-type systems can be found in premodern Europe, notably in the late eighteenth and early nineteenth centuries. The principle of elections has been traced back to Teutonic origins, and there seem to be clear precedents in the folk moots of early English history. However, it is probably not until the House of Commons became established as an elected assembly that we can definitely identify the emergence of a legislature. From England, the "mother of parliaments," the idea spread to other countries where similar bodies were established or created by the transformation of earlier types of assembly, council, or *parlement*. Within the early legislatures there were political factions and clubs, but these cannot be called political parties until they begin to organize the electorate and submit nominations. In this sense, political parties are closely linked to legislatures, and were invented shortly afterwards. We might even be justified in dropping the *L*-type system, and considering polities with legislatures and/or political parties as a single type. However, there seem to be some advantages to recognizing the emergence of *L*-type polities because of the historically important role they played as premodern systems, paving the way for the emergence of modern polities.

The final, *P*-type, polity can now be defined as any political system that has an executive, a bureaucracy, a legislature, and one or more *political parties*. Let us refer to the presence, in principle, of one or more political parties in a polity as a *party system*. It should be clear that virtually all contemporary polities, including the new states of Asia, Africa, and Latin America, have party systems as well as legislatures and bureaucracies. In this sense the modernizing countries of the non-Western world have governments that are structurally different from the premodern countries of the West. The addition of party systems may be assumed to have made a significant difference in the modes of operation.

Six Types of Polity

It is not easy to translate this alphabetical typology into English words. The *L*-type is not simply a *legislative-type* because it includes also a bureaucracy and an executive, and we would court misunderstanding to use the term *executive-type* for the *E*-type because readers would probably think immediately of some kind of modern state with parties and legislatures as well as executives. If we talk of *party-type* systems instead of *P*-type, we immediately suggest distinctions between one-, two-, and multiparty systems, and tend to ignore governments run by military juntas, even though they have (ineffective) political parties.

We might introduce the temporal categories, by making arbitrary definitions as follows. Let us suppose that we could redefine *folk polities* to refer to the *N*-type systems, *classical polities* to mean *E*-type, *traditional polities* to mean *B*-type, *premodern* to mean *L*-type, and *contemporary* to mean *P*-type. The relationships are quite close, but cases will come to mind where the temporal categories do not exactly coincide with the structural. Moreover, having gone to so much trouble to escape an extrinsic basis of classification, would we not be falling back into a trap if we now used a set of temporal terms for our structural concepts?

The temporal words also raise other difficulties. We are likely to associate classical with ancient or with Western, making it quite difficult to limit the meaning of the word to *E*-type systems. This is the same kind of

95

problem that Wittfogel (and Marx before him) encountered when they used the words *Asiatic* and *Oriental* for a particular kind of traditional bureaucratic empire. The word *traditional* itself is particularly rubbery. In present day usage it is likely to mean folk and classical and even premodern as well as the *B*-type systems.

If only five types of systems were to be distinguished, we might stop here and keep the alphabetical terms, which ought to be no more difficult to remember than Vitamin C, X-ray, and S-curve. However, the next stage in our analysis requires us to distinguish varieties of these basic types. We have already suggested that republic and monarchy are varieties of the *E*-type system, and feudalism and bureaucratic empires variants of the *B*-type polity. Among *P*-type systems we can go on to distinguish between modern and modernizing polities. Among the modern, we may draw further lines between democratic and totalitarian. Within the former category, distinctions already mentioned between presidential and parliamentary, between two-party and multiparty systems, are relevant. Some of these terms are functionally-oriented, referring to power distributions. Others are heavily value-loaded, making objective analysis difficult. We could try subscripts, distinguishing among *P*-type systems, between *Ps*, *Pt*, *Pv*, and so on, but this seems to be more cumbersome and difficult to remember than the adoption of new words. Accordingly, I have decided to make a rather shocking plunge and herewith offer a whole new set of words.

Hopefully this new vocabulary will not be too difficult to remember if we take it step by step. Moreover, relatively familiar Latin and Greek roots will be used with meanings not too divergent from the original. Only two basic roots will be employed, *cephal-* and *tonic*. The first term means head, and will refer to the character of the executive of any polity, as modified by other organs of government. The second term relates to tension, energy, balance, and hence may be applied to the capacity of a polity to exercise power, or the way in which it is used.

Let us start with *cephal-* and construct a set of terms for all the basic types already identified. First, however, we must put the root in the form of a noun. Unfortunately this must be artificial, since the root turns easily only into the adjectives *cephalous* and *cephalic*. Because we are referring only to whole political systems, we might use the phrase *cephalous polity*. However, if this expression is repeated many times, it will grow tiresome. Let us therefore reduce it to an acronym, which will also seem to be a noun-form of the root, namely, *cephaly*. The word *cephaly* may then be defined as any social system at the societal level characterized in terms of the presence or absence of an executive, and related structures such as bureaucracy, legislature, and party system.

We can now build up a typology by using prefixes for this root. Clearly since *N*-type polities lack an executive, we may use the root *a-*, meaning without, and create the word, *acephaly*. We may then offer the hypothesis that primitive folk societies usually have political systems that can be characterized as *acephalies*.

An *E*-type polity with executive but without bureaucracy, legislature, and party system may be referred to as a *procephaly*, using the prefix *pro-* in the sense of before, in front of. A corresponding hypothesis might be that classic polities, such as those described by Aristotle, are *procephalies*.

A *B*-type polity, with executive and bureaucracy but without legislature and party system, may be referred to as an *orthocephaly*, using the prefix *ortho-* in the sense of right, correct, proper. We can now hypothesize that governments in traditional bureaucratic and feudal societies tend to be *orthocephalies*.

An *L*-type polity, with executive, bureaucracy, and legislature, but without a party system, will be called a *heterocephaly*, using the prefix *hetero-* in the sense of other, different, and thereby pointing to the legislature as a new kind of power center capable of balancing that of the executive. Our corresponding hypothesis is that premodern states tended to have the form of *heterocephalies*.

The fifth or *P*-type, having all four organs, executive, bureaucracy, legislature, and party system, will be called a *metacephaly*, using the prefix *meta-* in the sense of along with, after. An appropriate hypothesis states that virtually all contemporary polities are *metacephalies*.

While engaged in this game, let us postulate a possible postmodern kind of political system in which some new basic institution of government will enable mankind to cope better with the wide range of problems with which the industrial and automation revolutions are confronting us. Such a political system might make possible a viable framework of world government. At least let us, quite speculatively, label such a hypothetical system a *supracephaly*.

The impatient critic who is concerned only with contemporary states, whether of the modern Western type or the modernizing non-Western type, is likely at this point to protest that, since he is only interested in metacephalies, why should he be bothered with all these other kinds of polities. The answer, of course, is that if one wishes only to study metacephalies, there is no reason why he should be concerned about other types, which might well be left to the historian and the prophet, to those who care to look backward and forward in time. He is likely, however, to engage in undue simplification, as when he lumps together under the general heading of "traditional" the wide range of divergent polities that we have identified here as acephalies, procephalies, orthocephalies, heterocephalies, and a possible supracephaly. Moreover, he is likely to engage in prolepsis, that is, the fallacy of attributing to an earlier age political characteristics to be found only in a later age, or the opposite fallacy of parachronism, namely, attributing to a later age characteristics found only in an earlier one. Unfortunately these fallacies are frequently committed by political scientists whose vocabulary is limited to the common sense words for political systems.

Perhaps even more importantly, if the scholar wants to understand the problems of political development, how one type of system is changed into another, then he cannot avoid looking at the kinds of polities out of which modern states have grown. In this context it becomes highly significant that the Western countries emerged out of heterocephalies, whereas this stage was skipped by the non-Western countries, which have jumped from orthocephalies into metacephalies. It may also be significant to be able to point out that, structurally speaking, all contemporary polities, both modern and modernizing, both Western and non-Western, belong to the same type, i.e., metacephalies. This is relevant to the great debate which has been raging in the field of comparative politics as to whether or not a unified theory can be applied to these two categories, or whether theories of a different kind are needed. My position is that basic qualitative changes are required for the statement of theories relevant to each level of polity, but that within each level much greater theoretical homogeneity is possible. Because, in ordinary usage, the terms *traditional* and *non-Western* are used loosely to include both metacephalies and earlier kinds of polities, which we might call pre-metacephalies (including acephalies, procephalies, orthocephalies, and heterocephalies), it is clear that generalizations about traditional and non-Western polities are highly suspect.

Since the taxonomy that has been presented so far is actually quite elementary, containing only six major categories, it is clearly inadequate for the requirements of systematic comparison of whole political systems. We must therefore proceed to examine each of these basic types in order to identify relevant subtypes, which in turn will also have to be named. The reader who finds neologisms particularly unpleasant is warned to stop here before he gets trapped in utter confusion. For those who may wish to proceed further, here is a summary table of the terminology used so far:

Table 3. The Six Basic Types of Polity

Acephaly	N-type	without executive, bureaucracy, legislature, party system
Procephaly	E-type	with executive; but no bureaucracy, legislature, party system
Orthocephaly	B-type	with executive and bureaucracy; but no legislature, party system
Heterocephaly	L-type	with executive, bureaucracy, legislature; but no party system
Metacephaly	P-type	with executive, bureaucracy, legislature, party system
Supracephaly	X-type	"all these and more besides?"

A Dialectical Paradigm

We have already seen that under each of the major types of polity formulated by structural criteria a variety of subtypes can be found. We noted, for example, Aristotle's discussion of monarchies, aristocracies, and democracies falling presumably under our category of procephaly. Similarly, we have seen that both bureaucratic empires and feudal systems may be found under the heading of orthocephaly. We have also learned that both modern and modernizing polities can be classified as metacephalies. Pushing further, we may distinguish among metacephalies in the modernizing category, some that are run by military juntas, and others that have a dominant party at the helm.

Two questions arise in relation to these subtypes. Why is it that some of them seem to be substitutes for each other? Aristotle was the first to observe this cyclical phenomenon, this apparent pendulum swing to one subtype and then back to another. Clearly a developmental theory ought to provide for system transformations within a single subtype.

However, it is also apparent that polities have been transformed from one of our major types to another. Bureaucracies have been invented and brought into existence where none existed before. Similarly, legislatures and political parties have each in turn made their historic appearance in societies that previously could not have known of their existence. A developmental theory, therefore, ought to explain how these forward leaps from one major type to another occur. Conversely, it perhaps ought to explain why some never succeeded in making such a system transformation, why they persisted over long periods without discovering or adopting the new governmental technology necessary to achieve transformation into a more complex type of polity.

One way of organizing our thoughts about these questions in a coherent fashion is in terms of a *dialectical paradigm*. The familiar notion of thesis, antithesis, and synthesis has been popularized by the Marxists, but it antedates Karl Marx, and there is no need to limit this logical framework to the particular applications which Hegel and Marx gave it. I believe it fits rather well the phenomena we are interested in here, with one modification. We need not assume that the antinomy between thesis and antithesis necessarily leads to a synthesis. Rather, the confrontation of opposed principles of government represented symbolically by the thesis-antithesis dichotomy can be thought of as a persistent conflict manifesting itself in cyclical or pendulum-alternations over relatively long periods. The movement of synthesis, involving system transformation, may take place only rarely and under very special conditions.

The basic dialectical confrontation is familiar in modern governments in the form of a *right-left* struggle. The *right* is typically thought of as a demand, normally by elite elements, for more order, stability, efficiency, and conservation of established principles. By contrast, the *left* is usually regarded as a demand, normally by sub-elite elements, for more equality, change, justice, and reform. We have many terms for this antinomy. In moderate form, it is

99

conservative against liberal; in extreme form, reactionary against radical. In terms of our key governmental institutions, the right is often linked with bureaucracy, with the principle of hierarchy, with administrative management and the norms of efficiency. The left is frequently associated with the legislature and party system, with demands for greater politicization of the population, for social mobilization, for increased participation in government, for social equality.

It is relevant to link this idea with current discussions of political development. The SSRC Committee on Comparative Politics has arrived at a consensus that the key ingredients in political development are *capacity, equality,* and *structural differentiation.*[7] It may not be stretching the significance of these concepts too much to suggest that the principle of *capacity* is similar to the principle of the *right,* the thesis of our little dialectic. The principle of *equality* may be linked to the principle of the *left,* the antithesis of our dialectic. The phenomenon of *system transformation,* involving the addition of a new basic organ of government, is an example of *structural differentiation,* and represents the dialectical stage of synthesis. It reflects the invention or borrowing of a new kind of governmental technology which makes possible the reconciliation of contradictory forces.

This formulation also enables us to see the developmental problem in a new light. In a sense, the goals of capacity and equality are among the most important "political goods" sought by the members of any polity. To a considerable degree they may be incompatible with each other in the sense that greater equality can be secured only by a reduction in capacity, and greater capacity only by a diminution of equality. Protagonists in a right-left struggle may see themselves as playing a zero-sum game, in which the winnings of one must be losses for another.

A system transformation involving greater structural differentiation, however, may make it possible for the members of a polity to secure more equality and more capacity. If more goods (both economic and political) can be produced, then there will also be more to go around. It is in this sense that the sequence of structural types presented in my taxonomy is developmental. It is not intrinsically more developed to have a legislature or a party system than not to have one. But if the introduction of these new governmental technologies makes it possible to secure more political goods, and to make the necessity of choice between rivals seem less brutal, then the consequences of this kind of structural transformation may well be developmental.[8]

It is possible to present the foregoing conceptions in a visual pattern as follows:

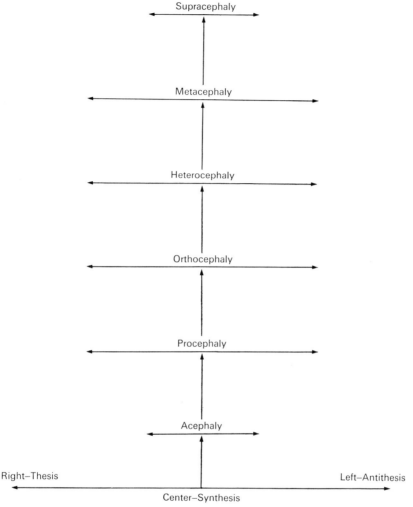

Figure 3-2. The Dialectical Paradigm

Three Epitypes

In thinking about the dialectical change processes suggested by this approach, we shall need some supplementary terminology. We might think of each of the five major terms introduced so far as basic types, each of which has a number of subtypes. However, this way of thinking about our subject is unnecessarily static. It may be better to think of the five terms as representing *archetypes*, each followed historically by a set of *epitypes*, just as the variations on a theme in music grow out of the original statement, but are not merely subcategories of it.

Fred W. Riggs

Let us distinguish two different kinds of *epitypes*. One involves movement to the right or left, horizontal modifications of the archetype involving a skewing of the political system in favor of either greater capacity at the expense of equality, or greater equality at the expense of capacity. Let us call these variations *antitypes*. They may be distinguished from each other by the directional words, right and left. Thus the *right antitype*, or the thesis in a dialectical sense, involves at each level an accentuation of the hierarchical principle of organization, centralization or concentration of power, enhancement of administrative effectiveness, and stability of organization. By contrast, the *left antitype*, or antithesis, involves at each level a strengthening of the principle of equality, the localization or dispersal of power, enhancement of political organization, and more widespread distribution of values, frequently at the expense of stability and order. Historically we may expect the right antitypes, the conservatives, to be victorious for longer periods than the left antitypes, which we may expect to be relatively ephemeral.

The other kind of epitype represents, of course, the movement of synthesis, the principle of system transformation. It can be looked at from two points of view. In terms of the next higher archetype in our paradigm, it could be regarded as a *prototype*. In terms of the preceding archetype, however, it could be treated as a *metatype*. We may expect the metatypes (or prototypes) to involve a balance between the right and left antitypes, and therefore in some sense to constitute a political center, an accommodation of contradictory tendencies, a compromise between the principles of capacity and equality, of stability and participation, of conservatism and liberalism.

It will be convenient to have a term for the whole set of an archetype and its epitypes. I shall refer to them as a *cluster*. Thus any archetype, such as orthocephaly, and the various antitypes plus the metatype associated with it may be called the orthocephalic cluster.

In the present context it is probably unnecessary for us to speculate about possible antitypes of acephaly. One might guess that the right antitype could be illustrated by extended patrimonial kinship systems, perhaps unilineal in membership. By contrast, the left antitype might consist of matrilocal and bilateral kinship systems. The metatype for acephaly could be thought of as probably a patriarchal system of limited extent, thereby facilitating the formation of political units transcending the family, with an executive recognized by a multiplicity of families. It is unnecessary here to consider further the probable characteristics of such a metatype, but let us call it a *protocephaly*, and regard it also as the protype of procephaly.

The Procephaly Cluster

It is easier to recognize the antitypes of procephaly. We are dealing now with city states, village republics, and perhaps some tribal societies.

Let us call the right antitype of acephaly, *monocephaly*, and the left antitype, *polycephaly*. The Aristotelian categories are relevant in this cluster. His monarchy and tyranny are both forms of monocephaly. A limited degree of centralization of power, which at other stages might not prevent further structural differentiation, tends here to inhibit the emergence of orthocephaly. An Aristotelian form of political decay or breakdown, the collapse of monarchy into tyranny, could be represented as a further movement to the right, from moderate to extreme monocephaly.

The contrasting left antitype, democratic forms of government deteriorating into ochlocracy (mob rule), illustrates the category of *polycephaly*. Whereas a monarch is the executive in monocephaly, an assembly of citizens forms the executive in polycephaly. Of course, only a small portion of the population may have the rank of citizens, whom the servile classes enable to engage in political and administrative activity. A number of officials may be selected to serve administrative functions, but in order to prevent the formation of a centralized authority, they are frequently rotated in office, and probably chosen by lot. History seems to bear out the proposition that left antitypes are short-lived for we have only a few examples of polycephalies, many more of monocephalies. The fact that Athens during the fifth century, B.C., became a polycephaly of unusual brilliance and creativity has given Westerners a distorted view of the salience, as measured by duration and prevalence, of this type of polity.

Aristotle seems to have favored aristocracies, and Plato's republic, with its Guardians serving a Philosopher King, might be regarded as illustrative of the metatype of procephaly, which may be called *anacephaly*. To find a historical example, however, we probably have to look, not at Greece but at Rome, where the rise of the Principate, in precarious balance with the Senate, made possible the emergence of bureaucracy in the West. Bureaucracy, however, had risen elsewhere and at earlier periods, notably in China, the Middle East, and India. To be classified as an anacephaly, we would expect a polity to display a balance of power between the executive on the one hand, with a rudimentary administrative staff of royal servants, and on the other hand, a college of hereditary nobles, an assembly or senate, and other centers of political influence. The power of the ruler and his staff represents the claims of capacity or stability and the political colleges typify the counterclaims of equality or participation.

We have now depicted the considerable range of variation possible with the procephalic cluster. Aristotelian theory can be applied quite empirically and meaningfully to an analysis of problems of political change within this cluster. But Aristotle could scarcely imagine the kind of problems and phenomena that would arise out of orthocephaly, the archetype that we can now regard as emerging out of anacephaly, but not out of either monocephaly or polycephaly.

Fred W. Riggs

The Orthocephaly Cluster

With the appearance of orthocephaly, we can again recognize two anti-types. The right antitype will be called *hierocephaly* because of the hierarchy of officials in the bureaucracy who become its primary power holders. Although the bureaucracy emerges in the court of rulers of the orthocephalic arche-type, appointed officials seek to enhance their own power so that they can gratify their own ambitions and self-interests. We can frequently discern, in historic empires, a movement from ruler-orientations on the part of the bureaucrats toward self-orientations. This entrenchment of the bureauc-racy as a self-serving ruling class is the touchstone of hierocephaly.[9]

The very effort to mobilize a large enough treasure, or "free floating resources" in Eisenstadt's phrase, to finance an overgrown bureaucracy tends to starve the autonomous social systems of such an empire, and the bureaucracy itself becomes so powerful that it can crush all potential sources of resistance within the polity. This leads to what Wittfogel calls "Oriental Despotism," a social system incapable of further endogenous evolution because it has exhausted its own inner springs of inventiveness and entrepreneurship.

The contrasting left antitype of orthocephaly may be called *paracephaly*, using the prefix *para-* for shield to suggest limits placed on the ruler's power. Descriptively, a polity marked by the proliferation of hereditary office-holding and the decline or disappearance of centrally controlled appointive staffs is paracephalous. Thus feudalistic societies, such as medieval Europe and Japan, can be regarded as paracephalies. Here the inability of the ex-ecutive to mobilize enough power to maintain control over a substantial domain and therefore to protect markets, build public works, and carry out developmental goals tends to prevent a paracephaly from evolving beyond a low ceiling which is self imposed.

These two orthocephalic antitypes may be studied in terms of proposi-tions advanced earlier. Clearly the hierocephaly, with its stress on bureau-cratic organization, has far greater capacities than the more equalitarian paracephaly with its host of relatively autonomous nobles. Yet the formal structure of government in feudalistic systems (paracephalies) is patterned after that of the bureaucratic, and the two contrasting principles of organiza-tion may also be regarded as alternatives of each other, liable to cyclical transformations.[10]

Neither of the orthocephalic antitypes, I submit, is capable of generating legislative bodies, and thereby creating a more structurally differentiated kind of polity. The hierocephaly has no need of legislatures because its bureaucracy is sufficiently able to deal with the major problems that con-front it, and so powerful that it can suppress all rival centers of power. By contrast, the paracephaly is unable to sustain centralized government over a sufficiently large domain to make possible the emergence of powerful middle classes. The requisite conditions for further differentiation emerged historically in states governed by absolutist monarchs which we have learned to call by such pejorative terms as *despotism* and *autocracy*. Our taxonomy permits us to give orthocephalic metatypes the neutral name, *autocephaly*. The best historical example is England, from the sixteenth through the eighteenth centuries. Comparable systems arose on the continent of Europe and in Tokugawa Japan.

In these historical instances we can discern a precarious balance between the growing power of centralized bureaucracy under the effective control of a self-recruiting hereditary monarchy, and the power of autonomous social systems, including courts of law, hereditary nobles, and an independent business community or bourgeoisie, organized in guilds, autonomous universities, and churches. The administrative function was well enough performed to maintain requisite standards of law and order and a minimal level of service over a domain in which relatively autonomous social systems could perform innovative roles.

The Heterocephaly Cluster

Polities organized as autocephalies exercised growing political power, paving the way for the appearance of a new archetype, the heterocephaly. The distinctively new governmental technique of heterocephaly was the appearance of legislative bodies as elected assemblies. Whereas such transformations have perhaps taken place at several times and places in history, I believe we can locate the first decisive transformation of an autocephaly into a heterocephaly in England with the rise of the House of Commons. From England, the institution spread to other countries in the West and eventually throughout the world.

Just as the earlier archetypes were vulnerable to transformations into antitypes, so the heterocephaly was also liable to its own deformations. The dangers were that the legislature would become too strong or remain too weak. In the former case, a legislature becoming excessively powerful overthrows the executive and proclaims itself head of government, as a convention. But the convention form of government, as France discovered during its revolution, and England under the Commonwealth, is a notably unstable and violent kind of government. As with other left antitypes, it does not evolve into a more differentiated form, but because of its instability, tends to dissolve into the right antitype of heterocephaly.

Let us call the left antitype of heterocephaly a *hypercollegial* polity, since we have run out of prefixes for cephaly. The words *legislature* and *convention* do not make appropriate adjectives, and so the word *collegial*, which can stand as an adjective for legislature, is introduced instead.

Fred W. Riggs

The right antitype of heterocephaly may be called, correspondingly, a *pseudocollegial* polity. Our reference here is to a legislative body created by a ruler and kept carefully under his control by a dominating bureaucracy. Bismarckian Germany might be classified as a pseudocollegial polity. Because the very existence of a legislature calls into being new popular expectations concerning the political process, the frustration of these expectations by a controlled legislature leads to growing tensions and the probable collapse of pseudocollegial polities.

The creative metatype emergent from heterocephaly can be referred to as an *epicephaly*. Historically, the leading case again is England where constitutionalism, despite many false starts, eventually stabilized in a form that made possible a lively balance of power between the king and bureaucracy on the one side and parliament on the other, with the prime minister as an effective executive. The key mechanism for achievement of this constitutionalist balance was the rise of the political party, providing machinery capable of expanding the popular base of legislative power as a more broadly representative organ of government. The party-controlled parliament also created a mechanism for the unambiguous selection of prime ministers and cabinets, once the hereditary monarchy could no longer fulfill this function.

The more or less contemporaneous evolution of constitutional government in the United States also generated an electoral party system whose effective political power was capable of balancing the administrative capabilities of growing bureaucracy. The epicephalic stage, therefore, gave birth to metacephaly, i.e., constitutional government with competitive political parties, as in the United States and Britain.

The Metacephaly Cluster

What, then, are the antitypes and metatypes generated by metacephalies? Again we find forms of government in which bureaucratic and political institutions exercise disproportionate roles. The *left antitype* of metacephalies may be found today in non-Western countries where a political party has seized power following the termination of colonial rule. These parties emerged out of revolutionary nationalist movements in countries where the ideals of constitutionalism had been spread by the imperial power, usually accompanied by the creation of colonial legislatures. I shall refer to such polities as *syntonic*. The word *syntonic* pertains to resonance, as when two radio instruments are put on the same wave length. As in any process of adaptation or acculturation, however, the syntonic system is apt to behave differently from its original metacephalic archetype. Characteristically, a syntonic polity is unable to maintain the legislature as an effective center of power, and the party tends to take over the government, reducing the administrative capacity of the bureaucracy by indulgence in patronage or spoils appoint-

106

ments. Thus the syntonic polity parallels the behavior of a hypercollegial polity.

We can distinguish two subtypes of the syntonic polity. A key criterion is the willingness of a ruling party to permit legal opposition parties. A utopian party, which considers that it has found the authentic answers to a country's political needs and destiny, may suppress any opposition parties as inherently heretical or treasonable. It will, therefore, forbid any candidates to run at elections except those nominated by the ruling utopian party itself. To perpetuate itself, such a regime must be able to count on a relatively effective police force and army in order to detect and suppress potential revolutionary elements. The great weakness of regimes of this type is their vulnerability to overthrow by *coup d'état,* notably one led by military officers. Let us call this kind of syntonic polity a *hypotonic* system. It may also be called a *movement regime.*

By contrast, a unity or conciliation party bases its claim to power on its ability to defeat rivals at the polls. This formal dedication to democratic ideals is reinforced by its inability to count on a corrupted and spoils-infested bureaucracy to ferret out its enemies. Consequently, a dominant conciliation party has to rely on its ability to coopt leaders of opposition groups. By permitting them to organize as political parties and nominate candidates, it is able to identify its most dangerous opponents quite quickly, and then to take measures to nullify the threat by offering them appropriate inducements. Since the consequences of this strategy are likely to debilitate both the party organization and the state bureaucracy, it seems appropriate to refer to such systems as *atonic.* It may be suggested, therefore, that *syntonic* polities appear in two main forms, *hypotonic* and *atonic.*

The *right antitype* for metacephalies may be referred to as *hypertonic,* corresponding to the pseudocollegial right antitype of heterocephaly. This kind of polity is also to be found in many non-Western countries, especially in those which have come into the twentieth century under the rule of hereditary monarchs. As the functions of the bureaucracy expanded, the ability of the rulers to maintain effective control over their own governments declined until, eventually, an uprising from within overthrew the kings or reduced their power, enabling military officers to name themselves executives.

Colonial regimes in which the effective center of power was a ruling administrative class can also be classified as hypertonic polities. It is convenient to think of hypertonic polities as appearing in two forms: *autotonic* when governed by self-elected military bureaucrats; *heterotonic* when governed by hereditary monarchs or by foreign powers, as in colonial administration.

In all these systems political parties tend to emerge in two roles, but neither one involves effective participation in the choice of the executive. Sometimes parties are set up by the executive as a front in the expectation that they will help mobilize mass support for an embattled regime. Sometimes revolutionary counterelites establish parties in the hope that they can change the system of government.

As in our previous clusters, a propensity for cyclical alternations between the right and left antitypes can be discerned. The breakdown of syntonic (party-dominated) regimes and their replacement by hypertonic (autotonic, or bureaucratic) regimes has by now become a familiar phenomenon in many countries of Asia, Africa, and Latin America. Normally, it is a military officer group or *junta* that seizes power in these transformations. However, as current events in Vietnam show, countermovements by popular demand to replace the military leaders with party control demonstrates the possibility of a countertransformation from a hypertonic to a syntonic polity. If we think of the former colonial territories as also being hypertonic polities, then we can recognize the emergence of nationalist movements which become the ruling parties in new states as additional examples of the transformation of hypertonic (heterotonic) into syntonic polities.

Some heterotonic polities seem more likely to be transformed into autotonic than into syntonic systems. It was pointed out that heterotonic polities may be ruled by foreign powers or by hereditary monarchs. We may hypothesize that monarchic heterotonic polities are likely to break down into autotonic polities (ruled by military officers), whereas it is more probable that imperial heterotonic polities will be transformed into party-dominated (syntonic) polities.

Tonic Polities

Let us call the metatype of metacephalies a *tonic* polity. We can recognize the presence of a tonic polity by the maintenance of a balance between rightist pressures for bureaucratic dominance and heightened administrative capacity, and leftist pressures for partisan dominance and greater equalitarianism. Operationally, let us specify two criteria, both of which have to be present in order for a tonic polity to persist. *First,* the *executive* must be named by action of the *party system*. He (or it) cannot be self-selected from within by bureaucrats (including military officers). *Second,* positions in the *bureaucracy* must be *protected* on a merit basis from arbitrary intervention by the dominant party. The first condition protects the political (left) interests of the polity and the second condition safeguards its administrative (right) requirements. If the first condition is not met, the polity cannot make political decisions that are adequate to meet the requirements of the political system for equilibrium and integration. If the second condition is not met, the polity cannot meet the needs of the political system for effective execution of public policy.[11]

The specification of these two criteria for a tonic polity enables us to recognize why the two antitypes fail to achieve the necessary conditions to become tonic polities. The syntonic polity results from left-ward pressures which enable it to select the executive through the party system, but it fails to meet the second condition. Its administrative capacities, therefore, are inadequate, leading to great dissatisfaction with governmental performance. By contrast, the hypertonic polity results from right-ward pressures, which enable it to protect the career interests of its bureaucrats, but it fails to meet the first condition. Consequently its public policies are insufficiently responsive to the needs of the political system, and even on the administrative side, the bureaucracy tends to become self-serving and hence as administratively inept as in a syntonic polity. In short, both the political and administrative functions are poorly performed in the metacephalic antitypes. This is the condition of poor integration in a relatively differentiated system which I have characterized as *prismatic*.[12] The hypothesis which follows from these considerations is that the countries of Asia, Africa, and Latin America in varying degrees and with notable exceptions tend to have either syntonic or hypertonic polities and to have political and administrative conditions that can be considered quite prismatic.

Turning to *tonic* polities, where the two criteria of political-administrative and left-right balance earlier specified are met, by definition, we can hypothesize that these conditions are found to a considerable degree in the so-called modern or developed political systems. It is within this category of polities, and this category only, that the familiar distinctions between presidential and parliamentary, and between two-party and multiparty systems, are valid.

Let us clarify these distinctions, however, in terms that arise naturally out of our taxonomy. We have indicated that the party system must select the executive in a tonic polity, but we have not specified the role of the legislature, which, by definition, must exist in all metacephalies. If the key vote on choice of executive takes place in the legislature, then such a legislature may be called a *parliament*. If the key vote on choice of the executive takes place through a general popular election, then the executive may be called a *president*. This key structural distinction enables us to distinguish between presidential and parliamentary systems, both of which are tonic polities.

These terms, although apparently simple, are actually confusing because they are used for institutions that do not meet the criteria specified. We can easily find, for example, legislatures in African and Asian countries that are called *parliaments* but do not, in practice, take the key votes that determine choice of the executive, even though they may go through the motions of making such a vote. If we decide to define a *parliament* as a legislature which votes on the choice of an executive, whether the vote is decisive or not, then we would have to say that both syntonic and tonic polities may be parliamentary.

109

To take another example, we can find examples of parliamentary tonic polities that have an official called a *president,* as did France under the Fourth Republic. The Soviet Union also has a "president" even though his selection is not effectively determined by either legislative or popular vote. Consequently, to call the two types of tonic polity, parliamentary and presidential, is to open the door to continued ambiguities which it has been our aim to avoid.

Let us, therefore, continue the quest for new names, and call a tonic polity in which the executive is effectively chosen by popular vote, after party nominations, an *isotonic* polity. The prefix *iso-,* meaning equal, is chosen to suggest the separation of powers between the office of the executive and the legislature which necessarily occurs if the legislature does not make the selection. The contrasting system, in which the legislature does make the choice, may then be called a *monotonic* polity, the prefix *mono-* being used to signify the unity of the position of executive as effective head not only of the bureaucracy but also of the party and the legislature.

Monotonic polities normally have a chief of state as a ceremonial office separate from the office of executive or chief of government. The chief of state may be a hereditary monarch or an elected president. This role, and the manner of its selection, does not affect the present typology. It may be useful to note in passing, however, that the ancient terms, *republic* and *monarchy*, are structural categories, and refer to the manner of choosing the chief of *state*. The chief of a monarchy is chosen by hereditary succession, the chief of a republic by a vote. Clearly all the types of political system identified in the taxonomy presented here can be either republics or monarchies. These terms enable us to distinguish between two kinds of ceremonial structure in any polity, but they do not help us to compare whole political systems with respect to the variables that interest us most.

Monotonic polities may be further subdivided into two more categories which correspond to the familiar distinction between two-party and multi-party systems. However, even this dichotomy generates ambiguities. Since syntonic polities also have parties, it easily leads to confusion if the terms are extended to regimes of this type. Moreover, the two-party criterion applies to isotonic (presidential) as well as to some monotonic (parliamentary) regimes. If a popular vote is the basis of electing an executive, there must be a majority party, even if a run-off multiparty system is used as in the French Fifth Republic. One suspects that if the institution of a popularly elected president is preserved in France, the competing opposition parties will unite, leading to the formation of a two-party system. At any rate, it does not seem particularly helpful to distinguish subtypes of monotonic polities by number of parties.

We are, therefore, dealing only with a subclassification of monotonic polities. The key distinction here is whether a coalition of parties in the legislature is necessary to secure the election of an executive, or whether a single party has a majority in parliament and so can control the choice of the executive. We may refer to the former system as a *coalitional* polity, and the latter as a *noncoalitional* polity, it being understood that these are subtypes of the monotonic polity.

An important question now arises with regard to the Soviet Union. How are we to classify this system? Can it be regarded as a tonic polity, or should we perhaps classify it with the syntonic polities, as something like the hypotonic (movement) regime? First, we must ask whether it meets the two criteria for a tonic polity. Certainly it meets the first criterion, for the executive is selected by the party system, not from within the bureaucracy. Does it meet the second? My guess is that, especially since Khrushchev, it does. This enables us to classify it as a tonic polity.

It is neither a monotonic nor an isotonic polity, however, for the executive is selected neither by the legislature nor by popular election, although formal ratifying votes are held. In terms of our taxonomy based on the role of three key organs, we can distinguish between those in which the legislature holds significant power and in which it does not. It is unnecessary to choose a term for polities in which the legislature holds significant power, but we can recognize both monotonic and isotonic polities as examples of such a political system. The Soviet Union is clearly an example of a polity in which the legislature, the Supreme Soviet, does not exercise comparable power. Let us now refer to such a political system as an *anatonic* polity, using the prefix *ana-* which means, variously: upwards, backward, anew, excessively.

Can we discover how the Soviet polity is able to maintain administrative rationality and the merit system, whereas hypotonic (movement) regimes conspicuously fail in this regard? The answer may perhaps be found in the internal structure of the Communist party. Here we find emerging, primarily perhaps in the Central Committee, reinforced by the organization of the Party Congress below and the Politburo above, a pattern of collegial decision-making which serves as a functional equivalent for the key role of legislatures in other tonic polities. Indeed, one might discern here something like an involuted or inverted parliamentary (monotonic) system. In both the English and the Soviet systems a ruling party governs, and in both cases this involves the imposition of control over the legislature. In the British case, however, control is temporary, and liable to be overthrown at any time by a parliamentary vote, whereas in the Russian case control is permanent. Where such control is permanent, we may suppose that no opposition party can ever hope to win a public election, so that any polity with a puppet legislature is certain to have a one-party system. However, the functional requisites of effective policy-making and administration seem to make necessary the creation within the dominant party of a second legislature, a double of the first, which had been converted into a dummy legislature. In effect, then, the anatonic polity is able to provide an equivalent kind of governmental capacity by introjecting a crypto-legislature in the body of the party system, replacing the formal legislature which remains as much a ceremonial facade as the royal chief of state in the British system.

We have now completed our taxonomy, since it is premature to speculate about the postulated supracephaly, or to guess whether any of the present tonic polities could serve as incubators of such a political system. In order to summarize and provide a reference point, the following evolutionary tree or dialectical chart of political systems is presented.

Ecological Hypotheses

In the discussion up to this point we have focused attention on structural characteristics of whole political systems with a view to establishing a useful taxonomy, and providing an adequate set of terms so that unambiguous statements could be made about the various kinds of polities identified. The mere formulation of a taxonomy, however, can be an idle exercise unless it lends itself to interesting applications. A taxonomy, like any model, may be useful or useless, but is not intrinsically true or false. One criterion of its utility will be the readiness with which it can be operationalized. By attempting to classify existing and historical polities in terms of this taxonomy, one could determine the extent to which it is capable of operationalization, and the extent to which there may be any political systems that do not fit anywhere in the scheme, or that could be placed under several headings. I shall not attempt to do this here, but clearly it is an important next step if the utility of the typology is to be tested.

Another step involves the formulation of propositions concerning the persistence and transformation of types of polities. Some hypotheses have already been presented relating to intrinsic characteristics of the models in the taxonomy. It has been suggested, for example, that transformations which involve an increase in the level of structural differentiation take place only when a balance exists between the right and left tendencies in political systems. This proposition can be further elaborated by specifying that this is primarily true of endogenous transformations, that is, changes generated by the internal dynamics of a polity. The hypothesis requires modification to meet the circumstances of exogenous change, when transformations occur in response to externally induced challenges, to threats and inducements emanating from other societies.

Regarding exogenous transformations, it is much easier to adopt a new governmental technology by emulation than it is to invent it in the first place. Consequently, unbalanced polities, classified under one of the antitypes, may well be able to increase their level of structural differentiation by adopting new technologies that were initially devised elsewhere. Changes of

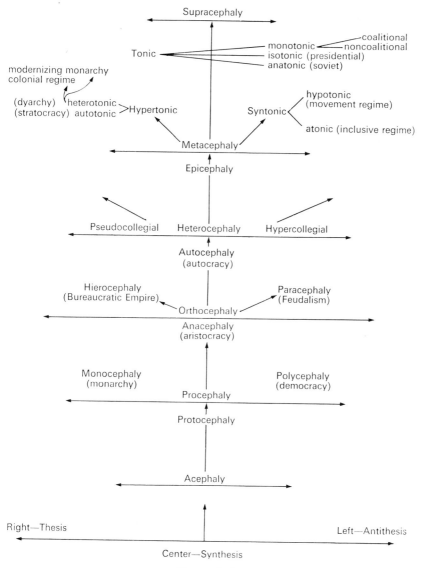

THE DIALECTICAL TREE

Figure 3-3.

this kind could be represented visually by drawing curved arrows from level to level on the sides of Figure 3–3, as shown in Figure 3–4.

Exogenous transformations, however, may well fail to provide the anticipated benefits which lead to their adoption. Structural differentiation should be distinguished analytically from the level of integration, or coordination between specialized structures, which is necessary for the successful operation of a differentiated system. It is often relatively easy to adopt a new

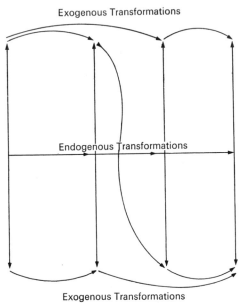

Exogenous Transformations

Endogenous Transformations

Exogenous Transformations

Figure 3-4. **Exogenous and Endogenous Change**

pattern of specialized structures or roles, but relatively difficult to secure the requisite integration between them. It is probably true that the problems generated by malintegrated but functionally specific (structurally differentiated) systems are considerably more trying than those created by less differentiated but more integrated systems. Indeed, it is precisely this discrepancy between increasing differentiation without an accompanying rise in integration levels which I refer to as *prismatic.*

The conclusion to be drawn from these propositions is that one cannot expect the same level of performance from all polities at a given level of differentiation. Great differences must be expected, in other words, in the inputs and outputs, in the efficiency and effectiveness, in the stability and continuity, of different polities of the same structural type, or, rather, of polities belonging to the same archetypal cluster. In order to explain such variations one would want to know something not only about the history of a polity in order to learn how its system transformations had originated, but also about many ecological variables that might also have affected its performance, its functional characteristics.

In addition to the phenomenon of system transformation involving increased levels of structural differentiation, it has been pointed out that cyclical changes between right and left antitypes are characteristic of each archetypal cluster. It has also been asserted that polities classified under the left antitypes tend to be far more ephemeral than those of the right antitype, and they tend to maximize values of equality and participation, whereas those of the right maximize capacity and stability. Correspondingly, the antitypes of the right tend to persist over relatively long periods of time, and may be viewed as having become well institutionalized, or achieving a condition of equilibrium. From the perspective of this taxonomy, however, these political systems can also be regarded as having broken down or stagnated. They have lost the power to innovate governmental technologies and are probably also unlikely to innovate in other spheres. Polities of the right antitype, therefore, are apt to be considered traditionalistic in the sense of having a high respect for precedent and tending to ritualize means and displace goals.

Some Environmental Variables

In an essay already too long, there is little space to work out hypotheses suggesting causal chains between environmental constraints and political system characteristics. However, a few ecological hypotheses will be presented in order to illustrate the kind of approach that might be fruitful.

Let us consider, first, a *temporal* framework for studying political development. It is characteristic of modern secular man to think of social change as inherently progressive, as moving over time from less to more developed. This outlook is, of course, by no means universal. Men in classical and traditional societies were more likely to look upon the past as a Golden Age, followed by increasing degeneration of the human condition. If we take a chronological framework, can we assign dates to the emergence of the various archetypes in our taxonomy? Or can we use a scheme of broad temporal and spatial categories instead? The latter seems to be a simpler approach. Let us first set up these categories in terms of the Western:non-Western spatial dimension, and a contemporary, past, and remote past temporal dimension. This gives us a simple matrix within which some quite familiar words can be placed, as in Table 4.

Although the equivalences are not exact, they are perhaps close enough to common usage to enable us to demonstrate a simple correlation. The following correspondences are presented as hypotheses, not definitions. We

Table 4. A Temporal-Spatial Framework

Spatial: Temporal:	Western	Non-Western
Contemporary	MODERN	MODERNIZING
Past	PRE-MODERN	TRADITIONAL
Remote Past	CLASSICAL	FOLK

are not defining tonic polities as modern, but asserting that tonic polities tend to be modern, and modern polities tonic. A set of these propositional correlations is indicated in Table 5.

These propositions, and others that follow, should illustrate a major premise of this paper, namely, that the structural typology presented here, by itself, explains little. But it does enable us to compare whole political systems, and it makes possible the formulation of hypotheses relating changes in political systems to change in environmental factors.

Table 5.
Time-Space Correlations with Polities

POLITY TYPES correlated with TEMPORAL-SPATIAL TYPES

Metacephalies	Contemporary
Tonic polities	Modern
Syntonic & Hypertonic	Modernizing
Heterocephalies	Premodern
Orthocephalies	Traditional
Procephalies	Classical
Acephalies	Folk

Because these are nondefinitional relationships, we do not expect to find perfect correlations. We cannot substitute words in the right-hand column for those in the left-hand column. But we can test these relationships by establishing a list of societies classified by temporal-spatial criteria, and another list by polity structures. We can then see to what extent the individual cases in one box match those in another box with which they are thought to be correlated. If the correlation rate is high, then the relationship may be considered significant, since the criteria for definition are quite different. Moreover, the exceptions which we can expect to find would be worth studying with particular care in order to uncover additional propositions or qualifications to add to the first set of propositions so as to make them more comprehensive.

Let us try another kind of environmental constraint and see whether or not further correlations can be discovered. A simple scale for communications technology may be employed. We are not dealing here with a single variable, but rather with a set of interrelated qualitative changes in the means of communication. All human societies presumably make use of speech to transmit ideas and instructions, but not all societies have known how to represent speech in written form. Many societies have writing but not printing. Again, not all societies with printing have been able to use electronic means for the instantaneous transmission of information over long distances. Let us arrange these criteria in the form of a Guttman scale as follows:

	A	*B*	*C*	*D*
Use of speech	+	+	+	+
Use of writing	+	+	+	−
Use of printing	+	+	−	−
Use of telecommunications	+	−	−	−

Figure 3-5. Developmental Scale of Communications

Let us now ask what relation this scale has to our taxonomy of polities. I think a pretty good proposition can be stated that communications type *D* is associated with the acephaly cluster, type *C* with the procephaly and orthocephaly cluster, type *B* with the heterocephaly cluster, and type *A* with the metacephaly cluster.

The association is not complete, in the sense that a new communications technique may be introduced before the appearance of the cluster associated with it, and polities identified in a cluster may also come into being before the use of the characteristic new means of communication. Nevertheless I believe the statistical correlation would be a strong one. This could indicate a pattern of circular causation. For example, the use of telecommunications may facilitate the emergence of metacephalies, and, reciprocally, the heightened political demands and administrative capabilites of metacephalies may be expected to stimulate the spread of telecommunications.

Economic Development and Political Transformations

A similar proposition could be formulated relating economic growth to polity types. Let us begin by constructing an economic scale, not in terms of per capita income, but in terms of the dominant pattern of economic activity. For example, let us assume a *first* stage to be one in which most of the population sustain themselves by *food gathering*, by hunting and fishing. In the *second* stage, most of the population consists of *agriculturists*. In the *third* stage a substantial portion, though perhaps never a majority, of the population is engaged in *manufacturing*. In the *fourth* stage a very large sector, perhaps most of the population, is engaged in the *services*, including under this term the advertising and distribution of goods, professional, artistic, and recreational services, administration, both public and private, and financial operations.

Bearing these stages in mind, we can guess that the first stage prevails

117

in the acephalous cluster and to some extent in the procephalous, the second stage in the orthocephalous cluster and probably also in the heterocephalous cluster. The third or fourth stage prevails in tonic polities but the second stage tends to persist in the metacephalous antitypes, i.e., in hypertonic and syntonic states. A serious effort is made in such polities, however, to speed the arrival of the third stage. It may be guessed that the fourth stage, especially with the expansion of automation in manufacturing, will prevail in any supracephaly.

These propositions are of the same type as those offered with regard to changing temporal-spatial and communications patterns, but they are more complex and less self-evident. They also illustrate possible patterns of *circular causation*. It is quite likely that a given stage of economic growth precedes the emergence of a polity type, but may also follow it. Economic growth may generate environmental changes conducive to the emergence of a new type of polity by creating both resources and needs that facilitate and heighten the urgency of an increase in the level of structural differentiation. But, conversely, a more differentiated system may also both create a demand for more economic goods, and make it possible to increase the production of such goods.

Economic changes, however, are related not only to rises in the level of differentiation. They may also be related to the *right-left antinomy* in our dialectical model. An economic category comparable to the political pressure for equality is a demand for more *consumption* goods, whereas the equivalent to pressure for greater capacity is the demand for a higher level of savings and *investment*. It will be seen that these demands are to some degree incompatible with each other at lower levels of economic growth, thus paralleling the incompatibility of the political pressures for equality and capacity at similar levels. But like the political pressures, the higher the level of economic development, the easier it is to satisfy the demands for both consumption and investment, just as the higher the level of structural differentiation of a polity, the easier it is to meet the pressures for both equality and capacity.

These countervailing economic demands can also be related to the cyclical movements between antitypes in our model. Let us consider the impact on the economy of a political movement to the left in a metacephaly. The formation of a syntonic polity marked by a substantial increase in equalitarianism and participation of newly mobilized populations brings with it an increase in demand for consumer goods at the expense of savings and investment. This means—quite apart from population growth which may also be assumed—an increasing discrepancy between rising expectations and relatively rigid per capita income levels. A countervailing pressure now arises to raise investment levels, which can be done only by reducing the level of equality and participation in the political system, and stressing the role of the bureaucracy, leading to the rise of a hypertonic polity. An example might be found in Russian history, which probably went through the first of these phases in the 1920s, and the second in the 1930s. Similar struggles are going on in other countries of Asia, Africa, and Latin America today.

Social Mobilization and Political Transformations

Turning to a social variable, we might consider the level of social mobilization and assimilation, as defined by Karl Deutsch.[13] A very broad generalization could be made to the effect that the level of social mobilization in a polity varies directly with the archetype level, moving from acephaly to metacephaly.

The degree of assimilation becomes relevant and important only to the degree that social mobilization occurs. Taking first the metacephalic cluster, we might observe a direct correlation between the level of assimilation and degree of tonicity. In other words, the tonic polities tend to be relatively assimilated, the syntonic and hypertonic polities to be socially differentiated, i.e., to have a low level of assimilation. Similar propositions, though to a lesser degree, might be made for the pre-metacephalic clusters.

Even more interesting correlations might be postulated with reference to the cyclical changes between antitypes in our model. Let us assume that a *left antitype* prevails in a given polity, at a given level of social mobilization. The stress on participation and equality which triumphs in this antitype now has the effect of raising the level of *mobilization* in the society concerned. This in turn means an increase in the proportion of the population pressing for full enjoyment of the privileges of equality and participation promised by the political system. A contradiction then arises making the left antitype increasingly incapable of solving its political problems. This, I should think, is the force that causes Aristotle's democracies to collapse into ochlocracies, and precipitates the dive into anarchy by a revolutionary convention government, as in France's First Republic. Such are the forces at work today in Asia, Africa, and Latin America where mass movement parties and participant policies in syntonic polities continually increase the number of people who demand to be heard.

The *rightist* reaction leads to the establishment of more hierarchic antitypes, dedicated to the norms of increasing capacity and necessarily also decreasing participation. Thus the right antitype promotes policies leading to *demobilization*. But previously mobilized populations resist governmental policies designed to reduce the mobilization level—those who have acquired a taste for political participation are reluctant to surrender their claims. The consequence of these pressures is an increase in the sense of alienation and discontent among disadvantaged but mobilized members of the population, culminating in revolutionary outbreaks, suppression, and further revolts, until eventually victory brings a swing back to the left antitype and a revival of participant and equalitarian norms.

It is clear that this dialectical cycle varies in rate. In some societies right or left antitypes seem to persist for much longer than in others. Can these differences be explained? One hypothesis can be generated from the preceding remarks about mobilization levels. Let us consider the degree of *particularism* or *universalism* in recruitment patterns in a given society as an independent variable, based on cultural norms and practices which we need not investigate here. Imperial China provides an example of a traditional society with an exceptionally high level of universalism as measured by social mobility rates throughout the society, but especially into the imperial bureaucracy. By contrast, Indian society was exceptionally particularistic, as measured by the rigidities of a caste system which made individual mobility almost impossible.

Let us now suppose that a right antitype of orthocephaly should come to power in a relatively universalistic society such as China. The effective use of an examination system for recruitment to the bureaucracy would, of course, be meaningless without this universalism, as the example of Japan shows, where admission to the Chinese-type examinations was limited to high status candidates. But in the Chinese case, the persistence of social universalism made it possible for an extremely hierarchic bureaucratic system to persist without pressure for lowering the rate of mobilization. Because opportunities were open for rising social elements to enter the gentry and bureaucratic strata, pressures from below for a change in the system in the direction of more participant institutions were minimized.

By contrast, in India relatively participant patterns of governance could persist, involving considerable intracaste equality and opportunities also for intercaste mobility. The bureaucratic principle of hierarchic recruitment never became securely institutionalized in premodern India. We can conclude, tentatively, that the high degree of social particularism counterbalanced the participant political institutions so that they did not have the usual effect of raising the level of mobilization and increasing political demands beyond limits that the system could satisfy. The result was a relatively high degree of institutional stability at the orthocephalic level in both India and China, but for quite different reasons.

In Europe, by contrast, the class system was intermediate in its mobility levels between those of China and India. The degree of particularism-universalism was, correspondingly, also intermediate. This means that as participant institutions were dominant in feudalistic left antitypes, the rise of newly mobilized populations occurred, notably in the form of commercial and artisan middle-class elements. Conversely, when right antitypes were in power, ruling officials tended to make their positions hereditary and resisted pressure for new social elements to enter the upper class hierarchies. This created a sensation of demobilization, increasing social tension and revolutionary sentiments.

The consequence was to make European institutional history far more dynamic than that of China and India. Of course, it also paved the way, whenever a precarious balance between the counterposed extremes was struck, for dramatic breakthroughs to a more differentiated level of political organization. Similar observations, incidentally, might also be made about Japan, whose institutional history is also more complex and mobile than that of China.

Conclusion

These brief observations and very tentative hypotheses are intended only to illustrate some of the possible contributions that the proposed dialectical taxonomy of political systems makes possible. Hopefully, further research will establish the utility of this taxonomy and lead to the general acceptance of a set of terms—which need not be the same as those suggested in this paper—sufficiently unambiguous and varied to permit systematic comparison between different kinds of polity, and to facilitate rigorous statement of testable and interesting hypotheses about the causes and consequences of diverse forms of government.

CHAPTER 4

Parsimony and Empiricism in Comparative Politics: An Anti-Scholastic View

JOSEPH LaPALOMBARA

Yale University

The complexities of the level-of-analysis problem emerge in bold relief when we listen to comparativists who are not enchanted by the whole-systems approach. They concede that the analysis of whole systems has focused attention on certain societal variables that political scientists used to ignore, and they recognize that such an approach has led to the development of some typologies that facilitate gross comparisons. But these critics argue that, despite the usefulness of whole-systems analysis on a limited scale, the approach harbors serious deficiencies, which render it unpromising for significant advances in comparative research.

The protestors against holism object to having some of the systems analysts treat the political system (or specified political factors) as no more than a dependent variable—the ineluctable result of the physical or cultural setting (or specific environmental elements) that operates independently to shape the contours and the essence of the political system. They prefer to conceptualize political factors as independent variables radiating influence upon the environmental

123

scene itself. Equally important, the critics of whole-systems are not attracted by the grandiose analytical schemes which some comparativists have unleashed upon the field. The abstraction inherent in such schemes, they feel, often conceals gaps in knowledge, which, if filled in, might have an effect upon the comparative result. They also complain that the concepts employed, though linked together according to the canons of logic, are usually difficult to operationalize, with the result that the theoretical formulations offered in the schemes can rarely be subjected to rigorous empirical validation.

Scholars who eschew the grand designs of whole-systems analysis hope to avoid or to minimize these weaknesses by turning the spotlight of inquiry to a different level of analysis. Their concern is with segments or subsystems of the total political system. By asking meaningful questions about political systems, interest groups, voting patterns, legislatures and legislative behavior, and certain political processes (such as decision-making), they seek to test middle-range theoretical propositions.

A vigorous critic of whole-systems analysis and an exponent of the political system research strategy is Joseph LaPalombara, who presents his views in Chapter 4. LaPalombara is Professor of Political Science at Yale University. His published works include The Italian Labor Movement; Interest Groups in Italian Politics; Italy: The Politics of Planning; Bureaucracy and Political Development *(editor)*; Elezioni e Comportamento Politico in Italia *(co-editor); and* Political Parties and Political Development *(co-editor). He has also published in professional journals in theUnited States, Italy, Germany, and Spain.*

TIME WAS WHEN political scientists looked sheepishly toward their colleagues in the other social sciences, apologizing for their own discipline's lack of theoretical sophistication and envying the presumably powerful theories that informed the work of others, particularly the sociologists. That period of autocriticism is relatively recent, although this may be obscured by the Babel of *theories, models, conceptual frameworks*—and the accompanying mountain of jargon and neologisms—that now confront us. With the partial exception of A. F. Bentley, Harold Lasswell, and those who pioneered survey research of voting behavior, the concern with empirical theory, behavioralism, model-building, conceptual precision, and rigorous methodologies dates only from the 1950s.[1] In comparative politics, the Northwestern University summer seminar, which triggered considerable stock-taking in the field, occurred in 1953; the Macridis critique, now considered by many to be a piece of antiquaria, was published in 1954.[2]

Those of us who were graduate students or young instructors in those years felt the excitement of what promised to be an intellectual revolution. Behavioralism was the common banner; even mere lip-service commitment to it was the password for admittance to the ranks of the profession's counterelite.

The assault on the Traditional Establishment was disorderly, to say the least. Some, reacting perhaps to Talcott Parsons' observation that there was no intellectual justification for the existence of political science, infiltrated sociology and borrowed (often uncritically) abstract, high-flown "theories" to be used in the war on Tradition. Others, closer to psychology, attacked with weapons of tightly controlled experimentation. Still others emerged from excursions into economics and other social sciences armed with game theory, decision-making models, and the heavy artillery of descriptive and nonparametric statistics.

It is difficult to assess in retrospect whether there was in fact a revolution and, if so, how successful it has been. Assessments range all the way from statements that we are now all behavioralists (which makes the behavioral umbrella a very large one indeed) to sectarian claims that only a particular kind of research or professional activity "genuinely" represents the revolutionary thrust.[3] My view is that the ferment of the last fifteen years or so has led to some interesting and important changes in what political scientists do and that the general direction of the profession will not be set until we have come through the contemporary reaction against scientism that is apparent not only among the more speculative and normative theorists but also among empirical political scientists and sociologists who take a dim view of so-called value-free theory and research.[4] I would also add that our better understanding of sister disciplines has served to reveal that they are just as theoretically chaotic and no nearer to so-called theoretical breakthroughs than is political science. Thus, the interdisciplinary excursions have been extremely salutary for political science, even if somewhat sobering for those who were dazzled by flamboyant claims and therefore unaware that the emperor was stark naked.

From whatever vantage point one views the changes in political science of recent years, they do not appear as unmixed blessings. It seems to me that this fact may be poignantly apparent when we reflect on the study of whole political systems. On the one hand, we are now able to conceptualize about such systems with the kind of sophistication born of discovering that there is much, much more to politics than constitutions, formal institutions, administrative law and organization, and the like. Not only have we been able to identify and to study the impact on the polity of so-called informal structures like interest groups, we have been able as well to relate to the dynamics of political systems, however defined, life experiences, attitude-formation processes, and aspects of society that were once thought to be far removed from what happens politically and therefore almost irrelevant. The published output of political science over the last decade or so would therefore suggest a degree of refined understanding—as well as methodological prowess—that would have been unthinkable or scornfully dismissed as nonsense an intellectual generation ago.

But we must also be willing to acknowledge that it is precisely in the area of concern and writing about whole political systems that we now find the greatest confusion, the most dizzying array of typologies of obscure utility, the most striking examples of historicism, unilinear notions of systemic development, cultural parochialism, lack of genuine concern with how one gets logically from broad theoretical formulations to indicated empirical research, and, if I may suggest it, a contemporary variety of scholasticism that masquerades as *systemic theory*.

The generous and most intellectually-open response to this problem is to stress that confusion, disorderliness, even chaos, is inevitable when the development of a science is in full ferment. Widespread and growing political instability coupled with the realization of how much about political organization and behavior we do *not* understand naturally leads many scholars to explore the widest range of explanatory, ordering "theories." Judged from this vantage point, theoretical efforts to capture and clarify the more elusive aspects of whole political systems appear courageous and praiseworthy.

A less generous reaction to a good deal of recent writing about whole political systems is that we have returned—armed with new terminology— to the ancient practice of generalizing about such systems (e.g., nation-states, republics, monarchies, democracies, oligarchies, regional or international communities) but without significantly narrowing the gap between theoretical abstraction and empirical reality. One doubtful claim about contemporary holistic approaches is that they represent explicit theoretical systems that carefully lay out the interrelatedness of concepts, hypotheses, and systemic dynamics. The more interesting of these efforts (e.g., the work of Parsons, Apter) turn out to be primarily exercises in logic, concerning which it is much easier to explore questions of internal rigor or consistency than it is to find one's way from theoretical formulations to empirical validation of theory. Other such efforts (e.g., Easton, Deutsch) represent fascinating but far from persuasive attempts to stretch the political system on Procrustean "models" derived from mechanics or cybernetics. Still other efforts (e.g., Shils, Almond, Riggs) represent not so much "theories" of political systems but rather somewhat novel ways of describing and defining qualities of such systems on the basis of which more or less useful typologies might be constructed and comparisons made. Although it is difficult to derive from any single or combination of these works an empirically testable (or probabilistic!) theory of politics, I shall suggest later how they have already served us well in our efforts to theorize about and conduct research on partial or segmented political systems.

Many of the problems I associate with the contemporary whole-systems approach to comparative politics can be traced to the work of Max Weber and more recently to the writings of Talcott Parsons. Neither of these seminal writers can be held responsible for the sometimes productive, sometimes silly ways in which Weber's ideal-typical authority systems or Parsons' pattern variables or four-sector analytic scheme have been applied.[5] Moreover, it is apparent that in the hands of political scientists like Holt and Turner[6] or Apter,[7] and sociologists like Lipset,[8] historical, empirical studies guided and disciplined by frameworks that derive from Parsons and Weber can be very illuminating indeed. Lipset himself, however, notes about the concepts of Parsons not only that they are "obviously subject to considerable refinements,"—a statement that seems to me to be delicately understated—but also that "little work has been done on the problem of linking such concepts to empirical indicators . . . ."[9] I would add that these are exactly the ingredients essential to the New Scholasticism and that nothing furthers it more than theoretical concentration on whole systems rather than on segments of the latter that may be somewhat more manageable empirically and theoretically.

I believe that much of our difficulty can be associated with something called *structure-functionalism*, which when indiscriminately imbibed can result in painful and embarrassing intellectual hangovers. However one may judge the value of his quantitative and aggregative-data efforts, it is striking that Karl Deutsch is one of the profession's handful of scholars who have manifested the courage to search out empirical indicators that might shed empirical

127

light on theoretical generalizations applying to salient developments in total political systems.[10] It is more than mildly amusing therefore that so much of the theorizing about whole political systems lends increasing authority to Barrington Moore's derisive comment about functionalists, namely, that they are forever packing their bags for a voyage they never intend to take. In short, we are now very long on whole-systems theories, very short on systematic empirical validation of them. The gap between what empirical researchers do and these theories remains huge and bottomless, essentially unbridged by incantations about how one moves (by logical linkages) from abstract theory to theoretical derived propositions for which empirical evidence (as opposed to illustrations) can be produced.

My purpose is not to provide a complete critique of the whole-systems approach to theory and research in comparative politics, or indeed to suggest that such an approach should be abandoned. Nor do I wish to restate all of the widely diffused caveats about structure-functionalism, although some attention to this matter is unavoidable. Rather I shall attempt to respond directly to the central question posed by the editors of this volume, namely, whether it makes any sense to adopt a segmented approach and what kinds of problems are involved in any effort to do so. I am also asked by implication to distinguish cross-national from cross-cultural research and therefore presumably to recognize that these two concepts are different and that what may be valid in cross-national research may not be so in cross-cultural comparisons. Because such an assumption is closely associated with structure-functionalism, and because it is an assumption I am inclined to challenge almost categorically, it is here that I shall begin.

Functionalism and Cross-Cultural Comparison

We seem to be agreed that a comparative political science that is not cross-cultural as well as cross-national would fall short of supporting the emergence of what Almond once called a "probabilistic theory of politics." The logic underlying this view is well known: Cross-national studies, whether of whole or partial systems, tend to be culture-bound. Where cross-national studies focus on institutions such as legislatures, political parties, interest groups, and the like, they may obscure the nature of politics in cultural settings where such institutions do not exist or, if they do, represent radically different meaning for the societies involved. Even where the phenomena subjected to comparative analysis seem not to be narrowly limited in time and space (e.g., decision-making, political socialization), failure to extend analysis across cultural boundaries is likely to result in misleading and inaccurate generalizations. In short, a probabilistic theory of politics can emerge only from a consideration of the full range of cultures and societies in which politics and political systems are found.

128

Parsimony and Empiricism in Comparative Politics

Although such statements seem obvious enough today, only in recent years were some political scientists liberated from the logical trap of assuming that the political process involves a given set of behaviors occuring within a given institutional framework. We may thus assume that it is unlikely today that political scientists who happen on a primitive tribe will conclude that legislation is absent where some concrete approximation of the House of Commons does not exist; that public administration is wanting where a *Conseil d'État* or a Weberian-type bureaucracy is not to be found; or, indeed, that political participation exists (or is meaningful) only when it includes "free" elections, or widespread public involvement in associations or political organizations ranging from the PTA to political party directorates.

We owe these recent insights to structure-functionalism. Regardless of what the individual political scientist may want to do (or not do) with functionalism, he must acknowledge that it is from this "theory" that we learned of conceptualizing the political system as a set of finite, interrelated functions essential to its existence and that the manner in which such functions are performed anywhere in space and time is not necessarily bound to a specific set of institutions (read "concrete structures"). We learned, too, that it is not merely a formal institution that may represent a "structure" of the political system but that other anlytically interesting and important patterns, such as value systems, economic allocation, attitudes toward innovation, and so on, can also be viewed from a structure-functional vantage point.

Our debt to functionalism does not stop here. We are increasingly aware of the applicability to comparative politics of the maxim—long ago offered us by Malinowski—that an artifact of one culture transferred to another in form may represent a radically different meaning and relate to a quite different function in its new setting. Thus Morroe Berger found, somewhat to his surprise, that a Weberian-type bureaucratic superstructure in Egypt did not in fact produce for that society the kinds of human interactions and consequences for the political system imputed to bureaucracy in the West.[11] Similarly, Riggs has gone to considerable pain to depict the survival in "modern" institutional settings of patterns of behavior deeply rooted in "traditional" cultures.[12]

Perhaps the best cataloguing of the kinds of lessons political scientists can learn from structure-functionalism is included in Gabriel Almond's widely cited introductory essay in *The Politics of the Developing Areas*.[13] A more recent and ambitious attempt is made by the British political scientist, H. V. Wiseman, whose concluding chapter is the best example I can cite of the impossible morass of jargon, fuzzy conceptualization, circularity of reasoning, truisms propounded as scientific wisdom, and appeal to mere scholasticism that characterizes the work of functionalists. That Wiseman is primarily involved not in a personal critique but in distilling the arguments pro and con of others serves merely to emphasize this unfortunate state of affairs. A reading of Wiseman's well-intentioned exercise quickly reveals why some political scientists find the structure-functional or other sociological approaches to systemic analysis extremely suspect. Consider, as one typical example, the following alleged contributions to the comparative study of political systems Wiseman uncritically accepts as having come from sociologists:

a. That the "nation" and the "state" are not necessarily the same thing.
b. That the concepts of *power* and *influence* are as important in comparative politics as institutional foci.
c. That "in the sociological sense," a legitimate government is one that has the support of those who are subject to it.
d. That "legitimacy" is never the sole basis of a government's power.
e. That the "effective government" of a society is always government by a small minority of the population or that "Rule is always the rule of the few."

To be sure, Professor Wiseman is reporting the claims of others, and is moved, regarding the first "sociological discovery" just cited, to suggest, "with respect," that such generalizations are not "peculiarly sociological."[15] My point would be that if structure-functionalism clearly led to the theoretical validation of even such insights or self-evident propositions, it would represent an important gain. But it seems to me apparent that such is not the case, that most of the telling criticisms of the structure-functional approach[16]— when the latter masquerades as a descriptive or dynamic theory—have not been satisfyingly rebutted, and that Wiseman himself succinctly reflects my reservations about it when he says about T. B. Bottomore's critique, "What is most valuable in the functionalist approach, he [Bottomore] concludes, is the greater emphasis and clarity given to the simple idea that in every particular society the different social activities are interconnected. It is then a matter of empirical enquiry as to which are the various social activities and how they are related."[17]

I am suggesting that once we have learned the important lesson of structural alternatives for functional performance and the multifunctionality of similar structures, little remains of structure-functionalism that is useful to political science, and much remains that can be damaging to comparative research. To return to the matter of cross-national and cross-cultural research, it seems to me obvious that the kinds of functionally "diffuse" or "fused" societies and political systems that are of great interest to anthropology are rapidly disappearing and that the nation-states do manifest an amazing amount of institutional similarity—they do have executives, legislatures, public administrative systems, courts, armies, political parties, interest groups, and many other institutional arrangements that we have come to associate with Western societies but which may in fact be simply the most probable way in which "concrete structural differentiation" occurs at certain stages of political development.[18] To be sure, the functional meaning or consequences of such institutions are not the same in Africa as in Europe, in Asia as in North America. Indeed, meaning and consequences of similar institutional arrangements may vary quite markedly in culturally homo-geneous areas, as well as over time within the same nation-state. This ele-mentary fact is not a discovery of functionalism; it was clearly understood by Aristotle, Hobbes, Burke, Rousseau, deTocqueville, and Bagehot, to name only a few whose writings appear to me to be particularly sensitive on this score, and who were concerned with whole-systems analysis.

The proliferation or diffusion of structurally similar institutions over much of the globe is also true at levels of government below the nation-state. It may be that some continents contain primitive local societies where politics is intermittent and where clearly political institutions are not easily discernible. Here functionalism may provide an important descriptive guide, as it might were one to research the local-level societies of Western antiquity. But villages the world over today appear to possess strikingly similar institutions like chiefs, elders, councils, and there is no reason for assuming that functionalism provides a better guide to the subtleties of the political process in such places than would, say, an approach that began with certain culture-bound assumptions about village government but then moved on sensitively to try to discern process variations in different settings. I shall return to this matter later when I try to indicate why one can fruit-fully engage in either cross-national or cross-cultural comparative research within a conceptual and institutional framework that is perhaps parochially derived from a limited cultural area like the West.

I would record one final difficulty in the study of whole political sys-tems, which, although not necessarily inherent in such a focus, is very much apparent in contemporary political science. I refer to the tendency to see the political system, no matter how well or poorly bounded, within a broader social, physical, and economic environment and then to assume that the political system itself is the more or less fatalistic outcome of environmental or ecological factors. I believe it is primarily, although not exclusively, among those who are concerned with whole systems that politics and political systems take on the qualities of exclusively dependent variables, the product of a wide range of independent factors including industrialization, political socialization, the degree of pluralism in society, the political culture, the distribution of information and energy in society, communications patterns, social stratification, even such things as the per capita number of telephones and radios, domestic and international flow of letters, telegrams, cables, or commerce manifested within any society.

131

There is thus more than a little truth to Sartori's complaint that systems theorists, functionalists or otherwise, have taken politics out of political science and have obscured the critically important fact that political institutions and political leaders constitute independent factors that manage to shape not merely the environment and some of the ecological factors but the operation and development of the political system (or parts thereof) itself.[19] Recent developments suggest that there is belated recognition of this problem, as witness the growing frequency with which we now read of the necessity of dealing more intensively with research on the "output" side of political systems. For all societies, that output side will include legislation, administration, and adjudication—the stuff of government from time immemorial, which remains the same old wine no matter how many new bottles theory produces or how many new labels one puts on bottles, old or new. It is in part because this is so that I believe theoretical parsimony and manageable, reasonably rigorous empirical research in comparative politics require greater attention to partial systems, or a segmented approach to theory and research. That this orientation to political science can never logically be the limits of our professional concerns will be apparent from my concluding statement in this chapter. But any brief for the emphasis on partial-systems in comparative politics necessarily requires some specification of how we might proceed and what problems are inherent in doing so.

Comparative Research of Segments of Political Systems

A segmented or partial-system approach to comparative analysis may be institutionally or behaviorally focused, morphological or analytical in its intention or execution. Comparisons may involve a search for similarities or of differences among nation-states regarding those aspects of the political system that constitute the focus of attention. Or the comparative enterprise may involve a more dynamic focus, such as that of identifying the determinants over time of aspects of the political process and discernible changes that occur in the latter. Today, for example, there is widespread and still growing interest in something called *political development,* which, however it is defined, involves an attempt to test whether specific institutional, behavioral, and process modifications within the polity can be related associatively (hopefully causally) with similar or differing but empirically identifiable factors.[20]

Such comparative research may or may not relate to theories concerning whole political systems. It may or may not be based on a carefully articulated and integrated set of propositions to be tested in two or more settings. Good research would require an understanding and specification of precisely what it is that is being compared and to what end. Now the end of any given piece of comparative research may and does vary considerably. How are laws made or enforced? How do formal occupants of political roles acquire them? What range of political participation is open to what segments of a nation's population and on the basis of what criteria? In what proportion of the problem-solving activities of society are formal institutions of government involved and in what way? What kinds of political decisions are centrally made, geographically diffused, hierarchically stratified, formally restricted to government officials or more widely shared—and through what sorts of patterned arrangements? What kinds of people "govern" formally, informally?

Clearly, the number of such questions one might pose for any nation is quite large, perhaps unlimited. This understanding, and the fact that we must choose among the questions about which data will be accumulated, naturally leads many scholars to insist that choice be disciplined by theory and theory-related propositions. Differently put, the caveat would read that neither a general or miscellaneous collection of facts about a political system, nor the restriction of fact-gathering activity to narrow-gauge problems that lend themselves to rigorous, laboratory-type experimental controls in comparative politics is acceptable procedure. Moreover, both structure-functionalism and political science's disillusionment with past emphasis on the collection of legalistic, formalistic data about governmental institutions extend this caveat to fact-gathering about the obvious political institutions of any society. The overshadowing question we must all respond to, therefore, is "so what?" in the sense of compelling us to ask what light our findings will shed on the *dynamics* of a political system.

Ideally, responses to the "so what" query would relate data-gathering and subsequent analysis to general theories pertaining to whole systems. For reasons I have already touched upon, we are a long way from such a desirable relationship between empirical research and theoretical formulations. At a somewhat more modest level of expectations, research on aspects of two or more political systems should be organized around a set of theoretical propositions relating to the *segment* of the total system that constitutes the focus for empirical scrutiny. Here, too, however, the danger of bogging down with "general theories" of organizational behavior, decision-making, conflict, institutional development, or change is very great, and it is just as likely that scholasticism can infect our discussions of partial systems as it is that it will (and has) infected our treatment of whole systems.

The seemingly verbal or semantic solution to this dilemma is Merton's now classical discussion of theories of the middle range. As applied to either whole systems or partial systems, I take Merton to mean that empirical research in the social sciences should avoid a theoretical fishing expedition and pretentious, impossible attempts to "test," say, the propositions generated out of Parsons' four-sector description of society and its subsystems. More specifically, Merton seems to be saying that comparative research is likely to be trivial unless the propositions one is probing empirically give us some (perhaps intuitive) reason to suppose that our findings will make the creation of general theories less impressionistic or deductive than they now so obviously are.

My preference would be that of formulating the kinds of theoretical propositions I believe Merton has in mind and restricting these propositions for the moment to institutions and institutional processes that are clearly, directly, and intimately involved in the political process. Such choice, I believe, is dictated not merely by considerations of parsimony; it is dictated as well by a growing realization that we are, as I have already noted, over supplied with general theory and much more poverty-ridden, not only on systematic empirical research but also on the possession of the most rudimentary kind of information on which the success of the enterprise of a modern comparative politics must finally rest.

Let us take a moment to illustrate some of what I have in mind.

One of the great problems we confront in comparative politics today is that of the enormous imbalance in the amount of subsystemic or partial-systemic information available for the United States, on the one hand, and the rest of the world, on the other. We speak of the West as containing political systems emanating from a common philosophical-historical tradition, little realizing that many of the things we would want and wish to know about the political processes of Western societies are simply not yet available to us. Our generalizations thus remain gross observations, obscuring or ignoring the more subtle aspects of political systems that seem to emanate from a common historical-philosophical matrix. To be sure, we know more, say, about the politics of England than of Egypt, of France than of Vietnam, of Germany than of China. But anyone who has tried to ask even the simplest questions aimed at drawing the most rudimentary comparisons among Western nation-states quickly discerns that the gap remains great and is in no wise closed by general theoretical constructs that beg certain relationships and processes presumed to be typical of Western political systems. Similarly, much of the work now available on non-Western systems tends to highlight the extent to which earlier statements about how different or exotic are the latter systems are simply not true.

Because our knowledge regarding the political systems of non-Western societies was very limited indeed, and because literally dozens of such systems emerged as nation-states only following World War II, we badly needed and have greatly benefited from works dealing with whole systems in Africa and Asia. At their best, such works provide a needed general orientation to the kinds of phenomena of interest to the political scientist, as well as a great many generalizations that have enriched the kinds of questions we now raise for comparative treatment.[21]

Nevertheless, we must secure more and reliable information about segments of these political systems before we can hope to push the enterprise of comparative politics much beyond its present essentially impressionistic stage. I find it instructive, for example, that political scientists are loath to make high-flown generalizations about the American political system (the one about which we have the greatest amount of information), whereas they will at the slightest stimulus generalize about large-scale societies in Africa, Asia, and Latin America, concerning which our lack of historical and contemporary information is perhaps the most striking thing we can say about such countries.

Filling these gaps is obviously essential. Doing so requires, I believe, attention to segments of political systems, whether these segments be institutional or behavioral in nature, whether their choice does or does not clearly relate to the validation or illumination of general systemic theories.[22] The comparative study of legislatures, public administrative systems, or political parties will serve as examples.

The comparative study of legislatures might range from the most traditional kind of formalistic and legalistic description of national legislatures and the legislative process to the most controlled kind of experimentation of legislative behavior, if, as is almost never the case in political science, the research site could be stringently controlled and manipulated. What we have by way of research findings today runs an interesting gamut of approaches; except at the most primitive level of post facto comparisons, almost none of what we have emerged from comparative research designs. At best, we are learning more things about more legislatures that relate to common theoretical concerns with such things as decision-making models, coalition behavior, conflict management, the role of parties and interest groups in legislative behavior, and the patterns of leadership and followership in such complex organizations.

I do not mean to sound excessively pessimistic here. As one surveys the literature, it is apparent that we have come far from earlier studies which naturally focused on legalistic analyses, in part because that was the easiest and also (lest we forget) an important way to begin. In many countries where roll-call votes are recorded, we have studies analyzing such things as party cohesion, the relationship between issues and voting or coalition patterns, and constituency-legislator relationships. Access to committee proceedings now means greater attention to variations in behavior as one moves from one legislative setting to another. From countries where direct interviewing of lawmakers is possible, we begin to get interesting information about personality and behavior, about the legislator's role, his self-perception, his views of third persons and organizations, even some information emerging from the administration of TAT's and Rokeach Dogmatism scales. We know more than we ever did about career patterns and recruit-

135

ment to legislative positions, about the social, economic, and professional characteristics of lawmakers, and how and why these characteristics have changed or remained stable over time.[23]

One can produce a similar roll-call of interesting studies for such institutions as bureaucracy, political parties, and interest groups. In each of these institutional sectors there are enormous gaps; for other institutions such as courts, the military, police, and local governments, our information is fragmentary at best, almost never susceptible to reasonably systematic comparisons across more than a few societies. A recent effort to organize a seminar on comparative legislative and electoral organization and behavior led me first to restrict the countries encompassed to the United States, Britain, Germany, France, and Italy. Then, as most who read these words will appreciate, the available data for continental European countries were found to be extremely limited, produced in relatively recent years by a very small handful of scholars. A good legislative study by Sartori in Italy is unmatched by anything available elsewhere in Europe; Mattei Dogan's work on French legislative elites and on the structure of political party support and membership can be compared with some work in Britain and the United States, but not efficaciously with other European countries; the work of the Nuffield group on British voting behavior is almost unique in Europe, not easily compared with the work of Rokkan and others in Scandinavia, or of Kitzinger in Germany. It is only regarding the last British elections, for example, that collaboration between the Nuffield group and Michigan's Survey Research Center will make possible systematic comparison between the United States and Britain. Comparisons now drawn between the United States, Britain, and France are at best approximate, notwithstanding that the Nuffield studies are often quite meritorious in their own right and that French electoral studies—beginning with the early postwar work of F. Goguel and extending to recent studies of French elections by the *Fondation Nationale de Science Politique*—reach a high level of sophistication.

Those political scientists who claim that we are deluged with randomly, unsystematically chosen empirical studies have never attempted, as I see it, to assess what is the nature of all of the supposed information we have about the political systems and processes of the West. Regardless of the range of one's linguistic skill and the resources of American libraries, it is frequently impossible to come by the most elemental information about the political institutions of other countries. If this is the case, it is obvious that we are often depending on impressions that may or may not be accurate. General theories of political systems based on such imperfect information must also be imperfect at best.

To summarize, one of the most pressing reasons for increasing research attention to segments of political systems is the information gap and our need for filling it before we can subject general theoretical formulations to empirical confrontation. But other persuasive reasons can be adduced. One of these is that we must greatly increase the number of persons in other countries who are engaged in comparative political research. As excellent as their individual studies may be, we cannot depend for our knowledge of Ghana or Nigeria, Burma or India, Argentina or Chile on the small number of American— in some cases European or indigenous—scholars who have been concerned with the political systems of such countries. We are moving in the direction of combining research and training in the comparative study of social and political systems with collaborative relationships between American and foreign students and scholars. Such collaboration should eventually emanate in increased numbers of Asians, Africans, and Latin Americans who contribute to our storehouse of knowledge. I strongly believe that the diffusion of the social sciences—certainly of comparative political science— is better served if initial joint endeavors focus on systematic work on segments of political systems rather than on speculative theorizing about whole systems, which would be, at best, supported by empirical impressions rather than what would pass for acceptable evidence.[24]

Another reason for focusing on partial-system analyses is that such foci better lend themselves to the articulation and testing of middle-range propositions. For any of the institutions normally accepted as intimately involved in the governmental process, we can produce a large number of interesting and important propositions, which, while not designed to validate general theory, would permit us to make more universally applicable generalizations when validated in a wide range of nation-states. I might add that such propositions need not be strictly tied to political institutions, but might relate instead to decision-making models, analytic functional categories, formulations concerning the relationship of personality or other psychological variables to organizational or individual behavior.

A third possible rationale for a narrower, more limited research focus is that it might bring comparative politics somewhat closer to policy-related problems. Now, I am aware that the profession has not yet settled the question of the "proper scope" of political science, and that more than ever before political scientists insist that the profession's scientific concern is with the *process* rather than the *content* of politics or political policies.[25] Although this is not the place to try to explore that kind of thorny issue in any detail, it is necessary to stress that I personally do not accept the notion that our concern is exclusively process and that, therefore, only those theories and methods that give us better leverage over process are worthy of our attention. One reason for stressing the concern of the political scientist with content or policy is that to acknowledge such attention openly helps to guard against several related dangers and, I believe, pitfalls. The first of these dangers is the assumption that political science—at least in its American configuration—now has the means of rising above "vulgar ideology" and qualifies for co-optation into the "scientific culture." A second danger would be that of "social engineering," which requires no further elaboration here. A third danger is that of indiscriminate fishing expeditions for data and what I would call the methodological escalation that accompanies the former. The political *process*, divorced from issues or problems of *policy*, has become such a huge umbrella concept (particularly in view of what various abstract theories now suggest are integral parts of that process) that I fear such a narrow focus would further the well-established trend toward removing politics from political science. In short, I would urge that reasons such as these can lead us to make parsimonious decisions regarding what it is the political scientist studies.

An additional reason for explicit concern with policy is that those who are policy makers (as well as our students!) expect modern political science to be aware of and hopefully to have something professional to say about the kinds of major problems that beset domestic and international societies. In voicing such expectations, it seems to me that policy makers are simply articulating what most of us implicitly understand, namely, that, more than any other field of intellectual or scientific endeavor, the social sciences are *not* expected to be merely "pure" sciences. I find it both amusing and ironic therefore; that those social scientists who speak with increasing authority to policy makers concerned with problems of nation-building or community development are the economists and sociologists, with a sprinkling of political scientists who, when consulted at all, often turn out to be experts in an outmoded, formalistic "science" of public administration.

To be sure, experts in comparative politics are also consulted, often with mutually distressing results. For the policy maker strongly needs the "translated" implications of theory and research and the political scientist—product of an intellectual pecking order that from time immemorial enthrones abstract theory—wishes to stress the elegance of theory and typology, leaving it to the men of public affairs to make what they can of such things. It is in such confrontations, I suspect, that the astronomical distance between our theoretical preachments and our research behavior is most strikingly revealed, and this may in part account for our tendency to shun policy matters.

The field of public administration is a very good example of these last points. We are now painfully aware that Max Weber's ideal typical formulations about authority systems and the patterns of public administration that accomapny them will not take us much beyond morphological description of empirical situations. We are equally aware that prescriptions about administrative organization that derive in part from Weberian notions of bureaucracy, in part from the norms of democratic Western polities, will not take us far in permitting policy makers to resolve problems of social, economic, and political development. One result of such understanding is that a number of political scientists interested in comparative administration have tried to devise new general theories of administration, or to construct typologies of political systems around certain differentiating criteria that are administratively based. Viewed from the vantage point of integrating a previously narrow, mechanistic, culture-bound public administration into the somewhat broader and dynamic field of comparative politics, such efforts are certainly praiseworthy. Judged by the measure of their contribution to a general theory of politics or indeed of administrative systems, such endeavors strike me as being of limited utility.[26]

Where they aren't essentially restatements of Weber, *cum* Talcott Parsons, they are nevertheless formulated at levels of abstraction that defy systematic comparative empirical application, and for this reason, among others, are of little or no use to those confronting problems of policy or operational alternatives. What differences ideal-typical morphologies adduce are generally gross; more often than not, both the typologies devised and the models of administrative systems suggested are based not so much on rigorously accumulated historical or contemporary evidence, but rather on illustrations which are themselves often impressionistic. Where attempts are made to draw operational axioms from such theorizing and model-building, they often result in curious justifications for whatever patterns of power and administration actually emerge in the so-called developing areas. Above all, the classification of nation-states by the presumed characteristics of their administrative systems and related conditions (environmental or ecological) that surround them generally results in grouping in single categories precisely those nation-states among which we must make refined discriminations before we can say anything meaningful of a probabilistic or prescriptive nature. In this sense, such efforts serve us no better than massive accumulations of aggregate statistical data about the world's nation-states, which, when subjected to high-powered, computerized analytical techniques, reveal that, say, Sweden, the United States, Britain, France, Germany, Norway, and Italy are in one group, the Sudan, Nepal, Afghanistan, and Tanzania in another. The only striking difference I have thus far detected in these two approaches is that the former, more impressionistic approach is (a) cheaper and (b) probably more sophisticated.

Are we then to abandon both grand theorizing and the accumulation of empirical data about bureaucratic systems? Clearly this is not what I intend, and the sector of public administration, as one segment of any political system, is one of the areas in which our empirical research can be fruitfully guided both by very important public policy concerns and by theoretical propositions of the middle range. We know, for example, that economic development in almost all of the developing nations is likely to take place largely through public-sector intervention, and that participation of government in such change-directed enterprises is also increasingly true

139

of the so-called developed countries. Now, while there is a vast and growing literature on the subject of planning provided by specialists in economics, political scientists have paid scant attention to this problem, except at the fringes of macroanalytic considerations. To be sure, as our theoretical out-pourings shift from the input side (where the political system seems to be abjectly dependent on elements in the environment) to the output side (where the institutions of government are recognized as having an independent impact on social change), one begins to read about the capacities or capabilities of the political system to achieve certain ends-in-view, including economic change or growth. No doubt it is important to acknowledge that political institutions must confront a wide range of challenges, from the maintenance of order and the provision of social overhead capital to the provision of the kinds of material and human resources (and their integrated coordination) that planned economic growth requires. In this regard, a number of writers have served us well, although I think it once again striking that several of these are either economists or sociologists, and that with rare exceptions political scientists have been late in moving in this direction.[27]

Much more needed, however, is greater attention by political scientists whose analyses of a partial political system, such as the bureaucracy, either explicate the bureaucratic process of a range of nation-states in considerable detail, or which deal comparatively with public administrative systems in terms of their problem-solving capabilities. One important step in this direction is the series of studies of national planning now under way at the University of Syracuse, under the general editorial direction of Bertram M. Gross. These national studies involve political scientists almost exclusively; the specific intention of Professsor Gross is to begin to fill the most serious gap in the planning literature, namely, what differences in the phenomenon are introduced by specific segments or aspects of the political system in different national settings.[28]

I have also recently suggested a comparative approach to the relationship of public administration to problems of development that would involve the construction of national profiles. Such profiles would require gathering data on the developmental and related goals of national policy makers, the total and kind of administrative resources available for goal attainment, the obstacles to the creation of whatever additional resources are needed for goal achievement, and the potentiality for overcoming such obstacles and of achieving a reasonable balance between goals and administrative capacity.[29] Although some of the data categories implicit in such profiling would have to be treated somewhat impressionistically, other potentially available aggregative data are available to the persistent researcher. Such data would not be accumulated merely because they are (correctly or falsely) easily available—a lamentable tendency only too apparent in the recent work of some political scientists. Rather, decisions as to where one will put his data-accumulating energies to work would rest very firmly on the articulation of empirically manageable hypotheses about the relationship of public administrative organization and behavior and development. I should add that, if the hypothetical statements involve concepts as broad as the "pattern variables" of Talcott Parsons, the empirical indicators that would permit scoring—hopefully ranking—each country on each of these variables as they apply to any sector of society would have to be carefully and persuasively specified. We have pretty much exhausted scholastic exercises about how much achievement orientation, universalism, collectivity-orientation, affective neutrality, and functional specificity is required, say, by economic modernity, or a public administrative apparatus conducive to economic modernization. For those who would in fact try to validate aspects of Parsons' theories, profiling of the kind I have in mind might be one potentially workable first step. Even for such scholars, I contend, an empirical focus on a segment of a whole political system would offer greater hope of succeeding than would a research enterprise requiring attention to the whole system.

In short, I remain skeptical about the whole-systems approach to comparative politics. My skepticism can perhaps best be summarized by two quotations from Heinz Eulau, whose capacity to deal imaginatively and creatively with partial-systems analysis is well known. About whole-systems approaches, Eulau remarks, with chacteristic bluntness, "But I have yet to read—and that includes David Easton's new book—a systems analysis from which one can derive testable propositions about politics."[30] About the most perplexing empirical problem of gathered data about whole systems, he remarks:

> How does one observe whole systems? Well, I would say that at the present time it is impossible to observe whole systems. I think that one can make statements about the whole systems, large systems, but that one cannot observe them.[31]

I would add that partial-systems comparisons of the kind I have discussed earlier should over time reduce the magnitude of the observational problem. In such a future, typologies will be less abstract, much more induced from reflections about empirical information gathered from carefully designed research on segments of the larger political system. No one will deny the desirability of a probabilistic theory of politics. My claim is that the quantum leap to the whole-systemic level of theorizing has tended to degenerate into a neo-scholasticism from which escape itself is difficult, and when escape occurs at all, it involves recurrence to partial-system analysis anyway.

Joseph LaPalombara

Problems in Comparative Research

It is easy enough to say that comparative research at a partial-systems level will contribute to an additive political science. But this approach, too, is not free of some perplexing problems, some of which affect comparative politics in general, some of which are highlighted or intensified when they emerge in partial-systems analysis.

If something less than the whole system is to be analyzed, the first and most obvious problem to resolve is that of the most important *unit of analysis*. My reference here is not to the empirical unit of analysis in that I assume that the individual, whether singly viewed or conceptualized in some group of associational context, is the commonly accepted empirical unit in the behavioral sciences. I am referring instead to the *theoretical* unit of analysis on the assumption that attention must be accorded this matter if we are to avoid falling into the crudest kinds of bare-facts empiricism.

The question of the appropriate theoretical unit should not be confused with what will be the independent or dependent variables in comparative research. Presumably, the determination of what theoretically causes, influences, or is associated with what, and for what reasons, comes at a later stage in the design of comparative research. Nor should we confuse "concrete-structural" or institutional units with what I intend here by theoretical. We may, for example, decide that we want to compare fruit, noncitrus fruit, or just apples, but for each of these choices it is necessary to indicate as well what will be the focus (or foci) of central theoretical concern. Likewise for politics, we might choose to study legislatures, legislative committees, or individual legislators, but it is important to specify around what single or combined set of theoretical concerns the comparative analysis will proceed. Such a procedure is required for several reasons, not the least important of which is that of anticipating the messiness caused by confusion as to the *level* of analysis at which research itself is directed. So many of our generalizations about the political process move with apparent randomness from the micro- to the macroanalytic levels that it is difficult to know when, for example, a study of legislative roles is designed to test psychological theories about individual or group behavior or sociological theories about the institution of the legislature itself. In short, we must be clear about occasions when we intend that the study, say, of individual legislatures, or of legislative committees, is intended to reflect in a microcosmic context propositions we intend to apply to legislatures, all representative organizations, all complex organizations, or vice-versa.

Clearly, the social sciences now provide a rich variety of theoretical units of analysis, from the broad "actor-situation framework" associated with Parsons to voting-behavior, where the act of voting can be conceptualized as illuminating theories about social stratification, communications,

142

personality, functionalism, decision-making, and so on. The most widely utilized theoretical unit in political science seems to me to be decision-making, and a vast range of the research output of the discipline can be subsumed under this rubric. Thus whether one asks who governs, or who gets what, or who has how much power and how is it exercised, or what variables seem to account for executive or judicial behavior, or what things are associated with distributions of popular votes, or how do political elites respond to historical crises, we seem to be posing as the generalized (independent or dependent) variable the making of political—or politically relevant —decisions.

To be sure, a great many political scientists are interested in change, that most elusive of the dynamic phenomena with which the social sciences are concerned. In today's world, we want to know as never before what difference (e.g., in reaching the take-off stage in economics, or in assuring legislative stability) a single-party or multi-party system will make in Ghana or Brazil, Thailand or Turkey. The problem of how bureaucrats should be trained, or whether the upper reaches of a bureaucracy should be dominated by generalists or specialists, *guardians* or *technocrats* as some would put it, has never been more poignantly posed than by political leaders and their followers who say that they simultaneously wish to promote man's material well-being and his freedom and dignity. For those who view political development as the increasing ability of political leaders and institutions to bring about a greater congruence between the demands they confront and the policy output of government, it is clear that, at one level of analysis, concern with how in specific concrete situations decisions are made and what are their consequences is inevitable.

Decision-making, of course, provides a very broad analytical framework and thus does not in itself resolve all of the difficulties inherent in comparative analysis. Yet, it seems to me that one of its striking advantages is that it directs our attention to the outputs of the political system and therefore to those aspects of the political process that involve formal governmental institutions. Functionalism on the other hand leads one to emphasize the input side of the equation and therefore tends to push research in the direction of such problems as the political socialization of children, which, although intrinsically interesting as an area of research, appears far removed from the political process. I might add, in addition, the political socialization research, where it does not concentrate on subjects who are probable future political elites, begs an important assumption that we have not yet succeeded in demonstrating persuasively, namely, that the values, beliefs, and attitudes about politics and political institutions held by the mass population make a difference.

To put this in terms of parsimony, I would prefer comparative research on decision-making in legislatures, bureaucracies, political parties—even in elections—to comparative studies of the political socialization of children, patterns of recruitment to governmental roles, or the system of communication found within society. It isn't that these latter concepts or analytical units are uninteresting or irrelevant; it is that their relationship to the output side of the governmental system remains extremely tenuous because we know very little in fact about what goes on in the black box that stands between inputs and outputs.

What I am suggesting is that a decision-making focus for the political scientist should also involve, for reasons of parsimony, a preference for obviously political institutional settings for research. Case studies of trade unions may perhaps illuminate the political process, but political parties should be preferred if they are accessible. If trade unions are placed under the empirical microscope, propositions about them should relate to some specific aspect of the political process and, more stringently, the making of political decisions. To put it simply, it is necessary to respond in more than vague or seemingly logical or self-evident terms regarding the relevance of research into nonpolitical institutions for the operation of political institutions themselves.

The selection of institutions or "concrete structures" as the focus for research leads to a second major problem, namely, that of the comparability of the empirical units selected for analysis. At least the problem appears at first blush to be more complex than would be the case were one to limit his focus, say, to decision-making, influence or power, communications or leadership in complex organizations. But, unless one is easily stampeded by what turn out to be scholastic objections by structure-functionalists, it is plain enough that whether one begins with concrete institutions or with an analytical concept like decision-making, the problem of comparability is essentially the same.

Let me push ahead with this line of argument to identify what is really our concern.

It is possible that, for some, the central theoretical concern would be simply the process or structure of choice—of reaching decisions—in a wide range of simple or complex formal organizations. For such scholars, I believe, comparative research would require the most careful specification and control over certain characteristics or parameters of organizations before meaningful comparative analysis can proceed. Assuming a large enough sample of organizations, such scholars would want to control for such things as number of decision-makers involved, degree of hierarchy and administrative differentiation of roles, the structure of internal communications, patterns of authority and sanctions prevailing, degree and kind of discretion or permissiveness in role performance, relationship to the organizationally external environment, and so on. Organizational theorists are able to draw research samples for comparative analysis from a much wider universe than is available to the political scientist—assuming for the moment that the political scientist is interested in politics, or, in the case at hand, in *political* decision-making.

This being the case, it seems apparent that the political scientist will by the empirical nature of things be less able to "control" for certain parametric conditions than will the person interested in organizational behavior. The comparative research that the latter does may greatly assist the political scientist in designing a research project and in interpreting his findings. One cannot ask of the political scientist, however, that he adhere to the same canons of maximizing the comparability of his research endeavors that would be justified for a scientist whose unit of analysis (in this case decision-making) encompasses a much wider range of empirical research sites.

I might say that essentially the same line or argument can be developed where, say, the theoretical unit of analysis is some aspect of functionalism and where the institutional focus for comparative research is the interest group or pressure group. As the work in the interest group field attests, pains are taken to abstract from the infinite number of group settings in which the individual might be found something called a *political* interest group. We need not be concerned with whether John Dewey was correct in insisting that all human behavior is group-centered behavior, or A. F. Bentley was right in declaring that if we fully comprehend the "group process" we will have comprehended everything about politics. But if the interest group is to be made the institutional focus for comparative political science, we must be concerned with the designation of criteria that will permit us to abstract from a potentially infinite number of groups those that are of particular interest to the political scientist, and which meet the minimal definitional requirements to be included in a sample. Because I have been unsatisfied with a number of efforts to do this, I attempted in my study of Italian interest groups to provide an operational definition of such groups that I believe would adequately satisfy the minimum canons of comparability. Thus, as a means of including and excluding groups from analytical treatment, I have insisted that they must manifest a *conscious* desire to have public policy move in a certain direction or remain static. Shared interests, even frequent interaction among group members, are not enough; my relatively simple differentiating criterion would exclude most groups, most of the time, from inclusion in the category of such organizations I would be interested in analyzing.[32]

The comparative political scientist, then, must be guided in the first instance by the central concern of what is political or what is relevant to the political process. If this is so, then it is unlikely, except at a very abstract and empirically unmanageable level I have associated with whole-systems analysis, to satisfy David Easton's thought that "Ideally, the units [of analysis] would be repetitious, ubiquitous, and uniform, molecular rather than molar."[33] Where, as in systemic and functional analysis, the units seem to be ubiquitous and uniform, they are molar, rather than molecular; where, as in group analysis and decision-making, they appear to be molecular, they are not uniform, and probably not minutely repetitious. The dilemma of comparative politics is that we have neither the availability of the particles or atoms of physics nor the price of economics to subject to comparative analysis.

The problem of the comparability of the unit of analysis is also apparent when one chooses such a seemingly obvious structure as political parties as the focus for research. The political party appears to be a deceptively stable unit concerning which much comparative research can be generated. Yet, it is obvious that little attention has been paid to the question what it is one is comparing when one looks analytically at parties across either national or cultural boundaries, or within a single nation-state. Voting studies in the United States, for all of their display of methodological rigor, have ignored this problem, as indeed they have ignored most questions of theoretical relevance until recently.[34] Nevertheless, those who purport to execute comparative research here must arrive at some workable and consistent definition of a political party if comparison is to involve oranges, apples, or lemons rather than a shifting combination of these, or fruit salad. Myron Weiner and I in a recent symposium attempted to respond to this problem. It is perhaps indicative of the state of the discipline that a number of our colleagues are willing to accept as political parties any organization whose leaders or members call it such, without regard to questions of definition.[35] I would simply rest here by saying that such resolutions will not do and that whenever we elect a segmented or partial-systemic approach to comparative politics, the kinds of problems I have raised here must be confronted and reasonably resolved.

A third major problem—not confined to partial-systems analysis—involves the nature of evidence, or the kind of data one will or can gather to validate or invalidate propositions. This problem is much too vast to pretend to treat here in detail, but a number of observations will help to round out my discussion.

First, I believe it is essential to recognize that some of the hypothesis-validating data we will need may not be easily accessible, or may not be available to us at all. This is true in part because of the areas of secrecy that surround many aspects of the governmental process. It is true as well because many nation-states look with increasing reservations, even hostility, to the legions of American field researchers abroad which the Golden Era of social science seems to have spawned in this country.

If we cannot get at the relevant or most immediately relevant facts, what then? Why, we will have to search for less direct indicators and do the best we can with what data are available. But this alternative means that we be careful about the alternative data-collecting choices we make, and above all that we not store data simply because they are available. It may be, as some claim, that the availability of vast quantities of data, when processed by high-speed computers, will help us to generate new theories, but for the present I find that expectation very doubtful.[36]

Second, it is necessary to pay more than lip service to the observation that much of the extant empirical information is not really comparable and that equally much of the seemingly reliable aggregative statistical data are just simply poor, that is, unreliable, subject to errors whose nature is neither random nor, if systematic, known to us. Such data, far from illuminating the processes we wish to study comparatively, may actually be totally misleading. I for one am doubtful that *The New York Times* publishes all of the news that's fit to print, or that more than a handful of nation-states are accurately reporting to the United Nations a very wide range of statistical information.

Karl Deutsch, recognizing that the quality of data available to us may vary considerably, ingeniously suggests that computers and new techniques of data analysis may help us to overcome the limitations inherent, say, in survey data or aggregative statistical information. If this is so, he says, " . . . truth may be thought of as a relationship between different streams of evidence. A statement is more likely to be true, the larger the number of different classes or kinds of evidence that confirm it."[37] This statement seems reasonable enough, so long as our decisions about the kinds of data to collect are made on the basis of propositions to be tested comparatively, and so long as we do not deliberately include in our "stream of evidence" data we know to be highly unreliable.

Third, as we look to history for information that will help us to confirm or disconfirm propositions about political and related development, we must have a better sense than we now do about what specific institutions (such as parliaments, interest groups, political parties) have meant over time in a single society. To say this is merely to restate the central problem implicit in comparative history as opposed to loose historical chronology: on the basis of what reasonably measurable criteria can we periodize societies and the institutions they give rise to. Among the many useful purposes this exercise will serve is that of permitting those of us who are interested in a *particular* kind of political development, namely, some variation of the democratic state, to identify with greater precision than we have possibly generalized or generalizable "stages" of democratic institutional development.

Conclusion

Is emphasis on partial political systems or segments of them the only legitimate or fruitful enterprise for contemporary comparative politics? Clearly not, nor have I intended to make this claim. If we are as far as most of us suspect from a probabilistic theory of politics, any closure at this time regarding levels of analysis, sectors of the political system to be analyzed, or methods to be utilized in the testing of theoretical formulations would be premature—childish in the fullest sense of that term.

My purpose, rather, has been twofold. First, it seems to me that we ought to be absolutely candid about what it is political scientists do. This requires above all that we not be deluded into thinking we have evolved empirical general theories when what we have are a number of impressionistic, somewhat abstract, deceptively empirical observations strung together by logical statements of varying elegance. Nor should we fail to note that, although ideal-typical constructs need not respond to empirical reality on a one-to-one basis, they are not very useful if we understand the real world to involve an infinite mixture of characteristics that ideal-typical constructs artificially separate, but in no way provide insights into possible or probable mixes.

My second purpose has been to suggest a rationale for emphasis on partial systems in comparative politics. Because I assume such research may serve to correct certain deficiencies in whole-systems analysis and therefore open the way to better empirical theories of whole systems, I may be said to have come full circle. That is, I am sure that most political scientists cannot—in any case should not—sidestep concern with what difference their discoveries make in our understanding of how political systems are evolved, maintained, and changed.

If I want to profile the conditions that impinge on the public administrative problem-solving capability of a sample of nation-states, my interest in doing so must surely reflect more than an abstracted scientific curiosity about the relationship between human, physical, and organizational resources and goal attainment. If some of my colleagues design a comparative project aimed at probing the relationship between a long list of social, personality, cultural, and related variables and what occurs in a national legislature, they are surely interested in something more than decision-making or power relationships in *that* kind of an organization. If another group of my colleagues seeks to understand the circumstances under which those who formally occupy religious or military roles begin to impinge directly on the policy output of political structures, they are hopefully interested in something more than the conditions that bring functionally specific institutions and role occupants into aspects of the political process where they presumably have no "logical" or "theoretically acceptable" place.

My point here is double-edged. First, I would agree with David Easton that, in considering the so-called behavioral revolution, we should distinguish very carefully between the impetus toward better methodology and the thrust toward better empirical theory. However we may resolve how we attack the problems of concern to the political scientist, we should understand that a second aspect of all of the ferment we are experiencing involves not merely method but a concern with theories about how political systems evolve and function and what influences these things. But I would go beyond Easton to insist that for most of the political scientists I know and respect there is great concern for the good society and how one can devise the set of institutions and behaviors that will enhance its development and survival. Although such normative concerns must be distinguished from the more scientific concerns of comparative political science, they should not be submerged to the point where we delude ourselves in thinking that we are more like physicists or pathologists than what we are. We are, I believe, the intellectual descendants of Aristotle, proud to share some of his major concerns and perhaps humbled by the understanding that we have not advanced our scientific understanding of political organization and behavior much beyond what he elucidated in *The Politics*.

CHAPTER **5**

Political Systems and Developmental Change

DAVID E. APTER
University of California, Berkeley

Since the emergence of new nations in the postwar era, specialists in comparative politics have increasingly turned their research efforts toward the study of political development and political modernization. Although lack of consensus among political scientists on the precise meaning of these concepts has resulted in different outlooks upon the problem and many different emphases, they all deal—explicitly or implicitly—with the phenomenon of social change. Modernization, with or without the adjective "political" in front of it, is a form of social change. A popular type of analysis is to view social change (and its influence upon the political system) as movement along a continuum, which reaches from the traditional society, through a transitional or modernizing society, to an industrial society. From this approach, scholars have developed some interesting typologies.

As research on modernization has grown more sophisticated, political scientists have gradually introduced refinements into their work, and some of them are building up a body of literature on the process of political modernization. Aiming to develop systemic theory, these scholars seek to determine not only how social change affects the political system, but how change is influenced by particular types of

151

political systems. In other words, political factors are dependent variables in some conceptual frameworks, and independent or intervening variables in others.

A leader in the conceptualization and investigation of the process of political modernization is David E. Apter, Professor of Political Science, University of California, Berkeley. Building upon, refining, and making more complex the models he constructed for field research in Africa and Latin America, Apter is interested in discovering why one type of political system rather than another is likely to emerge during particular stages of development and later to be replaced during a different stage. In Chapter 5, he clarifies some of the models he has presented in earlier works, he discusses the general model he is currently working with, and he formulates a hypothesis concerning the effect of differentiation in stratification-group competition upon the political-system type at particular stages of development, especially with respect to the characteristics of coercion and information.

Professor Apter's books include The Gold Coast in Transition; The Political Kingdom in Uganda; The Politics of Modernization; Ideology and Discontent (*editor*); *and* Comparative Politics (*co-editor*). *The ideas expressed in the essay below represent a particular phase in the development of Professor Apter's thinking. Future publication will reveal some modification in the position presented.*

THIS ESSAY IS one of several I have been working on recently that deal with modernization as a form of social change and particularly how the process is affected by different types of political systems. The papers share two general objectives: namely, clarification of a theoretical dimension relating to the study of modernization itself (clarifying the general models suggested in *The Politics of Modernization*[1]); and preparation of the ground for a broadly comparative empirical study of seven societies at different levels of development.

Here we are primarily concerned with the following question: Which type of political system is most appropriate for each level of development? The short answer is that the modernization process creates such problems of coordination and control that *democratic* political systems, in the usual sense of that term, are not very relevant. Moreover, their relevance appears to decrease as a society moves closer to the transition to industrialization. On the other hand, in contrast to modernizing societies, highly industrialized societies, by virtue of the need for multiple sources of information, have a systems-tendency toward some form of democracy. The key to this formulation suggests a proposition as yet unconfirmed; namely, that there is an inverse relationship between coercion and information.

The present formulation, which originated in my book on modernization, advances a theory that identifies expanding choice as the central consequence of modernization and suggests certain political types appropriate for the management of choice at different stages of political development. Development is seen as a continuous process of differentiation and increasing complexity, somewhat along lines recently suggested by Marsh, with stratification serving as its social measure by defining the group basis of political action.[2] In turn, political action, manifested by political parties and other concrete groupings, is seen as the link between society and government, through which the latter responds in terms of coercion and information. The relationship between coercion and information is considered crucial for the determination of how political systems change.

The original models employed a combination of concrete and analytical units, which seemed useful in carrying the analysis forward but proved less than satisfactory from a purely theoretical point of view.[3] A first essay dealt with the normative, structural, and behavioral aspects of choice in relation to politics.[4] A second focused on the relationship between government and society, concentrating on representation based on type of legitimate claim and elite access (rather than concrete groupings, such as party,

153

bureaucracy, or interest groups per se—although each of these, and others, could be fitted easily into the model of representation employed). This treatment specified the source of information in the relationship between representative elites and government as well as means for applying coercion. In this essay, the characteristics of information and coercion will be discussed more fully in relation to political types, although at the present stage, the presumed relationship between them remains speculative, extremely hypothetical, and necessarily very tentative.[5]

Perhaps some attempt to justify these efforts will help clarify our purposes. The comparative analysis of political systems is particularly difficult from two points of view. First, when dealing with the complex processes of development and modernization, virtually all aspects of social life come to have potential political significance. These may include recognizable political actions and familiar methods, as well as unfamiliar and remote ones. The point is that in each system undergoing modernization imbalances occur between norms, structures, and behavior, which we can describe as a lack of fit. To analyze this lack of fit is a difficult, but important, task of comparative analysis.[6] It is also difficult to find the appropriate intermediate conceptual level necessary, if we wish to make comparisons of modernization by the use of political studies that serve diachronically (through time) and synchronically (between systems). Moreover, such intermediate conceptualization needs to be capable of operationalization.[7]

Our efforts have included field work leading to explicit comparisons between different types of systems at various stages of development—synchronically; and—diachronically—to studies of systems with different, but culturally significant, historical experiences, e.g., Spanish, French, and English colonialism. Our research is still in a preliminary stage, and this manner of working back and forth between concrete research and conceptual reformulation has its problems. For one thing, it is certainly very slow. For another, many of the attempts at conceptualization prove too cumbersome or useless for research purposes. Nevertheless, despite the episodic character of events and the research rush produced when the fashion in governmental style shifts (such as a concern with single party systems or the military in politics), it seems worth the trouble. The speed of events is such that it is important to find that level of analysis which improves our level of analytical understanding by means of the comparison of many systems, even when we are not at the level of events themselves, and there is some cost in empirical efficiency. What events have clearly shown, however, is that the political aspects of development are far more complex than they appeared to observers a decade or so ago. It seemed at that time that the description of developing areas would throw into bold outlines the key variables of which all politics is composed, bringing us back to fundamentals in a fresh way, unencumbered by the orthodoxies with which we had become accustomed to study American or European governments. Now even the new fundamentals are lost in the bewildering array of political problems which succeed one another in Latin America, Asia, and Africa.

Consider the thinking a decade or so ago. Then the fashion was to regard decolonization as a process by means of which colonial authorities could devolve power to nationalist groupings, until the goal of popular government would be achieved. The approach, more common in Europe than the United States, sounds almost as quaint today as do the theories of nationalism, which as explanatory devices were more favored by American scholars. In the contemporary perspective, nationalism or socialism or even development itself represent fading strategic variables, because individually neither has explanatory power. We still lag behind conceptually, and this is particularly the case in structural analysis. The methodological promise of a few years ago has not sufficiently materialized. We still are caught by surprise by the rise and fall of governments, the failure of policies; not to speak of the effect on developing societies of those drastic alterations occurring within highly industrialized societies, the consequences of which are to create modernization itself.

Obviously, present efforts at reformulation will fare little better than the others unless we first establish some criteria to be met. The criteria suggested are as follows: first, we want to create a "systemic" theory that shows a "circular" flow of "causes and consequences." Such a chain of linked variables is what we mean by a systemic theory. Moreover, the variables themselves need to be analytical, whereas the units that are under study remain concrete. Second, the analytical variables should be operational, in the sense that they can be quantified. Several strategies for quantification are possible, but the simplest is to rank the concrete units on a simple scale to see their relative weights vis-a-vis the analytical variables. Third, the combination of theory applied quantitatively to concrete units should produce factored clusters of variables which correspond empirically as well as in terms of the theory, i.e., syndromes should be possible that can be inferred logically from the models for which empirical validation occurs. This remains our goal.

Before going on to a consideration of the problem of development and the types of political system optimally suited to a particular level, it might be useful to summarize the general model with which we are presently working. As matters stand now, we intend to use the structural models to be employed here for the analysis of differentiation and complexity due to modernization. Concrete groupings can be seen according to stratification; e.g., caste and ethnic strata; class based on occupation and solidaristic consciousness; another form of class based on multibonded factors, such as residence, income, occupation, education, and so on; and functional status. Elites representing these groups by their degree and type of access to government

155

provide the major source of information inputs and, as well, serve as coercive outputs. Different political systems have governments that handle such information differently. Cases under study include Senegal, Mali, Ghana, and Nigeria (early stage modernization) and Peru, Chile, and Argentina (late stage modernization). Each concrete group, e.g., landowners and peasants, army and bureaucracy, trade unions and intellectuals, will be ranked in terms of its predominant type of claim to participation in politics as well as the claim to access made by leaders on its behalf. Claims to participation are seen as popular, functional, or interest. Types of elite access to government decision-making are defined in functional terms as follows: goal specification, central control, and institutional coherence. The combination of empirical rankings can then be correlated with the type of system that prevails—mobilization, theocratic, reconciliation, or bureaucratic—in order to evaluate the types of information emerging at the governmental level and the degree of coercion applied. Part of the model is being tested on computers with coercion ranked on a multifactored scale.

Of course, despite the bewildering array of theories about development and, in particular, political development, there is no general agreement with regard to terms and categories or especially strategic problems. A concern for political stability as a problem focus is common, but there are many difficulties here. For one thing, indicators of instability (coups, armed revolts, secessionist movements, and so on) are very rough and lead an observer to emphasize more epiphenomenal variables. (Often, too, analysis is based on the simplistic assumption that stability is "better" than instability; that it is possibly the "silent" prerequisite of economic growth.)

Whatever the merits of these indicators, however, I would like to take a somewhat more complex position, if only because the causes of political development cannot be confined to or located in a single variable. Moreover, while political stability may be quite a good indicator and a desirable condition for certain purposes relating to development, it may also be undesirable for others and give misleading impressions, i.e., that societies with unstable governments are ruled badly. Our position is that during the modernization phase of the development process, a government's ability to affect development itself generally reaches an effective ceiling quite quickly. When this ceiling is reached, the system of government, as distinct from its occupants, will need to change. This approach follows from our original assumption that the political difficulties confronting government increase as modernization proceeds. To put it another way, a management problem is produced by modernization, which causes the political system to reach its ceiling rapidly. Then, once the ceiling has been reached, pressure will build up for the system to change.[8]

The Concept of Development

Before elaborating the model, some of the concepts used here should be clarified. *Development* is a generic term at the most general level of analysis, including various types of growth: economic (as in the increase in roundabout production), *differentiation* (which results from necessary specialization of function), and increasingly complex patterns of social integration (as in the formation of solidaristic groups). In this context, development has various indicators: such as, increased per capita income or GNP, numbers of civil servants, and the proliferation of specialized instrumental roles (financial, technocratic, and so on).[9]

Industrialization, as used here, refers to a specialized process in which the expansion of productive enterprise is the integrating factor in social life, creating a demand for both skills and education as well as providing the central allocative and distributive mechanisms. Industrialization thus defines utility. It produces certain structural and organizational uniformities. These structural similarities render obsolete certain once powerful distinctions, such as those between capitalism and socialism or between private and public ownership—particularly as organizational types. And although these distinctions are less and less significant, problems of bureaucratic decision-making, optimum organizational size, and efficient utilization of resources are common concerns of growing importance in all industrial systems. More significantly, perhaps, the United States is entering into a period of what might be called a *post-industrial* stage, in which the distinguishing feature is the generation and utilization of new information at an increasingly high rate. Several other industrial societies will soon find themselves in the same situation.[10]

Modernization, the process with which we are particularly concerned, is a special case of development defined by industrialization, but more general than the latter phenomenon. Here modernization is used primarily with regard to the spread and use of industrial-type roles in nonindustrial settings. We can diagram the characteristics of modernization as follows:

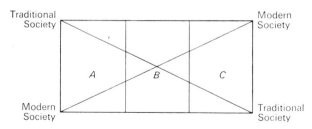

Figure 5-1. Stages of Development

It can be seen that the relationship between traditional society and modern society is such that the latter emerges at the expense of the former. However, it makes no sense to follow the same procedure in regard to the relationship between modern and industrial society. In other words, it cannot be said that as industrial society emerges modern society disappears. Quite the contrary, they merge and become the same. Hence the relationship between development, modernization, and industrialization is a logical progression resulting in the decline of traditionalism with modernization a consequence of industrialization.

This formulation has a number of advantages. For one thing, it can be operationalized. It is possible to examine the empirical spread and functional consequences of modern roles in traditional systems. Also it is possible to describe the general process as genetic and in terms of stages. If we consider Stage A early modernization, Stage B midpoint modernization, and Stage C the transition to industrialization; concretely, most African nations would fall in Stage A, most Latin American nations in Stage B, with a few—Brazil and Argentina—in Stage C.

In this context, development also implies change from traditional society, the base-point, to industrial society, the goal. However, this is a bit misleading; for, although we may think of development analytically as a shift from a traditional to an industrial society, the process of modernization works the other way around, i.e., from industrial to traditional. *Modernization*, thus defined, represents the spread of roles originating in societies with an industrial infrastructure, serving functional purposes in the industrial process, to systems lacking an industrial infrastructure. This is why we spoke earlier of a lack of fit in the system as well as a political management problem which intensifies with the proliferation of such roles in the absence (or very limited partial development) of industrialization.[11]

To reformulate our primary assumption: as a society experiences modernization, conflict produced in the absence of an industrial infrastructure requires government to organize and integrate the various sectors of the community. Hence the following proposition: the closer a modernizing country comes to the stage of industrialization, the greater the political problem of controlling and integrating the process. If this assumption is correct, the transition to industrialization requires an exceptionally well-organized political system, able to maintain a high degree of control. It is because the problem is so complex that I suggest that high control systems are necessary to make the transition to industrialization. However, after that phase of development has been completed, because the special emphasis of industrialized societies is on the generation, dissemination, and application of new knowledge at an ever-increasing rate, the need in post-industrial societies is for greater decentralization of high control systems. If the industrial infrastructure can also carry with it certain organizing properties so that they reduce the need for direct government control, a noncoercive, high information situation will result with government playing a mediating and coordinating role.

The central significance of the total development process is in its capacity to widen human choice and alternatives. This represents simultaneously a normative problem, how can choice best be widened? a structural problem, how can the system of roles be held together under various conditions of choice? and a behavioral problem, what constitutes the permissible levels of action as seen from the point of view of members of the system? At its widest extent, when development is linked with choice as the venue for contemporary political analysis combining normative, structural, and behavioral elements, it is possible once again to talk about fundamentals; and thus to fulfill the first step in the criteria for reformulation suggested earlier. Using the three main dimensions of the choice problem as our focus, we can suggest the following propositions:

(1) As societies modernize, the normative integration of the previous system begins to weaken, thereby widening the area of public meaning and reducing the area of prescriptive values. (2) From a structural standpoint, modernization creates more complex systems of roles which need to be managed. (3) From a behavioral point of view, there is more ambitiousness and less predictability in social action, producing greater uncertainty by individuals both of themselves and of the anticipated responses of others.

Modernization then is a direct cause of the lack of fit between normative, structural, and behavioral aspects of choice. It is the critical problem with which a government needs to deal. A solution requires political expertise under conditions of weak legitimacy and a low ceiling on political options.

Political Systems Types

Development and choice are the parameters within which a political system must operate. Development has been divided into three stages: traditional, modern, and industrial; and choice has been discussed in three dimensions: normative, structural, and behavioral. However, just as the process of modernization proceeds from industrial to nonindustrial systems, so the complexity of choice increases in the same manner, with rapid proliferation of contradictory norms, alternative role systems, and uncertain behavior. The political response to this is to control the normative and structural aspects of choice—on the assumption that this in turn will control behavior. As used here, a political system is a structural response to a behavioral problem of uncertainty resulting from randomness in public action. Such a response can be seen as a political type combining normative and structural variables.

Hence, the political system (which I define concretely as a relationship between society and government) responds to pressures of modernization, which, as reflected in the emergence of class and status conflicts, represent claims not only to redress and power, but also to key conflicts of values and interest. Such claims, whether based on values reflecting proprieties of rank in the society or interests in whose views should prevail and what groups should enjoy special advantages, may give rise to powerful ideologies, which political leaders wish to endow with much wider moral claims than ordinary proprieties. In conflict, these ideologies define the phenomenon commonly referred to as *legitimacy*, which, together with its values, forms one basis of our structural model of government. If these moral issues should reach such proportions that they define a new basis of legitimacy, we can say they embody nonempirical ends in which a high component of symbolic meaning is associated even with ordinary acts. We call such normative ends in application with empirical means consummatory values. They are commonly expressed in ideologies and represent a moral synthesis directly opposed to an appositive or antithetical moral synthesis.

The alternative situation is where ends and means are empirical. Ordinary demands, which are generated through the system during modernization, normally arise through the competition of groups, such as those based on interest, function, and the like. These are found in both the traditional and more modern sectors of the society. When competition of interest results in the identification and articulation of empirical means germane to empirical ends, what we can call a condition of instrumental values emerges. Most ordinary demands are of this nature. If consummatory values embody normative conflict, instrumental values embody interest conflict. Combinations of these are possible, as when ordinary issues are seen in a wider ideology with a hortatory or utopian objective enabling the ideological expression of a synthesis of consummatory and instrumental values: for example, the Catholicism of medieval Europe, Protestantism during the late Reformation and the industrialization of the West, Japanese nationalism with its high component of political religion, or communism with its elevation of the community to a sacred value. Such powerful syntheses are the moral punctuation marks of political life. They define the issues for all societies—whether accepted or rejected by individual governments—and have a great impact on structural and behavioral aspects of choice.

Two other variables of equal importance need to be identified. These are structural categories, which we call *hierarchical* and *pyramidal authority*. Here we refer to the degree to which a government is accountable to the public. If accountability is very low, we call this a condition of hierarchical authority. If it is high, we call the resulting authority structure pyramidal. Hierarchical authority is that authority analogous to a command system. Pyramidal systems have semiautonomous decision-making powers, as, for example, the several states of a federal system.

Putting these categories together gives us the following types of political systems:

Authority Type

		Hierarchial	Pyramidal
V **a** **l** **u** **e**	Consummatory	*A* Mobilization Types	*D* Theocratic Types
T **y** **p** **e**	Instrumental	*C* Bureaucratic Types	*B* Reconciliation Types

Figure 5-2. Political Systems-Types

As modernization proceeds the complexity of the process creates a need for more and more hierarchical authority to control the process. As I have suggested, this is partly because of the inequalities in a system (reflected in class and status solidarities and conflicts), which generate political grievances and can be exploited by political entrepreneurs, and because of heightened political competition, which creates estrangements preparing the ground for carriers of political consummatory values of either the left (as in Cuba) or the right (as was the case in Peron's Argentina). One characteristic response to the problem of modernization is seen when a government that is hierarchical in its authority and consummatory in its values comes to power and recates a powerful synthesis of consummatory meanings in instrumental acts. Such a government we call a *mobilization system* (Type *A* in Figure 5-2). Mobilization systems have a limited, but important, role, reaching optimum effectiveness in the transition from high modernization to early industrialization (as was the case in Russia in 1917 and is today in China). However, they have very limited utility for transforming traditional to early stage modernizing societies (as is shown in the cases of Ghana, Guinea, and Mali) and reach their ceilings very quickly. Such systems try to create a new synthesis between normative, structural, and behavioral dimensions by limiting choice and the criteria for choice to "morally valid" goals.

An alternative model, the reconciliation system (Type *B* in Figure 5-2), in which pyramidal authority and instrumental values prevail, is a common one during periods of modernization, particularly in Latin America. It has produced certain endemic problems, however. By permitting prevailing differences in the community to sustain themselves through the competitive conflict of interest groups, pyramidal authority results in an allocation of rewards in the system according to the strength and persistence of organized sectors of the society. As well, when there is a high degree of instrumentalism,

161

a situation that may be described as a gambler's choice prevails. The result is great inequality and very little commitment to the system as a whole. At best, the government's role is restricted to mediating between competing power blocs; and if it is sufficiently restricted in what it can do by high degrees of accountability, the result is stagnation. Such systems can work well only when one of two conditions is present: (1) when the system descended from a previous level incorporating highly consummatory values according to which a New Jerusalem had been defined in ethical terms (as was the case in the United States with its New England communities which had institutionalized the values of corporate responsibility so effectively that they spread throughout the system to act as silent monitors on instrumental behavior); or (2) when the system shows an exceptionally high rate of growth and a correspondingly high payoff (as is the case in Venezuela). Otherwise, the reconciliation system is likely to result merely in the rise of such inequality and its concomitant corruption in government that it produces little commitment to the society on the part of its members or its government. The relationships between norms, structures, and behavior are a result of a kind of political *laissez-faire*.

On the other hand, as industrialization proceeds, the conditions of a reconciliation system are produced in which the relevant conditions of success just described are likely to be present, especially if a "New Jerusalem" was created by a previous mobilization system. If, in addition, industrialization has produced the promise of a high rate of payoff, the result may be a well-functioning reconciliation system, which, although it may or may not be democratic in the sense of representative government, would nevertheless be characterized by the accountability of its government and the increasing primacy of its instrumental values. Thus, movement between A and B situations in the model is possible as a society goes from early stage industrialization to mature industrialization. More important perhaps, because they are more characteristic during modernization, are two other movements: namely, (1) from A or B to C and (2) from B to D. The first two shifts, from mobilization type and reconciliation type to bureaucratic type, recently occurred in Ghana and Nigeria. The second, from reconciliation type to theocratic type, is being attempted today in Chile. However, the long-term prospect in modernizing countries is a movement back and forth between bureaucratic and reconciliation types. Latin American countries have experienced this. Oligarchical reconciliation systems reach a certain stalemate, and a caudillo or military leader or other personalized figure takes over. He is overthrown and "democracy" is restored. The same situation is now coming to prevail in Africa in the form of military regimes.

The mobilization and reconciliation systems share one characteristic in common: they articulate a process that is the key to their functioning; namely, the organization and direction of the entire system toward given

162

goals in the first instance and the mediation and reconciliation of interests in the second. They have a certain political coherence.

The theocratic and bureaucratic types are "states of affairs" systems. They lack a political blueprint, but represent a more immediate and direct balance of forces. The theocratic system is based on a high behavioral commitment to consummatory values; and the structural form is whatever sustains that. The bureaucratic system is based on a powerful and effective organizational mechanism, e.g., army, bureaucracy, party, and so on. In this case, consummatory values are largely irrelevant; and, although behavior is controlled, all values are instrumentalized to serve organizational or structural needs. If the belief system of the one or the organizational subsystem of the other is threatened, the system will change.

This suggests that with the four types of political systems, we can speak of two "process" types and two "states of affairs" types and four criteria of maintenance. These criteria of maintenance are important because they can serve as a means to identify when a system-change takes place. To take two possibilities, if in a mobilization system the mobilization process falters and the system comes to depend on an organizational subsystem as the critical organizational mechanism and also the pattern of consummatory values begins to decline in favor of instrumental ones, then the system has shifted to a bureaucratic type. If in a reconciliation system mediation between various groupings terminates and a mobilizational process takes over with a particular subsystem assuming control over all the others in the presence of consummatory values, then the reconciliation system will have changed to a mobilization system.

To summarize the discussion so far, we have suggested that the modernization stage of the development process creates a widening of choice, which creates severe management problems in normative, structural, and behavioral terms. A political response is to combine normative and structural controls in political systems, each of which restricts behavior in some particular manner. Each political system reaches a ceiling in which the resources of development at its disposal are no longer capable of being redeployed.[12] The ceiling affects the process or state of affairs on which the system is functionally based, and a change from one type of political system to another becomes more likely. We can now turn to the political system itself in order to see how this situation occurs.

From the foregoing analysis it should be clear that there is no single best political system for a particular stage of development. Rather, what seems optimum is the system that has not yet reached its effective ceiling. Moreover, we can tentatively suggest that different types of systems will vary in their ability to prevent that ceiling from being imposed on them too rapidly. This suggests that there are possible optimum types for each stage of development. Mobilization systems are optimal for late stage modernizing societies in transition to industrialization. Bureaucratic systems are optimal for midpoint or intermediate modernization. Both mobilization systems and reconciliation systems are useful at the primary stages of modernization insofar as they create a framework for society; but both run into extreme difficulties produced by the transition from traditionalism to early stage modernization. Theocratic systems are not likely to be useful at any of the stages of modernization or industrialization, but the category has relevance historically, as well as in certain traditional cases.

It is now necessary to specify more clearly what we mean by *optimal* system. By *optimal* system I do not refer to the most democratic or most libertarian. My personal view is that democratic and libertarian systems work best in industrialized societies where the need to create and apply new information is critical. But modernizing societies can be more emulative, in the sense that they can observe industrial systems and utilize some of the information which they produce. The peculiar difficulty of modernizing societies, however, is that the more they modernize, the more roles are drawn from an industrial context, and the greater becomes the complexity of the system; yet the organizing functional principles of industrial society are lacking. Hence the goal of modernizing societies, i.e., industrialization, is a simple one, but the political problem, managing the complexity of roles, becomes greater the closer a country moves toward the goal. The best system, then, is that which handles this management problem effectively, allowing modernization to proceed in a relatively efficient manner.

I have suggested that a mobilization system shows relatively low accountability, which defines the basis of the hierarchical organization of government. Conversely, reconciliation systems show relatively low hierarchy, or high accountability, with accountability taking a concrete form vis-a-vis political parties, the military, civil servants, business enterprises, trade unions, international technical bodies, overseas missions, and so on. However, as modernization increases, the problems of coordination and control grow greater for both types of systems as previously described.[13]

Having described the political systems-types and the characteristics of systems-change, we can now restate some of these concerns in terms of several functional categories, relating these to the analysis of information as an input and coercion as an output of government. In the following discussion, it should be possible to see the relationship between the general model's formulation (in terms of mobilization and reconciliation types) and the responses of each system to the pressures of modernization.

Uncertainty, Information, and Coercion

We begin with a basic problem of system-change: when does a government reach its ceiling beyond which it cannot make major structural changes vis-a-vis human and natural resources? To answer this question, we examine the matter of systems-change in the context of several definitions and relationships. Although the analytical units are the political systems-types suggested, the concrete units are government and society. In mobilization and bureaucratic systems, government is the independent variable with society dependent. In theocratic and reconciliation systems, society is the independent variable and government dependent. Second, the link between government and society is what we call *representation*. Representation can be popular, interest, or functional, with different emphases prevailing in different systems-types; for example, mobilization systems emphasize functional representation, while reconciliation systems emphasize all three forms. However, every society shows some mixture of the three. Third, representation is carried out by representative elites who exercise three major functions: central control, goal specification, and institutional coherence. Central control refers to access to decision-making on a day to day basis. Goal specification refers to access to planning and the establishment of political objectives. Institutional coherence refers to mediation between organizational jurisdictions and ideological positions. These functions are the result of elite roles that concretely respond to problems arising in the stratification sphere and convert them into a series of inputs. This is why we say that representational elites have linkage roles between society and government. Nor are they merely passive transmitters of information. They may serve as triggers for government action, affecting values that have a wide moral significance (consummatory) as well as those with developmental significance (instrumental).

The relationship between type of representation and access to government differs depending upon whether government is the independent or the dependent variable. In a mobilization system there is minimum representation by type and minimum access. In a reconciliation system there is maximum representation by type and maximum access. The combination of access and representation is an index of participation. We can summarize the analysis so far in the diagram on page 166.

Several assumptions can now be specified: the greater the amount of participation by elites in government, the greater the degree of information available to government. The idea here is that elites create information by participation. In this context, *information* means that knowledge which reduces uncertainty, and *uncertainty* is the ability to predict a reasoned sequence of events. Given the foregoing analysis, we can recapitulate the problem as follows:

(1) The greater the degree of modernization, the wider the range of choice. (2) The wider the range of choice in a system, the greater the degree of normative, structural, and behavioral imbalance. (3) The greater the normative, structural, and behavioral imbalance, the greater the degree of

David E. Apter

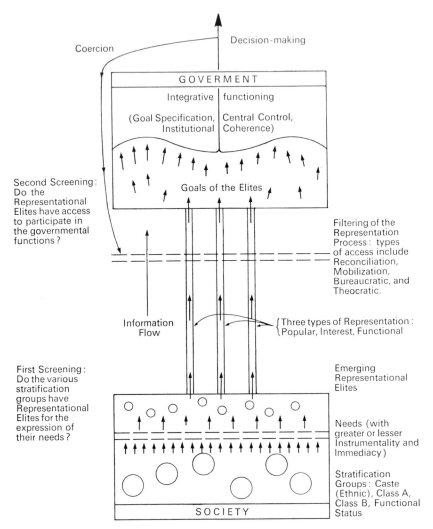

Figure 5-3. The General Model of Political Development

I am indebted to Professor Torcuato Di Tella for the organization of this diagram,

uncertainty. (4) It is to uncertainty that the various political systems-types respond.

To carry the analysis a step further, let us see how each of the two systems, *A* and *B*—mobilization system and reconciliation system—handle these problems. Let us assume that both types of system seek to maximize the information at their disposal and increase the efficiency of their decision-making. At any point in time the total amount of information available in a system is the product of consummatory values (normative preferences), instrumental values (interests), and technical knowledge. Moreover, modernization increases the total amount of information available in both the instrumental and technical spheres. Hence, the following propositions:

(1) The lower the degree of hierarchy, the more difficult it is for the government to act on information—unless there is a high degree of consensus from accountability units. (2) The higher the degree of hierarchy, the easier it is for government to act upon the information at its disposal. (3) In order to ensure freedom of action, hierarchical governments tend to maximize technical information and to employ coercion to control consummatory and instrumental values.

In other words, both systems attempt to increase their decision-making effectiveness through the application of coercion. In the case of the mobilization system, such coercion tends to be in the form of direct government control. It is applied in terms of the information already available. It is coercive, particularly in the sphere of consummatory values. Normatively, it restricts political values to a highly symbolic set of consummatory templates creating a special language or code. A high degree of symbolic coercion is prepared for violators of this code. They may be cast out of the community or put to death for violations of symbol. Political witches are publicly burned, especially those representing counterlegitimacy consummatory values. Instrumental values, more easily contained by police controls or a political party (the so-called single party system being one device employed), tend to be concentrated in two forms of interest: economic and political; but these interests stand for the community as a whole, rather than particular subgroups.

In reconciliation systems political leaders also desire to use centralized coercion. However, the key characteristic of pyramidal authority is limited power; and such limitation on coercion is imposed by the diversity and strength of accountability groups. Nevertheless, the tendency to coercion exists for many reasons. In the absence of coercion, there is likely to be considerable private corruption. Dislike of the government as well as other forms of resentment are common. Many interests compete; but this may weaken rather than strengthen the system as the danger that interest conflict may be converted into value conflict arises and prepares the groundwork for either a mobilization system or some other alternative, including take-over

167

by groups with a high coercive potential and instrumental values best represented in the military. Cases in point have been Burma, Pakistan, the Sudan, and most recently Nigeria.

In each case—mobilization or reconciliation system—the key to system-change is a functional change in the political system itself.

In *The Politics of Modernization* I put forward the proposition that an inverse relationship exists between political coercion and information. Increasing coercion will result in losses in information. Such losses are not necessarily direct and immediate; nor are they all of the same type. Losses in information from increased coercion are likely to occur in the following order: highest, in the sphere of counterlegitimacy consummatory values; and lowest, in the area of technical information resulting from industrialization itself. However, instrumental conflict is likely to be disguised and increasingly converted from interest conflict to value conflict. In other words, a two-step process takes place, including the loss of information about counter values and the increasing political significance of what would otherwise remain in the category of interest claims. This is the particular problem of the mobilization system.

The problem is the reverse in the reconciliation system. Thus, information about instrumental conflict is likely to be very high—so high, indeed, that it cannot be screened and evaluated. In addition, the content of the information is likely to be so confusing that a government is at a loss about how best to act upon it. With its sphere of action limited by diverse accountability groups, government is likely to find compromise necessary—itself a cause for that stagnation. This creates groups in favor of populist consummatory values that repudiate government or act as a regenerative movement against the government. If coercion can be applied against representatives of this moral force, it only reinforces their claims and gives them wider legitimacy. We can diagram these tendencies as follows:

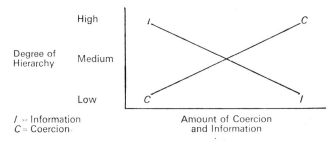

Figure 5-4. The Information-Coercion Relationship

Now, we can restate these assumptions in several hypothetical propositions:

(1) All governments engaging in modernization show a tendency to increase coercion to maximize the efficiency of decision-making. (2) The point at which this tendency terminates is where coercion causes such losses in information that effective decision-making is reduced. (3) Changes in the relationship between coercion and information produce changes in the type of government involved, not only in terms of mobilization and reconciliation systems, but also into two intermediate types involving hierarchical authority and instrumental values or pyramidal authority and consummatory values (the latter change occurring much less frequently than the former).

We can diagram these points as follows:

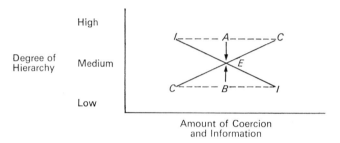

Figure 5-5. The Information-Coercion Relationship

The tendency A————$\rightarrow E$ illustrates the need for greater information on the part of a mobilization system, whereas the tendency B————$\rightarrow E$ indicates the need for greater coercion on the part of the reconciliation system.

Quite aside from their theoretical interest, these tendencies are significant for several reasons. As a practical point—particularly for countries in the early stages of modernization—erstwhile mobilization systems, such as, Ghana, Guinea, or Mali, which showed a high degree of hierarchy through the mechanism of the single party state as a vanguard instrument, did not apply much coercion in the first stage of their regimes. Moreover, having replaced colonially sponsored reconciliation systems (at least in the last stage of colonialism), they were exceptionally high information systems. However, as the pressure to pursue rapid modernization created problems of organization and discipline, the coercion outputs rapidly increased and the process of declining information manifested itself in several ways. In the Ghanaian case the conversion from A to C, as in Figure 5–2, occurred through a military *coup d'état*; while in Mali and Guinea it resulted in bureaucratic formalism and the drying up of sources of activity and enthusiasm.

In the case of a reconciliation system, the problem is too much information. The failure of the federal government of Nigeria to act on information

169

received was a result of the excessive degree of regional and local account-ability, which made necessary action impossible. The recent military take-over has resulted in the formation of a more hierarchical system with corresponding increases in coercion. Information previously available through the reconciliation system is still available for the new regimes; while the newly present coercive opportunities have been manifest in domes-tic military action against the Eastern Region.

I cite these cases because their theoretical formulations were worked out well before the actual changes in government occurred in both Nigeria and Ghana, and they are perfectly explicable by the model. Both new regimes have medium hierarchy and medium coercion and conform to the type I have called bureaucratic, which includes as subtypes military oligarchies as well as neo-mercantilist and modernizing autocracies. These can be des-cribed as *ABCD* in Figure 5–6;

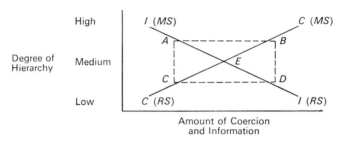

Figure 5-6. The Information-Coercion Relationship

The reasoning underlying both the concrete cases and the theory can be described in a number of propositions emerging from this formulation: (1) Increasing the degree of hierarchy narrows the circle of decision-makers and enlarges the excluded range of representational elites. (2) The greater the degree of hierarchy, the more concentrated the power of the decision-maker. (3) To maintain this power, decicion-makers may employ coercion or payoff. (4) To the degree to which potential representational elites are eliminated, competition for power between remaining decision-makers becomes greater, as does the need for manipulative skills on the part of the central leadership. (5) The greater the loss of representational elites, and the greater the competition between remaining decision-makers, the greater the loss of reliable information. (6) The greater the loss of information, the greater the need for a regulative coercive force, such as an army or police unit. (7) The greater the reliance on coercion, the more significant the role of the army and police, and the greater the need to control them.

170

To summarize:

(1) Increasing hierarchy—lower accountability
(2) Lower accountability—greater coercion
(3) Greater coercion—lower information
(4) Lower information—greater coercion
(5) Greater coercion—increasing hierarchy[14]

Conclusion

We conclude by restating the general hypothesis: As modernization grows in a system, the greater the complexity of differentiation in stratification-group competition, the more quickly a political system-type will reach its ceiling of effective response, and the greater will be the need for coercion. Thus, in early and middle stage modernization, we can expect a succession of political system-types, with the bureaucratic type providing the greatest degree of stability. If the goal of industrialization is central and overriding, during late modernization a mobilization system will emerge to take the society over the hump from late modernization into early industrialization. At this point, the need for information will grow and coercion will become increasingly dysfunctional to the system.

To recapitulate briefly, our task is to evaluate the political consequences of the differentiation of social structure from traditional to industrial stages according to stratification with caste (and ethnic), class based on occupational criteria and consciousness, class based on multibonded factors, and, finally, functional status groupings forming the basis of social life. These patterns of differentiation represent the empirical dimension of differentiation of choice, to be located and identified in particular group-related action in categories, such as landowners and peasants, army and bureaucracy, trade unions and intellectuals, and so on. Each one of these groups can be ranked in terms of its predominant type of claim to participation: popular, functional, or interest, as well as its degree of access to decision-making by means of goal specification, central control, and institutional coherence. The combination of empirical rankings can then be correlated with types of political system to evaluate what types of information emerge in relation to the degree of coercion applied. The general hypothesis is that if the level of differentiation reflecting changes in stratification increases, the political result will be more and more fragmentary changes in the political system-type until during late modernization when a mobilization system will emerge with the capacity to take the society from late modernization into early industrialization.

Cross-Cultural Survey Research
in Political Science

FREDERICK W. FREY
Massachusetts Institute of Technology

The first five chapters of this volume have concentrated largely on the conceptual and theoretical problems of cross-cultural, comparative research. In Chapter 6, Professor Frey addresses himself to the problems encountered in the cross-cultural use of a specific technique, namely, survey research.

However, even the discussion of a specific research technique when it is employed in a cross-cultural research design cannot proceed without some treatment of basic conceptual problems, which are covered in the first section of Chapter 6. Although these problems are not in principle different from those involved in research in a single culture, the multicultural setting of survey research greatly increases the magnitude of the difficulties. Frey discusses these problems systematically and suggests various strategies that may be employed to deal with them.

Although no attempt is made systematically to link the problems encountered in cross-cultural survey research to the conceptual issues treated in the earlier chapters, the reader will soon see the relationships. For example, Frey identifies what he calls a factorial matrix basis for country selection. In developing the dimensions one would use to build such a matrix, he would encounter precisely the problems Riggs discusses in Chapter 3 when he proposes a taxonomy of political systems.

A very important part of Chapter 6 discusses the administrative and organizational problems that anyone undertaking cross-cultural survey research—or any large-scale cultural research—would encounter. These are as formidable as the more strictly scholarly difficulties and suggest that the successful cross-cultural researcher must not only be an excellent scholar, but he must also be a skilled and sensitive administrator.

Frederick W. Frey is a Professor of Political Science at the Massachusetts Institute of Technology and is presently directing a major study of human factors in modernization based upon an analysis of selected attitudes and behaviors in four developing societies, two European societies, and the United States. Earlier he has done research work in Turkey and Venezuela. His publications include The Turkish Political Elite; "Surveying Peasant Attitudes in Turkey," in the Public Opinion Quarterly; and "Political Development, Power and Communication in Turkey," in Communication and Political Development.

CROSS-CULTURAL SURVEY research is a relatively new development in political science—indeed, in all social sciences. I suppose if one felt it important and were willing to rupture his imagination, he could discern in Aristotle's collection of city-state constitutions a precursor of today's cross-cultural surveys, in spirit if not in method. But such a tenuous connection would be satisfying only to those imperfectly weaned from philosophic authority. One cannot legitimately transform the infant that is cross-cultural survey research into a "2,000 year old man," no matter how one strains.

As we are dealing with an acknowledged youngster, a very brief introduction is perhaps appropriate, if only to make explicit my conception of the topic. Hence, in the first portion of this paper I shall confront three seemingly simple and basic questions: (1) What is cross-cultural survey research? (2) Why do it? and (3) How, if at all, does it differ from other survey research?

What is Cross-Cultural Survey Research?

The social scientist has a number of basic techniques for gathering data. Even an elementary catalogue would include documentary analysis, impressionistic observation, detailed case studies based on clinical techniques, key informants or participant observation, statistical manipulation of aggregate data, content analyses, survey research, simulation, and various forms of experimentation. Some of these techniques have a long and venerable history—for example, documentary analysis, impressionistic observation, and certain types of case studies. Others, such as content analysis, many forms of social experimentation, simulation, and survey research, are in essence only a few decades old. One hallmark of the more recent approaches is their emphasis on quantification and correlation, in contradistinction to the stress on qualitative classification and gross association featured in earlier analytic techniques.

Survey Research

Most writers on survey research have taken for granted a basic conception of the research technique under discussion, and rarely is any attempt made to define what is meant. Such a convenient tradition should not lightly be disregarded. Nevertheless, for the bold soul who is willing to ask the "simple" (and tough) questions, let me state that I conceive of survey research as *a method (or the products thereof) for systematically obtaining specific information from a relatively large number of individual sources, ordinarily through questioning.*[1] The important aspect of this conception is that survey research deals with an *appreciable number* of individual units *as individual units,* collecting unit-specific information about each. This is its strength vis-à-vis the case study, where the number of units is relatively small, and vis-à-vis aggregate analysis, where the clustering of attributes among identifiable individuals cannot be examined on an individual basis. Survey research involves gathering data in a visibly systematic manner in that the data collection procedures are kept as explicit as possible and that every feasible effort is made to eliminate or reduce the encroachment of bias and error into the data gathering process. This is its strength vis-à-vis more impressionistic efforts.

When we regard survey research from this perspective, we see that it differs from other research techniques employed by social scientists primarily in matters of degree—in the number of information sources manipulated, in securing data tagged specifically to each individual element of the population investigated, in the elaborateness of techniques supporting the generalization of findings or the reduction of bias, in the social settings appropriate to its use, and in the degree to which the variables of interest can be controlled.

I have defined survey research and its relationship to other research techniques in order to emphasize that it is one of several valuable devices in the investigative arsenal of the social scientist. Too often, we seem to stray into a fruitless debate emanating from whether one is pro- or anti-survey research. However, survey research has been so clearly demonstrated to be one of the most valuable research tools of social science that being implacably anti-survey research is ridiculous. At the same time, there are other unquestionably important social research devices, so that it is no less ridiculous to elevate survey research to a position of dominance. The only fruitful debate revolves about the most effective strategies for attacking various kinds of problems in social and political research.

The basic tools of social science are not alternative instruments but supplementary and complementary instruments. Thus, the competent survey researcher welcomes and depends upon insightful impressionistic analyses or penetrating case studies, particularly in a cross-cultural project. They are of inestimable aid to him in designing and interpreting his survey, just as the survey results are critical to more profound impressionistic forays and more telling case studies. Aggregate approaches can be valuable to the survey analyst in alerting him to possibly crucial correlations between variables and in helping him to introduce appropriate major controls into his survey planning. Similarly, the conscientious survey researcher, pursuing an important scientific problem rather than merely chalking up another survey, will be concerned with exploiting the possibilities which experimental techniques offer for pinning down the causal relationships that may underlie the primarily associational findings of most surveys.

176

Indeed, many projects obviously involve a mix of research techniques. Experiments frequently include surveys to ascertain the before or after psychological states of subjects. The aggregate data manipulated by the macroanalyst are often disinterred from censuses, which in turn are surveys. And, as I have pointed out, the survey researcher makes direct use of other approaches, even commissioning ancillary case studies to enrich his data, performing quantitative content analyses of his respondents' verbal output, and treating his survey as a quasi-experiment.

A major complaint regarding the orientation of sympathetic nonpractitioners of survey research in political science is that, although they agree that surveys are extremely valuable "in many instances," they tend to underestimate the subtlety and flexibility of the technique, and to restrict it unduly to glorified polling situations. As an example, let me invidiously select a colleague and an extremely able political scientist, Myron Weiner. Writing in the recent handbook, *Studying Politics Abroad*, Weiner poses the problem of ascertaining how a "dominant social and political group adapts itself to the demands of an emerging group entering the political system." He also is concerned with discovering the source of the dominant group's authority, locating the impetus behind the new group's entering the political arena, and the nature of the confrontation between the two groups (for instance, whether the established group closes ranks in an effort to maintain its power).[2]

"To answer these questions," Professor Weiner continues,

> survey-research techniques involving the use of a uniform questionnaire capable of giving results that can be tabulated would be inappropriate. Though some questions might be asked uniformly of both groups (particularly those involving the perceptions each has of the other), there are many questions which would be appropriate for only one of the two groups. Moreover, within each group there are important differences and a wide variation in political roles that may require that each interview consist of some unique as well as some general questions.[3]

It appears to me that, on the contrary, several of the questions posed can *best* be answered by survey research. Questions of the source of the dominant group's authority, of the impetus behind the new group's political activity, and whether the established group "closes ranks" are all essentially distributive attitudinal matters that are the meat of survey research. Moreover, the survey method permits precisely the technique described, namely, that of asking all groups certain questions, some groups other questions, and even presenting unique queries to selected individuals. Although format and inter-item contamination would have to be scrutinized carefully, the survey method is flexible enough to be adapted to this type of problem without distortion. I do not contend that it is appropriate in all situations; I argue

177

merely that many proponents of the "Yes, but" school too hastily under-estimate its adaptability, largely because they are less familiar with survey techniques than with more traditional approaches.

Cross-Cultural Research

Marion Levy has remarked that "Any worker in the field is sufficiently familiar with the bewildering profusion (of definitions of "culture") . . . Culture has been so defined as to include not only all patterns of action but also artifacts—all physical objects in any way altered by man. It has been discussed persistently as that element which differentiates humans from the other animals, and so has carried with it the faint whiff of the function performed for others by the concept *soul*."[4] After lamenting the difficulty of distinguishing the concept of culture from the concept of society,. Levy proceeds to define *culture* as ". . . the system of action of a society considered apart from its involvement of a 'plurality of interacting individuals,' apart from its operation. The study of culture in this sense is not a study of action but of the forms of action *as forms*." [5]

Kluckhohn and Kelly, in an influential formulation, defined *culture* as "all those historically created designs for living, explicit and implicit, rational, irrational, and non-rational, which exist at any given time as potential guides for the behavior of men."[6] Margaret Mead has distilled this into the "historically developed, shared, learned behavior of members of a society . . ."[7] Finally, Almond and Verba have defined "political culture" (perhaps more relevant for our purposes) as "the specifically political orientations—attitudes toward the political system and its various parts, and attitudes toward the role of the self in the system." They stress that they "employ the concept of culture in only one of its many meanings: that of *psychological orientation toward social objects*." They further state that "the political culture of a nation is the particular distribution of patterns of orientation toward political objects among the members of the nation."[8]

The fundamental difficulty in the concept of culture is vagueness, especially in its broadest anthropological usages. In those terms, one can legitimately speak of the culture of any social unit—family, community, tribe, nation, society, or the world. To jettison a little of this baggage, many writers like Levy and Mead have restricted the notion to the societal level. Others, like Almond and Verba, Rokkan and Duifker, and Boguslaw prefer to abandon the vagueness of "culture" and to talk more concretely of "cross-national" research.[9]

There is an important difference in perspective here. Cross-cultural research essentially refers to research in social units that differ to some usually unspecified degree in shared patterns of behavior and orientation. A nasty problem in this connection is that of designating the *amount* of sharing and

178

the specific *kinds* of behaviors and orientations that need to be examined in order to determine whether one is dealing with a single culture. Cross-national research, on the other hand, refers to research in social units of a given political level, regardless of the homogeneity, similarity or difference in their cultures, although it is commonly assumed that nations always differ culturally to some degree.

Whether the political scientist is interested primarily in cross-cultural or cross-national research depends to a large extent on the nature of the political topic he is investigating. Because the same kinds of methodological problems tend to arise in both instances, I shall not insist on the distinction in most parts of this paper. I should simply like to point out the generic class of *cross-systemic* or *cross-social-unit research*, in which there is sample clustering of respondents in specific social units and preservation of the distinction between units in the analysis, regardless of the level of the unit. One could refer to cross-legislature research, cross-political party research, cross-city research, cross-state research, and to many other kinds of cross-political-unit research in addition to cross-national research. Since political units ordinarily tend to display some cultural unity, when lower level units are all contained within some meaningful higher political unit one usually encounters less cross-cultural diversity. But when lower units are not all elements of the same proximate higher unit (as, for example, when one compares cities in Utah, Uttar Pradesh, Urfa, and Uzbek), or when there is no significant politically unifying higher unit (as ordinarily in the case of nations), then marked cultural diversity can be anticipated at least along some major dimensions. Political units and cultures are analytically distinct, if often empirically associated.

Why Engage in Cross-Cultural Survey Research?

Historically, two major developments in social science have converged to permit and provoke the political scientist's interest in cross-cultural survey research. The first is the improvement in survey methods and methodology. Quite naturally, when survey techniques were relatively untested and un-established, caution dictated modest aims. The beginnings were primarily in communities and organizations—studies of the London poor, prisoners, soldiers, etc. Later on national samples were attempted, with increasing sophistication and success despite (or perhaps because of) notorious setbacks in 1936 and 1948.[10] Cross-national or cross-cultural surveys may be said to represent a limited culmination of these efforts; they complete what might imperialistically be termed the *manifest destiny* of survey research in an extensive sense, and they have been fostered by the outstanding increase in technical survey skills. To cite but one example, multi-stage probability sampling techniques on an areal basis make feasible the accurate sampling of populations for whom no records are available and no quotas can be set, while the computer revolution enables us to perform deep multivariate analysis of large national samples which would have been unthinkable a few decades ago. In short, cross-cultural survey research rests upon hard-won technical advances which have become available only recently.

The second historic impetus to the political scientist's interest in cross-cultural survey research is the recent flowering of comparative politics, with its special focus on the underdeveloped world. One consequence of our concern with the emerging nations has been, as Almond and Verba have observed, that "the social scientist no longer assumes that the facts of social life are easily accessible through casual observation, introspection, or systematic reading. One questions not merely the interpretation of facts, but in the first instance the facts themselves."[11] As long as our inquiries were restricted to our own or even to Western cultures, it was relatively easy to take many so-called facts for granted, i.e., to assume them on the basis of our personal immersion in the culture. Confronted with strange and even exotic cultures in the non-Western world, however, the political scientist perceives his lack of basic factual resources more readily, particularly in the *attitudinal* realm where, at home, he feels a personal expertise. Under these circumstances, cross-cultural survey research gains salience as a research tool.

The political scientist's increasing self-consciousness about facts, which is reflected in his interest in cross-cultural survey research, is a very salutary thing. Surveys are often criticized for "proving what is already known." But a better formulation would be, "*confirming* what is already *thought*," and that is an honorable and important task. The history of science is replete with expensive wild goose chases for explanations of assumed "facts" that turned out to be false. Merton has written with characteristic vividness that,

> We need hardly review the long list of notorious episodes of this kind in the history of thought. Consider only Seneca explaining why some waters are so dense that no object, however heavy, will sink in them or explaining why lightning freezes wine; Descartes explaining why the pineal gland could exist only in man just a short time before Niels Stensen discovered it in other animals; Hegel solemnly explaining why there could be only seven planets and none between Mars and Jupiter just as Piazzi was discovering Ceres in that very region; the talented physiologist Johannes Müller explaining why the rate of transmission of the nerve impulse could never be measured just a few years before Helmholtz proceeded to measure it; J. S. Mill explaining the impossibility of sound statistical studies of human behavior long after Quetelet and others had conducted such studies. Episodes of this kind no doubt prompted Claude Bernard to insist on the obvious and compelling truth that "if the facts used as a basis for reasoning are ill-established or erroneous, everything will crumble or be falsified; and it is thus that errors in scientific theories most often originate in errors of fact."[12]

Whether it is indeed a "fact" that "errors in scientific theories most often originate in errors of fact" I should not like to say (without an appropriate survey, of course!); but cross-cultural survey research is, among other things, a self-conscious attempt to "get the facts" necessary for certain critical kinds of theory construction in political science, and in an area where we have had very few reasonably reliable "facts" up to now. Moreover, "it is often said that good theory leads to the discovery of new data, but it is probably no less valid to say that good data lead to the development of new theory." [13]

Stepping back a pace and taking a broader view, one can point out that comparison is essential to all science. Parsons has defined the experiment as "nothing but the comparative method where the cases to be compared are produced to order and under controlled conditions." [14] Survey research involves collecting cases rather than producing them, and conditions that are only as much controlled and "to order" as the natural setting and surveyor's resources permit. But its basic logic is no less comparative and scientific.

The great utility of cross-cultural research is that it dramatically expands the range of variation in the natural setting from which the survey researcher draws his cases. This increased range of variation is exploited primarily in two ways by cross-cultural research, as Sears has indicated. The first "is to provide a population sample, for testing hypotheses, that offers greater extremes on relevant variables, and broader variation among irrelevant variables, than can be obtained within a single culture." The second "is to provide appropriate conditions for the systematic variation of factors that cannot be varied within a single culture." [15] Thus, for example, if one is interested in the effects of various sorts of political protest experiences on political attitudes, he can (at least as of this writing) find only a limited range of protest experiences among the population of the United States. Individuals who have participated in revolutions, *coups d'état*, terrorist movements, and the like are largely lacking. Cross-national research would permit one to expand the range of this variable, perhaps critically. Other examples along the same lines abound. Cross-cultural research is required for a true probing of our generalizations, and an accurate assessment of their scope and qualifications.

Sears' second point reminds us of the fact that some of our hypotheses contain variables at a national or cultural level. These hypotheses, obviously, cannot be examined within the confines of a single nation or a single culture, except in the rare case where the hypothesis is universal and can be proven false by a single case. But whenever one wishes to scrutinize the relationship between a national or cultural variable and a variable at any other level, he must encompass more than one national or cultural system in his design. Only cross-systemic research can elucidate systemic effects. For instance, if one desired to examine the association between the number of political parties in national political systems and the incidence of feelings of national political efficacy, he would engage in cross-national political research. If he wanted to study the relationship between broad cultural norms regarding sibling aggression and preferred styles of political sanctions, he would ideally be led toward cross-cultural survey research. Since many of the variables employed by political scientists refer to characteristics of national political systems, one would surmise that cross-national research eventually will be strongly emphasized by political scientists. And because current concerns in political science deal so frequently with attitudinal and behavioral *distributions*, as reflected in concepts like *political socialization, political culture, idealogy,* and *consensus,* one would also predict that survey research will become increasingly prominent as an analytic tool.

To Sears' pair of basic reasons for engaging in cross-cultural research, I must add a few less weighty but nonetheless important points. The first is credited to Herbert Hyman. In a series of lectures delivered at the Inter-University Consortium for Political Research in 1963 on the topic of "Strategies in Comparative Survey Research," Hyman suggested that the political scientist is presently in a position not unlike that of the anthropologist who is rushing to obtain data on the world's rapidly dwindling supply of primitive or preliterate societies before they become extinct.[16] Similarly, one can see that it may not be very long before many of the traditional (to say nothing of primitive) political systems of the world disappear from view. What a tragedy it will be if we are unable or unwilling to secure survey baselines for subsequent evaluation of political change in these systems; what a pity if we lose forever any opportunity to obtain survey data on political attitudes and behaviors in systems and among peoples whose like may not be seen again. Indeed, this prospect seems to justify a feeling of some urgency toward improving our cross-cultural survey research capacities and opportunities, while of course avoiding rashness, haste, and panic, and with full respect for the sensitivities of the people being studied. But our chances for investigating political attitudes in a traditional ruling monarchy, among nations experiencing their first elections, in isolated tribes, in nations without political parties, in broad cultural areas without radio exposure, and so on, may be vanishing rapidly.

Another worthwhile observation regarding the utility of cross-cultural and cross-national survey research is that it is of great value even to one not strongly interested in the particular foreign country being surveyed. As many writers have stressed, the political scientist interested mainly in the United States tends to become a better analyst of American political phenomena if he can fit them into a perspective that includes evidence from other political systems. For example, one may be primarily interested in political socialization among school children in the United States. Even so, knowledge of the processes of political socialization among peasants in developing societies will aid him in fathoming those aspects of children's political socialization which seem to be due merely to the fact that they are children and not adults, and those aspects which seem due to the fact that they are politically inexperienced in the most elementary ways. From surveys that we have been conducting with United States school children and with Turkish and Venezuelan peasants, I have been impressed by the similarities in many phases of the political socialization process, even though the latter groups are newly politicized adults.

Lastly, cross-cultural survey research is worthwhile from a methodological perspective alone. The exaggerated technical problems that one encounters in cross-cultural surveys heighten his sensitivity to analogous problems in single-cultural studies—problems that he may have been glossing over in previous work. Sticking survey research tyros onto the difficulties of cross-cultural research, even if they intend to work solely within one culture ever after, would seem to be excellent training. For example, most United States research has indicated that serial error in panel studies (sensitization, crystallization) is not a major problem;[17] but one wonders whether research among people with much less gross familiarity with "surveys, polls, and samples" would alter this conclusion and alert us to the dependence of the United States finding on specific variables, such as exposure, education, or cosmopolitanism, that cannot be sufficiently varied in our modern culture. Experience with cross-cultural panel research would probably tend to make the survey researcher more vigilant in this respect. Maclay and Ware put the point succinctly and well when they say,

> Psychological instruments have most often been developed and validated in the context of Western culture. An important question involves the extent to which conclusions based on these instruments can be extended to human beings generally. This can only be studied by applying the instruments to a subject population consisting of persons with non-Western cultural backgrounds. An inevitable result of this approach is a fuller understanding of the limits within which the instrument is effective.[18]

Differences Between Cross-Cultural and Other Forms of Survey Research

The third introductory question posed was whether there are any differences between cross-cultural survey research and other forms of survey research. Essentially, this is a question that can be answered by a single word—no. There are no fundamental differences in principle or in logic between cross-cultural survey research and within-cultural survey research, under most conceptions of culture. Hudson and his associates, who have made intensive survey studies of youth in five Near Eastern nations, assessed

183

the situation accurately when they contended that "the methods of cross-cultural research are not in principle unique. They are different primarily in the sense that procedural precautions become more critical and some problems more difficult to identify and to solve than for within-culture studies."[19] Rommetveit and Israel, cross-cultural experimentalists rather than survey researchers, make the same point regarding their specialty: "We want to emphasize that we do not consider the difficulties to be discussed unique for cross-national studies. Rather, replication of an experiment in different cultural settings tends to accentuate some problems pertaining to empirical testing of social psychological theory in general."[20]

From one vantage, the point is that if inventories were made of the types of problems challenging cross-cultural survey research and the types challenging within-cultural survey research, the two listings would have virtually identical categories. One thinks immediately of problems like the translation of instruments for respondents in divergent cultures. Yet reflection will reveal a within-cultural counterpart for each such problem. Upper-class, middle-class, and lower-class respondents in the United States or England, for example, literally do not speak the same language, as the educational testing fraternity realized more than fifteen years ago.[21] Important "sub-cultural" variations between classes, educational groups, regional populations, and other social echelons plague the domestic survey researcher in a manner quite analogous to the more pronounced full-cultural variations that loom before the cross-cultural survey researcher. This is true in the areas of sampling, interviewer recruitment and training, instrument preparation, interviewer-respondent interaction, coding, and analysis. The differences are in degree and not really in kind.

These differences in degree—in the relative severity of problems, if not in their intrinsic character—do, however, have weighty implications for cross-cultural survey research. Not only are the problems more severe, but their existence is more conspicuous. One can ignore a mouse-like problem, but when it assumes elephantine proportions, one ignores it only at the peril of being overwhelmed. As several practitioners have asserted, cross-cultural survey research, more than other types, forces a concern with theory, with conceptualization, and with all the problems of measurement that intrude on survey operations. One does not have the easy out of saying, "Well, you know what I mean," relying upon many implicit within-cultural understandings. Almond and Verba have even construed this as a bitter sort of virtue, rationalizing that, "In fact, one possible methodological advantage of the cross-national survey is that many of the problems that can be ignored when one is dealing with a single nation must now be faced explicitly."[22] Noncomparability can enter the cross-cultural operation at any point where error or bias is possible, not just in translation or interviewer-respondent interaction. Thus, the cross-cultural survey researcher must take extraordinary pains in all phases of the survey procedure. But the difference lies primarily in the magnitude of the task and not in its inherent nature.

Two minor exceptions to these comments are needed. The first and more obvious one is that since cross-national and cross-cultural surveys are the only ones that vary systemic national or cultural factors, any special problems related to variables of this type may be unique to cross-cultural or cross-national surveys. Secondly, the cross-cultural survey faces all the problems of the domestic survey, multiplied by the number of nations studied.[23] Hence, it may be necessary to add some sort of *complexity factor*. In other words, there may be properties stemming from the tremendously increased complexity of the cross-cultural survey so that complexity itself must now be regarded as a separate, distinct, and essentially new or higher order problem.

For various reasons, mostly related to expense, complexity, the recency of its technical feasibility, and difficulties of access, relatively little cross-cultural survey research has been done. It seems fruitful minimally to distinguish bicultural survey research, in which the comparison is between only two cultures, and multicultural survey research, in which the comparison is among more than two cultures. The great bulk of the cross-cultural research thus far accomplished would seem to be bicultural. From the viewpoint of explicit confrontation of the methodological problems of cross-cultural research, bicultural research relates to multicultural research as single-cultural research relates to bicultural. In short, multicultural survey research demands the most direct assault on the most critical and characteristic problems.

Some idea of the kinds of multicultural survey research on politically related topics that have recently been conducted or are in process may be garnered from the selective listing that follows.

Some Completed Multicultural Surveys

1. Surveys of urban dwellers and peasants living near large cities in six Near Eastern nations (1949–1951) and focused on communication behavior, especially versus the mass media. Reported in Daniel Lerner, *The Passing of Traditional Society.*[24]

2. Surveys of the sense of threat and various political orientations of primary and secondary teachers in seven northwestern European countries (1953). Reported in a special issue of *The Journal of Social Issues* and in other journal articles.[25]

3. Surveys of national stereotypes among the adult populations in nine nations, six from Western Europe, plus Australia, urban Mexico, and the United States (1948–1949). Reported in William Buchanan and Hadley Cantril, *How Nations See Each Other.*[26]

185

4. Surveys of the foreign policy views of national legislators in seven nations. Reported by Lloyd Free in *Six Allies and a Neutral*.[27]

5. Surveys of the basic value systems of university youth in nine societies, developed and underdeveloped. Reported by James Gillespie and Gordon W. Allport, *Youth's Outlook on the Future*.[28]

6. Surveys of the connections between education, class, social mobility, and various values, including political, among twelve occupational, educational, and residential groups in four Latin American countries. Reported in K. H. Silvert and Frank Bonilla, *Education and the Social Meaning of Development: A Preliminary Statement*.[29]

7. Surveys of the impact of modernization on the attitudes of secondary and university students in five Near Eastern nations and the United States (1952–1956). Reported in a special issue of *The Journal of Social Issues*.[30]

8. Surveys of the civic attitudes of national samples of the adult populations of the United States, United Kingdom, German Federal Republic, Italy, and urban Mexico (1959–1960). Reported in Gabriel A. Almond and Sidney Verba, *The Civic Culture*.[31]

Some Multicultural Surveys in Progress

1. Sidney Verba and his collaborators are directing a project investigating political and civic attitudes in Japan, Brazil, Nigeria, and India. An attempt was to be made to secure national samples of the adult populations in all countries but India and Brazil. U.S. center—Stanford University.

2. Philip Jacob, Henry Teune, and their associates are directing a project investigating the political values (norms) of local level bureaucrats in selected communities of four nations: Poland, Yugoslavia, India, and the United States. U.S. center—University of Pennsylvania.

3. Daniel Lerner and Morton Gorden are studying the political orientations of various kinds of elites in the United Kingdom, France, and Germany. Panel and trend analyses are being undertaken, and the project is in its final phases. U.S. center—Massachusetts Institute of Technology.

4. Alex Inkeles is directing a study of the impact on traditional people of exposure to an archtypical modern institution—the factory. Data were collected in six divergent developing societies located in Latin America, Africa, and Asia. The project is now in its analytic phase. U.S. center—Harvard University.

5. Robert Hess and his associates are directing cross-national surveys of the political socialization of primary school children in several countries of Europe and in other parts of the world. The project is now in the pretesting and initial data collection phases. U.S. center—the University of Chicago.

6. Kumata and Gullahorn are conducting a study of communication behavior and other activities and orientations in five nations: Costa Rica,

Finland, Japan, Mexico, and the United States. The data are currently being analyzed. U.S. center—Michigan State University.

Obviously, this very limited catalogue of only recent multicultural survey research does not purport to be exhaustive—particularly as regards the enumeration of works in progress. It is intended to convey some of the flavor of efforts mounted thus far. Contrasting the projects completed with those in progress crudely suggests the recent swing to the developing areas in cross-cultural survey research. I should also point out that I have severely restricted the listing to deliberately cross-cultural and essentially academic research. Many data with cross-cultural implications have been collected by commercial survey organizations such as International Research Associates or the Gallup affiliates, and perhaps even more lie in the archives of government bodies such as the U.S. Information Agency. Tapping some of these sources, primarily the commercial ones, may be facilitated by the journal, *Polls*, sponsored by the World Association for Public Opinion Research (WAPOR). Of course, such polls are ordinarily framed with purely domestic purposes in mind, and from the viewpoint of cross-cultural research they become relevant only through arduous processes of secondary analysis.[32]

Finally, I should mention the dearth of cross-cultural methodological research. Although the problems of cross-cultural surveys are not in principle different from those of within-cultural surveys, in both particulars and severity, they *are* different. Methodological studies specific to the particular problems of cross-cultural research are sorely needed. The remainder of this paper will focus on many of these particular problems.

Initial Design Considerations

The fact that the survey is to be deliberately cross-cultural or cross-national affects the research operation from its inception. The processes of designing the survey are initially influenced most strongly along three dimensions: conceptualization, type of design, and country selection.

Conceptualization

The crux of the conceptualization problem for cross-cultural survey research can be expressed very simply: *cross-cultural research demands cross-cultural concepts*. "A comparative social science requires a generalized system of concepts which will enable the scientific observer to compare and contrast large bodies of concretely different social phenomena in consistent terms."[33]

Unfortunately, many of the concepts of political science fall far short of having this "transcultural" quality so vital to cross-cultural analysis. The observation is perhaps more palatable if it comes from a distinguished anthropologist: Clyde Kluckhohn commented that, "Our concepts . . . of

187

'economics,' 'religion,' and 'politics' have a large element of cultural arbitrariness. Probably the main reason that anthropologists have written so little about 'political behavior' is the circumstance that they have felt intuitively uncomfortable, unable to isolate in many cultures an order of phenomena strictly comparable to our category of 'government.' ''[34] The same comment would seem to apply to notions such as political party, interest group, the military, voting, and so on.

Salvage operations have been attempted for many of these traditional, Western political science concepts, but these operations are frequently not very satisfying. One such effort is to make currently *institutional* concepts more behavioral or, some prefer to say, *functional*. The difficulty here is that one either ends up with a concept that is still not applicable to a large number of societies or groups, and has merely glossed over this fact by saying that the rating for such societies was zero along the dimension, or one has confounded communication by stamping an established label on a totally new product. Thus, by the former tactic, all countries either have a government and free elections or they do not. The concepts are therefore technically cross-cultural in their application. But such procrustean categorization is not very fruitful; concepts with such large residual content are unlikely to lead to important theoretic developments.[35] By the latter tactic, one redefines *government* so that the concept can be applied to a family, a clan, a tribe, a school, a corporation, an army, or any society, thus making the concept truly comparative But one leaves a wake of confusion among readers who compulsively swim back to the established meaning. Indeed, many writers who engage in such redefinition themselves lapse back into more established connotations when the implications of the new conception become awkward or hard to sell.

A related problem can be discussed under the rubric of conceptual elaboration or the need for an analytic framework. For example, notions such as political culture, political socialization, power and authority, political recruitment, and so on, are at a level of abstraction that is clearly cross-cultural. However, almost never is research able to proceed at such a general level. Specific dimensions of political culture must be investigated—specific subjects or agencies of political socialization, specific types or aspects of power relations, and specific varieties of political recruitment. Although the most general level of conceptualization may be cross-cultural, very frequently the researcher is in danger of reverting to culture-bound notions at subordinate levels. Political culture sometimes seems to emerge from this process as merely a set of orientations toward a particular form of Western parliamentary democracy; political socialization becomes the inculcation of specific kinds of civic attitudes necessary for "participation," which is viewed as a special virtue; power and authority are again implicitly restricted to their governmental manifestations; and political recruitment is confined to rather formal legislative, executive, judicial, and bureaucratic roles. The truly

188

cross-cultural quality of the most abstract conceptualization trickles away in the parochial subordinate conceptualization that actually defines the research. The gap between very general conceptual domains and markedly less extensive operational formulations seems to be rather acute in political science. The dimensions of political culture have not been profoundly delineated. The components of political socialization have not been well articulated. The forms of power and authority have not been adequately classified, and recruitment processes often seem to be whatever has captured the fancy of a particular investigator in a particular country. No general and integrated subordinate conceptualization elaborates, but still trans-culturally, the most popular abstract formulations.

What has just been said by no means refers to necessary variations in measurement techniques in order to preserve functional cross-cultural equivalence of conceptual meaning. It refers to plain parochialism in conceptualization itself, apart from measurement problems. However, let us now consider very briefly the problem of operationalizing survey concepts, assuming that the concepts are truly cross-cultural in their basic reference. Since I shall return to this topic in considerable detail later on, I shall simply make a general comment now.

Some of the limited number of truly cross-cultural concepts in political science seem to achieve that generality through a loss of empirical significance. One can speak at great length about political participation and seem to be referring to a concept with cross-cultural applicability. It refers in some usually undefined way to taking an active role affecting "political decisions" (a phrase that is extremely Western in its common implications) or to influencing the allocation of power in some social unit, let us say, the nation. However, by any of these definitions we are plainly more adept at investigating some kinds of participation, such as voting or party membership, and so on, than other kinds, such as tacitly threatening a tribal leader, various forms of noncooperation or slow-downs, or spreading rumors, and the like. Almost unconsciously, the particular measures employed in relation to a seemingly cross-cultural concept reintroduce specific cultural limitations.

The result is that we have two levels of discourse: one that is truly cross-cultural but, in Angus Campbell's felicitous phrase, "virtually impervious to empirical test," and a second that is empirically based but that is really quite parochial.[36] The first cross-culturally-comparative-but-metaphysical level of discourse seems to be that which normally prevails at our conferences on comparative politics or political development, whereas the second level is more often that of our empirical journal articles and academic monographs. Between the two levels is a considerable chasm. One of our best hopes for merging the two levels of discourse more effectively lies in improving our ability to accomplish truly cross-cultural survey research.

189

Frederick W. Frey

It should be added that the specter of parochialism haunts not only the political concepts employed in cross-cultural research, but also most other concepts, including the standard demographic or social background factors. Surveys consistently classify individuals in terms of occupation and education, age and sex, and so on. Much effort is spent in holding such factors constant so as to inspect other relations without obfuscation. At other times our concern is to ascertain whether educated people, or males, or those upwardly mobile exhibit similarities of behavior. Background characteristics are the warp and weft of survey research. Nevertheless, such social background categories do not themselves hold still across cultures. The meaning of nominally similar social backgrounds in terms of experience and social stratification may vary surprisingly. The American military officer, for example, may be more similar in essential respects to the German businessman than he is to the German military officer. It is hard to locate a precise British counterpart to the American lawyer. Hence, the cross-cultural survey researcher has to attend not just to cultural variation in *political* conceptualization, but to such variation in every other concept employed in his analysis. Carried to an extreme degree, these considerations make him wonder if there is any certain and stable spot from which he can start to erect a reasonable investigation, any fixed point from which he can begin to move at least the social scientific world. Here as elsewhere in the research process he is called upon to exercise that elusive quality we call *judgment*, to avoid both nihilism and folly. The outcome is always a compromise. One consequence is that in many ways it requires nearly as much skill to evaluate cross-cultural survey research well as it does to accomplish it.

Type of Design

"By research design, or the proper planning of a total inquiry and the intelligent allocation of total resources of time, personnel, and money, one increases the likelihood: (1) that the study will be brought to some completion, (2) that it will yield unambiguous and relevant findings, and (3) that the errors that accompany all empirical inquiry will be reduced and measurable. These are, of course, the goals of all investigators everywhere, but a failure to achieve them is more painful when the labors have been so heavy," as they always are in cross-cultural survey research.[37] Thus Hyman adumbrates the role of proper design in survey research. This section will provide a rough panorama of some of the basic design considerations that impinge on the initial stages of a cross-cultural survey operation.

One useful tack in approaching the topic is to examine alternatives: What are the main kinds of cross-cultural designs from which the survey researcher can choose?

A principal distinction has already been mentioned—namely, the

190

number of cultures or countries in which the research is carried out. We previously distinguished bicultural survey research (comparative field operations in two cultures) from multicultural survey research (comparative field operations in more than two cultures). One bargains for a more than proportionate increase in expense and complexity as each additional field operation is added. However, against these drawbacks must be balanced the markedly greater analytic flexibility and evidential force that also attend the strategic inclusion of more nations. If the basic purpose of cross-cultural survey research, as opposed to within-cultural research, is to obtain greater range along critical variables and to open up the opportunity for investigating systemic national and cultural variables, then having more cultural or national instances is congenial to the motivating spirit of the inquiry. In principle, the number of cultures or nations surveyed will depend upon: (1) available resources of money, time, and personnel; (2) the within-cultural range of variation along the dimensions germane to the problem prompting the research; and (3) the access attainable to appropriate settings.

Some commentators have added a third category to our bicultural-multicultural classification. Hyman, in the same article, speaks of "pseudo cross-national" research, and Almond and Verba refer to "implicit comparison" between one culture where a survey has been accomplished and another culture that is known impressionistically.[38] I have excluded this category, though many examples of it are to be found, because it is not strictly cross-cultural *survey* research—survey data from more than one culture or nation usually are not being directly compared.

A second and extremely important design distinction has to do with the timing of the surveys. *Concurrent* designs, in which the surveys are executed approximately simultaneously in all the nations or cultures being covered, are distinguished from *successive* designs, in which a portion of the total set of nations or cultures being investigated is surveyed only after other portions of that set have already been surveyed.[39]

Some of the advantages and disadvantages of successive designs are as follows. They offer a limited set of researchers greater control. If three, four, or five field operations are under way concurrently, greater delegation of control and authority is required. The director of the project, for instance, cannot personally guide each operation. However, if the surveys occur successively, then it may well be possible for one or two highly skilled individuals to direct each field operation personally. How great an advantage this is depends upon the technical difficulty of the task and the willingness of the other participants to support such a visibly concentrated control structure. Moreover, since the project director in this case is unlikely to know all cultures well, there may be a sacrifice of the opportunity to have at the local helm someone possessing more familiarity with the given culture.

The successive design offers greater flexibility of approach in some

191

important respects. Things can be tried realistically in the first culture and then can be refined or abandoned as necessary, with consequent improvement in operations in subsequent countries. However, this is not all net gain; one pays a clear price for this advantage. A lesson may not be learned until operations are commenced in the *last* of the countries, and then it is too late to alter what has been done earlier. Again, the advantage or problem uncovered in the first country has to be judged regarding its generalizability. In a successive design, one does not ordinarily have extensive pre-test results from *all* participant countries to permit such judgments. To use a contract bridge analogy, the successive design offers the surveyor *full* information on *one* hand at the table, while the concurrent design with extensive pretesting offers him *less complete* information on *all* hands at the table. Which option is preferable depends upon the nature of the problem being investigated. If the trouble spots seem general and are anticipated at rather recondite levels of analysis, then the successive approach would hold the edge. But if the trouble spots can be more quickly ascertained and are more indeterminable in their location and incidence, then concurrent designs offer more promise.

The successive design aids access to many nations, since one can approach them with an example and, hopefully, a success story. It also minimizes risk because, if the project aborts, a reduced loss will be incurred than if all operations were simultaneously underway. Also, a far from negligible advantage is that the successive design minimizes the intricate administrative and logistical problems of cross-cultural survey research.

On the other side of the ledger, the successive design may be unattractive to the later participants because they are presented with something of a *fait accompli*. They normally will not have had as much voice in planning the research as the first-examined country. Or, if they have been included in the earliest planning stages, there is an unfortunate hiatus between planning and execution during which their ardor for research may cool or they may succumb to other blandishments. Furthermore, the later participants may well chafe under the necessity of including only partially successful items from earlier surveys simply to maintain comparability. Under pressure for numerous "improvements" and in an interpersonal setting where there is probably less commitment to comparison, the project directors may find their comparative opportunities slipping away.

In the same vein, the successive design may drag out the research project to a degree that is intolerable to nearly all prominent scholars. It is difficult to conceive of a major concurrent design in several nations that would run fewer than four or five years. Successive designs add appreciably to the duration of such enterprises, especially for the project director and the focal institution.

Although time comparability is an extremely elusive notion, it does seem true that major international events shape world political orientations to some degree. A Sputnik goes up, China invades India, the Vietnam war occurs, an H-bomb is invented and shown to the world. Events of this type are sufficiently pervasive, at least among elite sectors, that, other things equal, the researcher wants to choose the strategy that offers least risk of the intervention of events. He does not want a biasing intrusion in the middle of his field operation. Compressing the duration of the data collection period is one way of minimizing such risks.[40]

In sum, then, concurrent designs reduce the probability of unfortunate gross international interventions, provide truer participation for the major actors, bring evidence from all participant countries simultaneously to bear in shaping the interrogative instruments, shorten the duration of the project, and offer the administrative convenience (and difficulties) of having all operations in approximately the same stage of work at the same time.

One of the points sometimes made in favor of successive designs takes cognizance of the shrinkage factor in cross-cultural research. Not infrequently things "go wrong" in one of the countries involved, so that it has to be dropped. Clearly, the successive design can compensate for this quite easily by adding another country. However, there is a somewhat more basic point at issue that might be called the *directionality of design alteration*—a fancy expression for asking which way competitive research designs can best be converted. A concurrent design can always be converted into a successive design, but a successive design can never be converted into a concurrent design. On reflection, the greater flexibility of the successive design in handling shrinkage is illusory; one can always counter shrinkage by adding another country to a concurrent design and be no worse off than if he had originally planned a successive design.

In this connection one should also observe that many ingenious mixtures of the successive and concurrent principles are possible, producing combinations of the advantages and disadvantages I have discussed. A very simple concurrent successive design, for example, would be to survey four countries, two at a time. To evaluate the wisdom of such a strategy one would have to put weights on the considerations previously discussed—weights that will vary greatly from situation to situation.

Lastly, another word about the time comparability problem is required. It is quite obvious that mere chronological simultaneity does not guarantee comparability across the social, political, and economic contexts in which the surveys occur. Even though the surveys were to be conducted in two countries at the same time, if one country were on the eve of a national election and the other were not, the two settings might be quite different and the answers to certain questions consequentially biased.

In order to obtain even gross contextual comparability the researcher should have some a priori idea of the main dimensions that must be controlled or allowed for (such as domestic elections, wars, inflations, and so on). He usually tries to select a time when all or none of the nations are in the throes of such events, unless he is deliberately varying these factors. He has, in short, a mental checklist of flagrant environmental disturbances which he attempts to avoid. But the common constraints of time and resources permit him only limited discretion in this area, and all too often this checklist is implicit rather than explicit.

Just as international disturbances particularly plague successive designs, so concurrent designs seem to be more vulnerable to difficulties from domestic disturbances of the type just discussed. Under a successive scheme, the researcher usually can order the sequence of field operations so as to avoid predictable disturbances like elections. Using a concurrent design he must find a single period when the gross domestic situations in all countries are at least minimally comparable, and that may not be easy. In any event, his maneuverability with regard to the timing of field operations is reduced.

The significance of domestic disturbances can be illustrated by Scheuch's criticism of Almond and Verba's conclusion in *The Civic Culture* that the lower frequency of political conversations found in Germany, compared with the United States and the United Kingdom, could be attributed to differences in "political cultures." Argues Scheuch, "An equally likely explanation would be . . . that the surveys were carried out at a time close to national elections both in Britain and in the U.S.A., but halfway between elections in Germany. If I compare the 1959 data from Britain with the results for the same question in a nation-wide survey of ours just prior to the 1961 national election in Germany, the differences disappear."[41]

Among other design distinctions offered, Rokkan and Duijker have separated what they call "repetitive" designs from "joint development" designs. Actually, there are two main axes of differentiation here: the novelty of the design and the number of originators. A cross-cultural survey can be, at the polar extremes, either a replication of a design developed previously, in which case the major decision of the project participants is adoption, or it can be the invention of the participants. If it is a replication, one gains comparability with other research and ordinarily loses appropriateness, whereas the reverse is true if an invented design is employed. On the other axis, the design may be the handiwork of one of the participants who has persuaded others to adopt it, or it may be the joint product of several contributors. Obviously, these are the extremes of continua that permit many internal gradations. The fruitfulness of such a classificatory scheme is not transparent. Rokkan and Duijker seem to imply that the concurrent-joint development type of project is the rarest and perhaps the most difficult of all.[42]

Another design feature of all surveys, including the cross-cultural variety, is how they handle the time-change dimension; are they single-shot

194

attempts to gather data as of a given moment, or do they try to come to grips with attitudinal and behavioral change through time in some more direct fashion? If they do strive to grapple with the analysis of change through time, are they cast in the form of retrospective analyses, trend studies, cohort analyses, panel studies, or longitudinal studies? These are the main techniques for focusing on temporal change presently open to the designer of cross-cultural surveys.

All aspects of these devices for analyzing change through time obviously cannot be discussed in the present chapter. The paramount point at this juncture is that the cross-cultural analysis of change through time presents added difficulties. For instance, consider a concurrent design, and then consider a concurrent panel design, where each wave of interviews has to be accomplished at approximately the same time. The administrative problems are slightly staggering, though ultimately manageable with enough effort, access, and resources. We shall probably be seeing such an enterprise within a decade or so. Indeed, the Lerner-Gorden project previously mentioned may be a prototypical effort.

Given the instability of international relations and the suspicion, hostility, and chauvinism that often confront the cross-cultural survey researcher, trend studies and longitudinal analyses become perilously delicate. It may not be until we get attitudinal-behavioral surveys under regular international auspices that we shall enjoy sophisticated trend or longitudinal surveys of a cross-cultural character. However, a few variants of the panel technique, which usually has a much shorter life span than several other methods, are currently being employed in a partially cross-cultural way. The survey of the Turkish peasantry which we carried out in 1962 was designed as a combined trend-panel project. The original intention was to return to the field six or seven years later (about the time necessary to complete the original analyses!), and to utilize our large split-sample to accomplish both these objectives. One random half of the original sample was to be reinterviewed, making the study into a true panel. However, that half would no longer be an accurate representation of the adult Turkish peasantry, so that it could not support refined trend analyses for the rural sector of the society. Hence, the second half of a total sample equal to the original in size would be devoted to a new sample of the designated population. With a total second effort commensurate to the first we could procure both trend and panel type data.[43]

Another useful variant of the panel technique is what Hyman has labelled "selective experimental empanelling."[44] It essentially consists of selecting one's sample or panel on the basis of responses to a prior survey, perhaps conducted by another researcher. Leslie and Noralou Roos, for example, located several surveys that had been administered to students in the Political Science Faculty (civil service school) in Turkey some eight years or so previously. The erstwhile student respondents were now out in the Turkish bureaucracy, and the existence of the previous surveys afforded the opportunity to compare some of their university political orientations with those prevailing after a number of years of bureaucratic service.[45] Analogous research on a cross-cultural basis, while difficult, is surely conceivable.

As I shall emphasize later on, an invaluable approach to ensuring equivalence of meaning across cultures is the use of *system specific* variables. In other words, instead of comparing persons earning more than the local equivalent of one hundred dollars per week—which may be a relatively mediocre income in some societies or groups and an extremely good income in others—one compares persons who are *relatively* well-off or poor in the context of their society, regardless of their *absolute* level of income. I refer to this now not to elaborate this analytic technique, but merely to mention its design implications, both because of their intrinsic importance and to illustrate how the nature of the intended analytic treatment guides the survey design.

One of the foremost problems confronting the cross-cultural survey researcher is that of deciding upon the specific population of concern. Does he want a national sample of the adult population, a sample of peasants or city-dwellers, a sample of squatters, industrial workers, or teachers, or a sample of persons rating high on political efficacy vis-à-vis the national government? The decision on the population of concern basically influences the type of project established. One valuable strategy is to proceed highly "purposively," selecting apparently matched groups (e.g., in terms of occupation or education) rather than attempting to get large representative samples of broader strata. Such a strategy has much to commend it in terms of cost and precision.[46] But it raises the problem of how one ascertains that the groups are indeed matched in any way that is more than nominal.

Similarly, in attempting to ensure cross-cultural analytic equivalence through the use of variables with system-specific indicators, i.e., comparing groups with relatively similar positions in their respective systems, one requires considerable information merely to develop the system-specific placements. To obtain truly comparable groups one often needs information from rather large and extensively representative elements of the total population. As I have said, the true counterpart for a given group in one society may be a nominally very different group in another society, if we are to have more than formal comparability. We are usually interested in matching social *roles* or personality *types*. If extensive use of system-specific variables is contemplated, then the large national samples and rather broad interrogative instruments that superficially appear somewhat unsophisticated or costly may be the most sophisticated and economical approach possible in order to obtain attitudinally or behaviorally equivalent roles and types for analysis.

196

For example, one might want to ascertain empirically the relative social status of several groups in the cultures being examined. Then one could compare not nominally similar groups, but groups that had been empirically demonstrated to hold comparable relative status. Those with relatively high status in their respective societies would be compared, as would those with low status, and so on, regardless of their particular occupational or educational positions. Thus, more demonstrably equivalent and meaningful cross-cultural analytic categories would be employed and better social theory might be anticipated. But to perform this type of system-specific empirical matching, broad samples and broad instruments are generally required. In cultural areas where scant survey evidence has heretofore been collected, the broader approach may have more initial payoff. More economical purposive inquiries can be prepared afterwards. Of course, some purposive inquiries are planned in more than nominal terms. That of Inkeles, previously mentioned, is a good example. But these tend to be as expensive as larger and more representative surveys. Moreover, should the analysis yield serendipitous findings which prompt recombination and reanalysis of the data from an unanticipated perspective, that reorganization is likely to be much more difficult the more narrowly purposive the design. A more broadly representative design offers more flexibility in this respect, but frequently at the cost of depth in handling the original hypotheses. A sharply purposive design implies that one knows rather *precisely* what he is after, and there is nothing wrong in confessing that this is often not the case. A broadly representative design is more appropriate if the research has important exploratory aspects. Combinations of the two approaches will be discussed later.

It is readily apparent that the type of design chosen by the survey researcher must depend critically upon the nature of his research objectives. For instance, some topics will require essentially national coverage if not necessarily a national sample, whereas other topics will plainly demand focusing upon a much narrower group. In the first category one would place the investigation of the development of national integration, and the like. In the second category might be research on the impact of urban migration upon political attitudes requiring only a sample of such urban migrants and one or more appropriate control groups. The same holds for much of the research on various political elites.

A less frequently discussed point also refers to the type of analysis contemplated. Are the data going to be used for social simulation, and if so, of what kinds of processes? Our recent survey experiences in Turkey and Venezuela have illustrated some of the alterations in data collection that are required by simulation, at least for predictive policy purposes. One example will have to suffice. We can demonstrate to the reasonable satisfaction of the policy-maker the type of impact upon peasant attitudes that, say, radio exposure is likely to have in rural Turkey. We can tell him what kinds of effects an expansion of radio coverage will probably have. And our data can be used for—indeed, are critical to—a valuable simulation of the probable attitudinal consequences of various kinds of radio investment. But the simulator also needs to include a time perspective in his model, as does the policy-maker. The latter is not content to be told that five or ten years after the investment one could expect to find certain specified changes. He also needs to know the shape of the change curve—how much is to be expected the first year, how much the second, etc. Does change tend to occur rather quickly after initial exposure, is it evenly spread, or does the bulk of the change occur only after considerable gestation? Survey research can answer these questions, but only if the design specifically calls forth all the appropriate data. Among other things, simulation will probably tend to make the survey researcher appreciably more time conscious in his data collection. It may exert a major influence upon the shape of cross-cultural surveys to come, especially as we begin to simulate basic political processes.

Finally, in discussing these initial design considerations that are particularly weighty in cross-cultural survey research, one should emphasize the importance of precision regarding the level of generality of the variables employed. Of course this observation applies to all research, and I shall not dwell long upon it. But the added range of variation permitted by cross-cultural research makes the injunction particularly important.

Part of the training of a competent survey researcher is familiarization with the best-known schemes for social analysis. In such schemes, the crudest depiction of analytic levels is probably that distinguishing macroanalysis from microanalysis. In political science and sociology, however, these terms are very murky in their meanings. Microanalysis sometimes seems to refer to investigation at the level of the individual human being and macroanalysis to anything above that level. But other constructions have also been employed—for example, microanalysis referring to small group or local community research and macroanalysis to anything above that level.

A somewhat more refined scheme that has been extensively employed, with variations, is described by Mowrer, among others. Originally, it referred to levels of personality, but it has broader utility. Four main levels are distinguished: universal (panhuman), societal (society-wide), role (largely in terms of occupation and status), and idiosyncratic (unique-to-the-individual).[47] Each of these four levels can obviously be further analyzed. Thus, one can distinguish more or less extensive sub-systems in societies or in individuals. It is wise for the cross-cultural survey researcher to note the analytic level of each variable he is employing, largely to ensure that he has not overlooked vital intermediate linkages that are inherent in the conceptual model. Although he labors with too crude a macro-micro lexicon, Rokkan makes this point very well through a listing of eleven propositions about voting behavior largely derived from surveys, censuses, and voting records.

198

These propositions range in their combination of variables at different levels from the national or societal level alone ("Turnout rates for national electorates [are] higher in Western Europe than in the U.S.") to propositions involving national sub-systems and individual or role differences ("Educational differential[s] in political participation will be more marked the less partisan the politics of the locality").[48]

It is sad to see an otherwise carefully contrived survey collapse analytically because of insufficient attention to levels of analysis and to developing an overarching conceptual model of how the variables proposed for investigation presumably hang together. A crude example of the latter defect might be a study that focused on predicting traffic patterns from an excellent examination of tires and engines. Too many intervening variables are ignored—such as the sex of the driver—to make such an effort very fruitful despite adept handling of both the dependent and independent variables. The conceptual model adopted in the design stage was inadequate. The variables and hypotheses orienting the research must relate sufficiently closely to create a real chance of producing interesting findings; one must obtain enough of the data mosaic to be able to comprehend coherent patterns of inter-relationships.

Country Selection

The final aspect of initial design to be discussed is that of country selection. Four basic strategies of country selection are suggested to the cross-cultural survey researcher. The first and probably most often employed is that of *administrative convenience*. Countries are selected in terms of their proximity, the personal contacts of survey personnel, the fact that a scholar has accepted a Fulbright or other grant to teach abroad, expressed local interest in the research, or some other accident of increased access. Because difficulties of administration and access loom so large in cross-cultural survey research, this basis for country selection should not be maligned. The alternatives are frequently this form of cross-cultural survey or none at all. Thus, one can only symphathize with the lament of some of the researchers on the seven-nation OCSR Project: "The world being what it is and not as scientists would have it, these countries did not lend themselves to inclusion in clearly distinguishable cells of a neat design . . ."[49] Nevertheless, the methodological difficulties emanating from convenience designs are plain. To give but one example, such studies often attempt to comment on the relationship between systemic variables at the national or cultural level (such as democracy vs. authoritarianism) and other variables (such as the attitudes of minority groups). But there are so many uncontrolled intersystem differences (e.g., country size, wealth, climate) that it is virtually impossible to assign observed variations in other characteristics to any specific systemic trait. A

199

much more carefully controlled design would be necessary to pin down such systemic effects. On the other hand, convenience designs also tend to reduce the range of variation in lower level characteristics and thus blunt the other purpose of cross-cultural research.

A second basis for country selection is that of *maximizing similarity* along all dimensions except those of critical concern, after the fashion of a controlled experiment. The classic comparisons of China and Japan, France and Italy, the U.S. and Canada, and of the Scandinavian nations have been ventures in this direction. However, the problem is that even extremely similar countries still vary on more than those few dimensions which a very small number of research sites permits one to control. Still, there are occasions when surveys in three sub-Saharan West African countries or in three Central or South American nations might be rewarding, and the difficulty of securing variation in only those national and cultural systemic characteristics that are of interest while holding all other such systemic characteristics constant will plague all comparisons as long as national and cultural systems remain as diverse and few as they are. Given the scarcity of cross-cultural information, we cannot afford to be rigidly fastidious.

A third basis for country selection can be termed that of *maximizing diversity*. The aim in this case is to get countries that differ from each other as fundamentally and as extensively as possible. Then, if one finds across countries of such great diversity, regularities in the within-country relationships between variables, the generality of such relationships can be presumed. For instance, if perceived powerlessness is similarly associated with heightened political cynicism in nations as divergent as Thailand, India, Denmark, Uganda, Brazil, Yugoslavia, France, the United States, and Yemen, one might plausibly infer that such an association will prevail in most other nations. Coleman, for example, used this type of approach in investigating *The Adolescent Society* in ten Illinois high schools.[50] Its greatest drawback, however, is that if one does *not* find such cross-cultural regularities in within-cultural patterns, one may be hard-pressed to reap much cross-cultural value from the survey. It is an example of a fortiori reasoning and something of a gamble. Also, one can rigorously vary the diversity of only a few *combinations* of characteristics if he has access to but a small number of nations.[51]

The fourth basis for country selection might be called that of the *factorial matrix*. In this case one lists the systemic variables in which he is interested and the positions that can be taken along each such dimension. Thus, one might include the national party system (one, two, or more parties), the form of government (republic, monarchy, and so on), the style of elections (direct, indirect), and the like. These various dimensions would then be combined to yield a complete matrix of cells representing all possible combinations of designated characteristics. The survey researcher would attempt to classify nations into the cells of this matrix and select countries in

200

some unbiased way so as to represent each logical variant. A survey would be conducted in every country so designated.

Needless to say, the paramount objection to such an ambitious program is its cost in money, personnel, and effort. Moreover, the problems of access and administration would be colossal. The contemporary political climate in many nations today is not sufficiently open to permit worldwide survey research. And many of the cells would impair the estimation of the effects of different systemic factors. There may not be enough cases or enough variety among the nations of the contemporary world to permit us to unravel in this fashion the independent effects of some important systemic factors. Only with peace on earth may we begin to think seriously of a complete factorial design of this sort, although approximations to it may be forthcoming sooner than we think.

Whether he maximizes similarity along most dimensions or maximizes diversity, the cross-cultural survey researcher must decide which national or cultural characteristics are most decisive for his purposes. It is in this regard that aggregate analyses may be of signal use to the survey researcher. For example, if one wishes to maximize diversity he immediately encounters the question, "diversity along what dimensions?" One empirical tactic that might aid in specifying critical dimensions is factor analysis of the available aggregate data from a large selection of nations. If such data could be effectively reduced to a few potent and meaningful factors, then one might be well advised to make those factors the dimensions along which diversity was maximized. Aggregate analytic techniques can be conjoined with survey techniques to produce more effective cross-cultural designs.

As always, however, this research principle masks a number of practical obstacles. Although the diligent cross-cultural survey designer seeks aggregate data to aid in selecting social units and in checking and interpreting his survey findings, available aggregate data leave much to be desired. Frustrating differences in conceptualization, coding, and completion rates torment anyone making cross-national comparisons. The qualifications attached to the tables of international statistical compendia are often more intricate and more voluminous than the tables themselves. Many developing societies lack accurate data altogether, even on basic characteristics. Frequently, the aggregate data available for the design of cross-cultural survey research must be reduced to the lowest common denominator, and that is very low indeed. Moreover, pertinent political data, apart from electoral statistics, are among the most sensitive and consequently the most scarce. It is easy to perceive the potential significance of aggregate data for informed cross-cultural survey design, but it is often agonizingly difficult to acquire such data in appropriate form—usually more difficult than for a within-cultural survey.

A final comment about problems of country selection and access is

Frederick W. Frey

needed. Cross-cultural survey research is rather restricted in today's suspicious and contentious world. The cross-cultural survey researcher encounters ugly proprietary queries about "what these foreigners are doing asking questions of our people," and he faces accusations or insinuations of conducting an intelligence operation under the cover of research. Such problems will be discussed more fully in the next section. At present I simply want to note that survey operations, especially those involving American scholars, find it very difficult to gain access to certain types of countries. And the problem I wish to pose is whether our generalizations from the cross-cultural surveys we are able to undertake may not be in danger of bias as a result. Most of our survey work in the "third world," for example, omits an interesting set of inaccessible countries. We seem to focus disproportionately on India, Nigeria, the Philippines, Brazil, Mexico, Turkey, Israel, Japan, and a few other nations, and to generalize from them to the entire developing world. But these nations have in common that they are comparatively open polities and pluralistic societies, as developing nations go. To a considerable degree, that is why they have entertained survey research. We lack survey data from the more stringent regimes and the more controlled and xenophobic societies. Hence, we should be careful in our claims of "maximizing diversity" and in our generalizations about "developing societies." We may have a selection of such countries that is heavily biased by difficulties of access.

Sponsorship, Access, Organization, and Administration

An extensive multicultural survey demands the skills of a diplomat, financier, and administrator, as well as technical and theoretical expertise. Many of the most intractable problems of the cross-national survey lie outside the ordinary realms of data gathering and interpretation. Indeed, one recent practitioner has lamented that ". . . the sheer mass of . . . managerial problems connected with this type of research enterprise are so overwhelming that only the hardiest souls—or those ignorant of what lies ahead of them— venture to go beyond *proposing* such projects."[52] Matters of sponsorship and access, of organization and administration, bulk so large for cross-national survey research in this edgy world that they command special attention. They are significant not merely as preliminary hurdles which must be cleared before other more fundamental work can proceed, but as factors that pervade virtually all aspects of the survey effort.

Sponsorship and Access

Most cross-cultural survey research is formidably expensive. The real costs of questioning sizable samples of people in several nations ordinarily range from tens of thousands to millions of dollars. Formally reported costs,

202

though frequently lower and misleading, are not drastically different. Few academics can think of mounting such an effort with their own resources, even if they have a leading textbook in the introductory course. Research grants from their university's general funds are also inadequate to support all but the most modest and sacrificially cooperative projects. Hence, the cross-national survey is almost always a sponsored enterprise. Financial and other considerations demand that it be, although many troubles and a few vital blessings arise from such sponsorship.

The financial arrangements supporting cross-national survey projects vary from the fully cooperative enterprise in which the local collaborators in each country bear all the costs of their own activities to the completely subsidized project in which a single sponsor pays for the entire operation in all countries. Many intermediate arrangements are, of course, to be found. Frequently a basic grant is obtained from one source and is supplemented by contributions from other external sponsors and/or from the collaborating research institutions in the various countries. Examples of the financially fully cooperative framework are the Allport and Gillespie study of the basic value systems of students in nine nations, some of the cross-national investigations of political socialization, and the Multinational Comparative Time Budget Research Project coordinated by the "Vienna Center" of the International Social Science Council. Examples from the singly financed end of the spectrum are the Time International Survey, the Almond-Verba project reported in *The Civic Culture*, the Buchanan-Cantril study of national stereotypes which was sponsored by UNESCO, and the Michigan State–A.I.D. study of the diffusion of agricultural innovations in several developing societies.

Intermediate arrangements are probably most common, especially those in which substantial seed money from a single sponsor is supplemented by additional sources, including the research participants' own donation of services and equipment. Our survey of the Turkish peasantry, for instance, was supported by funds from the A.I.D. Mission in Ankara to cover the dollar costs of foreign travel and consultants; by funds from the Government of Turkey to cover interviewer expenses, printing, and so on, and by the Turkish Government's provision of the resources of its Test and Research Bureau of the Ministry of Education; by funds for data processing made available by M.I.T.; by a grant from A.I.D. in Washington covering some of the costs of data processing and analysis; and by analytic services furnished without charge by project consultants.

Our surveys in Venezuela were financed by the Ford Foundation and the Government of Venezuela. Moreover, both the Center for Development Studies (CENDES) of the Central University of Venezuela and the Center for International Studies at M.I.T. invested their own regular resources in the project.

203

Frederick W. Frey

One of the most interesting and administratively complex of current projects, directed by Philip Jacob, Henry Teune, and their associates at the University of Pennsylvania, examines the values of local level bureaucrats and political leaders. Funds from agencies of the U.S. Government, universities and research organizations in four countries, the Ford Foundation, and from governments in nations where the research was conducted were all combined to support a pioneering multi-national investigation.

Sponsorship and Control

As anyone who has faced the problem of funding a major cross-cultural survey will attest, putting together a workable financial package is far from easy, even if sponsors can be found who are willing to grant all or part of the funds. Perhaps the paramount problem immediately encountered is that of control. The adage, "Who pays the piper calls the tune," is found in one form or another in most cultures. The ready acceptance of this idea produces two kinds of difficulties: (1) problems in relations with contributing sponsors, and (2) problems in relations with various relevant publics. The sponsor may believe that he can and should control the researcher down to the most picayune detail, or the public may believe that the sponsor actually does so, regardless of the true character of the relationship.

The sponsor who invests resources in a project expects some kind of return. The critical question in every case is *what kind* of return—and what the sponsor does to ensure it. The so-called "return" can be as altruistic and noble as helping to generate a "contribution to knowledge" or "benefiting mankind" or as narrow and practical as "boosting sales," enhancing the sponsor's prestige, solving a particular policy problem, or exhausting allocations, which, if unspent, would lead to a legislative reduction in the sponsoring agency's budget for the following year.

The details of each sponsorship arrangement must be examined carefully. The cynical, who insist that the fact of sponsorship alone, or at least sponsorship by certain broad kinds of agencies (such as government departments, business firms, or foreign foundations), automatically implies a selling out—a loss of control—on the part of the researcher, and the gullible, who do not comprehend the kinds of pressures that certain sponsors can and do exert on researchers, are both unsophisticated interpreters of the sponsor-researcher relationship.

At the same time, whether these interpretations are justifiable or not, one has to live with them. For example, a widely held view that the true purpose of a cross-national survey is espionage or counter-revolution simply because the source of funds is the U.S. Defense Department, ignoring that Department's long history of supporting basic behavioral science research, may nevertheless be able to capsize an otherwise laudable research enterprise. The researcher must make his own calculation of the risks versus advantages of proceeding under various auspices—risks to himself, his colleagues, their institutions, future researchers, and even his discipline and his nation. At a minimum, most researchers would seem to endorse the principle that the sources of funds, the purposes of the research, and the freedom to share the data and publish the findings should be made fully explicit in survey research carried out by academic institutions. The professional associations of several major social science disciplines are currently attempting to suggest to their members general guidelines for sponsor-researcher relations. The purpose of the present discussion is merely to describe some of the more common problems directly encountered by the cross-cultural survey researcher in his relations with sponsors. A full treatment of the profound ethical, political, and educational issues in sponsor-researcher relations is beyond the scope of this paper.[53]

From many viewpoints, the single-sponsor arrangement probably engenders the fewest problems. The research is less likely to be pulled in several directions by competing sponsors. The researcher's relationship with the sponsor tends to be simpler and clearer. It is usually easier to maintain a designedly comparative focus under such an arrangement, since that goal will have been uppermost in the sponsor's mind when he agreed to support research in several nations. A high level of technical sophistication and control can more easily be ensured because the power of the purse is ordinarily vested in relatively few hands. When the theoretical and technical problems are severe and when great emphasis is placed upon maximizing comparability, the advantages of the single-sponsor arrangement are compelling.

Nevertheless, the disadvantages are also conspicuous. First, it is ordinarily difficult or impossible to find any single source of funds with resources bountiful enough to support a large cross-cultural survey project. Increasingly, it is only the U.S. Government, and its operating agencies at that, which can provide such funds. But when one accepts the advantages of the government's more ample financial support, he is frequently ipso facto incurring grave problems of access, an inappropriate image, and, in some cases, severe bureaucratic restrictions on freedom of operation.

Second, no matter what the source of funds, the potential power over the researcher of a single donor is often much greater than that of multiple sponsors. The sponsor who puts up such a large amount of money and knows that he is the sole support of the project may be especially prone to assume that the researcher is his minion or agent—that he has hired the researcher much as one would hire a gardener or fumigator. The academic researcher's outlook, on the other hand, tends to regard the relationship as more like that of grantor and grantee or, at worst, counselor and client. This is to say that within a very general agreement on overall goals, the researcher retains his

205

full autonomy and the sponsor is protected by the researcher's professionalism. These relations vary, of course, according to whether the project is conceived as being applied or basic research, but most cross-cultural survey research in political science has been and seems likely to continue to be more basic than applied. It is also important to recognize that "problems arise not so much because a scholar is told by his sponsors what to write but rather because a scholar may, wittingly or unwittingly, condition his manuscript to the assumed or divined values of his financial sponsors."[54]

A third disadvantage of the single-sponsor arrangement is that it may turn out to be what Alexander Szalai has called a "Safari type" of project.

> Some researcher has a big idea and is able to secure for its realization an important sum of money—possibly in the range of several hundred thousand dollars (which is, by the way, an order of financial magnitude for projects in which few social scientists beyond the borders of the United States can think— or even dream!). In possession of this big idea, and such an important sum of money, the researcher in question may now equip himself with a methodological armory of well prepared forms, questionnaires, sampling and interviewing instructions (all duly translated to the pertinent languages), and then set or jet himself on the way to the countries he had listed on his program. Having descended upon one of the countries he can assure himself of the help of the best native guides and sherpas, train them within a few weeks in the use of his superior equipment, and then with their help hunt down the needed data. The raw hides (filled-out questionnaires or perhaps punched cards) are then sent back, following precise instructions for packaging and addressing, to the home country of the researcher while he himself proceeds to the next country on his program. Having arrived home from his world tour, he can proceed—with the help of the best computers available, and with the assistance of his own home-based, highly qualified research team—to analyze all his findings: thus becoming much wiser and better informed about some aspects of social life in a number of faraway countries than those who have had to spend their lives there as natives.[55]

Szalai acknowledges that his description is an intentional caricature. But as such it suggests yet another problem which the well-endowed, singly-sponsored researcher may confront, viz., the sour grapes of his colleagues who are convinced that such funding would have been much more wisely entrusted to them, should they—God forbid—have been willing to prostitute themselves by taking it. He also notes the higher level of sophistication and standardization which such an arrangement permits and points out that the data "removed" by the "Safari" type of project are not really removed at all: "they have been in effect created within the framework of the project and for its purposes."[56] His argument about the great cost of the "Safari" type research obscures the fact that its real costs are no greater than under other arrangements, and probably are less. They are merely more visible because a single sponsor is bearing them. However, as I have already pointed out, extremely few agencies have the capacity to bear them alone.

But Szalai's main contention is the quite significant observation that, under the single-sponsor arrangement, control is often achieved at the price of a felt lack of equal or meaningful participation on the part of the national research teams. Their roles may well become merely those of hired hands carrying out someone else's orders in whose formulation they played no part. Resentment on the part of local scholars at such dependent casting is quite understandable and can jeopardize future research opportunities. The control permitted by the single-sponsor arrangement should be used to enable the original researcher to enlist a number of like-minded colleagues, not to purchase a small army of research mercenaries. Its utility is that it frees the researcher from having to make numerous ad hoc compromises to win this or that additional bit of funding—compromises that, in Szalai's words again, often reduce the level of effort to the "low common denominator of knowledge and experience possessed or attainable by all participants, some of whom are participants mainly by financial necessity.[57]

Obviously, to obtain funding and also to interest potential colleagues in joining a cross-national survey, some general proposal must have been formulated. Within that framework, however, cross-national research involving foreign collaborators increasingly requires the offer of full participation to those collaborators. This means bringing them into the design phase of the research effort as early as possible; otherwise, they are presented with the all too familiar request to help on what is really "someone else's project." It means participation in analyzing and reporting the findings as well as in collecting the data. Frequently, foreign researchers, upon completion of the data-gathering phase, have shaken hands with their local colleagues and abandoned them with the glib injunction, "Now you analyze your (punched) cards and we'll go off and analyze ours." But data processing facilities and analytic skills are perhaps the most conspicuous weaknesses in the survey capacity of many nations. Local colleagues are also quite sensitive about the fact that it is years before the research results of projects in which they have participated become available in the language of the country where the research was done, in addition to being available in English or some other foreign language. Sometimes this is because of publication problems in that country; but it is frequently a result of the "haves" only superficially considering the position of their less affluent colleagues. There is often a tacit cultural imperialism about cross-national research that can stifle continued collaboration. The singly-sponsored venture is particularly susceptible to its taint and special steps must be taken to counteract it.

Many problems of the multiple-sponsored project are patently the obverse of those just described. With different organizations and individuals trying to realize various goals through the project, the overall problems of sponsorship can become grotesque. Each sponsor sometimes seems to feel that his interests are being slighted in favor of others. Relations can be especially awkward when each of the several sponsors is primarily concerned with the work in a specific country. He may then be inclined to view the comparative focus of the research as a secondary goal and moan loudly when work in his country is delayed or must be adjusted to maintain comparability. A more satisfactory arrangement is for the multiple sponsors each to contribute to the general funding of the project rather than to its operations in a single country. However, it is difficult to negotiate such an arrangement, particularly since many of the contributions are in facilities and services rather than in cash. Hence, they must usually be specific to a given country.

Just as sponsors may differ in the relative importance they attach to the comparative versus the country-specific aspects of the research, so they may disagree over its other goals. One of the most common problems involves divergent emphases upon the production of research findings and upon institution-building. Such disgreement is likely to be most bothersome when the survey includes developing nations. The Western researcher is usually primarily concerned with accomplishing the theoretical and informational goals of the project. His colleagues in the developing world frequently seem to place secondary stress on the research goals and paramount emphasis on improving the research capacities of their nation and institution. They are interested in sending staff to Western universities for special training and in having foreign scholars teach courses at local institutes while the field research is in progress. They would like project funds to be used to make capital investments in their facilities. The developing governments and world-wide philanthropic foundations would often like to see the research largess and participation distributed very widely in the developing nation rather than concentrated in the local institutions that can perhaps do the best job. All these goals are laudable in isolation. But when one attempts to realize many of them in a single project, he quickly encounters incompatibilities. Discrepant emphasis on research findings and on institution-building seem to be a burr under the saddle of many cross-cultural projects. Some institution-building is a normal part of most such projects, but sponsors, especially governments and foundations, are wont to inflict unrealistic and burdensome institution-building goals on basic research enterprises.

The manner in which funds are to be dispersed is also frequently a point of contention in cross-national surveys. Local participants tend to press for outright grants to themselves, while the coordinators' predilection is toward keeping at least some residual control over local disbursements. No matter how this bargain is struck, trouble can be minimized if great care is taken to ensure that there is an explicit mutual understanding of each participant's contributions, obligations, rights, and privileges. Because personnel change and memories are faulty, it is a safeguard for all concerned to have these basic agreements with sponsors and with participants spelled out in writing, even though it may seem unnecessary or slightly invidious at the

208

time. Many a project has faltered because of oral agreements misunderstood or because of the transfer from the sponsoring or collaborating organizations of original negotiators with whom informal agreements had been made.

A related problem involves the management of time as well as money. Sponsors themselves have sponsors, so to speak. They must ordinarily account to other agencies or publics for their allocations of resources, and they are on a time leash as well as being on a resources leash. Many government agencies can commit funds for only one or two year periods, a span that is shorter than many cross-national projects. Most often such a legal commitment is extended informally by promises to do "all in our power" to secure continued funding in the next budget. But the researcher generally ends up going ahead on faith (which has not always been justified) or in trying to overcome these uncertainties through constructing an unwieldy series of financial contributions to cover the entire period of operation. Both procedures are unsatisfactory compromises from many perspectives.

Cross-cultural surveys are still pioneering ventures. Their methods are far from being fully established. Their planning involves many uncertainties, best guesses, and contingencies, with the result that they do not proceed with assembly-line predictability. Therein lies another source of sponsor-researcher tension. The researcher's best estimates of the time necessary to complete various phases and the project as a whole have large error factors. Researchers in their eagerness to sell the project to the sponsor tend to underplay these uncertainties, and the wishful thinking of the interested sponsor conspires to the same end. As the project drags on, sponsor-researcher relations often become increasingly strained. An initial awareness of the particularly uncertain character of cross-cultural survey research and the inevitable errors in time estimates would forestall many later conflicts.

Sponsorship, Access, and Image

There are many ways to categorize sponsor-researcher relationships, or the relationships between central coordinators and local participants. In very simple terms, these may be arrangements between one institution and another, an institution and an individual researcher, one individual and another, or some combination of these. Each of the cooperating institutions might be classed along a public-private dimension, and the private institutions might be further analyzed, for example, into commercial versus academic agencies. Commercial agencies generally offer the advantages of quicker mobilization, less encumbrance by governmental restrictions, greater willingness to carry out a prior design, and so on. They may present difficulties of more superficial work, an inflexible and primarily commercial approach, sour relations with the local academic community, and so on. Other organizational distinctions of this type can readily be drawn, but I shall not pursue them. The present point is simply that whatever type of sponsorship a project has—whatever the characteristics of local participants —these contribute to the image of the project held by various relevant publics. As William Hanna has suggested, ". . . the study and the investigator must occupy *some* roles in the host society."[58] The careful researcher recognizes this fact and tries to comprehend the image projected by his survey, what factors (including sponsorship) produce that image and what consequences it has for his work. He attempts to highlight those true aspects of his image or role that enhance the probabilities of success, and this effort extends to the consideration of sponsors and collaborators.

Hanna contends that the "ideal" study maximizes the satisfactions of participants and respondents, minimizes any inherent threat to them, and is conceived by the host population as legitimate. Obviously, the trick is to realize these very general goals in sensitive and divergent settings. For instance, in their own studies of influentials in small towns in Nigeria and Uganda, the Hannas tried to stress six aspects of their work: that it was nonpolitical, that it was one of several similar studies around the world, that it was informal, that it would be published, that it might be helpful to the hosts, and that it was "scientific-educational."[59] However, in shaping a desired image for his project, the researcher must be extremely careful to be accurate and not to create unwarranted expectations which later come home to roost. He merely strives to be sure he is putting his best foot forward—not in his mouth or on someone's back.

Political scientists appear to be relatively disadvantaged in dealing with several of these difficulties of access and image. The problems that interest the political scientist professionally are, alas, very similar to those that interest certain suspicious characters, such as the political observer from a foreign embassy, the journalist, and opposing political party leaders. Focal political topics such as the distribution of power in the country, recruitment to important political positions, satisfaction and dissatisfaction with governmental policies, propensities to violence, and orientations toward authority are likely to be disturbing and sensitive subjects. In a word, political science generally deals with the most delicate and threatening matters in the domain of social science. Thus, cross-cultural surveys in political science are particularly prone to problems of access and image.[60]

The frequency with which political scientists abroad find it advantageous to cast themselves as historians, sociologists, or anthropologists is testimony to the sensitive nature of their work and so, also, is the frequency with which they have to omit important variables because they are too threatening to permit inquiry. Unfortunately, in designedly cross-cultural research one is pushed toward the lowest common denominator, so that the conditions in the most sensitive nations tend to determine the level of the cross-cultural analysis. Perhaps fittingly, the political scientist has to develop special expertise in dealing with the political and diplomatic problems of cross-cultural survey research.

Very few studies have been done that focus explicitly on the effects of sponsorship on relevant publics. Nevertheless, a few basic facts seem clear even from the meager literature. The first is that the overtones of sponsorship are usually not uniform across populations. Reactions to a given sponsor ordinarily vary among subgroups of the host society. For instance, sponsorship by the local government may be quite palatable in some sectors of the society and quite unsavory in others. Foreign sponsorship may be of no interest to peasants and quite upsetting to university students. Or, the sponsorship arrangements may be of no concern at all to respondents, but they may subject the collaborating local scholars and institutions to such blistering fire from their colleagues, politicians, and the press that they have to abandon the venture. The researcher frequently must emphasize different facets of the project before different audiences and yet make sure that this does not lead to undue distortion. He must be aware that the problems emanating from sponsorship may differ from group to group and setting to setting. Sometimes they even change for a given group over the life of the survey, as the international relations of the countries change.

A second fact regarding sponsorship and image is that their overtones may not be uniform even for a single respondent or colleague. For example, sponsorship by the local government may induce respondents to greater candor in some responses and to reticence in others. Crespi, in his examination of sponsorship problems in Germany after World War II, found that surveys sponsored by the American Military Government and by German agencies did differ in their results in some respects. The American-sponsored data seemed to be more reliable in certain realms and the German-sponsored data more reliable in others, although it was often far from easy to ascertain which of two conflicting reports was more accurate or useful. Still more significant, perhaps, was the finding that though sponsorship differences were evident, only a small proportion of the questions was seemingly affected by sponsorship.[61] Two major types of bias appeared. One was a form of courtesy bias (respondents were reluctant to be critical in matters with which the sponsor was thought to be connected). The other was what I shall call an *interest bias* (respondents modified their answers in anticipation of obtaining some boon or redress of grievances through the sponsor, such as peasants, in reaction to local governmental sponsorship, stressing the importance of free fertilizer or understating their land ownership from fear of taxation).[62]

Hyman more generally observes that sponsorship bias tends to work through the respondent's idea that ". . . action in which he is concerned may follow from the research . . ."[63] Certain kinds of sponsors are more likely than others to evoke this idea, and bias may result whether the respondent's evaluation of the anticipated action is positive or negative. As Hyman suggests, sponsorship probably furnishes the respondents and others their main clue regarding the purpose of the research.[64] The researcher needs to know how that clue is perceived and how, if it is not satisfactory, other clues mitigating that of sponsorship can be provided. Nor can he rely on the ostensible significance of the sponsor, because respondents sometimes regard a formal sponsor, rightly or wrongly, as a cover for another agency. Thus, a little known foundation may be seen as a CIA front merely because it and its interests are little known. A commercial survey organization may be thought to be a minion of USIA or a local political party simply because its own role is not well established in the society. Respondents grope for some explanation of the sponsor's character and motivation which they can accept as plausible, and the survey researcher must adjust to this fact. His personal knowledge of the purity and utility of his venture and even his colleagues' affirmation of this verdict may be of scant import to the critical actors at the field research site.

It is possible to suggest a crude ranking of various types of sponsors according to the degree of alarm which their sponsorship would probably provoke in most nations, although such a listing is indubitably ephemeral and partially wrong or inappropriate in many nations. Nevertheless, impressionistic evidence indicates that in most countries local sponsors are less suspect than extralocal, and among the latter, international sponsors seem less suspect than a single foreign sponsor. Minor foreign powers are less potentially sinister than major powers.[65] Similarly, academic institutions and philanthropic foundations appear less suspect than commercial and formal governmental organizations. Nonprofit-making agencies seem less threatening than profit-making, and pure research agencies less threatening than action agencies. Of course, these are merely general and summary observations that are affected by other factors in every case. A gross and intuitive ranking of types of sponsors in terms of their suspiciousness to respondents might turn out as follows, in ascending order: indigenous universities and foundations, the indigenous government (national and then local), indigenous commercial polling agencies, international philanthropic foundations, international governmental organizations (e.g., UNESCO, WHO), foreign universities and foundations (i.e., of a single foreign country), and foreign governmental agencies (with those agencies bearing responsibility for foreign relations most suspect—i.e., the foreign ministry, propaganda ministry, defense ministry, and intelligence agency). Such a listing is intended to serve only a heuristic purpose, to alert the researcher to the kinds of considerations that enter into the evaluation of a potential sponsor's influence on the project's image.

A few additional admonitions are possible. The researcher must, of course, check carefully into the actual role of any potential sponsor or collaborator and not proceed solely in terms of gross considerations like those just presented. For example, some indigenous institutions that seem to be in an excellent position actually are poor risks because they have "too many foreign contacts." So many outside researchers have involved them in their projects that the institution's local base of support has eroded, either through jealousy or through lack of communication. Though formally well located, the institution has become known as a tool of the foreigner and any cross-cultural project working with it incurs disadvantages as a result.

Hitching a research project to an appropriate action program may facilitate access under sensitive conditions. Population (birth) control, community development, manpower allocation, educational reforms, informational campaigns, and the like can sometimes furnish a marvelously cooperative climate for basic research. The problem in this case, however, is to avoid being dominated by the action program's objectives and to skirt the dangers of bias emanating from association with the action program. One can frequently engage in very informative survey research efforts in conjunction with indigenous political parties. Such a tactic, though, carries with it difficulties of interesting the party in cross-cultural comparisons (indeed, difficulties of interesting the party in any publication of the results at all!) and problems arising from the researcher's identification with one political faction in the mind of other segments of the public. Nevertheless, sometimes this is the only way to obtain a more precise view of political processes in sensitive settings.

One should also be aware of the problem of unintended sponsors. In the field operation of a large survey one may inadvertently pick up self-appointed sponsors. We have had difficulty in some of our surveys in the developing world in persuading the gendarmes not to escort our interviewers into villages in order to "protect them from the villagers." Local bureaucrats sometimes like to act as if the survey were being performed at their behest. They try to use it as another example of how "in" they are with "the authorities." Even private individuals have sometimes pretended a special connection with the survey. Needless to say, some of these unofficial sponsors can have a pernicious influence so that the researcher must fend them off as best he can.

Local authorities usually have to be notified in advance that the survey will operate in their area, lest the interviewers be incarcerated as spies or vagrants. But one must be alert to prevent the local authorities from tacitly or explicitly adding themselves to the survey's sponsors. In some places the local authorities are so influential that respondents cannot be interviewed at all without the public concurrence of these authorities. In such cases the project unavoidably picks up another sponsor and must make the best of things, taking special pains to discover the significance of this added factor.

I have concentrated on the *problems* of sponsorship for the cross-cultural survey's access and image. Many of these problems, however, are but the negative side of situations that can have positive aspects. For example, although some forms of sponsorship may create a bad image for the project and make access difficult, other sponsors may create a favorable image that facilitates access. Some local authorities may be pestiferous but others may help the survey effort in many important ways. The focus on problems of sponsorship is merely a vehicle for discussing salient dimensions of the sponsor-researcher relationship.

Organization and Administration

If workable relations with sponsors can be negotiated, the cross-cultural researcher then confronts the problem of locating or creating an appropriate agency for accomplishing the research. Somehow, office space must be found, project directors, interviewers, coders, field supervisors, janitors, key punchers, computer programmers, consultants, and the like must be recruited; necessary clearances and permissions obtained; and so on through a formidable gamut of organizational and administrative tasks. Even the most important and technically sophisticated plan can abort if careful thought is not given to securing an effective research organization in each nation studied and at the central research coordinating site.

In almost every case, some forms of cooperation will be established with a local institution in each country, even if that institution has no survey experience and the survey apparatus has to be created virtually from scratch. Survey competence can often be imported, but not a "local habitation and a name."

Today, one can find in most parts of the world research organizations that specialize in survey techniques. Even a cursory glance through the *International Social Science Journal* for the past decade will impress one with the proliferation of such research institutions. This growth has taken place among public and commercial facilities alike, in Europe, Asia, Africa, and Latin America, and in developed and underdeveloped nations. For example, by 1964 in Western Europe (France, Italy, West Germany, and the United Kingdom), it is estimated that around four to five million interviews were being conducted every year by commercial agencies alone.[66] Granting unevenness in the quality of some of this work, it is nonetheless a gross representation of the considerable fund of survey experience and sophistication of certain agencies, and it also signifies an increasing public appreciation and acceptance of this type of research. Although the intensity of operation in most developing societies is below the European level, the rates of expansion and acceptance are probably no less, perhaps more. The cross-cultural researcher can usually discover some local organizations that profess interest and competence in survey investigations. In fact, he must frequently select from several candidates.

Four major considerations stand out in choosing local agencies with which to cooperate: their image, motivation, competence, and position. Image considerations have already been discussed. The researcher must remember that these apply to his local collaborators as well as to the general sponsors of the research. When he selects local associates he is donning their image in the local community.

Of the three remaining major considerations, I should rank motivation highest in importance. The local participants, as individuals and as institutions, must have goals that are similar or complementary to those of the research originators. The opportunities for friction in a large cross-cultural survey are enormous. Strong dedication by local agencies to the research aims of the project can overcome a multitude of obstacles; without that commitment even small problems can tumble the entire operation.

One sometimes overlooked but nonetheless vital component of motivation is trust in the academic integrity of one's associates. If I may alter a phrase from the law of equity, "he who seeks to do research must come with clean hands." The research originator must be scrupulously honest with his collaborators about his objectives and the nature of the research. They, in turn, bear the same obligation. Often, however, the international cooperation that is essential for cross-cultural research comes hard in this tense world. The Rudolphs furnish a graphic example of some of the difficulties from their work in India:

> Because of the value-laden aspect of much of Indian social science, there is a tendency to look for everybody's hidden premises. In the present not always cordial climate of Indo-American relations, what more promising premise offers itself than that some nefarious Western purpose is at work? The Indian experience with English social scientists has given their suspicions some historical foundation. While most Englishmen wrote scholarly and dispassionate studies of Indian castes and religions, some used analyses of social divisions in India primarily to justify the continuation of British rule. The suspicion remains that the foreign scholar may "want to understand us the better to manipulate us."[67]

The Rudolphs also note the strongly normative or ideological overtones of social science research in India.[68]

These same comments, *mutatis mutandis*, well describe the research situation in Turkey and many other nations. Suspicion of the good faith of one's colleagues is fundamentally corrosive of effective research cooperation. It takes care and candor on the part of the research originator and objectivity on the part of the local participants if the requisite level of trust is to be maintained. Ideological rigidities and indiscriminate xenophobic charges of hidden objectives pollute the research atmosphere just as badly as the research imperialism discussed earlier.

Next in major importance is the position of the local agency in its own society. With the best will in the world, some organizations are simply not well enough located in their own political structure to accomplish the research objectives. Cross-national research is ordinarily an extremely visible and somewhat controversial enterprise. Publicity and a certain amount of criticism are unavoidable. The local institutions engaged in the research must be powerful enough to stand the glare and the heat. Moreover, they must be able to muster sufficient influence to work their way through governmental and private roadblocks of various sorts. Their location in the power structures of their own society is critical.

Finally, the research competence of the local agency is obviously of major importance. Here, however, various adjustments are possible because technical expertise is, to an appreciable extent, importable, and because training of local participants can occur during the research activity. The ineluctable base must be intelligence and flexibility on the part of all participants. If this is present, it is often truly amazing and gratifying how quickly inexperienced local colleagues can develop considerable survey sophistication.

Two other aspects of the selection of local collaborators must be mentioned. They take the form of caveats. First, the research originators should be aware that picking one agency eliminates others. The selection process itself is invidious and may create problems for the project. One way around some of these difficulties, as well as a vehicle for obtaining additional talent not housed in the formally cooperating institution, is the use of advisory committees or the temporary seconding of personnel from one agency to another. I shall mention these devices again later.

The second caveat is to beware of overcommitment and faulty costing procedures on the part of some local agencies. Survey research is relatively new in many parts of the world. The infant survey organizations that have sprung up around the globe did not start with much experience in costing extensive survey operations. In some cases they have underestimated the costs of earlier work so that they are now in the position of having to use each new project to bail out the last, or to use the latest project to employ staff to complete previous commitments. The unwary cross-cultural surveyor can enter a jungle of inexplicable delays and expenses if he does not look into such possibilities.

Organizational Structure

As I have said, the realization of any cross-cultural survey requires a specific organization. This organization may, in some cases, be "purchased" by the researcher-client, as when he employs a commercial firm and relies completely on its existing structure. At the opposite extreme, an ad hoc organization may be created especially for the particular project, lasting no longer than it lasts. Other arrangements are also possible, such as grafting additional elements onto a commercial firm's organization or adapting an educational testing facility for survey operations. A single project's organizational forms can also vary from country to country. Commercial firms may be used in some of the nations studied, augmented governmental facilities in others, and newly created organizations in the remainder. In any case, the survey researcher must be concerned to find an appropriate organizational vehicle for his project.

Obviously, the structure of the survey organization will vary with the nature of the research objectives. For discussion we shall again take as our model a large, complex, multinational project since most of the important organizational features will be displayed therein. A chart depicting such a project's structure is presented in Figure 6-1. The chart is merely a hypothetical illustration of one possible organizational structure for a complex, five nation survey. I shall not discuss it in detail, but shall use it to suggest a few basic considerations.

Most multinational projects have a central headquarters—some resident organization that is the coordinating center for the project—plus a number of field teams, normally at least one in each nation studied. It may occasionally appear that there is no central headquarters, but closer inspection will ordinarily indicate that one of the country teams is actually doubling as the central organization. Although interteam contacts are encouraged in most cross-cultural projects, the usual communication pattern is the "star" or "wheel"—that is, messages tend to flow to and from the country teams via the central organization. The social scientist who is familiar with the research on communication patterns in task-oriented small groups will have some ready insights into why this should be the common pattern and what problems may arise. The "wheel" is one of the easiest structures to establish and probably the most efficient for many tasks in that it yields the quickest sharing of information for the least number of messages. It is especially effective for problems that demand coordination and synthesis of information. Since communication is probably the biggest organizational problem for cross-national research, it is not surprising that such research should tend toward the "wheel" form of organization, particularly in the early stages of its development. On the other hand, the same small group research indicates that one can expect morale problems among the more peripheral actors in the "wheel" structure. If they are relegated to the role of merely sending information into the central organization and receiving orders from that center, a justifiable disillusionment with their participation may result. Partly for this reason, most large cross-cultural surveys, especially those emphasizing voluntary cooperation, alleviate the centralization of formal communication by having a number of international conferences which bring all participants together in face-to-face interaction of a more satisfying, equal, and "free-wheeling" sort.[69]

The amount and relative formality of communication in a multi-

217

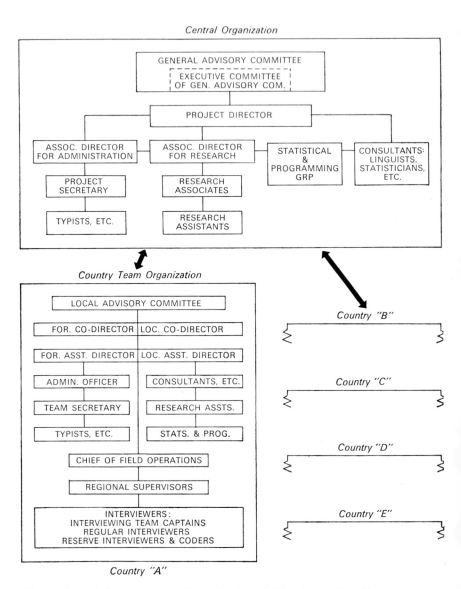

Figure 6-1. A Hypothetical Organizational Plan for a Five Nation Survey

national study go up almost exponentially with each additional nation. Because the collaborators are from divergent cultures, "every point has to be gone over and argued in detail since so very little is taken for granted or understood by implication."[70] Because the participants are so far apart and communication is relatively expensive, slow, and uncertain, a higher proportion of the understandings and instructions must be written, and what is normally written, such as coding instructions, must be especially elaborate. In the Multinational Comparative Time Budget Project, for example, over one hundred pages of instructions were necessary to define the main research procedures and coding scheme for all participants. The International Studies of Values in Politics Project has produced more than one hundred research and administrative documents whose mere catalogue runs into many pages.

A complicated cross-national study might typically demand more than half a dozen full international conferences at a rate of about two per year, dozens of meetings of all the main actors of a given country team, and hundreds of meetings of smaller groups. Organizing such contacts, recording their proceedings, and informing the entire research organization of what transpired is a truly difficult and complicated assignment. The person who is primarily responsible for this task occupies one of the most important positions in any cross-cultural survey project. Moreover, despite constant attention and high skill, communication snags still occur. But delays will be minimized and tempers remain tranquil if all parties keep the communication problem in the forefront of their minds. It is the chief organizational nemesis of cross-cultural research.

The Country Team Organization sketched in Figure 6-1 illustrates another basic organizational problem of cross-cultural research. There are usually strong tendencies toward bifurcation within each national team. Unless one finds a very high level of local competence, the local organization will have to include both domestic and foreign researchers—"insiders" and "outsiders," as Roy and Fliegel have labelled them.[71] The possibilities for tension between these two groups are manifold. Indeed, the very presence of the foreigner is a tacit implication of lower competence to local researchers. The ideal situation, as I have indicated, exists when local research expertise is such that no outside assistance is necessary. Unfortunately, in most developing societies and even in many developed societies, this is rarely the case. Local research capabilities must be supplemented by foreign technical assistance. In this situation, the researchers must guard against the potential local-foreign cleavage that can so easily appear. Moreover, the local-foreign split ordinarily parallels the division between the domestic goals of the project and its comparative and methodological objectives. Local researchers must provide judgments as to what is appropriate in the local setting, while foreign advisors generally furnish methodological and theoretical advice as well as an emphasis on cross-cultural comparability. These divergent tech-

219

nical orientations often provoke dissension among nationally homogeneous research teams engaged in within-nation studies. When they are exacerbated by international and intercultural differences, they can become divisive indeed.

Sometimes in cross-cultural survey research one runs afoul of awkward phasing problems in establishing the survey organization. Considerations of design, locale, and personnel are so interdependent that getting started can be difficult. For example, the design has implications for the selection of research sites and personnel. Problems of access feed back upon design, while the availability of personnel impinges upon both other considerations. Until one decides on the countries to be studied, he cannot effectively scout for high level personnel. But these high level personnel presumably will want something to say about various research sites. Although it sounds simple, getting a proper sequence of people, places, and plans often engenders many time-consuming and vexatious problems.

As I have noted, the quality of the research can be improved and the difficulties of access frequently minimized through the judicious use of various advisory committees, both for the Central Organization and for the Country Teams, as depicted in Figure 6-1. These committees ordinarily include well known researchers whose general monitoring of the project's progress is helpful plus assorted notables whose endorsement of the project facilitates access and whose contacts can help disseminate its findings. As noted, in many countries, if the researcher selects one local organization as partner, he ipso facto alienates others. The advisory committee affords a useful opportunity for bringing some of the potentially alienated people into a form of concrete involvement with the project. So long as one avoids creating "too many cooks," it is an extremely helpful organizational means of handling several difficulties.

The survey researcher contemplating cross-cultural work, particularly if developing societies are involved, can plan on becoming more or less ensnared in a Sargasso Sea of administrative complications. He must estimate the time needed to obtain the necessary clearances for his project as a whole, the difficulties of securing permissions for various individuals to participate, great turmoil over currency exchanges and customs disputes, barriers to travel in parts of many countries, and so on. An especially delicate problem is the matter of pay scales: The cross-cultural research project does not want to shatter the existing salary and fee scales of the foreign community. Flashing research funds around merely stimulates jealousy, encourages an improper basis for participation in the project, and reinforces a belief in the pecuniary naiveté of foreigners. On the other hand, one frequently desires a quality of work that exceeds prevailing standards. For instance, it may be imperative to attract relatively well educated people to be interviewers, rather than relying on the collection of factotums and process servers who may currently constitute the corps of so-called professional interviewers. To draw a better group into research activity one may have to pay more than established rates. Indeed, as an enterprise with a foreign connection, the project may be expected to pay at a somewhat higher scale than local organizations and may incur ill will if it doesn't. The trick is to find the middle line between rate-busting and ineffectiveness.

Finally, because it is often so large and so conspicuous, the cross-cultural survey project is forced to pay special attention to the local press. It is unlikely to escape the notice of local journalists, and, indeed, unlikely to escape virulent attacks from one source or another. Selection of a collaborating local agency which can withstand this pressure is one way of dealing with the problem, and coopting support through advisory committees and second-ing of personnel is another. A third is to pay very careful attention to relations with the local press. Generally, it is wise to face the fact that, however modest and academic one's aims, publicity will probably be unavoidable. In that event, the researcher is usually well advised to take the initiative himself rather than to be buffeted by events. He should examine his project from the perspective of its significance to the local community, trying to decide what will be "news" and what will not. Then, when he feels that some phase of the operation will receive publicity, he may decide to call attention to it himself rather than to wait for a possibly less informed initial revelation of project activity by others. Releasing full information oneself about the project often forestalls biased disclosure by another source for whom the project may be only a pawn in some larger and frequently rather desperate political struggle.

There sometimes seems to be widespread myopia in cross-cultural research organizations, especially in those newly formed from a mixture of local and foreign talent. Consciously or unconsciously, the various partici-pants generally push their own views and interests. Local scholars see research imperialism, callousness toward local sensitivities, misleading promises, dangers of espionage, the need for institution-building, unfair distributions of resources, "unequal institutional yoking," and so on. Foreign participants suffer no less from perceived xenophobia and paranoia, excess concern with local self-interest at the expense of broader research goals, hypersensitivity, internal power struggles, lack of research competence, ideological biases which distort research, and so on. It has long seemed to me that some of these self-centered perspectives might be altered if there were more opportunity to switch roles. In a cross-cultural project it is most useful to place a few of the participants from each nation in the role of a foreign scholar on the country team in another nation. Thus located, they frequently tend to get better perspective on the kinds of problems confronting the central organization of the project or the foreign scholars in any participating country. Similarly, it would be very healthy if scholars from other nations than the United

221

States and the countries of Western Europe were to have the experience of organizing cross-cultural research—of being the research originators and the "outsiders." In my opinion, it would be an excellent idea for the United Nations or even the United States alone to experiment with funding cross-cultural research that would be conceived and directed by scholars from those nations which are usually the subjects of research and only very rarely its source. Moreover, some of this research should involve the highly developed nations as the objects of foreign scrutiny and place Western scholars in the position of the insider. This proposal is in keeping with a consideration that is generally overlooked in evaluating research efforts—namely, that one of the principal payoffs of research is *the education of the researchers*. Some research that appears low in theoretic significance or policy implications is actually highly rewarding, because it contributes markedly to the development of the researchers themselves, furnishing them with urgently needed experience in the use of various research techniques, illustrating to them mistakes that can be corrected in future work, and providing contacts that lead to altered forms of future collaboration. In this sense we are only now gradually feeling our way into the establishment of more satisfactory organizational instruments for cross-cultural work.

Interviewers: Recruitment, Training, and Supervision

It seems necessary to say a few words about interviewers—the frontline troops of the survey organization. Three major issues arise—interviewer recruitment, interviewer training, and interviewer supervision. In most fundamental respects, these are no different in a cross-cultural project from a within-cultural project, but some types of difficulties are compounded.

If the research is conducted by subcontracting with an established survey organization, then that organization's field staff will be used, although it may have to be supplemented for an extremely large operation. In this case, the researcher's initial task is to evaluate the effectiveness of the field staff. A thorough probing of its capabilities is essential and will not be resisted by any first rate organization. The academic researcher must be particularly concerned over the ability of the subcontractor's staff to do the quality and kind of work the researcher requires. Many commercial organizations are quite efficient at market surveys and rather straightforward kinds of applied research, but frequently their staffs have very little experience at more theoretical work. Their interviewers, for example, may feel ill at ease in handling open questions demanding selective probing. To cover up their lack of experience with this kind of interviewing they may report all manner of difficulties and lay the blame on the instrument or on the design of the project. The researcher has to be able to distinguish these gripes, which cloak lack of competence, from real problems with the interview schedule or

the study design. There is also the danger that interviewers who have concentrated heavily on straight factual interviewing using closed items may
regard more open attitudinal items and selective probing as vague and
mushy academic research which does not really demand the high standards
set by their commercial research. They then tend to slack off and treat the
work as something of a lark. Just because one is employing "professional
interviewers" from a reputable survey organization does not necessarily
mean that there will be no problems with the field staff. The academic
researcher still should peer regularly and deeply into the field operation.

When the researcher must construct a survey organization on very
meager foundations, the creation of an effective field staff becomes a most
salient problem. First, he must recruit and select the group of interviewers.
The size and the diversity of the candidate pools in many countries are very
limited compared with the United States or Western Europe. Interviewing
involves interacting with many different kinds of people, all normally
strangers. The status structures of numerous societies are such that certain
classes, castes, or ethnic groups simply cannot obtain access to most other
strata and are thus barred from being interviewers except among their own
group. Again, because interviewing demands much public contact, it is
regarded in some societies as a morally and socially dubious occupation, thus
restricting the kinds of candidates available. Many societies are so rigidly
stratified into diverse sectors, whose members can be interviewed only by one
of their own stripe, that assembling a corps of interviewers for a broad sample
of the population becomes an extremely complicated task. One may, for
instance, have to have female respondents interviewed only by females;
peasant respondents may require interviewers who are from that stratum and
elite respondents may have to be questioned by their own kind; tribal
groupings may require interviewers from the same tribe; language groups
obviously demand interviewers fluent in the given language; regional conditions may be sufficiently different so as to require home-grown interviewers,
and so on. Such considerations make the job of assembling a large group of
prospective interviewers a most difficult operation.[72]

Armstrong divides the several main sources of interviewers in India into
four categories: (1) middle class and middle aged married women; (2) under-
employed white collar workers—middle class—ages 30 to 45; (3) under-
employed young men and women currently occupied as field investigators or
technical staff in research agencies, private and governmental; and (4) un-
employed pregraduates, graduates, and ex-graduates in the social sciences.[73]
His judgment is that the first group of married, middle class women is
"energetic and uncomplaining," neutral, somewhat rigid and authoritarian,
not quick to learn but diligent when something is once learned, undaunted
by high-prestige or low-prestige respondents, confident when trained, but
difficult to recruit. The second group has many of the same virtues but also

223

displays a tendency to inject orientations from their occupational positions into the interview. For many, it is just a second job performed perfunctorily. The third group is perhaps somewhat unique to India, depending on the sharing of interviewers common among Indian public opinion agencies. These are mainly young men who have completed M.A. degrees in economics at some university. Their background is usually in census-type enumerations, and their motivation is also likely to be weak because interviewing is again a secondary or temporary occupation for them. The fourth group, the students, is relatively easy to recruit but has little prior experience, includes few females, is highly moralistic and ego-involved rather than neutral, is strongly policy oriented, ideological and emotional, and is susceptible to status difficulties in dealing with many kinds of respondents, especially those lower in the social pecking order.[74]

My own conviction from work in Turkey, Venezuela, Chile, and the United States is that this evaluation of Indian students as interviewers has wide application. In addition to the problems already mentioned, students often seem to feel superior to the research effort and predisposed to regard it as a new form of holiday. As a result, they are very reluctant to do the hard work that is required, have to be watched for honesty, and have few qualms about shirking their obligations. Of course, these unfortunate attitudes are exhibited by only a rather small proportion of any group of interviewers, but that proportion is likely to be larger among students recruited as interviewers than among many other groups, and such attitudes can be quite contagious.

Especially in developing societies, the research organization needs to put as much effort into recruiting interviewers as it puts into training them. All too often the interviewer pool consists of those persons most readily available in the nation's capital or other cities—sociology students, social workers, housewives, and the like—people who respond to a newspaper advertisement or can be easily reached through helpful organizations. Sending such people into the hinterland to interview a peasantry that is highly suspicious of the urban elite is a great risk. To get around this kind of difficulty in our Turkish peasant survey, for example, we sent out members of the central staff to various distant parts of the country to search for appropriate interviewer candidates. School superintendents, county prefects, agricultural extension agents, village head men and teachers, local university staff, and other provincial figures were queried regarding prospective interviewers. These prospects were then interviewed and dossiers assembled on several hundred such candidates, about one hundred of whom were actually invited to the interviewer training course run in the capital. This effort seemed to be well reflected by the high quality of the final group of eighty interviewers. The best training program in the world cannot transcend the abilities and attitudes found in the general pool of interviewer candidates. Care in recruitment is no less vital than care in training, although it is much more rare.[75]

224

Unfortunately, there is no survey instrument or test that is very effective in predicting who will be a good or a bad interviewer. Various criteria for interviewer selection have been offered by different writers, and almost all such criteria must be employed in highly impressionistic fashion.

Discussions by American survey firms of a good interviewer's qualifications usually list a number of personal characteristics.[76]

1. Genuine liking for people of all types.
2. Honesty.
3. Above average intelligence, coupled with conscientiousness.
4. Ability to maintain a neutral attitude while interviewing.
5. Ability to distinguish between direct and evasive answers in open questions.
6. Adaptability.
7. A rapid writer of legible script.
8. Willingness to follow instructions to the letter.
9. Ability to be unhurried but in control of the pace of the interview.

Before hiring an interviewer, supervisors are sometimes instructed to ask themselves such questions as: Does she have a sense of humor? Would you like to know her better? Would she fit in with the other interviewers you have met? Do you think the reason she gives for wanting the job is sound? Is she the kind of person you would let in your house? Does she seem dependable in her other relationships as she describes them to you? Do you think she has a clear idea of the way she can organize her time to do an adequate job for us?[77]

Expressed recruitment criteria in developing societies range from Jorge Mendez' laconic but shrewd statement that "we choose them primarily not for their technical ability, but for honesty," to Michel Hoffman's experienced explanation that

> In selecting candidates [for interviewing in West Africa], we take account of the following factors: (a) the level of education, attaching greater importance to the knowledge of English or French than to the possession of diplomas; (b) a knowledge of the main vernacular languages used in the region; (c) professional experience, as the training period can be shortened in the case of investigators who have already taken part in surveys; (d) the results of an examination to test the level of understanding of a questionnaire in a limited period of time.[78]

To all these motivational and skill criteria one must add sheer availability (time off from other pursuits) and the physical toughness to stand up to the real rigors of work that is frequently quite literally "in the field." Small wonder that good interviewers or even interviewer candidates are hard to find.

225

Since the quality of performance demanded is relatively high and the fund of survey experience usually rather low, interviewer training is especially important in cross-national research. A fine group of interviewers can be realized from the pool of promising candidates only if they are properly trained and supervised. Interviewer training procedures among public opinion sampling organizations in the United States vary somewhat and provide only a limited guide for the academic cross-cultural research operation. For example, in the past, several polling agencies recruited and trained interviewers mainly by mail, whereas others required that the regional field supervisor play some direct role in the candidate's training. Much reliance was placed upon printed interviewing manuals, tests, and careful discussion by letter of the interviewer's completed schedules.[79] Because new interviewers were recruited sporadically into an on-going organization, to remain with that organization for a number of different studies, such a rather loose, individual, remote, and decentralized training procedure may have been adequate. The general organizational environment probably contributed significantly to the interviewer's training. But in cross-cultural surveys, particularly in developing societies, and when an entirely new pool of interviewers has to be assembled, more explicit, controlled, and intensive training procedures seem necessary. The importance of interviewer training looms even larger when we consider the aforementioned limitations on interviewer recruitment in many societies and the probable diversity of the interviewer pool required by the need to match interviewers and respondents, often within very narrow status and linguistic groupings. The cross-cultural survey researcher will ordinarily be training a very heterogeneous collection of people. This makes the training more difficult and requires extra time and staff.

Perhaps the best way of illustrating the additional demands which cross-cultural survey research can place upon interviewer training is to outline the kind of training program that might be used in a developing society for completely inexperienced candidates. We have, for example, employed in Turkey and Venezuela programs very similar to this sketchy description. Such a training program ordinarily lasts two or three weeks, about six hours per day. The candidates are paid for their time and instructed to take complete notes on all that transpires. They are warned in advance that their notes will be collected and evaluated near the end of the program. Our general experience is that a conspicuously bad set of notes predicts subsequently bad interviewer performance rather reliably, although a good set of notes does not guarantee good field performance. In any event, the main sessions (morning or afternoon meetings) of this type of training program would be scheduled approximately as follows:

1. Introductory session. The prime purpose of this meeting is to impress upon the interviewers the importance of the project and their role in it. An

attempt is made to have persons who are the most prestigious available and who are also adequate speakers give brief talks to the group of candidates. The main staff of the project is also introduced.

2. General description of the project. The project directors explain the major objectives of the project and the basic plans for realizing those objectives. An overview of the forthcoming research operations and of the interviewer training program is provided.

3. Principles of interviewing. At least two sessions are devoted to lectures and discussion on the general principles of interviewing—the nature of the interview, the role of the interviewer, prominent kinds of bias and inaccuracy, and so on.

4. Instruction concerning any sampling activities that the interviewers may have to perform.

5. Detailed examination of the research instruments. Item by item coverage is made of the interview schedules to be used by the interviewers. Expected interviewer performance, probable difficulties, and their remedies are discussed for every question. This procedure may take as long as a full week with complex instruments and inexperienced interviewers.

6. Demonstration interviews. Staff members first interview specially selected respondents or other staff members playing the respondent role in order to provide the trainees with a visible model of how they should proceed. These model interviews are discussed in some detail. Thereafter, further demonstration interviews from previously prepared tape recordings are played to the candidates, stopped to illustrate key points, and discussed. Also, we now have available an interviewer training film, which is shown at this juncture.

7. Practice interviews of each other. The candidates are divided into subgroups of no more than about ten persons each. Each subgroup is led by one of the staff members. The members of each subgroup take turns interviewing one another and critiquing those interviews. Several sessions are devoted to this.

8. Practice interviews of sympathetic outsiders. Each interviewer candidate interviews a sympathetic outsider of his own predesignated choice. This is usually a member of his family or a close friend, but it cannot be anyone associated with the project.

9. Practice interviews with readily accessible strangers. Each candidate interviews two people previously unknown to him but people who are readily available—persons randomly selected on the street or in dwelling units in the city where the training takes place.

10. First full scale field test. This is deliberately made easier in several respects than the anticipated daily work the interviewer will encounter in the field, but conditions otherwise approximate expected field conditions. For example, the candidates might be taken to villages which are reasonably

close to the city and required to interview only half of a regular day's assignment. In this as in all other field test interviews it is imperative to allow enough time and muster enough staff so that each interviewer's work can be scrutinized and discussed in detail with him on a personal basis.

11. Second full scale field test. In this, and a third field test if one can be managed, the interviewer candidates are placed into a setting that corresponds as fully as possible to the actual conditions of the field.

12. Final interviewer selection and discussion of logistical procedures. Any candidates whose performance is deemed unsatisfactory are quietly thanked for their participation, paid, and dropped. This action is unavoidably invidious and must be handled with care. The remaining group of interviewers is briefed regarding the logistics of the field operation—their interviewing team assignments, their supervisors and the frequency and manner of reporting, how they will receive their pay, mail, new interview schedules, and so on, how the completed schedules will be collected, what to do in case of illness or trouble, travel arrangements, and the like.

13. Final meeting. This involves an attempt to send the group out with high morale, dedication to the project, and zest for the difficult work they are to undertake. The most effective of the introductory speakers is often asked back to make some brief hortatory remarks. We haven't yet employed a brass band, but we do everything possible to send the group out in an enthusiastic mood. They usually need the recollection of such moments when they encounter the heat, dust, bed bugs, diarrhea, snakes, gendarmes, cranks, bad roads, and other offerings of the field.

Concern for the corps of interviewers, however, does not cease when they are sent off to the field. They must still be carefully supervised and their needs attended if good work is to result. The director of the *Reader's Digest* international surveys of magazine readership, one of the first cross-national survey investigations, long ago cautioned:

> In readership surveys in different countries, direct personal supervision of the interviewers is necessary; otherwise, it is hard to get comparability. For example, we have found estimates of readership in a given country to vary by as much as 30% depending on who did the research. It is not a function of the respondents, but of supervision. Inflated readership figures invariably result from faulty or distant supervision.[80]

Wilson and Armstrong offer similar advice:

> They [Indian interviewers] can only be safeguarded by completely trustworthy supervision—by "watchdogging" any survey from start to finish. Certainly this is not a problem that is confined to India alone. Professional interviewers in the U.S. are often far less than dedicated to the pursuit of scientific knowledge per se. But in India there is more than just a disdain

for what is thought to be a bit of a hoax. There we sometimes find a truly positive rejection of scientific norms out of an apparent belief that they are nonsensical and perhaps even amoral.[81]

Supervision of interviewer performance, like interviewer training, is compounded by the heterogeneity of the interviewer and respondent groups. Not only must the field supervisors handle quite diverse types of people, but many of the checks on interviewer performance become more difficult to apply because they depend on comparisons with empirically established norms. When the interviewer and respondent groups are very diverse, such norms and the comparisons which they support become increasingly tenuous. To give but one example, use of an interpenetrated sampling design to locate questionable interviewer behavior depends upon random assignment of respondents to interviewers so that the results obtained by any two interviewers should not deviate by more than a degree predictable by a probability model. However, when the interviewers must be very finely matched to the types of respondents, the applicability of such a control technique becomes greatly restricted. Respondents cannot be randomly assigned to interviewers except within rather severe limits. This same type of factor also affects other control devices, such as certain cheater questions, comparison of returned schedules, sampling performance, completion rates, and so on. Many control procedures depend upon comparisons of performance among interviewers. But to the extent that the interviewers have to be assigned very different types of respondents, such comparisons become increasingly uncertain. Most interviewers are encountering unique field conditions; hence their results can legitimately vary. The cross-cultural researcher, who needs to be most explicit in demonstrating comparability of interviewer performance, often finds such demonstration least possible.

Sampling

The matter of who to interview, i.e., designating the population of concern, is basically decided in the initial design phases of the cross-cultural survey. However, the armchair designation of the population to be sampled and interviewed is a far cry from actually accomplishing those tasks. Cross-cultural survey research, especially that which includes underdeveloped societies, rural populations, urban slum areas, and so on, is likely to pose many practical sampling problems. I shall deal selectively with a few of the most glaring difficulties.

The most critical problem is probably the lack in the underdeveloped world of all those aids and accouterments of sampling that have been produced in most modern industrial societies. Censuses, registers, lists, directories, records, biographical compendia, and most other convenient sampling frames are faulty or absent. Maps, aerial photographs, street guides, and the like are utterly out of date or nonexistent. Secondary data on community size, household size, and so on are lacking. Thus, as Elmo Wilson lamented, it is "difficult to apply any but the most primitive sample designs. For example, in setting up an area sampling of city blocks, one has to choose blocks with equal probability since estimates of population in the blocks are not available."[82] The economy and refinement of highly stratified sampling techniques, analytically so desirable, are frequently precluded because of lack of the necessary information permitting stratification. Moreover, the scarcity of statistical material makes the projection of sample survey data to broader populations much more hazardous. To quote Wilson again, "when such data are not to be had, one must estimate from the sample both the population and proportion who have a given attribute. This gives rise to two sources of error rather than one."[83] Finally, the absence of secondary data makes the validation of sampling strategies and survey results much more difficult.

The consequence of these difficulties is that one settles for a less sophisticated and accurate sampling performance, spends more money, time, and effort to sustain a given level of accuracy, or occasionally develops ingenious new solutions to specific problems. For example, the major problems of sampling a snarled urban quarter which houses squatters have to some extent been solved. One contribution relies on the critical fact that the warren of structures there consists, after all, of dwelling units. This in turn means that the residents must have regular access to their abodes. The *rancho, favela, callampa, gecekondu*, or whatever it is called in the particular country, is laced with paths permitting such access. Survey researchers have exploited this fact to plot systematic walk routes along these paths in such a way that the walk routes of all the interviewers taken together cover all the paths, and no portion of any path appears on more than one interviewer's route. Then a systematic sample of the dwelling units located on his walk route is taken by each interviewer.[84]

Actually, this sounds easier than it is, since the interviewers often have a very hard time tracing the walk routes which the survey researchers have laid out for them, frequently aided by architectural students or topographical surveyors. If one, for example, puts colored chalk marks on the houses to indicate each route, the residents may think one is putting the "evil eye" on them and wash the marks off (and Hansel and Gretel have exploded the bread-crumb technique). Therefore, at times we have found it necessary to have an architectural student or someone with similar training actually walk the routes with each interviewer until the latter memorizes his own. This is a laborious procedure, and one is grateful for the fact that only a limited portion of most developing populations lives in such squatters' settlements. I might add that it is often especially difficult to determine exactly what constitutes a "dwelling unit" in urban slums or in villages with continuous

230

walls lining each street and with doors opening onto inner courtyards of jumbled structures. Moreover, crowding, family problems, residential instability, and other factors contrive to make the enumeration of a "household" no less of a task in some places, even after the "dwelling unit" has been located. Problems involving the determination of "dwelling units" and "households" confront samplers even in the United States. They can be even more ferocious in other societies and in comparative research. Various practical answers can almost always be found for the difficulties of sampling under such arduous conditions. Areal probability sampling has been a great boon. The central problems for cross-cultural survey research arising from these sampling difficulties, however, would seem to be at least two, both involving the issue of comparability or equivalence. One of the local "answers" to sampling tribulations is to redefine the population if the sampling gets too formidable. In a single-cultural study this can be done without great anguish; but in a cross-cultural survey such ad hoc revision of the definition of the population has painful repercussions. Teams in other areas that are not experiencing the same difficulties may take a dim view of this "whittling down" of the planned research. Or, ad hoc sampling adjustments may be required in several countries and made in different ways in each, thus significantly warping the contemplated comparability of the cross-cultural survey data.

If the country teams remain steadfast to the original sampling plan and do their best within its constraints, another problem may arise. This is the problem of differential completion rates and sampling performances. The sampling plan, for example, may be more effectively executed in some nations than in others, producing conspicuous variety among countries in the incidence of nonresponse. In the Almond and Verba five nation study, for example, the percentages of the designed samples for each country that were actually interviewed were: United Kingdom (59%), Mexico (60%), Italy (74%), Germany (74%), and the United States (83%). Scheuch, for one, well argues that "If . . . the chance of inclusion in the sample is associated with participation in public affairs—which appears to be a reasonable assumption—then the highly different completion rates may account for some of the observed differences. This effect is especially worrisome for England, which (especially in respect to its differences from Germany) is of crucial importance to the authors' main line of argument."[85]

Similar differences in sample completion rates were found in the OCSR surveys of teachers in northwestern European nations, and in other cross-national studies.[86] Even under ideal conditions it is difficult to avoid some variation in completion rates. And, one might argue that 60% completions in survey-hostile Britain or Mexico is somehow "comparable" to 83% in survey-sympathetic U.S.A. He might even contend that the crucial comparison is how the completion rates for the given survey compared with

231

normal completion rates for that type of study in those particular countries, regardless of absolute differences in rates.

Such arguments, however, are only of secondary significance. Even if identical completion rates are obtained in all countries, the cross-national researcher must still make a detailed investigation of the nature of the sampling loss—the differences between designed and obtained samples in each country. In other words, if all countries displayed 80% completions, it might still be true that the nonresponding remainders would be quite different in all countries—and, thus, that the type of population to which generalizations could legitimately be made might change appreciably from nation to nation. For example, in one society the nonrespondents might be particularly inaccessible and in a third the nonrespondents might be mainly composed of migrants. *Even though the completion rates are identical, interpretation of the significance of non-response is still essential.* One might argue for the functional equivalence of these three samples on the ground that the underrepresented sector of the population consists of groups whose opinions are in low regard in each of the societies, despite other differences. Or, one might contend that regardless of equal completion rates and at least one dimension of similarity among non-respondents, these three samples are critically different. Such questions must always be resolved in terms of the analytic objectives of the study and not in terms of agreement or disagreement of numbers and labels. Furthermore, samples usually cannot be monolithically evaluated; two samples may be comparable for some purposes and not comparable for others. Blanket approval or rejection is usually misleading. All depends on the nature of the inferences to be drawn from the data.

Most discussions of sampling for cross-national surveys, like discussions of translation, coding, interviewer-respondent relations, and so on, make much of the notion of *equivalence*. Although not wanting to belittle the importance and desirability of equivalence, I think it essential to note that equivalence, in any ordinary sense, is *not* absolutely vital to cross-national comparability. What is absolutely vital is for the researcher to understand the full meaning of his operations, not for these operations to be totally equivalent even in a functional sense in all countries. If it can be obtained, equivalence enhances comparative possibilities. But valid and significant comparisons often can be made without full equivalence if the researcher knows the nature of the data he has collected—if he understands their meaning for his analytic purposes. In sampling, for example, the operation in one country may have resulted in an underrepresentation of the politically active while the sample obtained in another country more faithfully included that nation's politically active citizens. However, so long as this fact is known, so long as the nature of the two samples is understood, and they have some commonality of focus, certain kinds of comparisons can frequently still be made. Thus, if it turned out that the overall level of interest in politics was no less in the country where the politically active were underrepresented than in the country where they were accurately represented, and that political activity was positively associated with political interest in both countries, one might conclude that political interest would actually be even higher in the first country than in the second. This type of a fortiori reasoning is often possible with technically nonequivalent data, but only if the nature of the lack of equivalence is known.

Truly equivalent data, however, generally permit more sophisticated and powerful inferences than nonequivalent data. Most cross-cultural research attempts to generalize to similar populations in each of the cultures studied, so that at least functionally equivalent samples are desirable. Thus, one must specify both the populations to be regarded or intended as equivalent and the sampling schemes to be used to draw basically equivalent samples of these populations. In turn, this procedure implies that one can define, at least operationally for the purposes of the research, what the very conception of equivalence means. One must present the criteria in terms of which equivalence is to be assessed. And, finally, one must try to gather data necessary to *demonstrate* such equivalence, not merely nourish an intuitive conviction that it is there. How seldom is this done with any explicitness in cross-national research! How difficult this is, if one wants to be extremely fastidious!

Viewed from such a perspective, several problems immediately appear. For example, the similarities of the populations to be investigated are frequently specified on a largely intuitive basis, primarily in terms of social background characteristics such as age, education, place of residence, occupation, and so on. Understandably rare is the sample or population defined in attitudinal terms, for instance.[87] Yet a little reflection will reveal that even the demographic categories themselves are by no means of constant cross-cultural significance. One may speak blithely of "the adult populations" of countries X, Y, and Z. Operationally, this may be interpreted in each of the three countries as everyone over eighteen years of age, yielding a sort of nominal equivalence. But does it furnish anything more? The answer depends on a clear definition of what is meant by *adult* and the relationship of chronological age to that conception among the populations of each of the three countries. An eighteen year old may play an adult role in some societies but not in others. Or, let us take residence. One might want to sample the urban populations of the same three countries. But, as many researchers have noted, size of community seems to afford only a very gross measure of what numerous researchers want to mean when they employ the term *urban*. Stern and d'Epinay show that a town of 5,000 in Switzerland typically has more commercial and cultural activity than a town of the same size in

233

France.[88] My own experience in Turkey suggests that a Turkish "city" of 25,000 is likely to be less urbanized in most senses (cultural activity, commerce, transport, facilities, and so on) than an American town of 5,000. How does one locate comparable urban populations? Similarly, the educational system of one society may be so different from that of another that specifying comparable populations in the two societies, let alone producing equivalent sampling stratifications, becomes difficult indeed. It sometimes seems that one must already have done his study in order to do his study! One needs the information which his study seeks in order properly to carry out the research.

Another type of problem, and opportunity, confronting the cross-national survey concerns the most appropriate degree of clustering for the sample. Regardless of the over-all sampling strategy employed, any large scale study will probably involve several stages of sampling. States, counties, provinces, regions, cities, census tracts, organizations, and similar statistical and administrative units ordinarily constitute the primary sampling units. Intermediate units such as precincts, blocks, quarters, neighborhoods, work groups, and so on, are employed, and this is usually followed by clusters of dwelling units, households, families, and the like before one finally arrives at the individual respondent, if the individual is in fact the ultimate sampling unit. Although multi-stage sampling is essential from a cost viewpoint and is a nuisance from a statistical viewpoint, it offers two important opportunities. First, one can exploit the fact that the early stage sampling units are often administrative units. This means that they are units for which the government is likely to collect information on a regular basis. Not only does this create an opportunity to graft additional information onto the survey data (e.g., information on voting behavior or crime), but it also furnishes another validity check if the survey information is made to overlap in some degree with the governmental records. The researcher should, if possible, make a virtue of the need for multi-stage sampling by making the early stage sampling units be governmental units offering significant information for the survey. In this fashion, the clustering effect, while decreasing accuracy, may increase validation.

Second, multi-stage sampling also can be exploited through the use of what is commonly called *contextual analysis* or *configurational analysis*. Contextual analysis is essentially a technique for locating any given respondent in the social and cultural setting which surrounds him and gives shape to his attitudes and behaviors. For instance, the attitudinal and behavioral correlates of literacy may revolve about whether the respondent is one of very few people in his community who are literate or whether he resides in a community where nearly everyone is literate. Are the concomitants of political cynicism different if the cynic is surrounded by other cynics in his immediate environment as opposed to his being surrounded by less jaundiced views? The earlier sampling units in a multistage design quite often are appropriate contextual units for this type of analysis. However, the decision to engage in contextual analysis must ordinarily be made at the outset, because denser sampling of the contextual unit is necessary to perform this type of analysis on any extensive scale.

Of course, one problem engendered by multi-stage sampling is the cross-cultural comparability of the stages. Some nations, such as the Scandinavian or Japan, keep excellent and detailed governmental statistics that provide admirable sampling frames, enabling the researcher to skip certain sampling stages required in other nations with less admirable records. The resulting economies and costs enter into the researcher's calculations of sample size and accuracy, staff, and so on. [89] More significantly, contextual analysis is rendered less comparable by the difficulty in securing similar contextual units in each country. The equivalence or similarity for the resident individual of the U.S. county, British parliamentary constituency, Indian administrative district, Turkish and French prefectures may be difficult to determine, but those may be the units with which the researcher is stuck.

The basic decision regarding *whom* to interview depends, as I have said, upon the researcher's analytic objectives—the hypotheses he wants to test or the phenomena he wishes to describe. There can be no substitute for fundamental clarity at this level. However, there is unfortunately no automatic line of inference from clearcut designation of the population of concern to selection of the most appropriate sampling and interrogative strategies. Many diverse considerations enter into these lower level decisions.

Although nonprobability sampling techniques are occasionally useful, and one in particular, quota sampling, sometimes seems to give an economical result similar in precision to probability techniques, the researcher will want to use probability methods if he possible can. The advantages of making explicit error estimates with known confidence levels are too great to be ignored, and the inconveniences and expenses of many probability approaches are not significantly greater than those of quota sampling, the only non-probability competitor. Although occasional field studies show that the differences in results between conscientiously applied quota and simple random samples of the same population may be negligible, the only way the researcher using a quota sample can *certify* this for his particular field work is if the probability sample was also actually drawn. [90] Otherwise, there is only a subjective basis for confidence in the sampling result and no possibility of any precise error estimates.

There are, of course, many varieties of probability samples which are well described and evaluated in most basic texts on sampling statistics. [91] The researcher must determine whether he will attempt to use simple random sampling or systematic approximations to random sampling. Here, for example, he will have to consider such things as whether it makes any

235

difference to him if certain combinations of respondents (e.g., adjacent names on the sampling frame) cannot enter the sample even though each respondent initially has an equal individual chance of entering the sample. He must decide if it is possible and fruitful to stratify his sample and, if so, how. He must decide how clustered his sample is to be and what the clustering units should be. And he must do all these things with an eye toward cross-cultural comparability. Are villages as operationally defined in one nation absolutely or functionally equivalent to villages as defined in another? Is the conception of the family or household employed in one nation really a supportable counterpart to that used in another? Myriad demanding problems of this sort enter into sampling design at virtually all stages. Moreover, not only must all these decisions be made, but they must be effectively conveyed to listers, interviewers, supervisors, and higher staff so that uniform interpretations are used. This is a large order even within a single country, let alone to accomplish it cross-culturally. A well-conceived sampling scheme can trickle away quite easily in a series of bad decisions by field workers.

One often overlooked and basic point is that the cross-cultural researcher must try to think through his intended analysis in some detail in order to develop an effective sampling plan as well as to develop revealing inter-rogative instruments (questionnaires and interview schedules). He must know the main direct controls he will apply in the analysis so that he can ensure, through his sample design, that he will have enough cases to permit those controls. Almond and Verba, for example, have been criticized by Scheuch for using level of formal education as the keystone of their analysis in *The Civic Culture* while their sampling plan did not pick up a sufficient number of the relatively small percentage of European university graduates to allow for full inspection of that important group. A sample stratified in terms of formal education might have been more appropriate for their analysis. Similar comments could be made about many other studies. In my own research, our study of the Turkish peasantry would, I feel, be more effective if we had obtained information from a few illuminating control groups from other sectors of Turkish society. We did not adequately realize that we were not solely interested in variations *within* the peasantry, although such variations were of major importance to us. We were also interested in commenting on how peasants differed from other Turks. Focusing so completely on the peasants and excluding other groups has made the latter portion of the analysis much more difficult.

Moreover, even at the sample design stage the researcher also must know in some detail the kinds of observations and measurements he will need to validate his ratings and placements as well as to test his hypotheses. Thus, while greediness leading to an attempt to gather too much information on too many topics in the course of a single survey is the undoing of the novice, too narrow a focus prevents the researcher from demonstrating the construct

236

validity of his concepts and from subjecting many of his hypotheses to an appropriate test. Detailed knowledge of the kinds of data that will be required to support the analysis is critical even for adequate sample design.

In this connection, let me inject one additional observation regarding the utility of broadly representative samples. A query that must be directed to any proposed sampling scheme is this: What possibilities does it offer for analytic flexibility? What opportunities will there be for reanalysis and recombination of the data from another perspective? In other words, is the study so narrowly focused that only the hypotheses originally articulated can be investigated? Or, is it the case that the sampling design and interrogative instruments are constructed so that alternative hypotheses can also be investigated? If one employs a highly purposive design focused on occupational groups, for example, and his hypotheses regarding the significance of occupation are disappointed while at the same time the data suggest that educational factors are unexpectedly influential, to what extent will the data support an appropriate shift in the analytic focus? Such a consideration is obviously more important in some types of studies than in others. In the early stages of descriptive investigation of a problem it may be quite important. Moderately stratified and large national samples sometimes offer the researcher an unusual opportunity to have his cake and eat it too.

Another point regarding sample size is relevant here. Large national samples may be extremely cheap compared with any other kind of extensive sample. This is merely another way of saying that the marginal 'cost per interview may be very low in cross-cultural research, particularly in developing societies. The overhead costs incurred in mounting a major survey in many societies tend to be extremely high. Facilities must be established almost from scratch; interviewers must be trained in several languages; regional operations must be installed, and so on. Getting a qualified interviewer out to remote parts of the country is relatively so costly that it seems wasteful not to have him operate maximally while he is there and not to keep him in that general vicinity for a significant period if possible. Moreover, because studies of cross-cultural processes demand so much deviant case analysis, large samples may have a high theoretical payoff, especially if they can be interestingly stratified.

One of the dangers besetting cross-cultural survey research in particular is that of untimely interruption of field operations in one or more of the chosen sites. As a result, sampling procedures to minimize such risks have been developed. The general strategy is to divide the total desired sample into component subsamples by random means. The smaller each subsample, the greater the reduction of disruptive risk. In the Turkish peasant survey we split the total sample of approximately 6,500 respondents into rough halves. This meant that at the end of half our field work we had in hand an independent take of half the full number of interviews. If operations had to

237

cease after that point for any reason, we should still have obtained a sample whose only deviation from that designed was in size, not in basic representativeness.

The price paid for this insurance was slightly increased travel and interviewer expenses, since some diseconomies resulted from having two independent subsamples over the same area. The interviewers had to cover the country twice instead of once. Other surveys have employed as many as twenty-five such subsamples. The smaller the geographic area covered by the survey and the easier and less expensive the transportation, the greater is the opportunity to exploit this strategy. It also offers the advantage of furnishing some useful measures of variation due to interviewer fatigue or initial inexperience (should earlier subsamples differ more than randomly from later subsamples). And, as Bonilla has remarked, it gives ". . . the research team an early estimate of what over-all sample performance is likely to be," thereby permitting timely introduction of corrective measures. Without random subsamples, the first results sent back to the central survey office will probably be quite unrepresentative and the directors will not know if response performance among such a group is likely to prevail among other respondents.[92]

In some settings, as I have mentioned, the dangers of interruption are attended by dangers of poor interviewer performance, despite proper recruitment and training of interviewers. Once again, sampling tactics can provide some assistance. Respondents can be assigned to interviewers randomly, within certain limitations, so that possible variations in interviewer performance can be detected by response variations between interviewers' respondents that exceed chance expectations. This is generally called an *interpenetrating* sample design. It does not *prove* interviewer failure or cheating, it does not pin down which interviewer was the deviant in certain cases (especially when only paired comparisons are possible), and it is revelatory only after the field work is completed and through fairly involved analytic procedures; but it is a valuable and unobtrusive after-check on the quality of interviewer performance, to be used in those instances when one's suspicions have been aroused. Moreover, it permits a certain substantive pinpointing of the items most affected by interviewer failure.

Finally, I should mention that several writers have questioned the "assumption" they see in survey research that ". . . the unit or source of opinion is the individual," the egalitarian model of one man, one opinion.[93] In other words, this suggests that we should not slavishly demand that our ultimate sampling units or study units be equally weighted individuals. For certain purposes, a more sophisticated sampling plan might be to weight individuals according to some index of their power or influence in the community of concern. It is additionally argued that, "Where life is lived more communally, opinions are likely to have a communal base. The unit of opinion is more likely to be the extended family, the sub-caste, the village, etc., than the individual . . . To the extent that it is, it is not easily accessible to random sample survey technique."

On the whole, I believe that these comments are rather misleading. Regarding the first point, it is certainly an interesting idea to sample respondents according to the influence of their opinions or to weight their opinions by an index of their influence. The trick lies in coming up with precise and reliable weights and indices to use. We are very far as yet from even appearing to be able to do this, Moreover, survey research based on individual responses seems to be a basic tool in most attempts to develop such a capacity.

The second point, that the unit of opinion is likely to be the family or village, seems to me to miss the mark. First of all, it is an empirical question whether this is true or not, and one that can only be answered by survey-type research at the individual level. Moreover, in Turkey, for instance, our research among peasants indicates that in many attitudinal areas it is emphatically not true. Sex, for example, is one of the best general predictors of a peasant's orientations and behavior, which is merely another way of stating that women have markedly different attitudes from men on many topics, even though they are from the same families. Young people, to a lesser extent but still significantly, differ from their familial elders. Peasant families and villages are not ordinarily the attitudinal monoliths that many have made them out to be. Certainly, great familial and village consensus does exist in some areas. But this is far from being so extensive that one can assume consensus and adopt a strategy which precludes finding otherwise. Taking the terms literally, it is hard to interview a *clan* or an *extended family*! One must always interview one or more of its members or representatives, unless one wishes to conduct a group interview, which has its own special problems. Survey research and probability sampling techniques are perfectly suitable for interviewing only household heads, clan leaders, village headmen, or any other distinguishable spokesmen when such a sampling unit seems appropriate. On the whole, more of our problems lie in how well we use the survey methods we have than in the lack of an appropriate method in our repertoire.

Interrogative Strategy

Having determined the basic design of the research, located the necessary sponsorship, established an effective organization, and worked out a feasible sampling plan, the cross-cultural researcher then faces the hurdle of developing an appropriate interrogative strategy. Knowing whom he is to interrogate and why, he must decide specifically *what* is to be asked and *how* it is to be asked. Questions must be constructed, tested, and organized into survey instruments (questionnaires and interview schedules). In addition, the posture which the interviewers are to adopt vis-à-vis the respondent, i.e., the desired character of the interviewer-respondent relationship, must be clarified and the most likely obstacles to its achievement must be anticipated. If sampling and some aspects of data analysis can be considered the more scientific facets of survey research, here surely is its more intuitive and impressionistic side. What is perhaps the best introductory book on the subject is aptly entitled *The Art of Asking Questions.*[94]

As I have previously cautioned, this essay does not purport to be a primer on survey research. Although we sorely need a more advanced sequel to Payne's valuable work on question design, that is not our present purpose. Our focus is rather on those problems that become particularly acute in cross-cultural surveys. After a few comments on the notion of equivalence, I shall concentrate upon three major problems of developing an interrogative strategy for cross-national research: (1) general problems of equivalence in survey instruments, (2) several special interrogative approaches, and (3) the problem of translation.

On the Notion of Equivalence

Since we once again confront the ubiquitous notion of "equivalence" in cross-cultural research, let me briefly elaborate a fundamental comment made earlier in connection with equivalence in sampling. First, equivalence is never total. Equivalence is not identity. The objects, situations, phenomena, or processes that are said to be equivalent are nevertheless distinguishable, which implies that there is at least one respect in which they differ. Since it is not total, when one speaks of equivalence he must specify the *dimensions* along which equivalence is asserted. And, if he wants us to take his work seriously, he must indicate their *relevance* for the theoretical or practical problem he is attacking. For example, he must tell us the respects in which his samples are equivalent and why those respects are critical to the investigation—i.e., why other plausible sampling criteria were not needed. Thus, he might say that his sample covered Negroes and Spanish-Americans in the United States and Kurdish, Arabic, and Greek-speaking citizens of Turkey because his hypotheses involved the concept of a nation's major minority groups. Even in this instance further elaboration of the meaning of that critical word "major" would properly be required. Are not the Jews a major minority group in the United States? Perhaps not, if the criterion is the proportionate size of the group, but certainly yes if the criterion is their contribution to various specified aspects of national life.

Similarly, the researcher might justify comparing a sample from one nation of all persons aged sixteen years or over and a sample from another nation of all persons twenty-one years or over. He might do this on the grounds that, although age ranges of the two samples obviously differed, they were equivalent in that each represented the adult population of its society. In one society the adult role was ordinarily thought to be assumed by about age sixteen while in the other society that transition was at twenty-one. He might add that this dimension—adult role—was important because many of the basic hypotheses of the research involved the concept of an "adult," i.e., theoretical relationships were predicated only of adults, not of adolescents, children, or infants.

Obviously, the two kinds of sampling strategies just described produced samples which were equivalent along some dimensions (minority group position and occupancy of an adult role) and different along other dimensions (race or color, linguistic knowledge, chronological age). The additional assertion was made in each case, as it always is, either explicitly or implicitly, that the equivalent dimensions were those critical to the purposes of the investigation and the differing dimensions were irrelevant to the investigation. Whether these assertions are true or not is, of course, another matter.

The same considerations apply to equivalence in interrogation and in all other aspects of the cross-cultural survey. For example, the researcher must show us the ways in which this set of specific questions used in this country is equivalent to that set of specific questions used in that country, and he must contend that these two sets, at best only equivalent in some respects and not in all, are equivalent in those very respects which are crucial for his problem. Thus, a question used in one country about the perceived pecuniary dishonesty of politicians may be regarded as equivalent to a question in another country about the perceived impiety of politicians. Both may be taken as tapping a tendency toward cynicism regarding the personnel of politics, as expressed in terms of values known to be salient in each society. A "modern" nation may place high value on honesty and low value on piety, while a "traditional" society may care little about peculation but much about adherence to established religious forms. The questions might be equivalent in tapping respondents' tendencies to perceive politicians as lacking or possessing at least some of what each culture regarded as important moral qualities. On the other hand, it might be that the meaning of the term "politician" varied in the two societies. In one it might have strongly negative overtones that were lacking in the other. A critic might fault the researcher on this basis for using questions that were equivalent only in some of the theoretically critical dimensions but not in others.[95]

From this viewpoint, we see that the debate, if there ever really was one, over "functional" versus "formal" equivalence was silly. Equivalence must always be "functional" in the sense that the notion of equivalence intrinsically involves reference to the purposes of the research. "Formal" equivalence, which presumably means the employment of mechanically identical procedures (e.g., literally translated questions or slavishly copied sampling procedures), is interesting only when it leads to "functional" equivalence. Uncritical reliance on "formal" equivalence can be intellectually respectable only if one has no other information at all on which to establish some degree of "functional" equivalence, a most unlikely situation.

A second point for reemphasis is that full equivalence, within the scope of the research objectives, is exceedingly desirable but not absolutely essential for cross-cultural surveys. What is essential is: (1) that the significance of the research procedures as they relate to the purposes of the research be deeply understood, and (2) that the procedures have enough in common so that they are critically comparable. One can compare apples and oranges as different species of fruit, but it is a strain to compare apples and explosions or oranges and prejudice. Some parallelism, some interesting underlying dimension of comparability, must be present.

In the discussion of sampling, the point was made that the samples in any two different countries do not have to be fully equivalent, i.e., represent functionally identical populations so far as the purposes of the research are concerned. Useful comparisons can frequently be made among samples which differ along important dimensions so long as the nature of those differences is known and the populations have at least some relevant similarities. The same is true for survey instruments and interviewing procedures. An item used in one country may be relatively easier for a given personality type to answer affirmatively than an item which was intended to be its counterpart in another country. But if the nature of this difference is known and if the items tap the same attitudinal realm, varying only in the points at which they divide the latent attitudinal continuum, then useful inferences can ordinarily be made. Full equivalence permits more precise and sophisticated inferences, but recognized and meaningful variations in procedure will also support rewarding analyses. Realization of this fact becomes especially important in the secondary analysis of diverse cross-cultural data, which are by their nature seldom fully equivalent.

The basic research problem is to *devise* such equivalent samples, items, coding schemes, interviewing procedures, etc., and to develop procedures for *demonstrating* that equivalence. Unfortunately, equivalence cannot be demonstrated through the researcher's testimony that he feels he has obtained it, although all too often we have no more than this to rely upon. The point is that the researcher needs not only to develop an interrogative strategy which will produce equivalence in questioning, but that this strategy must also furnish as much information as possible to demonstrate that equivalence. Practically, this means that in the survey instruments one usually needs to include questions whose specific purpose is to demonstrate equivalence along with questions which obtain the substantive information originally sought. Thus, if one wants to regard honesty in one society and piety in another society as equivalent in the sense that both are highly valued moral qualities, he may need to include in his survey selected questions which directly establish this fact, i.e., questions which elicit the relative importance of these moral qualities, compared with others, for the respondents. He may then, in turn, confront the problem of which other qualities constitute the most appropriate and *equivalent* comparisons.[96] He thus encounters one of the deepest difficulties in comparative research—that of finding some sure ground, some known equivalences, from which to start. Equivalences must be demonstrated in terms of other equivalences which are already known. But how are those prior equivalences to be established? Considerations of this type are what drive cross-cultural analysts to moan that ". . . the most serious problem in attempting to attain equivalence is that there is no way of recognizing it when one has attained it."[97] While this may be an ex-aggeration, it is true that our demonstrations of equivalence are always approximations which rest increasingly on faith or subjective judgment as one probes further and further back into their empirical support. However, this too is a pervasive problem in empirical science; it is simply more acute in cross-cultural research.

General Problems of Equivalence in Cross-Cultural Surveys

The paramount purpose of survey instruments and the efforts of inter-viewers is to present known and controlled stimuli to the respondents. The significance of the survey lies in its analysis of how various respondents react to these stimuli, and in making inferences from the respondent's answers to survey items to his behavior in other settings of importance. Obviously, if the meaning of the respondent's reactions is to be understood, the researcher must know the nature of the stimuli to which people are responding. And, if the researcher is to make precise comparisons among respondents and avoid incredible analytic complexity, the stimuli presented should be as equivalent as possible for all respondents. One's aim is to observe important differences or similarities in the responses to equivalent stimuli among various types of people. Moreover, one must worry about *equivalence in response description and interpretation* as well as equivalence in stimuli and their presentation.

One approach to these problems is to ask what kinds of stimuli are presented to the respondents. What are the outstanding ways in which variations in stimuli might occur? What kinds of stimuli do we want to present to the respondent and what kinds of noise, static, irrelevancies or disturbances do we wish to keep out?

As with sampling, the general nature of the desired interrogative stimuli presumably will have been determined by the basic research design and objectives. The hypotheses to be tested and the concepts for which measures are sought will be explicit or implicit in the project's goals and plans. The immediate question is how to devise a specific set of stimuli that can be uniformly presented to diverse groups (since we cannot tailor-make a complete instrument for each respondent) and that will be related in a regular and convincing way to the concepts guiding the research.

The nature of the relationship between specific stimuli and responses, on the one hand, and more abstract theoretical concepts, on the other, is the problem of validation. Are we measuring what we want to measure? For example, does the question, "What would you do if you were Prime Minister?" really reveal a person's political empathy (his ability to project himself into the political role of another), or is it instead primarily measuring his level of political knowledge (his familiarity with what Prime Ministers are supposed to do)?

The problem of the constancy of the stimuli is the problem of reliability. Will the measuring device consistently produce the same results in the same situation? Is our yardstick made of steel or rubber? Will a respondent with a constant degree of political empathy respond identically each time he is confronted by our question as to what he would do if he were Prime Minister?

The problem of noise or static among the stimuli is in part the problem of unidimensionality. Are we measuring only one thing or several? Does the question concerning empathy also reflect, to some unknown and varying degree, the respondents' attitudes toward the particular political role of Prime Minister in addition to their basic empathic capacity? If so, then people are responding to different and uncertain stimuli.

Of course, in the deepest sense, if one has complete validity in an instrument he will ipso facto attain reliability and unidimensionality. If the instrument or item truly measures what he wants it to measure and only that, other objectives will be realized. But needless to say, such complete validity is virtually never attained in survey research.

Probably the ideal method of developing an effective interrogative strategy for a cross-national research project would be to assemble a group of perfectly trained scholars representing all of the nations included in the study, have them come to a full understanding of the purposes of the research, the concepts and hypotheses to be investigated, the main research techniques to be used, and the resources at hand, and tell them to return to their nations and proceed. With a complete and common understanding of the theoretical concepts to be studied, utmost methodological sophistication, and maximal knowledge of their own societies, each scholar could be relied upon to develop the most valid specific indicators possible for each comparative concept. Detailed questions and tactics would vary from nation to nation in accordance with differences in culture and environment, but these variations in specific items would merely be the means of ensuring that equivalent conceptual measurements were being taken in each country. Political participation might be measured in part by formal voting in Turkey and by passive resistance to a tribal chief in Truk, but each informed researcher would fully comprehend the concept of political participation and develop the best possible indicators for that concept in the context of his society. Even so, although we could be confident that we had attained maximal equivalence under the circumstances, the precise degree would remain uncertain.

Obviously, this approach to cross-cultural research remains an ideal rather than an actual or even feasible procedure. Such knowledgeable, cooperative, and perceptive scholars with a shared conceptual framework live only in more Elysian realms. Yet this is the model to which our research efforts aspire. In determining an interrogative strategy for cross-cultural surveys the basic procedure is to assemble a research group (including consultants, formal and informal) possessing deep familiarity with the nations to be studied and with existing research techniques. This group must agree upon the objectives of the research and reach a mutual understanding of its major concepts and hypotheses. Such joint comprehension of purposes and conceptualization is a sine qua non for effective comparative research, and time or effort spent in fostering it is well invested. Then, once a common theoretical orientation toward the research is established, work can proceed on the development and discussion of specific indicators.

Too frequently cross-cultural research projects seem to start out with a detailed survey instrument developed for research in one country or by authors thinking largely in terms of one or a few countries. The interrogative strategy of such a project is often simply to translate and administer this instrument in the remaining nations. Having an instrument that seems appropriate for at least one nation studied can be quite a boon. Many of its items and indicators may be well suited to other settings. Inspection of its questions and format may suggest counterparts for use elsewhere and may also contribute to further understanding of the underlying conceptualization of the project. But such an instrument must be viewed heuristically, not taken as providing an automatically appropriate set of questions which must merely be translated into other languages. Indeed, I shall argue again later that deeper insight into equivalence and comparability, while posing many recondite issues, renders the problem of translation somewhat less acute since mere translation of an instrument prepared for one culture into the language of another is an increasingly crude and unsatisfactory strategy. The real task is rather to share a full awareness of research goals, concepts, and techniques, and to construct for each culture fitting survey instruments which can be validated. The main route to instrument equivalence is through clear and uniformly understood conceptualization plus item and index validation for each society.

245

Types of Equivalence

For interrogative purposes it is useful to distinguish two types of equivalence: direct and relative. Direct equivalence exists when two procedures or results can be directly equated without reference to any other factors, although the procedures or results may themselves be quite complex. Relative equivalence exists when two procedures or results can be equated only through reference to their relationship with equivalent other factors—that is, only through standardization which comes from reference to norms. For example, consider two particular survey respondents, one from the United Arab Republic and the other from the United Kingdom. One could compare the absolute number of hours each had spent watching television in the week prior to being interviewed. Forgetting for the moment such things as equivalence of media content, the psychic meaning of watching television, the conditions of viewing, and so on, one can compare the absolute number of hours these two respondents spent in front of the television screen. At this level, assuming the respondents are willing and able to furnish the information, one direct question to each of them is sufficient: "How many hours did you watch television last week?" The equivalence that is sought is simple and absolute. The same procedure might suffice for ascertaining absolute levels of monetary income, years of formal education, number of voluntary associations joined, whether the respondent formally belonged to a political party, and so on.

On the other hand, we might be interested in a different type of information. We might feel that for our inferential goals we needed to know not the absolute number of hours spent watching television, but whether the respondent was, relative to his society or community, a frequent or infrequent viewer. We might feel that the accessibility of television was so different in the two societies that simple absolute comparisons meant little. We might be more interested in how each respondent's viewing frequency compared with some relevant norm for his environment. Is he, compared to others in his community, more or less exposed to such broadcasts? If such information is our goal—and in one way or another, especially in cross-cultural comparative research, it usually is—then we cannot always get by with direct and limited questions. We must at least ask ourselves whether our survey instruments are going to provide the information necessary to make our relative interpretations, i.e., to establish the appropriate norms. Often the mere fact that we have asked everyone in our sample a given question, such as how often he watches television, permits us to generate relevant norms or standards. We can plot the frequency distribution of television viewing for our entire sample and then classify each individual respondent in relation to that distribution. Thus, for instance, we can note that this respondent listens more often than 89% of all respondents, while that one only listens more often than 23%.[98]

Other types of relative equivalence, however, must be specifically planned during the preparation of the survey instruments. This is true when comparison is made to unsampled sectors of the population using the respondent as an informant regarding those sectors. For example, one might be interested in the frequency of the respondent's exposure to television compared with that of his spouse or his father. Ideally, one would like to include such other individuals in the sample in order to get a direct report from them, and the sample would have to be appropriately designed to do this. But such is not always possible. In that event, one might have to rely on the respondent's report of others' behavior, always cognizant of the limitations and possible biases of such reports and taking special precautions in question formulation that can minimize these difficulties. Nevertheless, if reports are necessary to establish a desired equivalence, they obviously must be foreseen and included in the survey instruments. It is discouraging how easy it is to overlook what is so "obvious" and find out only in the analytic stage after the data have been gathered that a bit of information critical to the establishment of relative equivalence is missing.

An extension of this point is perhaps even more significant. Almond and Verba, for example, point out that although voting is often readily taken as an index of political activity, there can be no automatic assumption of equivalence regarding its meaning as such a political act in different settings. ". . . (T)o one individual it may be a highly affect-laden protest against the current government, to another it may be traditional conformity to family voting patterns." "Surely the Southern Negro in America who registers and votes at great personal risk is participating in a much more intense way than is the voter who lives in a situation where voting is relatively easy and expected."[99] The essential point is that when the researcher needs to know not only whether a respondent engaged in a particular behavior, but, for equivalence of interpretation, also needs to know the meaning of that action for the respondent, he must make certain in advance that his survey instruments obtain both types of information. He must secure direct information on the behavioral pattern and also secure the attitudinal information necessary to confirm or deny the assumption of equivalent psychological factors underlying ostensibly similar behaviors. Moreover, if such behaviors are shown not to be absolutely or grossly equivalent, the additional interpretive information can be used to establish more limited equivalences. For instance, types of voting in various contexts might be defined.

Still more generally, considerations of this nature lead one to observe again the constant interdependence of interrogative strategy and data analysis. In fact, this relation is so interactive that it is difficult to write about one without delving into the other. The interrogative strategy is planned largely retrospectively in that the researcher attempts to envision the nature of the analysis he wants to do and works back from there to determine the kinds of data he will need and the interrogative strategy requisite to securing those data. All this was said earlier in the comment that the objectives of the research dictate the interrogative strategy just as they dictate the sampling strategy. But the relationship between analysis and interrogation is even more specifically interdependent than such a general statement suggests. Both in the process of research as a whole and in the confines of a particular survey the vital rhythm must be to generate and test, revise, and test again. A research project is formulated, accomplished, and evaluated; this leads in turn to further research, hopefully more sophisticated and focused if its predecessor was successful. Within a single survey, though clearly on a reduced scale, the process must be to form an interrogative strategy and then pretest it, to make refinements and then pretest those, and so on until the researcher is reasonably satisfied that he can safely proceed and is in no danger of exhausting himself, his funds, and his time.

Establishing Validity

If the road to equivalence is through clear and common conceptualization and paramount emphasis on local validation for each national operation, then the cross-national researcher must orient his interrogative strategy toward maximizing the possibilities for validation. There are, in general, several techniques for doing this. He should examine each one carefully to ensure that he is systematically exploiting all his opportunities. Far from being what one writer has condemned as "the last refuge of a methodologist attempting to escape social responsibilities . . .," validation is the key to comparative survey research.[100]

The first and most tenuous technique for determining validity is to obtain as full information as possible about the conditions under which the interview took place or the questionnaire was completed. Like most other techniques but even more conspicuously, this is an essentially negative tactic. It enables us to eliminate possible causes of invalidity rather than to make a positive demonstration of validity. Nevertheless, we know that, for example, certain interviewing conditions decrease the probability of securing valid responses. The presence of unwanted third parties who might kibitz during the interview, noise and confusion in the environment while the questions are being asked, interruptions, a respondent who seems especially apprehensive or insincere, having to conduct the interview in a great hurry, and so on are all conditions which reduce the likelihood of valid interrogation. The cross-cultural researcher therefore attempts to discover as much as possible about the conditions under whch the data were gathered. He devotes extra attention to the "face sheet" sections of his instrument where such information is explicitly obtained. He tries to devise ingenious ways of using his interviewers as observers in addition to using them as questioners and recorders. Thus, he works hard to train the interviewers in making observational ratings and tests their reliability in doing so. In every way possible he attempts to devise an interrogative strategy which will give him maximal information about the circumstances under which the data were obtained.

The second and perhaps most obvious method of ascertaining validity is to compare the survey data with similar data obtained independently from some other source thought to be accurate. Thus, one might compare survey respondents' voting claims with appropriate official electoral data. He might compare reports of political party membership with the parties' formal records of their membership. Assuming that these independent records are accurate (by no means an assumption that is always true), one can often secure valuable insight into the validity of the survey. Several limitations, however, quickly appear. This type of validation is ordinarily possible for only a few social background characteristics and certain limited and rather formal or conspicuous behaviors. One can check respondent reports of age, education, literacy, and the like, against official statistics, and one can frequently compare respondent reports of church attendance, voting behavior, media exposure, and so on, with governmental and organizational data on the same topics. The opportunities for such validation of the survey are limited to the range of data available from these presumably reliable outside sources of information, and that is usually quite a restricted range indeed. Moreover, the comparison is usually between aggregated external statistics and survey data, not comparison at the individual level. Even more, the portion of the survey instrument which most needs validation is perhaps the psychological and attitudinal, yet this is the very area where independent external validation is least likely to be available. In fact, if such data were independently available, there might be no need for a survey. Sometimes one also encounters the contention that many of these independent validational data have themselves been collected through survey procedures, such as censuses. Any biases inherent in the use of the survey technique for collecting information will therefore be present in both data sets. The comparison of the two sets of data cannot eliminate invalidities arising from the survey method itself (e.g., distortions caused by sensitivities intrinsic to the interviewer-respondent relationship or the approach through apparently direct questioning).

Nevertheless, validation of at least some key items by comparing the survey data with trusted independent data is a valuable, if limited, tool for the cross-cultural survey researcher. He must try to exploit it as fully as possible, which, once again, requires foresight and planning. The researcher

249

will have to familiarize himself with the various possible data sets which permit such validational comparison and then must include in his survey instrument items which are articulated with the kinds of information externally available. As was pointed out previously, one excellent way of maximizing such validational opportunities is to make an administrative unit for which the government regularly collects and publishes many types of information (e.g., a county, district, census tract) one of the early sampling units in a clustered, multi-stage design.

Philip Converse has well expressed the rationale behind this approach to validation by reminding us that ". . . we have an obligation to feel uncomfortable about an untested methodology (including a new survey) until we see that it can reproduce some simple characteristic of the real world . . ." in which we have confidence.[101] The independent, external data constitute, in this case, our presumably reliable information as to what the real world is like. However, this perspective on the problem suggests another tactic of this method of validation. It is to have respondents with known attitudinal or behavioral characteristics answer our survey instrument to ascertain if it makes the expected discriminations. Thus, some of the earlier instruments designed to tap fascistic tendencies were partially validated by having persons of known fascistic sympathies, as well as others without any apparent fascistic leanings, respond to them. Assuming one has confidence in the original fascist vs. non-fascist characterization of these respondents, a valid instrument should permit the researcher to distinguish the two groups. The same technique can be employed to locate political actives, to investigate the propensity to violence, or to validate a scale of innovational inclinations among bureaucrats. In principle, this is the method used in the development of measures of need/Achievement, need/Affiliation, and need/Power.[102]

Another variant of this approach to validation is to employ wherever possible several methods of obtaining important information. If findings from surveys, experiments, content analysis of textual materials, and case studies by participant observers all point to the same conclusion, our confidence in that conclusion is markedly increased. At least for certain critical findings in his analysis, the cross-cultural survey researcher is well advised to try to augment his survey efforts with findings from research using other methods. The link between surveys and field experiments is particularly fruitful.

The third, most difficult and probably most important approach to validation which I wish to discuss is that usually labeled "construct validity." Once again, the logic of validation involves checking the results obtained from the new and questionable measure against other related information in which we have some degree of confidence. In this instance, however, the other information does not come from some independent source but rather from the other items of our survey plus accepted theory. Existing theory leads us to predict that certain relations will hold between the measure to be validated and other variables tapped by our survey instruments. If these relationships turn out as theoretically predicted, then we have increased confidence in the validity of our measurement. If they do not, then either our measurement of the given variable is invalid, our measures of the associated variables are invalid, or our theory is inaccurate. Obviously, various combinations or all of these unhappy situations may exist. As is generally true in survey research, negative findings are extremely difficult to interpret. Validation basically involves demonstrating that the new technique or hypothesis conforms to what we already know.

A few examples may be useful. In one of our surveys we asked peasants about their views of the life of rural migrants to the city—were such people happier, more prosperous, lonelier, more immoral, etc.? The answers revealed a fairly high proportion of "don't know" responses. Whenever the researcher encounters a high incidence of "don't knows" (about 25 per cent in this case), he must ask himself if it is likely that the rest of the responses were superficial—"off the top of the head." The "don't knows" may be merely the visible portion of the iceberg of disinterest or uncertainty and the remaining replies no more informed. To check on this possibility, we cross-tabulated the "don't knows" against information on whether the respondent had ever visited the city and whether he had any relatives living there. Most of the "don't know" replies came from the group with less exposure to urban life and to rural-urban migrants, a most plausible result in terms of our "theory" regarding opinion formation among peasants. After such a finding, one gains confidence in the validity of these data.

In the same study, we were also concerned to develop an index of the peasant's "propensity to innovate." We assumed that it was realistic and meaningful to conceive of a generalized propensity to be early, relative to one's associates, at adopting new practices. In other words, we assumed that innovation was not completely specific to the particular practice involved but also reflected a generalized behavioral tendency. An attempt was made to measure this tendency through three items: (1) whether the peasant stated that he would be willing to be the first person in his village to adopt a new and useful method of farming; (2) whether he would be willing to accept an innovational recommendation from his son; and (3) when he perceived at least some innovational conflict in his village, whether he usually sided with the group that wanted to do things in the new way or in the old way. We were gambling that such a limited and general set of items would still be able to tap a generalized propensity to innovate. How could such a measure be validated?

First, we examined the intercorrelations among our three items. If they are measuring the same attitudinal propensity, the three items should be fairly well correlated with each other (although the translation of "fairly well" into a specific acceptance-rejection cut-off point for a correlation coefficient is essentially a matter of judgment). The items should not be too highly correlated, however, because each would then add little to the others. Three perfectly correlated items, for example, could be replaced by any one of them without loss of information. In this case, all three items were moderately, positively and statistically significantly (at the .05 level or better) correlated. However, one of the correlations—that between choosing the "modern" side in village innovational conflicts and willingness to accept a son's recommendation—was clearly lower than the other two. Further analysis, moreover, indicated that the item involving the son was definitely not unidimensional. It seemed to be tapping the male respondents' notions of familial proprieties as well as their innovational propensities. The male literates, who turned out to be the most innovational group for the other two items, fell below the female literates for this item, and the same inversion was noted when the male illiterates were compared with female illiterates. Apparently, the sex and parental role images contaminated this particular item. A revised index might exclude it.

Nevertheless, the three-item index was run against the other items in the survey which directly offered construct validational clues. The theoretical reasoning was essentially that if we had actually obtained a crude but valid measure of the peasant's propensity to innovate, certain other relations could be predicted. For instance, holding sex constant, we should predict that illiterates with a relatively high propensity to innovate would be more interested than other illiterates in learning to read and write. Such proved to be the case. Further analysis, after controlling for sex and literacy, showed clear positive associations between the propensity to innovate measure and reported consultation with an agricultural extension agent, use of government agricultural credit, receipt of government agricultural supplies, perception of innovators in the village, rating the provision of more seed and fertilizer by the government as "very important," wanting more irrigation aid and more agricultural credit, expressing interest in homemaking training for village wives, expressed willingness to participate in a village project, avowed interest in a village vocational course, viewing city returnees as likely to have good ideas for village improvements, expressed intention to invest rather than consume or save a hypothetical windfall of money, heightened nationalism, and so on through a considerable list of expected relationships. At the same time, a few of the predicted relationships failed to appear, though never was there a reversal of a prediction. Those with a high propensity to innovate, according to our measure, were not more likely to have taught themselves to read and write (contrary to our prediction), were not less likely to use a wooden rather than a metal plow, were not more interested in birth control, and were not less likely to look to the village headman for farming leadership. As usual, the validational picture is not completely cloudless. But, in this case, four of every five predictions from a total predictive set of over two dozen hypotheses turned out to be true for the propensity to innovate index, and so we felt justified in asserting its essential validity. It is from such detailed analysis that construct validity is established.

Validational Difficulties

Several snares await the cross-cultural survey researcher attempting to demonstrate the construct validity of his items. One of the most obvious problems is that of avoiding various types of respondent "sets." By "set" I refer to a respondent's tendency to react to survey questions not individually and in terms of their specific content but en bloc and in terms of some fixed orientation that is irrelevant to the purposes of the questioning. Rather than distinguishing, considering, and answering each question, the respondent gives the same type of rigid, generalized, and inappropriate response to entire blocs of divergent items. The most egregious example is probably simple perseveration; for instance, the respondent persists in answering all questions from a "yes-no" series of items affirmatively, regardless of changes in the content of those items, much in the fashion of the foreigner who doesn't really understand English and answers all questions with a smiling "*si*." The reasons for the foreigner's stream of "*si*'s" and the survey respondent's perseveration in a particular response are usually the same, namely, lack of understanding of the questions.

Another, related pattern is "acquiescence set" or the "courtesy bias." In this case the respondent fails to consider and answer each particular question because his paramount concern is to please the interviewer or the authors or sponsors of the survey. He repeatedly says what he thinks his interrogators will want to hear. In its crudest and most obvious form, he agrees with any assertion made to him. In its more complex forms he articulates whatever he believes will accord with the opinions of the researchers, or their sponsors, though his replies may vary considerably pursuant to his notions of his interrogators' values. But, in any event, he is responding basically indiscriminantly or irrelevantly to all the items rather than specifically and appropriately to each.

A third type of respondent set involves his reaction to the questions in terms of the "social desirability" of his response rather than to the items' real content. In other words, the respondent in this case replies not to please the interviewer or researchers, but to please some different reference group, some "generalized other" of importance to him. He strives in his answers to do the "done thing" in his culture, to appear to have admirable and proper orientations whether he really possesses them or not. Thus, if it is widely held in his community that the good citizen votes, that voting is socially desirable, he will say he votes regularly whether he really does or not. His general strategy in answering all items, regardless of his true posture, is to maximize his social acceptability as he sees it.

Sets of these types are a problem not only because they preclude valid measurement, but also because they may produce a false appearance of validity. For example, the survey items forming a putative scale may show a satisfactory degree of inter-relatedness because they are truly all measuring the same underlying variable, or because they are all blighted by the same type of response set. Moreover, we also know that certain strata and groups are more likely than others to be afflicted by response set, so that the unwary researcher may sometimes find additional correlations with other items which seem to confirm the validity of his measure but which are really due to this same response set. In short, response set may produce both the within-variable inter-item correlations and the theoretically plausible correlations with other variables that make up much of the evidence for validity.

Probably the most common illustration of this difficulty is that of shortened versions of the F(ascism)-Scale in underdeveloped societies. In some surveys validity has been claimed for the F-scale on the grounds that the component items correlate with one another (as they should if they were all tapping the same underlying attitude) and on the grounds that the scale as a whole correlates predictably with other variables such as education, social class, and certain motivations of the respondents. Unfortunately, both these findings might well be artifactual—the result of response set produced and undetected by the survey procedures. If the questions are not carefully selected, the intercorrelations of the scale items themselves obviously could be produced by response set. Moreover, it is now fairly clear that such response set is more likely to occur among the less educated, lower social classes who are often poorly motivated to respond to surveys. But this is the very stratum which existing theory leads us to suspect of authoritarianism. Thus, assumptions of validity or response set might both equally well "explain" such findings, at least superficially.[103]

A carefully developed interrogative strategy can do much to reduce the danger of response set and to permit its discovery if it should occur. Threatening, monotonous, and ambiguous items increase the likelihood of response sets. A string of items which yields a series of "don't know" replies from certain types of respondents may be so discouraging that it induces them simply to continue replying "don't know" to other items for which they do have a more appropriate response. More generally, the survey researcher attempts to vary the directionality of meaningful responses so that the perseveration and acquiescence types of response set can be readily discovered. He constructs his questions in such a way that the truly cynical, truly fascistic, or truly liberal person (as the case may be) must answer some of the items of the cynicism, fascism, or liberalism scale affirmatively and some negatively, some items "strongly agree" and some "strongly disagree." Even then, in the latter instance, he might worry about a response set toward selecting extremes, and so he might even try to have the "mildly agree" or "mildly disagree" responses to a few items also be those most appropriate for his measure. Batteries of questions which are designed to constitute an index or scale are formulated in such a way that any pattern of answers produced by response set yields a result that is meaningless or conspicuously inconsistent in terms of the variable being measured. For instance, the person who answers "yes" to positively phrased items that politicians are good and also "yes" to negatively phrased items that they are bad will therefore not possibly be categorized as either cynical or naive, and the combined uniformity and inconsistency of his replies will alert the researcher to the danger of response set. Similarly, the researcher who has reason to fear social desirability biases should conduct preliminary studies to attempt to develop response categories of matched or comparable social desirability.[104] In general, since response set tendencies are clearly not randomly distributed across cultures and across groups within cultures, they may produce, if undetected, spurious substantive findings which will in turn confound the validation of related measures. Hence, detecting and avoiding response sets is a major concern in the development of an effective interrogative strategy for cross-national research.

Another basic type of interrogative decision confronting the cross-national survey and related to validation has to do simply with the number of items needed to measure each variable. In this instance, the researcher has to make a series of frequently difficult trade-off judgments, and he must try to be as clear as possible about the bases for his decisions. The overriding fact which occasions this difficulty is that the researcher has access to a very limited amount of the respondent's time and almost always wishes to ask far more questions than the respondent will suffer. Given this restriction on obtainable data, the matter of how much time, energy, and good will to allot each of the variables under investigation becomes critical. To handle the problem wisely, the researcher must have a very good idea of the relative importance of each of his variables and the relative difficulty of measuring them with acceptable accuracy. What level of accuracy in measurement will be acceptable obviously depends upon the types of hypotheses which guide the research, so these, too, must be clearly formulated and evaluated for this purpose. For example, if the research hypotheses involve possibly curvilinear relationships or threshold phenomena, then the elaboration of each relevant variable must be sufficient to provide evidence of curvilinearity or threshold effects. Dichotomization of response categories, for example, precludes such analysis.

Ideally, one should always obtain as much elaboration as possible for each variable. Such a statement expresses a general guideline—one that is important and too often neglected. However, the guideline is of limited help in determining the specific number of items and response categories best devoted to each variable. The essential trade-off is between demonstrating reliability and unidimensionality, on the one hand, and demonstrating construct validity and producing interesting findings, on the other. To employ split-half reliability checks and to use most of the well-known scaling procedures for demonstrating unidimensionality, one usually needs numerous items to measure each attitudinal variable, anywhere from a minimum of about six to several dozen, with ten or twelve items per variable frequently stipulated as adequate. The precise number of items minimally required obviously will depend on the types of reliability checks and scaling procedures used. Nevertheless, strict adherence to certain textbook canons of reliability and scaling implies that the researcher will be able to investigate very few variables in the twenty to ninety minutes that he ordinarily wins from the respondent. Moreover, merely because a battery of items has scaled in some sense with one sample or one population at one time does not mean that it will scale with a different population or with the same population at another time. That a set of items constitutes a unidimensional scale is an empirical finding which must be demonstrated for each separate survey. It cannot be assumed on the basis of previous results or results from different populations.

Unfortunately, if the researcher devotes such a large portion of the small total of items on his survey instrument to demonstrating reliability and unidimensionality, he leaves little room for other items which are necessary to demonstrate construct validity or to produce important substantive findings concerning the relations among variables. For construct validity and substantive interest, the researcher wants to use as few items as possible to tap each variable so that he can have ample resources for investigating many variables. Thus, as I have said, a crucial problem for the researcher is to decide the relative importance of each of the variables being considered for inclusion in his survey instruments and also to judge their difficulty of measurement. He will strive to allot more of his limited number of questions to those variables that are most important for his main hypotheses and, within that framework, to those variables that are most difficult to measure. Needless to say, such judgments are painful, and they demand a clear conception of the analytic output envisioned from the survey.

In this connection, it is essential to note that item validation, on the one hand, and scale or index validation, on the other, are not necessarily the same. The researcher must concern himself with both. For example, let us suppose that an index of political participation is composed of six items, one having to do with voting, one with party membership, one with campaign activity, and so on. The researcher first of all confronts the question of whether he has obtained accurate information from each of the six items, e.g., are the respondent reports of their voting behavior accurate? If the component items do not yield valid information as items, then the index as a whole will be misleading. At the same time, the individual items might all be valid and yet the index as a whole might be invalid in that it might not be measuring what we wish to measure; in other words, the items have been poorly chosen and do not relate appropriately to the theoretical concept we wish to employ. In this instance the items may be too formally political, and we may be overlooking many informal types of political participation which are included among the referents of our concept but which are not found among our items. The index may be valid only for the urbanized elite of the nation and yet our hypotheses may be intended to apply to the entire nation. The researcher must be concerned with the validity of both component items and composite indices, not with items alone.

The Need for Prior Knowledge of the Phenomena Under Investigation

Cross-cultural research also rather vividly points up the researcher's need to have a deep familiarity with the substantive matters which he is investigating through survey techniques. Embarrassing and wasteful errors can occur if the interrogative strategy is not grounded in sophisticated knowledge of each country's mores and practices. One of the very first cross-cultural surveys with manifest political content, the *Time* magazine international survey in 1948, illustrates how easy it is to go astray. The interview schedule for that study contained an item asking people to choose the two most important civil rights from a list of five such rights. The researchers were surprised when in Sweden 52 per cent selected "the right to say and write what one believes without fear of punishment," and 75 per cent selected "the right to vote in a fair and free election to decide who shall govern the country," while in Switzerland, "the oldest democracy of the world," this relationship was reversed, 55 per cent choosing "free speech" but merely 41 per cent selecting "the right to vote." On going back to their open-ended interviews, however, the researchers realized that under the Swiss system of government there is ready and frequent use of the referendum, so that any controversial issue can be brought before the people. Hence, many Swiss respondents were answering from a frame of reference not adequately taken into account in the closed form of the question. Their attitude was, "It is not very important to whom a government salary goes; whomever we elect into office, on every important issue we are going to tell him by people's vote what should be done." "The right to vote in an election to office is not so important; the important thing is the right to vote on every important issue and expenditure."[105] True equivalence in interrogation or response interpretation in this case obviously depended upon deep knowledge of the differing constitutional provisions and the popular attitudes toward them in each country.

The experiences of Hunt, Crane, and Wahlke while interviewing political elites in France, Austria, and the United States led them to stress this same need for profound familiarity with the systems being studied in order to draft effective survey instruments. With admirable candor, they report ". . . some conspicuous failures which reflect the necessity for thorough knowledge of institutions as a precondition for effective behavioral research. Some questions (taken by simple translation from the American interview schedule) were totally irrelevant for Austrian legislators. For example, questions on legislative decision-making, such as how legislators make up their minds how to vote, are meaningless to legislators who have no 'free votes' and who act almost entirely as decision-legitimizers."[106]

As a final example I might again refer to some of our own work in Turkey. Even items which have long been used in some cultures and seem quite transparent in their interpretation can take unexpected twists in yet another culture. In a study of the value systems of secondary school students we were using the well-known item: "In general, concerning your own personal future, would you say that you feel enthusiastic, hopeful, indifferent, resigned, or embittered? (Select one.)" In previous research in Western cultures, these response categories were seen as being arrayed in descending order of optimism. Moreover, the Western respondents reacting to them could usually be relied upon to perceive them as an array, i.e., as a ranked sequential ordering. When we pretested this item in Turkey, however, our respondents clearly indicated that this implicit ranking did not hold. The Turkish students felt that being indifferent to one's future was worse than being embittered. In the latter case one was at least still engaged with life and the future, while the indifferent person had given up. Furthermore, the students had no prior experience with surveys on which to draw helping them to perceive that a descending ranking was intended. The entire weight of the response-decision fell upon the specific wording, not upon a combination of both the words and a certain general sophistication at answering survey-type questions. Any interrogative instrument which cursorily proceeded to use this rather standard item for comparisons involving Turkish students, without understanding their lack of survey sophistication and the overtones of terms like "indifferent" and "resigned" in a Muslim culture, would court serious error. Every effective survey instrument must be based upon carefully prepared information about the social systems and behavioral practices which the survey seeks to investigate. It is rarely appropriate to start a completely new area of investigation with a survey. Ordinarily, the survey technique is most productive if employed only after considerable impressionistic and case study information has been collected.

Deep familiarity with the people and practices under investigation is

258

essential not only to obtain the information that is technically required for the problem under investigation, but it is also crucial for another reason. We have become increasingly aware of the degree of instability and superficiality in respondents' answers to many types of questions.[107] Some of this superficiality is undoubtedly an accurate reflection of the state of political opinion on many so-called "issues." However, in numerous instances it is a product of mechanical and cursory interrogative procedures. Questions must be designed which "take" with the respondent, which engage and interest him, and which are in his idiom. Otherwise, he may answer, but superficially and capriciously. It is my conviction that much of the static in attitudinal measurement could be eliminated through greater effort in preparing items which really mean something to the respondent, a feat that can only be accomplished if the researchers have a direct and deep familiarity with the people being studied. Lip service is always paid to this ideal, but the actual investment made is often as limited as the questions that result!

A particular dilemma is that increasing the impact and interest of the survey questions usually involves making them more concrete and more firmly in the vernacular of the particular respondent. But, this concreteness and colloquialism—this styling of the item to make it especially meaningful in the particular world of specific respondents—opens the door to various biases and seems to make it even more difficult to secure equivalence of stimuli. There is no automatic answer to such problems. Nevertheless, great stress on formulating items that truly engage the respondent is absolutely vital to effective survey research. It is often neglected, especially in cross-cultural enterprises where no single individual can be extremely knowledgeable about all the nations, classes, subcultures, and groups under investigation.

There is a related practical point which, though pedestrian, is of major theoretical consequence. One of the reasons for wasted opportunities and ineffective interrogative approaches in cross-national surveys lies in the insufficient time and resources allowed for penetrating *analysis* of data from the pretests of the survey instruments and interviewing procedures. Most pretests are used to train interviewers and to detect any flagrant faults in the survey instruments. The researchers check for offensive questions, vague and ambiguous items, "giveaways" (items for which almost all respondents give the same "obvious" answer so that the stimulus does not distinguish among respondents as desired), and so on. Such checking of the instruments and interviewers is usually restricted to special pretest probes or post-interview sessions with selected respondents to elicit their interpretations of the more dubious items, and to inspection of the pre-test marginals looking for any conspicuously high incidence of "don't knows" and refusals or any unwanted gross distributional pattern in answer to certain questions. Alas, only rarely is the pretest analysis carried to any depth. Very seldom is there analysis of more than marginal results. At a minimum, fairly extensive and intensive cross-tabulation is necessary to see if the questions really "took," as indicated by plausible connections among the responses. Sponsors who press for rapid results at cut-rates may be as much responsible for inadequate pretest analysis as researchers who rush to get the survey completed and the book published. Whatever the reason, provision for more than superficial analysis of pretest results is one of the basic ways of obtaining survey instruments and interviewers who secure more than superficial answers from the respondents.[108]

Special Interrogative Approaches for Cross-Cultural Research

There are a few interrogative strategies and a few special techniques whose particular appropriateness for cross-cultural applications has been claimed. The devastating epithet "culture bound" has been cast at so many standard instruments that novel interrogative approaches seem to have extra appeal for cross-cultural researchers. Although I should argue that no completely "culture free" interrogative technique exists or is likely to be produced, the struggles to develop one are interesting and a few of the approaches invented are valuable even if they fail in some of their claims to avoid the usual problems of equivalence.

One basic strategem in the search for "culture free" instruments revolves about the attempt to locate cross-cultural uniformities—activities, perceptions, or social structures which exist in every culture. These could then become the critical dimensions for establishing equivalences. Although in a few cases these uniformities are only theoretically inferred, more often they are asserted both on the grounds of their theoretical plausibility and because they have been discerned in every society which the author's evidence encompasses. Anthropologists using the Human Relations Area Files have probably been most prominent in this work, but psychologists such as Raymond Cattell were on the same quest as early as 1940, and similar efforts can be found in other disciplines.

Obviously, the empirical discovery of nontrivial cross-cultural uniformities, which can then be used as the matrix for establishing other equivalences, involves the same type of vicious circle I referred to earlier. How can one demonstrate that the measures supporting the empirical assertion of certain cross-cultural uniformities were themselves equivalent? The anthropological assertions rest largely on the observations of anthropologists, missionaries, officials, and the other ethnographic reporters whose data constitute the Human Relations Area Files. These writers, in turn, frequently relied upon informants, whose representativeness and possible biases are often well examined. Rarely is there any replication of previous work.

260

Although many of the studies are painstakingly honest and some are theoretically sophisticated, it is difficult to contend that the problem of equivalence has been as consciously confronted by them as it has in the survey realm. Nor is it easy, even if one accepts the asserted universality of some of the activities, perceptions, and structures described, to know how to utilize this information to develop further equivalences. Awareness of the nuclear family as a "universal human social grouping" does not automatically suggest how this fixed point, if indeed it is one, can be used to move the cross-cultural research world.[109] The same measurement problems and interpretive difficulties apply to the psychologists' suggestions regarding the universality of spatial abstractions, Oedipal complexes, or frustration-aggression responses.

Nevertheless, it seems reasonable to assume that some objects, actions, and experiences are more widespread than others, and that equivalence is probably easier to establish in relation to those that are more widely known. The cross-cultural survey researcher should be concerned to exploit the best available judgments about what experiences or perspectives his respondents are most likely to have in common. He may strive especially hard to demonstrate basic absolute equivalences in these areas and then utilize such information to establish additional equivalences through scrutiny of the associations of other variables with the basic variables. However, with one possible exception discussed later (involving the pooling and scaling of all data from all countries), this strategy remains more of a gleam in the eye than an actual practice.

Projective Techniques

Probably most outstanding among the claimant special interrogative techniques for cross-cultural use are the leading projective tests such as the Rorschach Test, Thematic Apperception Test, Sentence Completion Test, Szondi Test, various drawing and painting tests, and role-playing and psychodramatic techniques. In general, political scientists have made little use of projective devices, although a few younger scholars have engaged in some promising forays with the Thematic Apperception Test (TAT).[110] Instead, it is the anthropologists who have most extensively adopted projective techniques for cross-cultural research. Interestingly enough, they have used them mainly to investigate topics that are also of considerable concern to political scientists, namely, national character (modal personality) and acculturation (the relationship between culture and institutions, on the one hand, and individual personality, on the other). Some anthropologists, indeed, have argued that projective tests alone of all psychological tests have the freedom from specific cultural content and have the invariant categories for interpretation that these researchers feel are necessary for successful cross-cultural comparison.[111]

Projective measures are so labeled because they confront the respondent with relatively general and/or ambiguous stimuli which he must further define for himself in greater or lesser degree. The stimuli are usually rather remote from his daily reality, thus eliminating many concrete constraints and pushing him in the direction of fantasy. It is theoretically assumed, largely on psychoanalytic grounds, that in this fantasizing the respondent will tend to project many deeper, basic and more covert aspects of his personality.

Lindzey has characterized a projective technique as

> . . . an instrument that is considered especially sensitive to covert or unconscious aspects of behavior, it permits or encourages a wide variety of subject responses, is highly multidimensional, and it evokes unusually rich or profuse response data with a minimum of subject awareness concerning the purpose of the test. Further, it is very often true that the stimulus material presented by the projective test is ambiguous, interpreters of the test depend upon holistic analysis, the test evokes fantasy response, and there are no correct or incorrect responses to the test.[112]

Many of these features are attractive to all survey researchers and some have a special appeal to the cross-cultural survey researcher, at least superficially. The fact that the projective instrument is particularly sensitive to covert or unconscious factors, that it obtains a wide variety of data, evokes fantasy responses, and has no correct or incorrect responses may or may not be attractive to a given researcher. However, these features are more important for his other research goals, such as examining latent motivation, than for the cross-cultural aspects of his work. But the general nature of the stimuli and the possibly standardized interpretive procedures might be characteristics offering real advantages to the cross-cultural researcher. They warrant a somewhat closer look.

An immediate point is that there is marked variation among projective tests along the dimensions enumerated above. For example, the Rorschach Test seems to be more culturally general in its stimuli than the Thematic Apperception Test in many of its variants. The Rorschach again seems to make it very difficult for an intelligent but untrained respondent to discern the researcher's intent and interpretive scheme, while the Blacky Test appears much more transparent. On the whole, however, projective devices do seem to offer better screening of the researcher's measurement objectives and greater facility in handling sensitive topics than is permitted in the usual survey instrument. However, they often do so at the cost of greater difficulties in several areas: mass-application, interviewer or examiner training, response interpretation and validation, the magnitude of associated coding operations, and remoteness from the concrete setting that may be all-important for many political activities.

Although the cross-cultural survey researcher contemplating use of a projective device will have to consider many detailed features of these tests, we cannot examine all such considerations here. The major methodological problem from our perspective revolves about the related characteristics of (1) stimulus generality or ambiguity and (2) uniformity of principles for response interpretation.

The claim of greater cross-cultural applicability for projective techniques depends, first, upon the asserted generality of the stimuli used. Inkblots, rather vague pictures of human beings in various situations, photographs of clouds, cartoons of a family of dogs, garbled sounds suggesting human speech, photographs of a collection of human faces (actually, of people with known psychiatric disorders), a blank sheet of paper on which a man is to be drawn, dolls with which to play, colored blocks with which to make patterns, and similar stimuli initially do seem to be less culture-bound than most standard interview questions formulated in a typical survey (if there is any such thing). Nevertheless, careful examination suggests that although projective devices have interesting characteristics that offer special advantages in the assault on certain research problems, they have no overall comparative advantage in cross-cultural survey research per se. On the contrary, I would even argue that projective techniques have some conspicuous limitations in cross-cultural work and that the approach to cross-cultural equivalence through attempts to develop "general" culture-free stimuli is quite dubious.

Several considerations lead to his conclusion. First, in most instances a little probing will reveal that the supposed generality of the projective device has critical limitations. The original set of TAT cards, for example, has one showing a boy contemplating a violin on a table before him, another depicts a woman with books in her hand, a third shows a boy lying down against a couch with a revolver on the floor beside him, another has a man smoking a pipe, yet another contains the barrel of a rifle and portrays a surgical operation in the background, while still another includes a woman with magazine and purse. Clearly, these items, not familiar in all cultures, create a probability of culture-based differences in the nature of the stimuli presented to respondents. Moreover, researchers in the field have encountered the well-known problem of having to alter the facial and bodily features of people in the pictures as well as their dress so as to make them appropriate for specific cultures other than those for which they were originally devised. To these perhaps more manageable difficulties one must add the major problem that in certain cultures, although the storytelling role is well known, the visual interpretive conventions, such as foreshortening and perspective, on which the stimuli depend are unknown or different. Discussing the use of TAT's in Africa, Sherwood points out the need for cultural appropriateness in the pictures and the researcher's *uncertainty concerning the very requirements of appropriateness* for the Swazi and other African cultures. Biesheuvel also reminds us that:

> Preliminary investigations indicate a profound unfamiliarity with the conventions of graphic representation, even among fairly well-educated Africans. The rules of perspective drawing are not understood. A group of industrial operatives, presented with a picture of cattle grazing in a field, correctly identified those in the foreground, whilst those in the background, drawn smaller to simulate distance, were sometimes seen as hyenas or similar animals. A workman, standing on a box obscured by fellow-workers whom he was haranguing, against a background of factory buildings and chimney stacks was seen by some as a giant catching the smoke that emanated from the stacks. . . . Conventional graphic details in the postural or facial representations of persons frequently suggested mutilation or blindness.[113]

There is no intention to "pick on" the TAT. Analogous examples could be furnished for most projective tests. The dogs and cartoon conventions of the Blacky Pictures are very Western. The supposedly characteristic pathological features of the photographs used in the Szondi Test are unquestionably European, perhaps even inter-war Central European. The Draw-A-Man Test has obvious difficulties of application among peoples who do not know how to hold a pencil or who have not been culturally conditioned to see a page as a natural boundary or who have a religious injunction against visual reproduction of the human form. Even with the Rorschach, which seems to be more truly general in the nature of its stimuli, the very activity of devoting so much attention to "silly inkblots" is more resisted in some cultures than in others. The extent of the true generality of the stimuli presented in a projective test is always a matter for serious concern and empirical demonstration, just as in the case of a standard survey instrument.

Let us, nevertheless, assume for the moment that the stimuli in the projective test are more widely applicable than those used in other types of instruments. At least the inkblots do not have to be translated, even though they alone do not constitute all the stimuli presented to the subject. One must not forget that an integral part of the Rorschach and many other projective tests is a set of questions from examiner to subject—in other words, an interview. This interview, "clinical" or not, is subject to all the major problems of translation, interviewer effect, response recording, physical setting, and so on, that beset the usual survey interview. Skilled projective analysts are very aware of these problems, although recent converts and less skilled practitioners often seem to forget them.

Nevertheless, it might be argued that the apparent generality of the inkblots themselves, perhaps evidenced by the fact that they neither require translation nor depend upon artistic conventions, is no small advantage. Here, however, we must make some further distinctions among stimuli. A distinction can be drawn between what might be called "objective" and "subjective" stimuli—between what observers and experimenters would agree was presented to a subject and what the subject actually perceived. An inkblot, for example, has generality in the sense that it is a visible form, some of whose characteristics are measurable, e.g., its maximum length or width, color, area, shape, etc. Confronted with two inkblots, one could obtain wide agreement among researchers as to whether they were identical (equivalent). But the dimensions of equivalence here are very limited. In another sense, the inkblots (as symbols) are very definitely not equivalent for most people. Respondents might agree with the researchers that two inkblots were or were not identical, but that is not what they are asked to do. The inkblots are to be treated as symbols and suggestions, and as such they are far from equivalent. They are ambiguous, which is to say they mean different things to different people. In part, that is what gives them their interest. Far from being general, their symbolic "richness" and diversity mean that they have almost unique significance for each respondent. Hence, we can say that along certain manifest dimensions the stimuli are general, but very limited; along other subjectively mediated dimensions they become ambiguous and quite specific, but very rich and suggestive. Indeed, the interest of the Rorschach Test lies in seeing how certain objectively identical stimuli become very different subjective stimuli for different types of people. Ambiguity and generality should not be confused.

In one sense, it can be said that the difference between objective and subjective stimulus is itself a response. Hence, at least for the Rorschach and perhaps a few similar tests, we do have cross-culturally equivalent stimuli and interesting variations in response—i.e., an appropriate instrument. From one perspective this may be true. Elementary differences in perceptual responses can be established in this fashion. But what is the significance of such information? So the Englishman tends to perceive a given blot as a butterfly and the Persian sees it as a stork. So the Russians perceive motion in a blot and the Chinese do not. So the South Africans have a high incidence of animal responses and the Americans do not. These are variations in perceptual response at a level that is extremely remote from an understanding of personality or behavior. Critical inferences must be made from these perceptual dimensions of form, movement, color, whole, and detail to basic personality characteristics. A tremendous burden is placed upon response interpretation, which must be independently validated for each culture. The presumably general perceptual dimensions are relatively few. Other dimensions such as the originality vs. popularity of the response, shading (including perception in three vs. two dimensions), the incidence of "bizarre" responses, etc., have been developed. Many of these obviously depend on cultural and other norms. But, most importantly, the interpretive canons for transforming such general and remote data into predictions about personalities and behaviors have been developed in a few Western cultures. Even there, many

265

fundamental questions exist about the validity of such interpretations. Their validity in widely variant non-Western cultures is even more uncertain. Effective cross-cultural usage of techniques like the Rorschach depends utterly upon within-cultural validation of a complex, far from intuitive scheme for interpreting the extremely remote stimuli and responses that are involved. Taking all these facts into consideration, it does not seem that the projective test is any master key to cross-cultural equivalence. For certain purposes it is an extremely useful tool, a valuable addition to the researcher's kit. But it is not, as has been claimed, a unique answer to our interrogative problems in cross-cultural research.

At an even more basic level, there seems to be a fundamental trade-off between stimulus generality and difficulties of response interpretation. Up to now, stimulus generality has been achieved at the price of remoteness, with consequent uncertainties of response interpretation. At the other end of the continuum, ease in response interpretation seems to be achieved at the price of increased cultural specificity of the stimuli. In either event, the validational problems that must be solved in order to demonstrate item and response equivalence appear to be roughly constant and comparable. One can shift them more to the Stimulus or Response side of S-R equation, but one cannot dodge them to any significant extent.

The Semantic Differential

A second interrogative technique hailed as particularly useful in cross-cultural research is the semantic differential. Developed by Charles Osgood and his associates, it is said to lend itself "admirably to work with a number of cross-cultural problems."[114] The original inspiration seems to have come from Osgood's earlier work on synesthesia, the linkage of certain sensations belonging to one sense (e.g., sight) with those of another sense (e.g., hearing). Thus, high notes in music might regularly be envisioned as bright or red, while low notes might be pictured as blue, dark or somber.

Researchers on synesthesia began to employ polarized adjectival pairs such as "hot-cold," "wet-dry," and "young-old" to study synesthetic tendencies. For instance, subjects were asked to describe their reactions to a piece of music in terms of their first impressions of the degree to which it suggested one or the other of such adjectival opposites. Rather striking consistency of response among various types of subjects was noted. Osgood perceived the possibility of using this approach to get at broader problems of conceptual connotation, e.g., as he and his associates suggest, *The Measurement of Meaning*.[115]

Essentially, the semantic differential technique involves presenting a group of *subjects* with a series of *concepts* (such as "Democracy," "Me," "Russia," "Nixon," "The War on Poverty"), usually one concept at a time.

The subjects are asked to react to each concept in terms of a set of polarized adjectival *scales* (good-bad, strong-weak, fast-slow, active-passive, etc.). A seven position rating metric is ordinarily used for each scale, usually in the following format:

Justice

good	X :	:	:	:	:	:	bad
active	:	:	:	: X :	:		passive
fast	:	:	:	:	: X :		slow, etc.

The numbers arbitrarily assigned to the seven possible responses typically range either from $+3$ through -3 or from 1 through 7. In the example above, the respondent's check marks might be scored respectively $+3$, -3, -2 or 1, 5, 6.

The technique is relatively easy to administer, requires very little special skill on the part of the interviewer or examiner, permits widespread application, and has the major virtue of eliminating the arduous coding operation necessitated by many other approaches. Moss has suggested that it is easy for the subject to "malinger" (dissemble) with many of the present adjectival scales, but points out that it is possible to compensate for this by using less obvious scales when the scale/concept relationship becomes too transparent. For example, if the respondent is reacting to the concept "Me," the volatility dimension might better be scaled metaphorically through adjectives like "fluctuating-level" instead of the more obvious "calm-excitable" or "emotional-unemotional."[116]

Rosen has observed that "the sole major difficulty would seem to be that of administering the semantic differential to groups of low intelligence or education for the technique requires a certain abstractness of attitude on the part of subjects."[117] Similarly, there might be some question about its ease of application with illiterates who could not read the scales. Against this concern, however, one can point to the fact that the semantic differential has been applied with apparent success in illiterate and very poorly educated groups. Suci, for example, reports the use of the semantic differential in four Southwestern U.S. cultures: Spanish-American, Hopi, Zuni, and Navaho. The three American Indian groups were illiterate and had to be given the material verbally, individually and in their own languages. Moreover, the rating scale metric had to be adapted from the general form previously described to a six-inch line with the ends and middle marked. Positions on this line metric were determined by measuring the distance in tenths of an inch from the left end of the line to the respondent's check mark. With these adjustments, the technique seemed to work quite well.[118] Maclay and Ware also comment that "even if the tests are administered orally and individually an impressive amount of data can be collected in a relatively short time; Hopi subjects marked scales at the rate of about 250 per hour."[119]

267

The logic of the semantic differential permits three basic types of variation: in subjects, in concepts, and in scales. Ordinarily, the researcher desires to control at least one of these three variables and systematically investigate fluctuations in the others. He may be interested in comparing what connotations the concepts "National" and "Local" have for samples of urban Danes and Italians. In cross-cultural research we frequently wish to compare respondents from different cultures in terms of their responses to equivalent concepts and scales. Hence, in evaluating the semantic differential, as with other interrogative approaches, we again encounter the problem of assessing and demonstrating equivalence. This time, the two problem areas are equivalence of concepts and equivalence of scales. Equivalence of subjects is also a matter of concern, but those problems have already been discussed in the section on sampling.

The "concept" variable of the semantic differential can be regarded as the main initial stimulus to which the subject responds in terms of the scale categories made available. It can be a word, phrase, or paragraph, a verbal, visual, or tactual representation, etc. It might be a word like "socialism," a slogan like "better Red than Dead," or a party symbol like an elephant or donkey. The general injunction is simply that the concepts investigated by the semantic differential should produce individual variations in response, should have unitary meaning (unidimensionality), and should be familiar to the subjects (otherwise there may be a spurious regression toward the middle of the scales, 0 or 4).[120] Obviously, these desiderata also apply to standard survey questions.

In its verbal forms, the semantic differential involves the researcher in problems of the cross-cultural translation equivalence of the various concepts employed. He wishes to present subjects in various cultures with equivalent concepts and note any connotational variations for those concepts. Therefore, he confronts the problem of demonstrating as best he can the basic equivalence, for his purposes, of translations like "government" and "*gobierno*," "rule" and "*regle*," "friend" and "*freund*," or "prep school" and "public school." In the long run, once a foundation of established equivalences has been laid, the semantic differential offers much promise in helping to demonstrate further translation equivalences. But at present this problem must be tackled in a fashion that is no different from that used in regular cross-cultural survey research. Back-translation is the tactic most frequently adopted. Sometimes uncertainties regarding the equivalence of concept translations have affected the interpretation of empirical findings.[121] One possibly significant advantage for the semantic differential, however, is that in most instances only the meanings of single words or phrases must be equated. Extensive passages and full sentences or paragraphs are not ordinarily involved. And, as Kumata and Schramm have noted, syntactics (and pragmatics) can be omitted—only semantics are at issue.[122]

Matters get a bit more complex when we turn to the "scale" variable of the semantic differential. The scales can be regarded roughly as the set of response categories in terms of which the subject reacts to the initial stimulus, the "concept." Many of the problems mentioned in discussing the "concept" also apply to the "scales." Obtaining and demonstrating translation equivalence for each element of each scale is one example. In Japanese, for instance, the translation of "light" (*karu-i*) refers only to weight and not to illumination, as in English. "Calm" refers only to emotional states and not also to weather, while the Japanese translation of "fast" (*haya-i*) implies "early" as well as rapid.[123] Thus, certain connotations may appear to be present or absent in some cultures solely as an artifact of the linguistic possibilities inherent in nonequivalent scaling words.

If the semantic differential is to yield insight into the connotational meaning of a concept for different groups of subjects, the scales employed must furnish an adequate sampling of the main dimensions of meaning for that concept. If we are interested in intergroup variations in reactions to the term "politician" we must cast our net of scales widely enough to pick up the basic aspects of such reactional variations. If all our scales are focused on the evaluative dimension (good-bad, happy-sad, kind-cruel, nice-awful, honest-dishonest, etc.) and none on the potency dimension (strong-weak, hard-soft, rugged-delicate, large-small, and so on) we may miss important considerations. Hence, unless one has some special reason to be concerned with only one aspect of connotational meaning, he encounters the problem of ensuring that his scales represent the main dimensions of meaning relevant to the concepts under investigation. It is a far from trivial difficulty.

This problem of obtaining a representative selection of antipodal scales becomes especially critical when the semantic differential is applied in a new cultural setting or for new concepts. In the United States the adjectival scales were first selected on the basis of their frequency of usage among 200 undergraduate students responding by free association to the forty nouns on the Kent-Rosanoff list of stimulus words. Later, understandably worried about the possible unrepresentativeness of these first scales, Osgood and his associates resorted to *Roget's Thesaurus*, extracting the most common antipodal pair of adjectives from each classificatory category used by Roget. I mention these details to indicate how the problem of scale representativeness was handled in the country of origin of the semantic differential. The same problem must be attacked in each culture where the technique is to be applied, at least until we become quite confident of the generality of a set of dimensions of meaning. Indeed, one of the most attractive and instructive aspects of the semantic differential for the cross-cultural researcher is the attention which its proponents have paid to cross-cultural validation. On the whole, they have recognized the need for detailed local validation for each application, at least in the early stages of the technique's development, and they have been relatively assiduous in attempting to secure that validation. The logic of cross-cultural validation for the semantic differential is no different from the logic for the validation of a standard survey instrument, as previously discussed.

In addition to providing the subject with a representative and balanced set of dimensions of meaning (semantic space) for the concept being examined, other criteria also enter into the selection of scales. One is that the scales must be germane to the concept involved. Irrelevant scales lead to a disproportionate incidence of middle (0 or 4) choices. Scales should also have semantic stability across concepts, e.g., the sense of the terms "high-low" should remain reasonably constant if they are to contribute to an appreciation of the differences among concepts. Furthermore, the scales should certainly be linearly polar, i.e., functional opposites.

Once certain base points have been established, the semantic differential itself becomes very useful in checking these criteria. For example, if a set of basic scales has been validated by other methods, then additional scales can be tested in part by the semantic differential using the basic scales. The polarity of two new scalar adjectives can be partially demonstrated by showing that they have opposite connotational configurations in terms of the basic scale semantic differential. If "good" is seen as "kind," "true," "harmonious," "grateful," etc., and if "bad" is really the polar opposite of "good," then "bad" should be seen as the polar opposite of the associated adjectives, i.e., as "cruel," "false," "dissonant," "ungrateful," etc. This can be empirically checked through the semantic differential. As usual, once a beachhead of equivalence has been established, it can be exploited to gain ever increasing areas of equivalence.

Perhaps the most intriguing and promising aspect of the semantic differential is that empirical research to date, both among diverse components of the United States population and in other societies as well, suggests that there is great interpersonal regularity in the major dimensions of connotative meaning. Many dimensions of meaning have appeared in the research literature on the semantic differential. Factor analyses of the intercorrelations among scales have produced at least the following types of factors: evaluative, potency, activity, anxiety, aggressiveness, tautness, novelty, stability, chaos, receptivity, inept insecurity, personal-social misery, and sociability. However, in most of the studies completed so far three of these factors stand out from the rest in importance. It is thought that these three may be the primary dimensions for the organization of human judgments.

The most important dimension of connotative meaning (semantic space) is *evaluation*. Virtually all investigations have revealed a pervasive evaluative (good-bad) factor which accounts for approximately half of the total extractable variance in response to the semantic differential. The second major fact has usually been the *potency* (strong-weak) factor, which ordinarily accounts for about half as much extractable variance as the evaluative factor. The third dominant factor, roughly equal to or slightly smaller than the potency factor in variance explained, is the *activity* (active-passive) factor. When additional clear factors can be extracted, they commonly account for less than half of the variance attributed to the potency or to the activity factor.[124]

The consistency with which these three major dimensions of connotative meaning emerge in a wide variety of studies is quite impressive. Work in the United States revealed the same basic structure for extremely diverse groups including college students, Indians, schizophrenics, various I.Q. levels, authoritarians, males and females, voting groups, and so on. The basic dimensions also emerged when the scales were presented in their standard verbal form and when they were presented in terms of non-verbal pictures and drawings (e.g., dark vs. light circles, thick vs. thin lines, crooked vs. straight lines, etc.). They appeared again when the "concepts" used were naval sonar sounds rather than more ordinary words and phrases. And, of greatest significance to our present concerns, they have emerged in studies of monolinguals from the United States, Japan, Korea, Greece, Italy, Hopi culture, Zuñi culture, and Navaho culture. Recently, further cross-cultural applications have been made with samples of students from about forty different nations.

All in all, both the extent of the cross-cultural testing of the semantic differential and the apparent stability of the evaluative, potency, and activity factors have been striking. They provide a valuable example of successful cross-cultural research which has yielded important findings, showing that persistent, sophisticated, and ingenious use of a promising approach to cross-cultural survey research, coupled with willingness to make numerous specific checks into validational problems, can produce marked advance. The brief history of the cross-cultural application of the semantic differential illustrates the kind of effort that can and should be made.

A cautionary note must also be sounded. Although the development of the semantic differential furnished much needed inspiration to cross-cultural survey research, it too is still in its infancy. As noted earlier, the total extractable variance from factor analysis of responses has not been large. There are probably dimensions of connotative meaning that we have not yet tapped successfully. Moreover, understanding and labeling the factors that do emerge is difficult. Researchers using the semantic differential are wont to say that the first factor unearthed in their analysis "is clearly evaluative" so long as it includes the "good-bad" and three or four other prominent evaluative scales, despite the fact that it may include numerous additional scales that were not previously highly loaded on the evaluative factor in other studies. After much careful quantitative analysis the perception of intergroup similarities between factors is often disconcertingly subjective. The careful consumer of this research is always well advised to look beyond the often debatable factor labels chosen by the particular author into the detailed scale composition of each factor.

We have already discussed the sticky problems of concept and scale equivalences. The researcher must also grapple with various scale instabilities across concepts. In other words, the factorial relationships of particular scales sometimes change with the concept being judged. "High-low" may be primarily an evaluative scale for one concept and an activity scale for another. Greater scale stability across concepts would be most welcome. The output limitations of the semantic differential must also be recognized. There is a certain remoteness to the procedure and considerable limitation of focus. It obtains useful information but only a portion of what most political analysts will want to realize from cross-cultural survey research. It cannot generally replace standard survey items. Finally, and more trivially, in administering the semantic differential the researcher must guard against response set just as he must in standard surveys.

Obviously the semantic differential is no panacea. Nevertheless, empirical evidence promises that it will be a particularly useful tool for cross-cultural survey research, both for attitudinal research and in helping to establish connotational equivalences for key concepts in standard survey instruments. In fact, as Tannenbaum has suggested, ". . . the researcher may also use his ingenuity in adapting the SD as an indirect measure of other variables—e.g., as a measure of empathy, identification, etc."[125] The cross-cultural survey researcher would do well to familiarize himself with this interrogative technique.

The Self-Anchoring Scale

A third interrogative approach to cross-cultural survey research, and one that has been somewhat in vogue recently, is the self-anchoring scale developed by Hadley Cantril, Lloyd Free, and Franklin Kilpatrick. Prompted by the precept of transactional psychology that the individual does not merely *react* mechanically to his environment but *transacts* with it as an active agent, the technique focuses on what perspectives the individual brings to this transaction. As Cantril and Free describe it:

> Very simply, a Self-Anchoring Scale is a means for getting a person to define, on the basis of *his own* assumptions, perceptions, goals and values, the two extremes, or anchoring points, of the spectrum on which scale measurement is desired (e.g., the "top" and the "bottom"; the "good" and the "bad"; the "best" and the "worst"); and then to employ this self-defined continuum as a measuring device.[126]

More specifically, the respondent is asked to imagine his future in the best possible light and to describe what this best possible future would look like. He is then asked to imagine his future in the worst possible light and describe what that would be. Once these anchoring termini are established, he is shown a drawing of a ladder (or, if that instrument is unknown, an analogous illustration, such as levels up a hillside). The bottom of the ladder is numbered zero and the top is numbered ten. The spaces between the rungs are accordingly numbered from one through nine. The respondent is asked to think of the best possible future for himself, as he has defined and described it, as being at the top of the ladder (10) and the worst possible future as being at the bottom (0). He is asked where, then, in that self-constructed perspective does he feel he personally stands at the present time. Where did he stand five years ago? Where does he believe he will stand five years in the future?

The same general procedure has frequently been repeated for the respondent's views regarding his country as well as for himself or his family. Matthews and Prothro, for example, have used it to examine feelings about race relations, while my associates and I have been employing it to elicit self-ratings of influence, prestige, communications centrality, and popularity in well defined concrete groups such as schools and other organizations.[127] Additional applications of the self-anchoring idea are easy to suggest.

In the strictly cross-national domain, Cantril, Free, and their colleagues report applying the Self-Anchoring Striving Scale to national samples of the population in the United States, Brazil, Cuba, the Philippines, the Dominican Republic, Israel, and Yugoslavia, with plans to include Poland, India, and Nigeria. Lloyd Free, moreover, utilized the same tool in research on samples of national legislators in nine countries: the United States, Brazil, France, Great Britain, India, Italy, Japan, West Germany and the Philippines.[128] Sidney Verba and his associates have also been using the self-anchoring approach in their survey work on political participation in India, Japan, Nigeria, and the United States. They employ it mainly to get at comparative perceptions of power and community contributions.

As its formulators would probably be the first to suggest, the self-anchoring scale is, in many respects, hardly new. Survey researchers have long used the technique of getting the respondent to define a situation and indicate his self-perceived place in it. Reference group theory, for example, is predicated on such principles. Judgmental scaling procedures such as those of Thurstone and Stephenson involve a similar approach. What the self-anchoring scale contributes, however, is to help focus and sharpen inclinations which have often been haphazard and crude. It is practical and economical and manifestly designed by scholars with profound field experience. The approach helps in the attack on the equivalence problem through, at its best, a kind of *standardizing* of stimuli and response interpretations. A relative equivalence is explicitly sought. Assuming that the terminal points are meaningful to the respondent and that he can really grasp the equal interval scaling concept, we can compare individuals who see themselves in similar positions relative to their own personal perceptions of the range of variation in their environment. The restriction of focus necessary to obtain this comparability places definite limitations on the applicability of the tool to many problems, but this is true of any interrogative technique.

I have already mentioned what seem the most worrisome limitations of the self-anchoring approach. The first is that some respondents appear to find the conceptualization of the required termini very difficult. Their confidence in their choice of features as characterizing the "best" or "worst" situations sometimes does not seem great. Gentle probing appears to induce some people to add or subtract features with little hesitation. In short, even though they have defined them, the termini—the ideal descriptions—seem not to be very meaningful to some respondents. The researcher must be quite wary of interpersonal variations in this respect. The coding process can be used to alert him to problems of this type. Especially meager descriptions of the terminal situations may reflect a lack of impact by the self-anchoring approach in general for a given group of respondents.

Second, as I have suggested, while the ladder symbol is probably as good a way as any to communicate the notion of an interval scale, the researcher must still be concerned about the degree to which that notion really "took" with the respondent. Also, the time span for questions on future expectations and past recollections must be scrutinized with extra care for many ill-educated populations. Five years, the span on the original instruments, should not be mechanically adopted. It would seem clearly too long for certain groups. Finally, the researcher should be aware that use of the self-anchoring approach to investigate pictures of the desirable and the undesirable usually commits him to an extensive coding operation that he must think through and organize as he would a standard survey with many important open items. Cantril and Free have provided us with considerable help in this respect by publishing the detailed codes they developed for their research.[129] But each researcher will have to digest the underlying principles of the Cantril-Free codes, adopt them, modify them, or construct new codes for himself. Needless to say, in any form such decisions must involve a great deal of labor. On the other hand, the self-anchoring scale can be used without securing an extensive elaboration of what the termini meant to the respondent. But if that is done, the researcher has little protection against the possibility of relatively meaningless, superficial termini that was discussed earlier. In some instances, he may decide that the ideas are so entrenched in the culture and vernacular (e.g., "most powerful man in the village" and "least powerful man") that he can take the risk. But this too should be a conscious and explicit decision.

The Problem of Translation

I shall take up only a few selected topics in the area of cross-cultural translation of survey materials. Two factors permit this economy. First is the presence in this volume of an excellent treatment of linguistic problems in political analysis that covers a number of important points. Second is the previously expressed view that translation problems are essentially problems of validation, which have already been generally examined. I strongly concur in Anderson's observation that "it is important to recognize that the question of translation equivalence is a special case of instrument validation."[130]

Nevertheless, at least as a starting point in the process of instrument construction and validation, the cross-cultural researcher frequently does become involved in the translation of survey instruments and instructions. Therefore, a few comments on outstanding problems seem required.

Back-translation: Simple and Complex

The necessary translations for cross-cultural survey research have been accomplished in many different ways. Simplest and probably most dubious is the practice of having one bilingual read the original and produce a translation that the researcher adopts largely out of faith or sloth. Sometimes the same basic procedure is followed with the exception that a group of people make the translation, rather than a single individual, discussing any disagreements as they arise. Perhaps more typical and certainly slightly more fastidious is the technique of back-translation. In this case, one or more bilinguals translate the instrument into the second language and then other bilinguals, completely independent from the first translation, retranslate it back into the original language. A critical comparison is then made of the two versions of the instrument in the original language. The translation is deemed acceptable if the original version survives its trip out into the second language and back with a minimal amount of reentry distortion.

More elaborate variants of the back-translation technique are known but have rarely been used by cross-cultural survey researchers. They apply particularly to multicultural projects. One is what Casagrande, after Voegelin, calls "serial translation." In this, a message in language A is translated into language B, which is in turn translated into language C, and so on, and then the penultimate version in language N is finally translated back into the original language A and the two versions of the instrument in language A, the first and the last, are compared. In "parallel translation" an instrument in one language is directly translated into two or more related languages and the translations in the several target languages are compared to reveal basic problems in the translation of the original language.[131]

Actually, the multicultural survey seems to offer special opportunities for a frontal assault on the translation problem. A technique somewhat between the serial and parallel approaches appears most efficacious. Let us assume that work is undertaken in five nations and in eight languages. The discussions among the researchers and an original questionnaire have been accomplished in language A. It would seem fruitful to develop a dyadic series of back-translations from language A into each of the other languages and back again (ABA, ACA, ADA, AEA, AFA, AGA, AHA). Obviously, one could go further and develop a complete matrix of all possible translations—and such a strategy has much to recommend it, even though it would be extremely laborious and possibly expensive. However, the vital feature of such a process is to make the inter-instrument comparisons as extensive, systematic, and even quantitative as possible. All too often the back-translations are merely intuitively and impressionistically compared and no record is kept of the nature and incidence of discrepancies found. With more comparisons and more explicit records, however, patterns in the frequency and location of difficulties might be discerned and guidelines developed forewarning researchers of troublesome areas. Up to the present time, translation problems in cross-cultural survey research have been attacked in a very haphazard and ad hoc fashion, so that we have even very little retrievable lore, let alone empirical knowledge, accruing from our labors.

Back-translation, of course, is but one method of inspecting the translation equivalence of survey materials. Other devices are available, but virtually no use has been made of them. For example, statistical checks on the level of redundancy in each version of the instrument are promising. Examination of the comparative frequency of usage in each language of the instrument's most critical terms could be added to the more standard semantic concerns. Syntactical considerations could be investigated as strongly as the simple semantic considerations now probed. As pointed out previously, the semantic differential could be used to indicate the degree of basic, cross-cultural connotative similarity among the survey's focal concepts.[132] Adjective-verb-noun ratios, the length of sentences in the different language versions of the instrument, the amount of use of the subjunctive— these and other aspects of the translation equivalence of the survey instruments might be examined to give us better insight into the comparability of the instruments. Unfortunately, a rather mechanical and certainly very limited back-translation has constituted the translation procedure of most cross-cultural survey work. That it has often "worked" does not mean we cannot or need not do much better.

276

The Use of Bilinguals

Interest in the development of additional systematic indicators of translation equivalence is quickened by an increasing awareness of some of the problems in using bilinguals. Recent research has indicated that there are several forms of bilingualism. The most critical distinction for our purposes is that between the *compound* and the *coordinate* bilingual. The distinction revolves about whether the individual has learned the two languages in associated or dissociated contexts. The compound bilingual, for example, might be a person who learned both languages at home in his family, the two languages being used relatively interchangeably. The coordinate bilingual would be a person who learned the two languages in quite different contexts, such as one at home and the other as part of his graduate education in another country.[133] For the compound bilingual the two languages are essentially two different ways of encoding the same set of meanings and experiences. For the coordinate bilingual the referential meanings encoded in the two languages differ to a considerable extent.

The precise implications of the compound/coordinate distinction for cross-cultural survey translation are at present rather difficult to assess. Carroll, in his review of the research literature on bilingualism, concludes that "this [compound/coordinate] theory leads to the expectation that there would be more interference between languages in the case of the compound bilingual, but that the compound bilingual would be better able to translate from one language to the other."[134] The compound bilingual has had much more experience at translation since it was a constant feature of his language learning environment, while the coordinate bilingual has learned his languages in two separate cultural realms. The latter situation is regarded as more desirable for pure, idiomatic absorption of the second language and for communicating in the given culture, but less beneficial for the purpose of translation. In short, coordinate bilinguals are more likely to have functionally independent language systems.

Against this interpretation, however, is the conclusion that, ". . . for the selection of translators in comparative research . . . coordinate bilinguals, especially those with bicultural experience, can render translations more equivalent in meaning than can compound bilinguals, because their mode of language acquisition sensitizes them more to the real differences in meaning across cultures."[135] Indeed, Osgood and Sebek contend that the compound bilingual can never produce a truly cross-cultural translation since, although he knows two languages, he does not know two cultures.[136] The translator needs to be bicultural, not merely bilingual.[137] Moreover, at least some of the empirical research by Lambert and his associates fails to show any correlation one way or the other between the type of bilingualism and the facility and

277

speed in translation, although it does reveal clear differences between the two types of bilinguals in terms of other linguistic attributes.[138]

If nothing else, the compound/coordinate distinction alerts us to the fact that it is necessary to know one's bilingual. People who speak the same two languages well may differ not only in how they learned the languages but also in dialect, social background in the two cultures, subject matter competence in the two languages, and their general personal posture in each different culture. They often do not speak both languages with comparable fluency, and the very fact that they possess the rather rare skill of being bilingual makes them somewhat unrepresentative of either culture, possibly even in their speech patterns. They may, for example, be prone to introduce words, phrases and constructions from one language into the other.[139] Certainly, it is highly probable that the bilingual translator will be unlike many of the survey's respondents. It is wise, therefore, to have the translation put into its final usable form, even for pretesting, by more representative monolinguals from the given culture in consultation with the bilingual translator and the survey directors.

On occasion, bilinguals have been used in the preparation of survey instruments not directly as translators but as key pretest respondents. The bilingual answers the proposed survey items as accurately as possible in both of its translated forms. Then the response equivalence of his answers to the two versions is examined and used to provide insight into the equivalence of the translation of the instrument, always allowing for the possibility that recollection of the first-language administration may provide extra clues to the meaning of the items in the second-language administration.[140]

Other General Problems

Knowledge of the structural characteristics of the two languages being translated alerts the researcher to areas of probable difficulty. For example, the absence of certain parts of speech in one of the two languages may signal problems. Thus, in some languages such as Turkish the speaker is pushed by the structure of the language to specify his degree of certainty in making an assertion while in other languages this is not required. In some languages a generalized, indefinite pronoun (such as "one") is available and in other languages it is not. Some languages require an indication of the relative social statuses of actors being discussed while other languages do not. The researcher can anticipate difficulties in these basic areas of structural differentiation among languages. Indeed, some interesting peoples have a purely oral tradition with no established written form of their language. Furthermore, these fundamental inter-language differences are compounded by the fact that the respondent makes his own distinctive selection from the set of expressive opportunities afforded by his language. Indeed, it has been observed that some respondents, e.g., certain African children, know *no* language well. "Besides a mother tongue, used with their parents, and a lingua franca used with their fellows outside the family circle, these children learn a European language. The result of this bi- or trilingualism is that no language is known thoroughly; the vocabularies are poor, the exact significance of words is rarely known, the grammatical rules remain rudimentary."[141] Similar deficiencies exist among portions of the populations of most nations. However, since extensive discussion of these various problems can be found elsewhere, I shall not pursue the matter further.[142]

At the deepest level, there is a certain initial vicious circle in translation that not surprisingly is analogous to the basic problem in validation. As Nida has indicated, we cannot understand the meaning of terms unless the relevant culture is understood, but we cannot understand the culture unless we can understand the meaning of its terms.[143] What we should like to have is a universal "metalanguage" that we could employ to query respondents and understand the differences and equivalences in the current specific languages of the world. Lacking such a metalanguage, we are compelled to study a language empirically through methods that are in one way or another dependent on that language. Similarly, in construct validation we must use some existing theory to obtain the necessary validation testing predictions. Yet, how are we to get this existing theory with which to start? What we have confidence in knowing is often quite limited and does not permit wide construct validation. We can only proceed by a slow and initially quite tentative process, establishing, as I have said, our limited beachheads, laboriously exploiting them, and gradually gathering momentum as our base of knowledge expands. It is for this reason that the present rather early work in cross-cultural survey research takes on added importance and that it requires a special fastidiousness. It should be the foundation on which further research can be accomplished.[144]

Data Analysis

The theoretic utility of cross-cultural or cross-national (more generally, cross-systemic) research, as was stressed earlier, is that it permits (1) greater elaboration of important variables and (2) the investigation of interesting systemic effects. Actually, the second value can be reduced to the first. Cross-systemic research permits analysis of systemic effects precisely because it permits the greater elaboration of *systemic* variables—i.e., it permits more than one type of system to be examined. The critical analytic problem of such research is to exploit these opportunities for the elaboration of focal variables, individual or systemic, without foundering in complexity.

Not surprisingly, in view of the above, the greater elaboration of variables and the consideration of systemic effects are analytically intertwined. The researcher has proceeded to the cross-cultural or cross-national level to expand the ranges of crucial variables. Unfortunately, not only the variables of direct concern are elaborated by this process. Many other variables as well may be affected by the inclusion of a different culture or nation. New factors, absent in the initial culture, may even be encountered. The introduction of another system to the analysis, which permits the desired elaboration of focal variables, also tends to produce an undesired elaboration of other variables. The researcher then confronts the grave problem of maintaining appropriate controls. He needs to determine that the relationships among the cross-systemically elaborated focal variables are not spurious or misleading—that is, not attributable to undesirable changes in other (control) variables which have also been affected by the change in system.

For example, suppose we are interested in the hypothesis that political alienation is associated with exposure to certain mass institutions of modern society, such as the factory, the large public school, or the mechanized army. Alienation might be engendered by the anonymity and massivity of these institutions. To examine such an hypothesis, we might adopt a cross-national approach. We could thereby obtain a wider range of respondent exposure to modern mass institutions. If the original nation considered were modern, the additional nation might be transitional or traditional in level of development, thus affording a number of respondents, unavailable in thoroughly modern societies, with little or no exposure to mass institutions. We could then make a comparison of the political alienation of respondents with more widely differing degrees of mass institutional exposure.

Alas, however, many other variables may also have been affected by the cross-national shift. Among these may be numerous systemic and control variables. The presence of these new or more elaborated other variables creates additional hypotheses alternative to those which the researcher was originally considering. He must make analytic adjustments to examine these additional competing hypotheses, if indeed such analytic adjustments are possible. Sometimes the cross-cultural or cross-national gap is so large—the intersystem differences so great and similarities so few—that effective comparison is virtually precluded. So many variables in addition to those of focal interest are introduced or changed that a plethora of alternative hypotheses is created—a snarl too great for the researcher to unravel. Thus, definitive survey examination of many hypotheses in an ultra-modern and a Stone Age level society might be almost unthinkable, so many and large are the possible contaminating factors and so few the number of systems (viz., two). This type of comparison is likely to be fruitful only when one is reasoning a fortiori and obtains a positive finding, in other words, when his hypothesis of a positive (rather than null) relationship is supported despite the great differences and many obfuscating factors separating the two systems. Needless to say, betting on such a finding may be rather risky.

280

Some of the possible complexities can be illustrated by returning to our first example. Suppose that, contrary to our hypothesis, political alienation turned out to be no less among the traditional population than in the modern society whose citizens are more exposed to anonymous mass institutions. We might initially feel that our hypothesis was unequivocally falsified. However, if this particular traditional society (and one always examines some particular traditional society) were an exploitative monarchy, it might be argued that the political alienation found was due to this systemic difference. If this factor were controlled, the expected lower level of political alienation in the traditional society might be found. Unfortunately, a convincing control for such a pervasive systemic factor can be extremely difficult. Yet another hypothesis, for example, might be that the effects of having more than seventy percent of the nation at the poverty level produced the unexpectedly high political alienation in the traditional society. Obviously, further arguments of this sort might develop a long list of plausible and analytically difficult hypotheses.

Of course, I have deliberately aided my case by using negative findings as the illustration. Positive findings confirming a positive hypothesis place the analyst in a much better position, but essentially the same problem remains. Indeed, part of the art of designing cross-systemic research is to select systems which are optimally different—different enough to yield informative elaboration of crucial variables, but similar enough to avoid horrendous analytic problems. An overlapping gradation of differences is often most attractive in a multicultural project. Nevertheless, even in the best of cases, the primary analytic problems of cross-systemic research are establishing equivalences and handling unwanted variation produced by the fact that whole systems or sub-systems of variables (i.e., real persons or nations) must be added to obtain the desired elaboration of only certain variables. It would be pleasant if we could selectively add only cases which expand the ranges of the focal variables alone and of no others. Nature does not allow us this convenience, but the researcher attempts to approximate it through cunning design and to complete the job through careful analysis. From an ultimate perspective, of course, all that has been said can once again be translated into the attempt to maintain equivalence in all respects other than those where variation is desired.

Two Practical Problems

How is the researcher to accomplish this difficult goal? What major problems does he encounter and what strategies seem most effective? One battle the analyst fights almost from the start is to save himself from foundering in data and complexity. He has the task of psychologically getting on top

281

of the data. This is manifestly difficult in most large scale surveys, but it is especially difficult in the multicultural venture. The computer can generate tables, matrices, arrays, and graphic presentations faster by far than the researcher can digest them. If he does not learn to discipline this monster, he may find himself in the unwelcome role of the Sorcerer's Apprentice. He must shape the analytic procedure to his intellectual purposes and have a strategy for so doing. What particular strategy he adopts depends on many specific factors of preference and facilities. But some coherent and organized approach is essential. In our work we have usually adopted a very deliberate approach to data analysis which includes the following basic stages.

1. *Gross marginals.* We obtain first the percentaged answers for every item from the largest meaningful collection of respondents. In a representative cross-national study this would ordinarily either mean all respondents for each nation or, possibly, the entire pool of respondents. If the samples are less global, then even at this level there will be many separate data sets to examine. The gross marginals are inspected primarily to note response distributions whose skewness might limit further direct analysis, to get an impression of how well the instrument "took," and to gain a very vital initial gestalt of the substantive nature of the replies, that is, to develop some very broad and tentative first impressions of the main characteristics of the groups studied.[145]

2. *Controlled marginals.* If the original gross marginals were pooled for various reasons, the first additional breakdown would be to get national marginals—the percentaged replies for each national sample. After that, other controlled marginals are usually obtained for major social background characteristics such as sex, education, age, literacy, occupation, urban/rural residence, and so on. Simultaneous rather than alternative controls are frequently then applied for a few of the most critical background variables. Thus, sex and literacy might both be controlled at once, generating percentaged replies for all items from four groups: male literates, male illiterates, female literates, and female illiterates. This procedure helps the analyst to make a first judgment regarding which controls he may have to employ for which items in subsequent analyses. It also further refines the crude and tentative picture suggested by the gross marginals without prematurely inundating the researcher in complex data. To avoid analytic indigestion, information must be fed to the researcher at an appropriate and controlled pace.

3. *Index and scale construction.* The researcher presumably has designed his instrument with certain constellations of items in mind, and has framed his research to emphasize certain variables which he must now finally operationalize. The next move is usually to some form of initial scale and index construction using the well known techniques for assessing reliability, unidimensionality or homogeneity, and validity. (I shall return to this problem

in a moment.) After this stage, the remaining stages can be shuffled in their order or can occur simultaneously, depending on the style of the analyst.

4. *Specific cross-tabulations to test hypothesis.* Items, indices and scales are cross-tabulated and correlated at increasing levels of multivariate control in order to test the more explicit and specific hypotheses of the research.

5. *Empirical cluster search.* While one is testing specific, a priori hypotheses, he is also concerned to see if other unanticipated but fruitful and more parsimonious cuts into the data might be made. He thus becomes interested in factor- or cluster-analyzing his data, using a more empirically and less theoretically oriented approach than that implied by specific hypothesis testing through cross-tabulation (including under the latter term any statistical analysis of specific relationships such as analysis of variance and covariance, regression and correlation, as well as categorical bivariate analysis). Moreover, he has probably already become involved with such an approach since it is useful in index and scale construction. Ideally, the more empirical factor- and cluster-analytic approaches and the more theoretical cross-tabulational approaches will coincide in their findings, each thus supporting the other. In fact, however, at least a few rather awkward and disquieting discrepancies are usually uncovered—factors which have no apparent theoretical meaning to the analyst or theoretically important hypotheses which are in the right direction but disturbingly weak. These try the mettle of the researcher.

6. *Analysis and reanalysis.* Such empirical/theoretical discrepancies and the fact that the analysis itself almost always leads to new ideas and inspirations not completely envisioned in the original research design both lead to sequences of deeper reanalysis of the data. These involve the generation of new scales and indices and the pursuit of new cross-tabulations. Hence, the last three phases of the analytic operation may be run through a number of times in a complex multicultural survey. This is one of the reasons why the analysis sometimes takes so long; it is usually a very big and demanding task.

A second very practical problem facing the cross-cultural survey analyst is simply that of where the analysis should take place and who should do it. In a large multicultural project, the gross marginals and the controlled marginals are frequently prepared by the individual country teams. Such analysis is straightforward and essentially within-cultural. It can often be the basis for a preliminary report to impatient sponsors which gains time for more penetrating analyses. However, after this stage it is extremely useful if all the principal researchers can be assembled to conclude the more difficult and truly cross-cultural portions of their assignment. Cross-systemic analysis demands either common processing of data or, more usually, at least continuous and intensive communication among the researchers, since they are striving to develop equivalent system-specific indicators for shared concepts. One can, of course, try to do all or part of this by mail. In fact, such a communication pattern, augmented by occasional international conferences, has probably been the most common arrangement in large scale cross-national research up to the present. But the research inevitably suffers both protraction and loss of quality as a result. The profoundly shared conceptual and methodological approach which is so vital to cross-cultural researchers ordinarily depends on frequent, intensive, and rapid interaction throughout the analytic phase. Assembling all the principal researchers in one location to complete the analysis increases their level of fruitful interaction tremendously.

Analyzing Equivalence

Two fundamentally different but compatible approaches to the analytic demonstration of equivalence in conceptualization and measurement are currently available to the cross-cultural survey researcher. One can be christened the approach through *unidimensionality* (or homogeneity) and the other the approach through *validity*.

The Approach Through Unidimensionality

In one sense, we have an equivalence problem in most within-cultural research whenever we employ attitudinal scales. We want the items comprising those scales to be equivalent in that they all tap the same attitudinal universe and, to a preponderant degree, only that universe. In other words, we want the scale to be homogeneous or unidimensional. Similarly, in cross-cultural research we want the presumably equivalent items used in the various cultures to measure one and the same thing. Accordingly, one of the methods for analyzing equivalence involves demonstrating, if possible, the cross-cultural unidimensionality (homogeneity) of the items in question.

Przeworski and Teune have provided the most explicit description of this strategy, based on the prior discussion of Scott.[146] The approach requires designating a total set of all items to be used to measure a given property (e.g., attitude) in any and all systems being studied. This total set of items should have two subsets: (1) a subset of items common to all systems and (2) a different subset of items specific to each system or to a few but not all systems. The subset of common items should consist of questions which are "identical," except for translation, across all systems. The remainder of the total set will consist of questions which are system specific.[147]

All respondents from all systems are then pooled, thereby disregarding nationality, culture or other systemic differences. Responses to the formally identical items by the pooled samples are subjected to an analysis of their scalability to determine unidimensionality. This can be accomplished by testing their homogeneity, as the authors recommend, or by other forms of item analysis, Guttmann scaling, Likert scaling, and similar procedures. If a set of demonstrably unidimensional items can be obtained from the set of formally identical items, with systemic differences ignored, then this set can be defined as equivalent across the systems. The degrees of equivalence of the remaining system-specific items can then be gauged by analyzing their correlations with the standardized group of equivalent, formally identical items. "Those indicators which are specific to each country and which are correlated with the identical indicators are maintained to have equivalent cross-national validity."[148] Unless the degree of scalability (unidimensionality or homogeneity) turns out to be so high that the possibility of a national anomaly is precluded, the careful researcher will probably want to check the scalability of the set of formally identical items in each nation as well as for the pooled group of respondents, especially if the national samples differ appreciably in size and the scaling criteria are not very strict.

In short, then, what this approach involves is creating an initial beachhead of cross-systemic equivalence and then establishing equivalences through correlating other items with the items of established equivalence. The presumably "identical" items and pooled respondents are necessary to move from within-system scalability to cross-system scalability. Showing that one group of four items (A, B, C, D) scales for one national sample and that another group of four items (W, X, Y, Z) scales for another national sample is obviously of little help in demonstrating cross-systemic equivalence, even though the researcher might intuitively feel that the items were equivalent. By using items that can at least initially be presumed to be "identical" in a known if formal fashion and by pooling all respondents, the door is opened for a try at establishing cross-systemic equivalence through general unidimensionality demonstrated by scaling. Of course, only equivalence and not validity is at best indicated by this method. Moreover, one must recall that a few a priori decisions still ineluctably enter the picture. For instance, only the correlations of the previously designated subset of system-specific items with the identical items are considered, not any and all correlations between the identical items and other variables. In other words, an initial and limiting assessment of likely equivalence has been made on other grounds. This is useful in excluding accidental or irrelevant correlations. All techniques, moreover, appear to involve this type and degree of extra-empirical intervention.

To the manifest attractions of the approach to equivalence through unidimensionality must be added a few other uncertainties. The method requires a set of at least formally identical items and this simply may not be possible across some divergent groups of systems for some important properties. In light of our previous discussion of "Interrogative Strategy," one can also understand the uneasiness of some researchers over the very concept of "identical" items. Beneath the formal identity produced by translating the same core questions into several languages may lurk a very real lack of identity. Against this one could respond that if such lack of real identity is the case it will be revealed when the set of formally identical items fails to scale. While this is a protection, the researcher then is led to wonder how often a scalable set of core items will actually be obtained from the formally identical subset of items. The demands of the approach may be so great that it may not be very widely applicable. It would appear possible that in many instances, (1) a sufficient number of presumably identical items cannot be developed, (2) the set of formally identical items that is developed will have many real nonequivalences lurking beneath the surface and will not scale, or (3) the attitudes of the populations will be so different as to preclude international scalability for the pooled group of respondents. Nevertheless, these are empirical questions and such reservations can be dispelled by widespread success in actual field use of the unidimensionality approach. Certainly it has promise and there is such a dearth of alternatives that much experimentation with it is fully warranted.

The Approach Through Validation

The approach to equivalence through validation has been more widely employed than the approach through unidimensionality, although it has usually been applied implicitly rather than explicitly. In the unidimensional approach, a core equivalence is asserted on the basis of showing that the *same set of items* (formally identical) hangs together across systems, i.e., that the items exhibit similar, nonrandom patterns of relationship *among each other* without regard to system. In the validational approach, equivalence is asserted on the basis of demonstrating that *different system-specific sets of items* all measure a variable which is similarly and predictably related to *designated other variables* in each system.

To illustrate the validational approach to equivalence, let us take a fairly tractable example. Suppose we are interested in the variable "level of political information" and wish to develop equivalent measures of it in several countries. After Matthews and Prothro, we might use a set of seven items to tap this variable in the United States, the items asking about the party affiliation of Franklin Roosevelt, the identity of the governor of the respondent's state, the length of the governor's term, the name of the county seat of the respondent's county, the term length of a U.S. senator, the number of members on the U.S. Supreme Court, and the names of the last two states admitted to the United States.[149] Obviously, however, these items would be inappropriate in another country. But, no less obviously, it seems perfectly possible to develop an analogous though specifically different set of items for each country studied. One might ask about presidents in one case and premiers or prime ministers in another, about the length of an official's term or about the frequency of referenda, about the names and programs of political parties or about who debated whom on television. Each country would have a formally unique set of items, but these items could presumably be functionally equivalent. The problem is how to demonstrate such equivalence.

The validational approach depends upon having a sufficient theoretical base to permit predictive confirmation of the presumed equivalence. In other words, it requires that we know enough to make the following type of statement: "If we have validly measured the same variable, X, in each country even though we have used formally different specific items, then that measured variable X should display certain stipulated relationships with variables A, B, and C." If those stipulated relationships, those common and expected patterns among distinct variables, are indeed found in every system, then we assert the equivalence of variable X (and sometimes even A, B, and C) across systems. Put crudely, we reason that the probability that such a set of predictions will hold across divergent systems by chance even if we have measured non-equivalent variables rather than equivalent ones is so low that it can be rejected. Our confidence in making this assertion clearly depends upon the number of systems involved, the number of variables, and the precision of the theoretical predictions or expectations. As these go up, so does our confidence.

To demonstrate the equivalence of different specific indicators of the variable "level of political information," we might proceed as follows. Our theoretical expectation is that political information should be positively correlated with such variables as formal education, exposure to certain content in the mass media, literacy, interest in politics, political activity, and I.Q. It should be negatively related to political cynicism and feelings of inefficacy. If our theory (which, in the early stages of empirical research, is often a euphemism for common sense or shrewd guessing) is sophisticated, we could stipulate expected ranges in degrees of association among these variables as well as direction. If these expectations prove true in all systems being investigated, then we have increased confidence in the equivalence of our concepts and measures. If the findings are negative, then we are unsure whether the fault lies in our theories or our measurements, as explained previously.

Implied in this discussion is a manifest limitation of the validational approach to equivalence—we may not have enough accepted theory concerning a given variable to allow such validation. Another drawback is visible when the researcher obtains partial or inconclusive validation. Clear standards of what constitutes an acceptable validational test are even more lacking than consensus on the tests of unidimensionality. In many cases we are not far beyond simply having to accept the subjective judgments of the researcher. This is reflected in the analyst's frequent squirming to find ad hoc reasons excusing failure of a validational prediction in order to salvage the equivalence assertion he wants to make. It is also reflected in the development and enunciation of the validational expectations *after* the data have been examined rather than prior to inspection of the data.

Finally, it should be noted that the unidimensionality and validational approaches to demonstrating equivalence are, as mentioned earlier, eminently compatible. The careful researcher is likely to employ both, especially since the unidimensionality approach does not necessarily imply validity, which must be separately demonstrated. At best, if the researcher shows both that a set of formally identical items can be scaled for the pooled groups of respondents and that this identity set plus highly correlated system-specific sets of items actually reveal precise and complex relationships among variables according to accepted theoretical expectations, then he has taken a major stride toward confident assertion of cross-systemic equivalence of concepts and measures.

Levels of Analysis

The cross-cultural survey researcher has willfully plunged into multilevel analysis and sometimes suffers dearly for his temerity. Any cross-systemic survey obviously involves at least two "levels" of analysis, the individual and the systemic. In most instances, numerous intermediate levels are also distinguished, such as small groups, generations, communities, status categories, organizations, institutions, and regions. Some of the conspicuous problems about levels that have confronted cross-systemic research have been confusion over the conceptual definition of the levels of analysis, lack of operational equivalence of the levels across systems, and improper inference from one level to another. Nevertheless, human life is organized into various environments of great importance, and multilevel analysis is required to understand those contexts.

Levels of analysis are probably most often and perhaps most fruitfully distinguished in terms of the property of inclusion, though there are various dimensions or types of inclusion. The individual is included within the family, the family in the community, the community in the region, the region in the nation, and so on. Structurally embedded levels of this type open up critical possibilities for contextual analysis. Other interesting levels, however, are distinguished on analytic grounds, such as the relative sizes of the units, their complexity along some dimension such as structural elaboration, and their comparative amounts of prestige or authority. There is no universally preferable criterion for distinguishing levels of analysis, and the onus is always on the researcher to demonstrate the utility of the distinctions he has chosen.

Galtung, after Lazarsfeld and Menzel, suggests the following scheme for characterizing any unit within a given level:

1. By reference to itself only (absolute or global description),
2. By reference to other units within the level (comparative),
3. By reference to the structure of the units within the level (relational),
4. By reference to subunits included under the given level, and
5. By reference to superunits above the given level (contextual).[150]

Such a scheme is of value primarily in alerting the researcher to the types of analysis possible with multi-level data.

One fundamental point which the analyst should keep in mind is that insofar as possible he must have a clear understanding of the theoretical significance of each level of analysis he employs. In this sense, residual levels are unfortunate and should be minimized. Teune makes this point effectively in discussing the status in comparative research of national level terms like "the Indian political system."[151] Such terms are disguised residuals for the comparative analyst. They reflect the, hopefully temporary, inadequacy of his theory rather than its power. Much of his effort is devoted to replacing such idiosyncratic *names* with more universal descriptions of levels and systems. Thus, instead of talking about "India" he wishes to be able to talk about a national political system with characteristics $A, B, C, \ldots N$. Only when he can do so will he display true theoretical understanding of the level he is discussing. Needless to say, however, we shall reach such sophistication only gradually and by small incremental steps. The goal, nevertheless, must remain before the researcher.

Once he has determined the possible levels of analysis permitted by his data, the analyst encounters the problem of deciding at which level he is going to seek the explanation for a given empirical variation. His analysis may be basically oriented to a dependent variable (i.e., he is interested in the causes of a given phenomenon), or it may be more oriented to an independent variable (i.e., he seeks the consequences of a given phenomenon). Furthermore, the focal dependent or independent variable (and this may be a relationship) can be at any analytic level. Be that as it may, the analyst is usually well advised to adopt the strategy of proceeding upward from the "lowest" and least complex level. Ordinarily, this means proceeding from the individual level through levels of ever-increasing complexity. In principle, he does not want to introduce into his explanation any analytic level higher than is needed to provide an acceptable explanation of the variance which concerns him. For example, some of the attitudinal and behavioral differences among Italians, Englishmen, Americans, Germans, and Mexicans are said to wash out or be greatly reduced when education is controlled. If that is true, national systemic variables may be unnecessary for an adequate explanation of such differences.[152] Similarly, much of the variance in political participation in those five nations may be explained by patterns of social status and organizational involvement, so that variables describing national political cultures need not be invoked.[153] Terhune criticizes some of the national character studies for neglecting lower level demographic explanations of international differences in personality because of the analyst's eagerness to adduce cultural factors.[154] The analyst may still have to consider higher level factors if critics plausibly argue that the explanation of variance in the dependent variable provided by the lower level independent variables was spurious or that those lower level variables were actually only intervening between some higher level independent factors and the dependent variable. But the principle of seeking the lowest level of explanation which satisfies the mind is a useful guideline.

The existence of different analytic levels in cross-systemic survey data permits numerous errors of inference to occur, all of which might be labeled the fallacy of the misplaced level.[155] The error consists in making illegitimate inferences from data at one level to conclusions at a different level. Taking the simplest case where we have only two levels—let us say, the individual and the systemic—then two basic errors of this type can occur. One is naively to infer the characteristics of individuals directly from data which are only at the systemic level, and the other is naively to infer the characteristics of systems directly from data which are only at the individual level. The former error (misplaced inference to a lower level) has been called the "ecological fallacy," the "sociological fallacy," and the "group fallacy;" the latter error (misplaced inference to a higher level) has been called the "individualistic fallacy," and the "psychological fallacy," although some minor distinctions exist even among these terms. It should be noted that these inferences are not necessarily false. They may actually be true under many circumstances, but they are generally dubious until empirically proven true.

It has been noted that the greater the distance separating any two levels, i.e., the greater the differences in size and the larger the number of intermediate levels, the greater the probable discrepancy between the correlations obtained at the two levels. In fact, analysts use this principle in estimating the magnitude of the ecological fallacy. Interlevel differences in correlations are observed for all levels available, and this pattern is then used to estimate the magnitude of such differences between available levels and unavailable levels. Estimates of this kind are difficult, however, since they depend upon an ability to determine the distances between levels or an arbitrary assumption about such distances, e.g., that they are equal. When levels are distinguished in terms of the relative sizes of the units, empirical estimates of distance can plausibly be made. But similar judgments for levels distinguished in other terms, such as authority, are quite uncertain. In any event, we can say that useful inferences from one level of analysis to another can frequently be made, but they are not automatic nor even easy and they must usually be explicitly tentative.[156]

Ordinarily, because he has deliberately gathered data at the individual level, the cross-cultural survey analyst is less likely than many other researchers to fall into the ecological fallacy, especially if he follows the analytic strategy of proceeding upward from the lowest level. On the other hand, he is particularly prone to tumble into the individualistic fallacy or else to leave his analysis without indicating its systemic relevance. In other words he is likely to infer systemic or other higher level characteristics from data solely at the individual level, or to say nothing about the higher level significance of his findings. If we know anything it is that there is no easy inference from such information as the percentage of "democratic personality types" in a group to how democratic the group's structure will be, or from the desire for political participation of individuals to the degree of participation manifested in the group. The information about individuals is a necessary input but far from sufficient. Many contextual, structural, and group properties must be included before such higher level inferences can validly be made. Yet those inferences are of great interest. What, then, can the survey analyst do to become more effective in exploring systemic and subsystemic topics? A well-designed survey is one of the few vehicles available for gathering and exploiting relevant data at a series of levels from the individual upward to the nation or culture. How can this opportunity be handled analytically? A major part of the answer seems to lie in the further development of two related types of analysis which can be called contextual and structural.

Individuals in social systems experience as part of their environment many of the characteristics of other individuals in that system. For example, it often makes a difference to the behavioral manifestation of a pro-government attitude whether one is in an environment where nearly everyone shares similar sentiments or whether most other people disagree and oppose the government. In short, individuals with the same basic attitude may behave differently according to the attitudinal context (climate of opinion) in which they find themselves, while individuals with different attitudes may behave similarly under certain contextual circumstances. When he moves from the individual level of analysis to a higher level, the researcher wishes to introduce not only "global" properties unique to the higher level (e.g., type of party system, number of trade unions, existence of nuclear industrial capacity), but also what have been called "compositional" or "contextual" factors which have higher and lower level manifestations (e.g., the proportion of authoritarians, the number of persons strongly attached to the group, the incidence of literates). Certain systemic properties may be threshold phenomena, that is, may only appear after a certain critical point in the incidence of an attitude or other individual characteristic is reached. Contextual

291

analysis offers the survey researcher who seeks to "move on up a little higher" some valuable techniques for dealing with such phenomena. However, it is a fairly recent development and many problems remain.[157]

One difficulty emerged rather quickly relating to the use of very limited categorical controls for continuous variables. Early contextual analyses basically involved obtaining individual and group data for an independent variable of interest, and a dependent variable. Let us say that the two variables were how often a villager discussed his problems with village leaders (independent variable) and his level of satisfaction with village politics (dependent variable). The initial contextual analysis might yield the results shown in Table 1.

Table 1. Hypothesized Average Political Satisfaction Scores of Peasants, by Individual Frequency and Village Rate of Discussion of Problems With Village Leaders*

Individual Peasants Who Discussed Their Problems	Villages Where a Majority of Peasants Discussed Problems	
	Rarely	Often
Rarely	.38	.71
Often	.63	.86

*The table indicates, for example, that the average political satisfaction score of peasants who as individuals discussed their problems "often" with village leaders but who lived in a *village* where the majority of peasants reported discussing their problems "rarely" was .63.

From these data one might readily conclude that there was a contextual effect. A peasant's satisfaction is not solely related to his individual frequency of discussion of his problems with village leaders, but it is also apparently affected by the rate with which other peasants in his village discuss their problems with village leaders. However, these results may be entirely spurious. The individual and village dichotomization of the frequency of discussion (a continuous variable rather than a dichotomous attribute) may mask a tendency for the more frequent discussants *within* either dichotomized category to be in the villages whose rate of discussion was "Often." In other words, the individual variable was not really held constant, and its residual variation accounted for the findings. The same considerations also apply in reverse to the village variable.

Responses to this difficulty include: (1) using only truly dichotomous variables, (2) using correlational methods which furnish a much more elaborate breakdown of continuous variables, and (3) only regarding as interesting those cell differences which exceed the highest possible results that could be spuriously obtained.

The approach to contextual analysis through multiple correlation and regression has special appeal in this case because it helps handle another even more severe problem. The initial isolation of contextual effects requires control or allowance for related individual and group properties of a non-contextual type. Direct control of such factors requires a prohibitively large and dense sample.[158] Hence, the analyst is led in the direction of statistically allowing for these factors which need to be eliminated rather than attempting to control them directly.

An illustration may help. In our Turkish peasant survey we sampled individual peasants in village clusters, roughly sixteen randomly selected respondents per village. We can use this sample to generate estimates of the climate of opinion in the village, estimates not possible from any other data. We can then ask contextual questions such as, "Is the peasant who has a high individual sense of communal responsibility and lives in a village where there are many others like him more prone to be interested in politics than another peasant who also has a high individual sense of communal responsibility but lives in a village where there are very few others like him?"

When we attempt to answer such questions, we try first to eliminate individual level factors which would be associated with both variables and produce a spurious contextual effect. For instance, those with high communal responsibility in the village with greater communal responsibility might be disproportionately literate. Literacy might also be associated with interest in politics, so that when a control for literacy was introduced, the contextual relationship between communal responsibility and political interest would disappear. Similarly, on the village level one might argue that those villages where there was a high degree of communal responsibility would tend to be the larger, less isolated, better developed villages, and that political interest would be greater in such villages regardless of the incidence of feelings of communal responsibility. Ruling out such a hypothesis would demand controls for village characteristics. But when the researcher attempts to apply such individual and village controls, he finds he needs a large sample not only of individuals but also of villages (the primary sampling units)—too large in many cases to be practical. Hence, he is led in the direction of statistical techniques which get around the need for direct physical controls. Even so, a profound contextual analysis on any large scale requires extremely careful design and highly sophisticated multivariate analysis. Various models for contextual analysis have been suggested, depending on assumptions of linearity or non-linearity of the contextual relationships and the directness or indirectness of relationships between contextual and individual variables. Much more work remains to be done, but surely this is one of the most promising approaches to squeezing more systemic significance from the survey data which we so laboriously and expensively collect. Since the cross-cultural researcher is likely to be particularly interested in multiple level analysis and inter-system differences in contextual configurations and effects, this approach will probably have a special appeal for him.

Contextual effects have been mainly conceived in terms of attitudinal characteristics. The research conducted so far has dealt largely with climates of opinion. A related and no less essential type of survey research involves what I have called structural analysis. Sometimes "structural analysis" has been used as a term synonymous with contextual analysis, but I employ the term to refer to the sociometric attack on relational problems of group structure. I refer to gathering through survey procedures individual data on interpersonal influence (power), communications, prestige, friendship, liking, etc.—data which are normally displayed through a matrix or directed graph. It seems critical to ascertain not merely what attitudes the respondent has on a certain topic nor even what behavior he is likely to engage in, but also enough about the structure of interpersonal relations in which he is enmeshed to be able to grasp the probable consequences of his behavior for relevant others and the behavioral implications of their actions for him. In cross-cultural research the likelihood of widely variant structural environments for individuals holding similar (or different) attitudes is probably increased. To interpret the social as opposed to the personal significance of attitudinal information the researcher requires structural data which the survey technique can provide. At present most of our attitudinal findings are structurally unanchored in any but the crudest and most formal sense. Since forms in particular are likely to be deceptive across cultural boundaries, more realistic structural information is specially important to the cross-cultural researcher. He will therefore tend to become more deeply immersed in problems of matrix manipulation, path analysis, the location of indirect chains of relationships, and so on. Many of these problems are so new that they are not yet well covered in the literature, but the survey technique holds promise of permitting a much more precise and quantitative approach to the analysis of social structure beyond the small group level, than we have managed up to now. Such a development would enable the cross-cultural researcher to transcend some of the limitations which now hamper him in investigating the systemic significance of attitudinal characteristics.[159]

Although this long essay has necessarily focused on all kinds of difficulties and problems, they should be taken in perspective: I would simply repeat that none of these is distinctive to cross-cultural research. Nor have I intended to encourage a paralyzing perfectionism. On the contrary, cross-cultural research already has its modest success stories, established by careful scientists who overcame the difficulties. Fascinating international regularities in occupational prestige structures, the patterning of attitudes toward population control, national stereotypes, the impact of the mass media, structure of connotational meaning, political socialization, and the distribution of achievement aspirations have already been glimpsed. The problems discussed have their solutions, and the theoretical promise of cross-cultural survey research to political science and to other social sciences is truly exciting.

294

CHAPTER 7

Linguistic Aspects of Comparative Political Research[1]

DELL HYMES
University of Pennsylvania

Since the end of World War II, scholars in the field of comparative politics have been noted for the multidisciplinary nature of their work. Many have read widely in anthropology, economics, sociology, and other fields, and they have incorporated both theoretical and empirical work from these fields into their writings. Given the prominence of this new multidisciplinary focus, it is surprising that few scholars have paid any attention to the relevant work in linguistics. This is particularly surprising in view of the fact that a researcher doing work in a culture in which he is not a native speaker of the language undoubtedly encounters the problem of obtaining comparability of meaning as he moves from the language of field research to the language of publication. The difficulties involved when working in just two languages are greatly multiplied when comparative studies are undertaken in several cultures, each with a different language. Yet political scientists engaging in research that cost hundreds of thousands of dollars have dealt with the problem of linguistic comparability in the most simplistic and naive manner.

295

Chapter 7 is Professor Dell Hymes' answer to the general question, "What can the expert in linguistics tell the political scientist about the linguistic problems of comparative research?" In addressing himself to this query, he raises other questions. First, "Does language affect politics?" (In other words, is politics conducted in Swahili different from politics conducted in French simply because of the differences between the two languages?) Second, "Does language affect what one finds out about politics?"

Although the political scientist must take note of the answer to the first question, few, if any, have the theoretical and research competence to cope with the problems if the answer were strongly in the affirmative. (Fortunately, it is not.) The political scientist, however, cannot fail to come to grips directly with the implications of the second question. One does not have to read far into Hymes' work to realize that linguistic comparability in research instruments is a major problem which must be handled. Simplistic techniques, such as back translations of questionnaires, are inadequate in dealing with this problem.

Hymes identifies all of the dimensions of the problem of linguistic comparability, and suggests the feasibility of a "linguistic pretest," which would enable the comparative researcher to explore the implications of each dimension for his specific research instrument.

Political scientists will find the subject matter of this chapter largely foreign, but it is a highly pertinent treatment of one of the most important—and certainly the most ignored—of the methodological problems of comparative research.

Dell Hymes is Professor of Anthropology at the University of Pennsylvania, and Curator of Linguistic Anthropology in the University Museum. Major publications include the editing of Language in Culture and Society, The Use of Computers in Anthropology; *and* Studies in Southwestern Ethnolinguistics. *A book of his* Essays in Linguistic Anthropology *is in press.*

296

FOR THE STUDENT of language, the world's diversity of language is an opportunity. For the student of politics, such multiplicity may be an obstacle, if not a curse. The very diversity that offers the linguist a testing ground for theory may seem to the political scientist something that interferes with testing. The data of comparative research must of necessity come from users of different languages, yet the sophisticated political scientist is aware that such data may be uncertainly valid, uncertainly comparable, just because the languages are different.

Put rather crudely, there are two questions:

1. Does language affect politics?
2. Does language affect what one finds out about politics?

The first question has to do with the role of language as a determinant of political thought and behavior. In one sense it is a question in the sociology of knowledge, and in any case it is methodological: the scholar's research strategy will vary with his answer. The second question has to do with choice of language in which to work—translation, interviewing, and the like—matters of method that arise when one must work in another language, whatever his strategy.

In this essay I shall take up the two general questions in turn, sketching a series of critical and practical considerations. At the end I shall suggest that in coping with diversity of language a comparative political science may encounter not only problems, but also opportunities.

Interpreting Linguistic Diversity

It is hard to imagine political life without speech. Without speeches, perhaps; but not without the coordination and control, the modes of influence, persuasion, and conflict which speech makes possible. But if use of language is a prerequisite of human social life, and hence of its political dimension, does it matter which language is used? Does acquisition and use of one language, rather than another, shape thought and values in a particular way? Is political life in French different from political life conducted in Swahili, just because of differences between the two languages?

We touch here on a question that has had a long history and many names. During the eighteenth century there began a shift from an emphasis on the universal logic of all language to a deepening concern with the individuality of each language. In this as in much else, Herder was a seminal figure. In his philosophy of history Herder focused his concept of development upon:

> ... the *Volk*, as the most "natural" socio-political unit, identifying it with a community sharing the consciousness of its own distinctive socio-cultural traditions, the determinate feature of which he sees in the possession of a common language. ... The chief medium of transmission in this educational process of social interaction is language which ... Herder regarded as the most distinctive element in a *Volk's* cultural heritage. It is through language that a community's sense of its separate existence is both awakened and sustained. Language and education, therefore, constitute for Herder the most determinate factors in the fashioning of a community's social consciousness by which it becomes aware not only of its own existence but also of that which differentiates it from the rest of humanity ... A *Volk's* language, for Herder, was not something detachable, for he saw in it the embodiment of a *Volk's* inner being, its inner Kraft, without which it ceased to exist.[2]

Here we find two viewpoints that were to become fundamental to a long line of subsequent thought, not only political, but also linguistic and anthropological: equation of a people's identity with linguistic identity, and singling out of language as a central embodiment of a people's psychological character.

In the early nineteenth century, Herder's mode of thought was developed by Wilhelm von Humboldt in such a way as to make him the classic reference point for all subsequent concern for the relation of linguistic differences to other differences among mankind. From W. von Humboldt effectively stems the tradition of seeking clues to national character in specific types of linguistic feature. The tradition played a major part in the foundation of social psychology by Lazarus and Steinthal, and in the work of the man who presided over the birth of experimental psychology, Wilhelm Wundt; it entered into the theoretical basis laid for modern French sociology and anthropology by Durkheim and Mauss; and it motivated the work that signals the beginning of modern American linguistic anthropology, Boas' *Handbook of American Indian Languages*. In recent years in the United States the subject has been variously referred to as the *Whorf, Whorf-Lee,* and *Sapir-Whorf hypothesis;* the *Weltanschauung* problem (the German name being recognition of the role of von Humboldt); *linguistic relativity;* and it has been the whole or partial subject-matter of "metalinguistics," "psycholinguistics," "ethnolinguistics."[3]

The surge of American interest in the 1950s, sparked by posthumous attention to the writings of Whorf, has been followed by relative neglect in the 1960s, the linguistic *Zeitgeist* having shifted from a Herderian focus upon the differences among languages to focus upon what languages have in common, accompanied by a revival of interest in the logical and rationalist standpoints of the sixteenth and seventeenth centuries (dubbed *Cartesian*

298

linguistics). Shifts of *Zeitgeist*, however, tend to dispose of problems by forgetting, not answering, them. The problem of the shaping role of language remains a genuine one for serious comparative knowledge of the determinants of social and political life.

I cannot pretend to thrash out the entire problem here, but I can sketch the perspective that I believe evidence and experience to warrant. My ultimate purpose will be to refocus the problem by showing that it is fundamentally a problem, not just of the content of a language, but of its use. The content of languages, however, is what has been typically at issue, and must be considered first. If one imagines a political scientist who is planning research in another country, and who has been apprised of some interesting facts about the language of the people he intends to study, one will be considering in large measure the position from which most of the theoretical discussion of the *Weltanschauung* problem has been conducted. It has been essentially the "study of culture at a distance." Even when the discussant has obtained his own data in the field, his or her interpretation of the data is usually made at home. Sometimes superficial, sometimes profound and penetrating, *Weltanschauung* discussion has been pretty much an armchair one of interpreting cognitive import of reported linguistic traits in the light of general assumptions about the distinctive and central role of language. Scholarly interest has usually been more sophisticated and systematic than lay interest, but on this score it has most of the time been methodologically in much the same boat.

Some Common Pitfalls

Let me now review some of the considerations that arise if one attempts to interpret linguistic traits as signs and causes of thought and behavior. Put otherwise, given some interesting facts about the language of a people the researcher intends to study, in what ways can he go wrong in assessing them? Ten topics can be distinguished (somewhat arbitrarily) with ad hoc labels. All are variants on the theme of not interpreting data out of context.

(1) *Presence of a word.* It has long been a popular habit to single out striking facts about particular words. It has been maintained, for example, that a key to German national character lay in the existence of a word, *Schadenfreude*, for which other languages lacked equivalent. Some have said that Russian aims could be better understood when one realized that for them to seek *mir* could mean not only *peace* but also *world*. One might recall that St. Thomas Aquinas thought it necessary to the perfect bliss of those in heaven that they be able to observe the suffering in hell, and succeeded in having and expressing the thought in the trans-European tongue of the time, and I wonder if it has occurred to the Russians that for an American to speak of his world goal as *peace* might involve a *double entendre* in English too.

It is not that certain words may not be crucial in the shaping of action and to its understanding. The French lexicologist Matore has done interesting work on the *mots clef* of periods in French history,[4] and Raymond Williams introduces his valuable study of English *Culture and Society, 1780–1950* with the observation:

> In the last decades of the eighteenth century, and in the first half of the nineteenth century, a number of words, which are now of capital importance, came for the first time into common English use, or, where they had already been generally used in the language, acquired new and important meanings. There is in fact a general pattern of change in these words, and this can be used as a special kind of map by which it is possible to look again at those wider changes in life and thought to which the changes in language evidently refer.[5]

The words Williams traces are *industry, democracy, class, art,* and *culture.* Notice that the social history of England is not read off from the presence of the words; rather, the words are used as foci for investigation.

(2) *Absence of a word.* The report that people X have no word for Y has been taken sometimes as indicative of the absence of a concept. American Indian languages usually had no word answering to our *freedom;* must they not have been unfree? This type of question has been reinforced by the habit among linguists and anthropologists of speaking of a language's lexicon as an index to culture, of language as a "perfect symbolism of experience." The truth of the matter is that a language is always a selective index to a culture, always a partial symbolism of experience. Language itself is a clear example. Every competent speaker of a language operates daily with an intuitive knowledge, complex and precise, of grammatical concepts, e.g., transitive, negation, nominalization, and so on. Yet for most of human history no language has had terms to denote such concepts. The principle holds for social life generally. Basic concepts of entitlement among the islanders of Truk, for instance, have no Trukese labels.[6]

Perhaps it would be convenient for comparative research if a dictionary could be treated as a complete index to concepts. The fact that a lexicon is a partial index, if less convenient, is however ultimately scientifically more interesting. Automatic lexical expression would be a sort of miracle to be accepted on faith. Selective lexical expression permits controlled comparison and covariation to get at the dynamics underlying the role of vocabulary in social life. If in a given society the shared understandings and concepts pertaining to political life may be, but need not be, lexically tagged, it becomes possible to study the conditions under which lexical tagging does and does not occur, thus perhaps adding depth to one's understanding of political process.

Linguistics and anthropology have no general theory of vocabulary to offer at the present time. Studies of semantic change, of lexical acculturation, and of semantic fields contribute insights into the basic factor, communicative need. The central question would seem to be, what needs determine the degree to which a message must be explicit? Sapir states the principle with regard to interpersonal communication: the more two participants share by way of understanding of a situation, the less their messages need be explicit about it. The same principle might apply to the role of vocabulary in the use and storage of information in the brain, if knowledge of words is viewed as a way of communicating with oneself over time. Number and kind of audiences (including oneself), of settings, for the transmission and retrieval of lexically coded information would be the key.

Many other types of interpretation of vocabulary are variations on the theme of presence or absence of a word. Some can be singled out here.

(3) *Many-one explanation in dictionary style.* It often takes several words in one's own language to explain a single word in another. This fact has often been exploited for amusement and sometimes for intellectual inference, the implications being that the other language is interestingly odd in the presence of a single word for the elaborate meaning in question. It is important to notice how much the interest of the examples depends upon the style of presentation. Sometimes the style is straightforwardly humorous, as when one Yiddish word is explained as meaning "a guy who's always trying to get ahead of you," and a second as "a guy who's so far ahead you'll never catch up and still keeps trying to get ahead of you, because that's the kind of guy he is." Sometimes the style is more patently dictionary in vein, as for the Kiowa Indian word translatable as "the hair on the back of a baby buffalo's knee." The gloss is a suitably rhythmic phrase. A typical Indian explanation: "hair, a kind of hair; you find it on baby buffalo on the back of the knee; they're the only ones that have that kind of hair" would be less likely to amuse. And if English had a single word equivalent (no doubt rural or dialectal), there would be no question of interest arising; one would simply say that the Kiowa word means "tarl," just as one casually says that German *Kopf* means "head." In either case (humorous or dictionary style) the interest depends partly on the explanation fitting aptly into a verbal genre of our own culture. Such aptness itself is no guide to the semantic values of the word in question, any more than would be a felicitous account in Navaho of the meanings of English *brown-nose* or *lapel*.

Clearly the number and kind of meanings of a word, the oddness or obviousness of its main meaning, its humorousness, quaintness, or richness do not depend upon the glosses that can be imagined for it in another language. Its semantic values depend upon its place in its own system. In point of fact, a specification of the ways in which common, analogous words (e.g., the counterparts in various languages of *democracy* and *socialism*) are not quite equivalent might be far more revealing. In any case, when an important word is without close equivalent in one's own language, it still is necessary not to focus upon it alone, rich and ineffable as the word may be, but to work both ways between the two most nearly corresponding sectors of the vocabularies in question.

(4) *Opposite meanings.* The type of absence represented here of an expected word has gained special attention. Freud was much impressed by the researches of a nineteenth-century philologist, Abel, into Coptic, an extinct language of Egypt. Coptic seemed often to express two opposed meanings in one word. Freud and others have seen in such cases an example of a more primitive mode of thought. The difficulty is that the appearance of two opposed meanings packed into a single word depended upon translation in which the two meanings were expressed by separate words. Consider Latin *altus*, which is translated into English sometimes as *high* (e.g., the sky), sometimes as *low* or *deep* (e.g., the sea). What of the possibility that the Latin word indicates not two things, but one, having to do with magnitude of distance from a vantage point, and hence rendered as *high* or *low* according to the context (e.g., as seen from below, *high*; as seen from above, *low*)? Such is in fact the case. The Latin word has a consistent semantic value within its own system. Latin is not lacking a word where it needs two, but merely using a word with different semantic value. (Nor would it be just to say that English is using two words where it needs but one without comparing the two systems of reference as wholes).

(5) *Confusion of meanings.* The interpretation of Latin *altus* as equivalent to English *high* or *low*, according to context, illustrates a general phenomenon. A classic example has been with regard to color terminology. Many American Indian languages, such as Navaho, do not have separate terms for what is distinguished in English as *blue* vs. *green*. Are the Navaho unable to distinguish the two? Apparently not; if a distinction is wanted, they use their single term (*X*) in the phrases "sky *X*" for *blue*, "grass *X*" for *green*.

(6) *Concrete vs. abstract terms.* Differences in vocabulary have often been interpreted in terms of this overworked dichotomy. Some languages have been said to have many concrete terms in an area of experience, but to lack abstract terms; inferences as to cognitive abilities have been drawn. Several points can be briefly made. First, it is often possible to develop abstract terms in a language, if the occasion arises. Boas succeeded in having Indian informants abstract kin terms from the elements for personal relationship with which they normally occurred. Second, the noticing of a lack of abstract terms depends upon the linguistic background of the observer. From the standpoint of some Indian languages, English lacks common terms for "writing-instrument" (covering pen, pencil, and so on) and "flying thing" (covering airplane, butterfly). Third, the presence of an abstract term may be missed, because of the common practice of using the term for the most typical member of a set as the term for the set as a whole as well. Compare English *duck*, "female" as opposed to the male *drake*, but also serving for

both when sex is indifferent or abstract from; *man* "male" as opposed to the female *woman*, but also serving for "human being" in general. (Technically the term restricted to a single role is called the *marked* term, and the term that may serve two roles is called *unmarked*.)

Finally, the notion of the abstract may itself be misleading. One must distinguish vagueness of reference from superordination.[7] A term designating a vaguely defined area may be abstract without being proof of intellectual prowess. Plenitude of particular terms may show power of observation and analysis. What is pertinent is the elaboration of terminology such that one term subsumes others, as in our examples of *man: man, woman,* and *duck: duck, drake,* or as in English *parent: father, mother.* The test for superordination is that one can ask the correlative questions, "What kinds of X (e.g., parent) are there?" and "Of what is Y (e.g., father) a kind?" and receive standard answers. (Much current anthropological work in semantics has gone into exploration of structures of this kind.) With superordination one has definite evidence of cognitive relationships, and rather well worked out techniques for getting at them, although the proper cognitive interpretation may well require going beyond the structure of superordination itself.[8]

To return to concrete vs. abstract: the most interesting and illuminating recent comparative treatment of the issues to which the contrast is addressed is *La Pensée Sauvage* by Claude Lévi-Strauss. The main point to be made here is that the seeming predominance of concrete or abstract terms is not in itself an index of cognitive capacity or character. The adequacy of existing terms in a language can be evaluated only in relation to the needs the terms serve. Depending on needs, preponderance of either type may be equally well adaptive or maladaptive. We know only too well that abstract terms may unify a nation but equally well condone a crime.[9]

(7) *Poverty and elaboration of vocabulary.* The present topic is a more general form of those preceding it. It has often been noted that languages differ in proliferation of terms for different sectors of experience: the Lapp have many words for reindeer, the Nuer for cattle, the Aymara for potatoes, the Ponape for yams, the Samoans for elite communication, and (the classic example) the Eskimo have several words for kinds of snow. Such proliferation would seem to reflect a focus of cultural interest. Conversely, paucity of terms would seem to reflect a lack of cultural attention.

A great deal can be said for close examination of the degree of elaboration of terms for a given sector, say, political roles, types of leadership, elite communication, and the like. The topic is one of the most important in a general theory of vocabulary, and has come to be called technically the question of the degree of *terminologization.*[10] In the interaction between political systems of different origins, differences in the degree of terminologization of political life might be quite significant.[11] In the making of comparisons, however, a serious caution must be exercised. The apparent richness or poverty of a set of terms may be an artifact.

The Australian aborigines provide an important example of specious richness of terminology. The elaborateness of Australian terms for kinship has often been contrasted with the relative sparseness of American kinship terms. The comparison has been thought to refute evolutionary theory, which should expect the more "primitive" Australians to be simpler in such respects. Recently the comparison has been shown to be misguided. The Australian terminology serves not only as a way of keeping track of kin, but also as a verbal matrix for most of the statuses and roles in the society, which are handled in terms of the idiom of kinship. The proper comparison is not to American kinship terms alone, but to the American status and role terminology as a whole. When this comparison is made, elaboration of terminology is seen quite obviously to go hand in hand with socioeconomic complexity.[12]

For specious poverty of terminology, there is a revealing African example. The legal terminology of "primitive" peoples has often been held to be sparse or nonexistent. At first glance the Barotse would seem a case in point. There is etymologically but one basic term for the concept of property and ownership. One may suspect some mistake when he realizes that the Barotse have a quite thoroughgoing system of jurisprudence. The mistake lies in overlooking the fact that the Barotse are not dependent upon "property" terminology for handling disputes about property. They have a highly developed terminology for rights and statuses of persons, and when the basic concept of property relationship is placed in the context of specific relationships among types of person, its implications become accurately defined for the case in hand.[13] Similarly, the forms of Trukese entitlement, although unlabelled, are inferrable from the named forms of transaction that give rise to them.

Often enough one cannot freely compare whole societies and languages. Brown has pointed out that American skiers, as well as Eskimo, have quite an active vocabulary for types of snow.[14] With regard to the elaboration of terminology for elite communication in Samoa, Goodenough has pointed out that there exist sectors of American society into whose terminology the Samoan terminology is easily translated.[15] Indeed, one of the basic facts about linguistic evolution since the emergence of modern science is that there exist specialists whose collective responsibility it is to provide a tag for everything in the universe. In principle, no plant should go unnamed by botanists, no artifact by students of material culture, and so on.

In general, then, one must establish the functional equivalence of what is compared in each language, partly by specifying the social group whose use of each language is in question.

(8) *Metaphor, dead or alive.* Cognitive interpretations of linguistic

differences often cite descriptive expressions that imply a particular orientation. One example discussed in the literature is the Chiricahua Apache expression for a "dripping spring," analyzed literally as "as whiteness, water moves downward."[16] No doubt the Chiricahua who coined and accepted the phrase thought of whiteness, and of water as embodying it. There can be no certainty that a Chiricahua who uses the term today connects a dripping spring with whiteness, or with any particular assumption about the mode of relationship between a quality and that which manifests it. The description may be a dead metaphor.

Consider an English example. How often does one think of a morning meal as the breaking of a fast? The written word can be seen to contain *break* and *fast*, and the connection might be joked upon ("Breakfast at our house is a fast break, all right"). For most intents and purposes, the original description is lost and there is left but a single term, a frozen idiom. The make-up of the world enables us to infer something about the outlook of the past, not the present, users of the language.

Every language has a sector of such frozen idioms. Their constituents display one facet of the general fact that a language deploys its stock of morphemes in multiple ways, and that specialization in separate uses may divert different occurrences of a morpheme from any common meaning. To find a political term recurring in some other field of discourse is not in itself warrant for using the meanings of the one to illuminate those of the other. Consider a Martian linguist trying to interpret Republican politics on the basis of *Grand Old Party, Grand Central Station, grand piano, grandfather,* and *ten grand.*

The leading edge of live metaphor in a language is an important source of insight into the orientations of those who do the coining and accepting. But what is live and to whom must be established.

In interpreting expressions in another language, we may be misled also by metaphors and descriptive terms of our own devising. Having restated facts in grammatical terminology, we may read into the terminology a cognitive significance which it does not have. Not too long ago, for example, a linguist sought to interpret concepts of possession among the peoples of a number of Pacific islands. He did so by examining the ways in which nouns in the language were marked for "possession." Goodenough has shown that the "possession" of nouns and the concepts of property and possession of the Trukese (one of the peoples in question) have nothing to do with each other. In fact the concepts of property and possession must be analyzed first in their own terms before their linguistic expression can be properly understood.[17] The so-called "possession" for nouns is quite analogous to the case in English, where I do own "my book," and perhaps "my life," but hardly "my father," "my school," "my church," or "my home town." The so-called possessive is a relational category, some of whose uses do involve ownership, but many of whose uses do not.

This point brings us to the problem of grammatical categories, on which has been concentrated much of the interest in inferring cognitive characteristics from language. The description and interpretation of such categories is extremely complex. Here I can only continue in the same vein and point out certain methodological considerations.

(9) *Part-whole.* The label, part-whole, may suggest two common problems that beset inferences from grammatical categories. The first is illustrated by the gender of nouns in several European languages. All nouns are assigned to a gender, and some cases clearly show a correlation with sex, hence the sexual labels *masculine, feminine,* and *neuter* are extended to the whole. For the larger portion of the vocabulary, however, and in most uses, there is no sexual force to the gender.[18] This fact has led some to dismiss semantic interpretation of such categories as arbitrary, and others to deny any relation between such categories and thought: does a person whose language has sex gender think more about sex? The case is more subtle and difficult. The existence of clear cases of sexual meaning for the gender classification makes it possible for such meaning to be extended and exploited. The force of the classification is a possible, rather than a certain, thing.[19]

The case seems to be similar with gender classification in other languages. The Algonquian language, Ojibwa, for example, has two major classes of nouns, animate and inanimate; that is, these labels are assigned to the classes as wholes on the basis of clear cases. The word for *stone* belongs with animate nouns. In point of fact, stones may be treated sometimes as if inhabited by spirit. The grammatical classification is seemingly a rod along which the semantic lightning may or may not flash.[20]

The second part-whole problem has to do with linguistic typology. In the development of cognitive interpretation of differences among languages, the classification of languages as belonging to one or another grammatical type played a major role. From it stem such typological terms as *isolating, agglutinating, inflectional, polysynthetic,* and the like, and the standard use of Chinese, Turkish, and Sanskrit as contrasting examples. The type of a language, however, was sometimes defined in terms of the make-up of the verb. The error is the same as that made in comparing Australian kinship terms to American kinship terms. The verb word is not functionally equivalent in all languages. Some psychologists, for example, have talked about English in terms of tense, because tense is the category most obviously marked in the verb word itself (*run: ran, talk: talked*). In the theory in question, English was held to be developmentally more advanced than a language whose major category was aspect (designating, not the time of an action, but its character as completed, incomplete, beginning, and so on). Yet the grammatical categories of the verbal type in English depend not on the verb alone, but on a set of words in the predicate as a whole. (As a complex example, consider the predicate of "(I) *would have been about to get going.*") The English predicate has modal and aspect forms of importance, and it has some aspect markers that might well seem to represent the growing edge of the system, as having but recently been specialized in aspect function ("*keep* going," with *keep* no longer the same form as in "keep it," but marking continuative aspect; "*get* going," with *get* no longer the same form as in "get it," but marking inceptive aspect).

The main point is that no one portion of a form class or a sentence can suffice a priori for judging the cognitive capacity or character of a language. The relation between functions and means is not one to one, but a multiple mapping in both directions. Proponents of cognitive differences have often seized upon the fact that the same means, say, the verb, may serve different functions in different languages. Too often the fact that different languages may serve the same functions by different means has been ignored. A meaning or relationship not marked in the verb may be marked in the noun or pronoun, or by order of words, or lexically. It is possible to say something about the cognitive cut of a language, but only on the basis of a more comprehensive consideration of its resources.[21]

(10) *Multiple resources and codability.* The matter of resources brings us to the major issue for any attempt to infer behavior or thought from language. The difficulties taken up so far might all in principle be met. Rash inference from presence or absence of a word, or the style in which a word is explained; rash imputation of a special type of thinking (opposite, con-confused, concrete, or abstract); misleading comparison of poverty and elaboration of vocabularies; misreading of metaphor and etymological connection; inappropriate taking of a part for a whole—suppose one were to avoid all such difficulties, what then? Would languages appear so variable and complex that nothing could be said about cognitive differences among them?

I do believe that languages have characteristic cognitive differences, and that such differences may play a part in the cognitive worlds of those who use the languages. There are so many common ways of making too simple an approach, however, that one has to be especially scrupulous, both to be accurate and to avoid raising the hackles of those who have reacted against such errors by preferring to view languages as almost wholly independent of such considerations.

We can get to the heart of the matter by taking up what has been a focus for serious students, the question of obligatory categories. Suppose all difficulties of ethnocentric perception were removed. Languages would still differ in their grammatical cores. Even if it should be demonstrated that all languages share certain underlying universal grammatical features, the salient differences would remain. And of some of these differences it can be said that they are obligatory for users of the language. A person may choose to be silent, but if he speaks, he will in English almost always have to specify a noun as singular or plural, a verb as present or past in form; in Russian, a noun as to gender, a verb as to perfective or imperfective aspect; in Kwakiutl, a verb as to whether the information is directly known or hearsay; and so on. Presumably children learning a language in which their attention is forced to certain categories will be more attentive to those categories than will children learning languages for which the categories are marginal or absent. Presumably as adults they will reflect this learning experience in those modes of thought and behavior dependent upon linguistic means.

There has been comparative research that has yielded positive results. In the American Southwest, Navaho is a language in which the use of a verb may require one to specify one among a set of categories for the shapes of objects; Zuni is a language for which this is not the case. Users of Navaho have been found in fact to sort objects more frequently according to form or shape than users of Zuni; and insofar as they are bilingual, to do this in direct proportion to the extent to which Navaho is their dominant language.[22]

Another important line of research has concerned lexical categories, such as common terms for color. Such terms are not obligatory in the same sense as grammatical categories, but within their own domain are analogously so. It has been shown that the speed with which colors are named, recognized, and recalled varies with their degree of "codability" in the language used by the subjects, that is, the degree to which the colors are good instances of the portions of the spectrum designated by the simple color terms. The effect is particularly striking when a color central to a simple term in one language falls between the colors central to two simple terms in another language. If the color is, say, a yellowish-orange that is a "good" instance of a standard Zuni term, users of Zuni will name, recognize, and recall it much more readily than will users of English, who will also have difficulty agreeing on what the name should be ("yellowish-orange," "orange yellow," "sort of between yellow and orange," and so on).[23]

There is indeed a good deal of evidence that particular differences in linguistic habits go together with particular differences in thought and behavior. It would be strange if it were not so, if so thoroughly practiced a set of tools were without effect on what was done with it.

Where, then, is the difficulty? If one knows that a language has particular categories of grammar and lexicon, on the one hand, and one knows that particular differences in linguistic habits can make a difference, why hesitate to put the two together, and to anticipate thought from language? The difficulty lies in considerations indicated by the tag, "multiple resources and codability."

Take codability first. Tests of color perception have found little or no difference among users of different languages in their ability to discriminate. *Potential* ability to recognize, recall, and name shade of color is much the same throughout mankind. Where language may make a difference is in the ease and readiness with which a particular shade of color will be handled. Much of the job of language in ordinary life is to enable us to recode the infinite variety of experience into the finite set of conventional categories on which we usually rely, making such discriminations as suffice in the context of what is taken for granted. Commonly, it is enough to ask for the red book (not the blue or green one) without concern for the exact shade of red. We could not and need not be continually as exact in reporting as our abilities permit us to be in perceiving. It is in "naming as we run," recording experience into habitual categories, that language can and does most influence our thought and behavior. But it always remains possible to be more exact and to go beyond the habitual verbal means. It is also possible to go beyond the habitual verbal means in speaking, by being more flexible, employing a tactic of identifying something to another person by whatever ad hoc attribute will suffice, or resorting to some strategy, such as an elimination of possibilities in a certain order, and so on.

It may be that the habitual means [including here perhaps the habitual ways (additional words, supplementary phrases) of being a step more precise] prevail. Indeed, in daily life, to persist after more precision than common understandings call for is to annoy, perhaps disrupt. In the potentiality of transcending habitual verbal means, there might seem only a margin for adaptation and change that does not much qualify the general effect of the habitual means at a given time. One could accept then without further probing the position which I take to have been that of Boas: in the long run, a language adapts to cultural needs, not conversely, but in the short run, a language does shape the thought of those who acquire it. On a Herderian view of the cultural distinctiveness and centrality of a language, such a position would be justified. In terms of what we know about communication in culture and society, however, the Herderian view is inadequate. There may indeed be cases to which it is a close approximation, and the recognition of potentiality of change would not be alien to Herder's belief that individuals must both acquire and struggle against their inherited culture. But the plain fact is that the potentiality of going beyond the fixed grooves of one set of habitual linguistic means is not constantly employed cross-culturally: it varies with the language situation of a community, and the attitudes and energies of those who compose it. *Because it can be neither postulated in advance nor inferred from language as such, it must be investigated in its own right.*

The potentiality of which I speak may indeed work either way, away from or into the grooves of a particular code. A semantic possibility, usually dormant (e.g., gender), may be vitalized (say in poetry); a semantic habit, usually fixed, may be transcended (say, in poetry). It may be possible to specify for a given community or set of persons what the degree of potentiality in either direction will typically be; but to do so requires a knowledge beyond that of the language itself, as has been said. Once such questions have been broached, one is launched into the investigation of habits of speech as well as habits of language, and beyond that, into the investigation of the particular place of any one set of language habits within the range of communicative means available to the community in question.

A Second Type of Diversity: Use

Such a step breaks with the Herderian assumption that has so long been characteristic of American linguistics and anthropology. To put the matter in terms of what Kenneth Burke would call "representative anecdote," the Herderian view takes as norm the case of "one language—one culture." It ideally imagines a world parcelled out among a set of such "language—culture" units, each developing through time its distinctive way of viewing and organizing the world. Notice, too, that the view of the importance for thought and culture of the differences in the content of two languages implicitly assumes that the functional role of language in the two cases is the same, namely, that of shaping thought and culture. Relativity based on content presupposes a functional universal; but in fact this functional role is itself the subject of a second, more fundamental sort of linguistic relativity.[29] Much fine work has been done in terms of the Herderian tradition, and probably it is not accidental that the tradition has been so prominent in the idiom of a scholarship strongly German in background, and much concerned with the description of patterns about to be levelled out of existence by the spread of industrial civilization. Then, too, a central methodological problem has been to obtain validity through accurate knowledge of categories different from one's own, and the one language—one culture idiom readily lends itself to that kind of problem. Nevertheless, the Herderian tradition elevates to the status of theoretical norm what is at best one empirical possibility, with regard to the central role of language, and, more particularly, of *a* language. What I shall now say on this point may seem obvious, but it has not been obvious in the context of discussions of the social role of language, in either anthropology or sociology. (See, for example, the discussion of the problem in the first major American book on the sociology of language.)[25]

With regard to the central role of language as such: a language is never the only means through which members of a society acquire their habits of thought, and the degree to which it is the means varies. Basic adult skills and understandings may be verbally transmitted, or may be acquired almost wholly by observation and imitation (e.g., among the Athapaskan-speaking

310

Kaska of northwestern Canada). The central religious effort in a young person's life may be elaborately prepared and instructed verbally, or verbal preparation may hardly enter at all (as among the Souian groups, the Hidatsa, and the Crow, respectively). Socialization pressure may be withheld until the child is old enough for accompanying verbal explanations (the Wishram Chinook), or may be imposed before the child can be able to understand (the Hopi and Zuni). The presence of children in settings in which political matters are verbalized, as in adult gatherings generally, will vary. The prospective importance of verbal skill in political matters is likely to vary as between male and female children, as does the importance of verbal skill generally. [In many societies public discourse is almost entirely a male prerogative, and women may be able to take public communicative roles only in the privileged guise of singing (Araucanians of Chile), chanting (Bihar of India), or providing a vehicle for the supernatural (again Araucanians).] Explicit verbal training of boys for political discourse may be emphasized (Ashanti of Nigeria, Araucanians) or nil (the Abipon of Argentina). And so on. In general, then, the role of language in socialization with respect to sectors of life may vary within a society and between societies; this holds for the role of language in political socialization as a special case.[26]

Not only may such involvements of language vary, but so also may the attitudes toward a language. Contrasting outcomes of acculturation among American Indian groups indicate that language has had differential value for them. Some have held onto their language at the expense of territory; some have held onto territory and let language go. Some regard their native language with pride, cultivating its use; some regard their native language as useful only for excluding whites; some experience ambivalence. The attitudes toward language in relation to statehood seem quite different in Africa today than in India and from what they were in nineteenth-century Europe.

Cultural practices indicate that verbal means are differentially valued. Some societies elaborate verbal explanation of their customs, others not (e.g., the Hidatsa and the Crow, respectively). The sensory modality given first rank in ceremonies may be verbal (prayer, incantation, and so on) or not (e.g., a tactile means such as pulsing). Normal conduct may call for filling uncomfortable silence with talk or for avoiding unnecessary talk with silence.[27]

Such considerations point to the fact that language is not magically ubiquitous, but a resource which different societies allocate differently. It is but one of the communicative resources available. There is the accompanying code of vocal gesture in intonation, tone of voice, and the like; manual gesture; visual art; dance; instrumental music; and the genres built partly or wholly out of the resources of language, but organized at levels not necessarily reflecting its internal structure, such as song, myth, and drama. As a selectively utilized resource, language is never the adequate expression of the whole thought of a people. That it might in principle suffice, as urged by many theorists, has to be set beside the fact that it never does suffice. It would indeed be difficult to account for the existence of the actual plurality of modes of communication if all but one were superfluous.

Even in a one language—one culture situation, then, one must first assess the patterning of the use of the language before being able to assess the opportunities the language has for shaping thought and behavior. As a first approximation, one would expect the content of language to be less influential the less it entered into a sphere of activity. Such a consideration might not be expected to affect the comparative study of political life, if political life is thought of as pre-eminently verbal. It may be the case, however, that the understandings basic to political life are not verbalized, or that they derive from sectors or activities relatively unmediated by language. What gets talked about as politics may be exactly what is not most important to understanding and shaping what is said. In any event there is no assurance that political discourse is assigned the same role in every society. Its place among other speech events, as to style and function, may vary from full "semanticization"—language being used to its cognitive utmost—to a heavy loading of aesthetic and entertainment values. Its weighting relative and conjointly with other modes of communication (visual, symbols, music, and so on) may vary.[28] (A typology of modes of political communication may exist; if so, I apologize for not citing it and should like very much to see it.)

Perhaps the most salient inadequacy of the one language—one culture tradition is the fact that there never is effectively but one language, if by one language we mean a homogeneous grammatical and lexical system uniformly used. This point must be made on two scores. First, there is obviously the prevalence of multilingualism over much of the world. In most areas the question for comparative research cannot be, "Does language affect thought?", but "Do the languages affect thought?" (and if so, which, how much?). The national political life of a good many countries is carried on in a language which is not the first language of many of the participants.[29] Before an investigator can assess the influence of language, he must learn the linguistic history of the individuals and communities concerned.

Three examples from comparative research on the Whorfian hypothesis can be briefly cited. Recall that the degree to which bilingual Navaho were influenced by the shape categories of the language varied with the extent to which Navaho was their dominant language. It has also been shown that the degree and nature of bilingualism affect the structure of semantic associations among Navaho.[30] Finally, a particularly interesting case has recently been examined more closely by Bright and Bright. In northwestern California have lived several Indian peoples of quite similar culture and quite distinct languages. The case has provided a stock instance of noncongruence between culture and language. What does such an instance indicate for the Whorfian emphasis on the role of language? Contrasting two of the peoples (the Yurok and the Athapaskan-speaking Smith River), the Brights found that linguistic structure does correlate with a difference in cognitive style. Yurok syntax is flexible, and so is the Yurok handling of folk taxonomies (lexical classifications of the plant and animal world); Smith River syntax is rigid and so is the Smith River handling of the folk taxonomies in question. The general contents of the folk taxonomies of the two peoples, however, are quite alike. No doubt the similarity has been induced by the common elements of the environment, but it has also been significantly influenced by intertribal bilingualism, itself carried in large part by intermarriage. (As David Aberle has pointed out to me, the intercoordination of the kinship systems among these linguistically different communities must reflect the same process.) Bilingualism, then, can induce a commonality of semantic structure superficially belied by contrast of syntactic and phonological form.

Bilingualism is indeed not a unitary thing. No single assessment of its influence can be made, because such influence must vary with the variety of conditions of its occurrence. The crucial difference that bilingualism makes to the Whorfian interpretation of language content can be quickly summed up, however, in a hypothetical example. Imagine having an account of interesting facts about a major language of an African country, and inferring a distinctive cognitive outlook from them. Imagine then learning that the white man from whom the data came had first learned the language at age 35 and used it only in visits to the local capital. How much of the distinctive cognitive outlook is likely to be his?

The hypothetical example is in fact close to the mark for all the cognitive characterizations of language that have been associated with the Whorfian hypothesis, including my own work with the Wishram Chinook. For Wishram I found several lines of evidence pointing to a particular cognitive orientation, one that tends to express experience in terms of relationships between two poles or terminals. (The word coined in the nineteenth century for *window*, for example, is quite distinctive: "They-two-see-each-other-through-it.") Yet I hesitate to impute the orientation to the men living now from whom the data came. They are bilinguals who hardly have occasion to use the language apart from answering questions of a visiting anthropologist.

In such a case one can see both the justice and the limitations of the tradition of concentrating upon the cognitive implications of obligatory categories and descriptive words. The fact that languages differ significantly in these regards must mean that selective modes of reporting of experience have over time become incorporated in a common instrument. On the basis of appropriate linguistic data, we can characterize languages cognitively

313

as historical products. What we cannot do on the basis of language alone is to characterize the users.

Less glaring than multilingualism, but at least as important, is the fact of diversity of use within a single language. The general structure of a language is something like a checkbook which users cash in various ways. Some ways become socially standardized, so that an individual must recognize *styles, levels, varieties, registers, keys,* and the like (to mention some of the terms that have been employed).

In even the most homogeneous of speech communities, there are at least formal, common, and slang levels of usage, associated with distinct attitudes, occasions, and individuals. Within a complex society what is considered one and the same language may be associated with systems of usage, speech codes, which are quite different in their cognitive import. Perhaps the most often cited study of this sort in the United States is that by Strauss and Schatzmann on cross-class interviewing.[31] Basil Bernstein has used English experience and sociological theory to develop an "ideal-typical" contrast of major significance between "elaborated" and "restricted" codes. Restricted codes are considered to be oriented toward the status basis of a social relation, and to limit the verbal signalling of personal difference; given the social context, the verbal component of the message is highly predictable; new information is made available through extraverbal channels, which become objects of special perceptual activity; discrete intent can be transmitted only through variations in such extraverbal signals; through such restrictiveness the code reinforces the form of the social relation. In ideal type an elaborate code is the opposite, being oriented toward the personal basis of a relation and the signalling of personal difference and intent; the verbal component is not highly predictable, and the verbal elaboration of experience is focused upon. The one is associated with a positional social control (couched in terms of status, social category), the other with a personal social control (couched in terms of personal traits).

It is Bernstein's contention that children of equivalent intelligence, but some inducted into the one type of code, some into the other, will differ markedly in their abilities to perform on the usual intelligence tests, to perform in certain social roles, and so on. He has found evidence for the contention. His work is the most striking demonstration today of the fact that not language structures, but socially organized patterns of use of language, are what is critical.[32]

Bernstein is properly concerned to keep the concepts of elaborated and restricted codes from becoming simplistically identified with middle-class ("good") and working-class ("bad") modes of speech, respectively. Wherever the appropriate social relations exist, either of the two types may emerge in varying degree, and all of us enter into one or the other in different situations. Much greeting and organizational communication is in a form of restricted code. A striking example of relevance to political behavior is found in an account of factional conflict in an Egyptian village.[33] Most communications within the village are stereotyped in verbal form, which is attended to only to the extent of noting that the form and the sender are acceptable according to traditional norms. What is closely attended to are the qualities of voice, accent, modulation of words, and the like—phenomena that are taken as conveying "friendliness" or "enmity" with regard to shifting factional alignments. Messages from the government tend to be interpreted in these terms, whether heard over radio or from being read aloud in the coffee-house by a literate villager. Communications from persons of other cultures are evaluated in the same way, and drastically different receptions may be accorded them, depending on how they mesh with the local mores. Complimentary remarks may be taken as disdainful, slighting remarks as friendly.

Let us sum up the question of the effect of language in the following way. With regard to the principle of linguistic relativity associated with Whorf, and having to do with differences in the structure of languages, we can say this: there is a more fundamental principle of linguistic relativity, that of difference in the functions and uses of languages. Insofar as the issue has been posed as lying historically between the Herderian and the Cartesian traditions, we can see that both traditions fall short. Both have a portion of the truth: there are indeed distinctive cognitive patterns crystallized in the structures of languages (the Herderian emphasis) and there are universal cognitive patterns (the Cartesian emphasis) underlying these. Both traditions, however, and linguists generally, have tended to pose the question as if the role of language were everywhere the same and the whole story, so that different linguistic structures would mean different minds; like structures, like minds. Either that, or language would have to be said to have nothing to do with the matter. We have seen that no universal answer is to be given. Because the role of language is not everywhere the same nor ever the whole story, the question changes from one of the place of language in culture to one of the place of speech codes in societies.

When the question of the effect of language is posed in terms of speech codes and use, I think that a significant effect may indeed be found. We have seen some evidence of this. I share the view of most anthropologists and linguists that in the long run of history, the exigencies of human needs and situations generally prevail to control the instrumentalities by which they are expressed. In the short run, however, there is always dependence on present needs and situations and the communicative means already in play. Spontaneous wholesale change is no more usual here than in other spheres of life; to a great extent the existing means are relied upon, and so persist, and so shape common discourse and reflection, while being gradually, more or less unreflectingly, adjusted through changing use. Change that is intentional and even sudden may occur, and a conscious struggle may be waged to determine the communicative terms in which political life will be conducted, from a matter of the speech code as a whole to a matter of a set of terms (as Jeremy Bentham pointed out), each with its own implicit valuation of what is supposedly being neutrally described. Such struggle in itself dramatizes the point: the assumption that possibility of human action shapes communicative means, and the assumption that such means, once shaped, themselves play a shaping role.

The answer to the question, "Does language affect politics?" has dealt mostly with the relations of language and thought, and has been a qualified "yes." Clearly languages as symbols of identity and as boundary mechanisms also have important political effects, and there is here a recognized and important field of investigation. Something more will be mentioned relevant to these matters in the next section. In all these respects comparative research must concern itself first of all with discovery of the sociolinguistic patterns of the groups to be studied. On this score, the answer to the second question, "Does language affect what one finds out about politics?", is a strong "yes." The relative strength of the "yes" in each case may be the result of an impression that there is danger of overestimating the effect in the first case, and of neglecting it in the second. In any case, let me now turn to considerations of the second sort.

Coping with Linguistic Diversity

The matters to which we now turn have long been discussed by linguists, but have not been at the center of linguistic interest in the present century. The main concern of modern linguistics has been with analysis of the structure of language, such structure and the science of its study being conceived as autonomous. The virtue of autonomy has tended to develop into the vice of isolation, or at least into an attitude of rejecting much having to do with speaking and the actual diversity of speech communities as unworthy of a structuralist's concern. The nature of the social role of language has been taken for granted, or rejected as of no concern to linguistics, or its investigation put off as not opportune. Recently these tendencies have been counteracted by interest in what is now called *sociolinguistics* (earlier, "sociology of language"), in some respects, "ethnography of speaking." Much of the current effort has had to go into establishing the relevance to linguistics of social factors, and into conceptual rethinking.

There thus exists no synthesized body of sociolinguistic research and theory on which to base "engineering" recommendations. There do exist a variety of studies and experiences that bear on what I take to be the two primary (and interrelated) questions confronting the political scientist in planning comparative research: what code (or codes) to use? and, how to use it (them)?

316

Choice of code

In choice of code the essential questions have to do with (a, b) functional scope (demographic, topical) and (c) value:

(a) whether, and to what extent, a given code is known;

(b) whether, and to what extent, the topics under investigation are easily, naturally expressible in the code;

(c) whether, and to what extent, the symbolic connotations of the code affect responses in and to it.

Let us consider first the question of what code or codes will be needed simply to communicate with those the scholar wishes to study. The question might be viewed as one of determining the language of the country or region. Such an approach might be encouraged by the practice of mapping languages and dialects on flat maps with solid lines between them and solid colors distinguishing them, as if the language world were parcelled out in such a "flatland" way. As we know, such is hardly the case. Every country is sociolinguistically complex, not only as to historically derived linguistic resources (dialects and languages), but also as to their organization into functional varieties (levels, styles).

The sort of difficulty that may arise simply in determining what relation holds between linguistic affiliation and cultural and social identity is well illustrated in a recent paper by Moermann on a people of Thailand. Moermann shows that ethnic affiliation is impermanent in that individuals, communities, and areas change their identification, and that where the origins of groups are political, as in parts of Africa and in Thailand, one should expect changes to be fairly common. Moreover, it cannot be assumed in advance what institutions and criteria will be essential to ethnic identification, and where the nonmembers of a group are likely to use ethnic terms differently, either as to literal meaning or as to semantic system in which contrasted, or both. In situations of "ethnolinguistic mosaics," interpenetration, or continuous variation, "objective ethnical characteristics," including language, are likely to fail, and the researcher's best strategy is to analyze the folk taxonomy, the labels used by the people themselves, as a guide to the real entities, together with the actual boundaries and networks of communication with regard to types of interest.[34] Moermann quotes from the late S. F. Nadel's account of the Nuba a statement that applies among the Northern Thai (and no doubt elsewhere).

> We shall meet with groups which, though they are close neighbors and possess an almost identical language and culture, do not regard themselves as one tribe . . . ; and we shall also meet with tribes which claim this unity regardless of internal cultural differentiation . . . : Cultural and linguistic uniformity, then, does not imply, and cultural and linguistic diversity—at least within certain limits—not preclude, the recognition of tribal unity.[35]

317

The key terms in linguistics for demarcation of units are *language* and *dialect*. Yet, as Einar Haugen has discussed in a very useful article, no simple answer can be given to questions such as "How many dialects are there in this country?" The two terms, to quote Haugen, "represent a simple dichotomy in a situation which is almost infinitely complex.[36] In terms of the utility of a dialect in communication, purely linguistic measures of similarity and difference will not suffice. Whether or not the dialect of one group will be understood and accepted among others is mutually a function of linguistic differences and of attitudes toward them. A linguist working in Nigeria, for example, found that members of one group declared themselves unable to understand the speech of another as soon as they had heard enough to recognize it.[37] In terms of the convention of regarding mutual intelligibility as evidence of belonging to the same language, the investigator would have to regard the two dialects as separate languages; yet obviously the lack of intelligibility is the result of social attitude, not linguistic difference. In contrast, one may find mutual intelligibility maintained in the face of considerable linguistic difference.[38] Where linguistic similarity *is* a simple index of mutual intelligibility, it is likely to be in cases of a dialect continuum within which mutual intelligibility is directly proportional to geographical distance, and not directly related to political and standard language boundaries.[39]

The language that will reach the greatest number cannot be chosen always on the basis of its prestige. Sometimes a pidgin without prestige in the eyes of any of its speakers will be the lingua franca of an area. Nor will prestige always accrue where one might expect it, for example, in urban centers as against hinterlands. In some respects Arabic peoples may regard the language of the nomads superior to that of the city-dwellers.[40] Sometimes so much of actual talk may be in a contact language as to excuse the investigator from dealing with the native language, whatever the respective status of the two in native eyes. On the other hand, lack of prestige may pose a problem for use of a language or dialect in research. The choice may put the field researcher in the position of having taken sides. A prime example is the type of situation analyzed by Ferguson under the heading of *diglossia*. There may coexist a high and a low form, specialized to distinct contexts, with the high form being used in written communication, including that of the government, on formal and public occasions, and in the classical literature that provides a focus for cultural values and identity. The low form will be originally confined to oral use and usually the first learned form. Only some of the population will have learned the high form through special training in schools. The large sector of the population not literate can be reached directly only through the low form, yet attitudes towards the low form may discourage its use (it may not be considered really a language at all) or identify the researcher with the modernizing wing of political life. As a case in point, one investigator in India had great difficulty in having schedules printed in the colloquial forms of Telegu and Tamil appropriate to his purpose. Equating graphic form with high form, the printers attempted to "Sanskritize" the schedules (that is, amend them so as to represent the literary language). (See Ferguson's excellent discussion of the linguistic and sociopolitical characteristics of diglossia situations and their likely political futures.)[41]

In a diglossia situation, those who control the high form also usually control the low, switching back and forth as occasion requires (even in the course of ordering in a restaurant, reading the "high" form from the printed menu, and asking the waitress for the corresponding "low" form). Such code-switching is a commonplace in many societies, quite apart from diglossia proper. Notable work on it has been done by Gumperz, who has compared a North Indian and a Norwegian village community in this regard. Gumperz defines two types of switching, associated with two types of interaction, the transactional and the personal. (The two concepts are close to Bernstein's concepts of restricted and elaborated codes in terms of the underlying social relations distinguished, but cross-cut, in that either transactional or personal switching might employ either restricted or elaborated use of a code.)

Fundamental to Gumperz' work, and to a sociolinguistic perspective, is his notion of *verbal repertoire*. Such a notion breaks at once with the one language in one culture outlook, and takes as its starting point actors in a social system of whatever degree of linguistic complexity. Whether multilingual or monolingual, persons have repertoires comprising distinguishable varieties of usage. (The ways in which shifts within verbal repertoires covary with topic, networks of relationship, and other factors of speech situations amount almost to a definition of the field of sociolinguistics for some of its pioneers.)[42] One result obtained by Gumperz is that in Norway differences in code-switching correlate with membership in different types of friendship networks, "closed" (friendships restricted to the village) and "open" (having relations with both villagers and city dwellers). Members of "closed" networks carried on discussion among themselves entirely in the local dialect, regardless of topic (switching to standard Norwegian only in the transactional situation of dealing with outsiders), whereas members of "open" networks used a high proportion of standard Norwegian forms among themselves wherever the topic was supralocal, e.g., national politics. This usage might be judged as putting on airs by others, as allusion to sophistication by themselves.

One must look behind the labels for codes to the exact nature of the linguistic differences between them. Analogous differences in function may be maintained by quite diverse degrees and kinds of linguistic difference. The diacritic indications of a shift in code may range from alternate shapes

319

for common morphemes (e.g., "going": "goin' "), and modifications of the frequency of certain consonants and vowels (e.g., in the mutual adaptation of Czech conversation between standard and colloquial, or in the value-laden levels of speech in New York City); through shifts in vocabulary and syntax; to shifts as between whole languages. One of the most pervasive and important kinds of shift is that on the dimensions of what Roger Brown has called "solidarity and power"—between a level typically used between intimates and to subordinates, and a level typically used between those not intimate and to superiors (the subject is, of course, more complex than this brief summary). Speakers of French choose between pronouns and verb endings ("vous êtes," "tu es," and so on); it has been proposed that Paraguayans choose between Guarani and Spanish in the same way. Sometimes the appearance of shift between the whole languages may be misleading; syntax and pronunciation may remain the same, for example, and only vocabulary shift, as in some Indian communities bilingual in Dravidian Kannada and Indo-Aryan Marathi.[43]

The historical circumstances under which a multilingual situation has developed may profoundly condition the uses to which a given code is naturally or even possibly put, as *diglossia*, for example, shows especially well. In his analysis, Ferguson has taken into account the ways in which modernization generates pressure for national affairs, including politics, to be discussed in the "low" form of language, but such effort may not be fully successful. Social scientists must not be misled by the slogan of modern linguistics that "anything can be said in (translated into) any language." This slogan refers to the *potential* equality of all languages, as expressions of human nature. As expressions of social and historical experience, languages are not equivalent. One must reckon in research with the *actual* inequality of languages. Not only is it easier or more difficult to say some things in some languages; within the present resources of a language it may be impossible to say certain things that can be said in another. The officials of developing nations themselves recognize this fact in their planning of language use in education and administration in the light of financial means, demography, international ties, requirements for skilled personnel, and the like, sometimes opting for training in a language not native to those who will use it, as against the long delay of developing a native language to the point at which it can be used in the same function. On political matters, Alexandre has observed (what follows is an abstract):

> European colonization established administrative and political systems in Africa which are today manned by leaders of the new states; the diffusion of native languages capable of expressing these systems has not always followed a parallel development. The result is a situation marked by discontinuity, in fact, if not intention, between the political expression at the top (i.e., leaders who use European languages), and the political expression at the base (i.e., the mass of

the population who know only African languages, often highly diversified). In fact, the African languages, worked out in given social structures do not permit, at least in their current state, expression of political doctrine conceived in European terms. The introduction or transference of political techniques are often made with such speed that there is no time for the conceptual instrument to be "Africanized".[44]

As was indicated in the first section of this chapter, languages are not neutral instruments, but are subject to evaluation by their users like every other aspect of a culture. Pride in a language, loyalty to it, concern for a given standard in its pronunciation and other facets—all these dimensions of attitude are cross-culturally variable. The choice of a language, or of code level within a language, carries with it inevitably a semantic value, for the speech code will be associated in the minds of respondents with the persons, purposes, and situations for which it is typically used. As the Spanish-Guarani, Norwegian, and diglossia situations show, members of a community may themselves choose among speech codes to express these meanings, thus defining identities, intents, and occasions.

Clearly it is not enough to know in a general way "the language of the country." To plan comparative research wisely, a scholar needs to know the set of languages and dialects; the semantic resources, topical scope, of each; the symbolic meaning of each. He needs to know, in short, how the standard verbal repertoire is organized and utilized.

The ideal handbook for planning comparative research would contain a complete set of national sociolinguistic profiles along these lines. For each country of the world, the profile would indicate what languages are in use, their spheres of use, what part of the population uses them. Typical verbal repertoires for each significant sort of social group would also be given. Nothing of the sort exists. For the characterization of nations in terms of major languages and their spheres of use, Charles Ferguson has been developing formulas and standard modes of description.[45] The work so far can give one a good idea of the types of national linguistic situations one may encounter. With regard to use of languages, some new statistical measures for estimating the linguistic diversity and commonalty of a population have been developed.[46] For perspective on multilingual situations, a recent collection of papers is helpful, including an outline typology and discussions of specific situations.[47] Still a basic work, and especially stimulating, is Weinreich's *Languages in Contact*.[48] For a survey of linguistic phenomena from a social point of view, the best book-length special treatment remains one in French, that by Marcel Cohen.[49] With regard to types of verbal repertoire and their modes of use, little is formally known in the literature. Insofar as political science research demands knowledge of such matters, political scientists may find themselves contributing to sociolinguistics by investigating such phenomena themselves, or by reporting information obtained from others.

321

Use of Codes

Let me now turn to the question of how codes are to be used in research. I take it that the question of how to evaluate information obtained in a code is to be answered in terms of one's knowledge of how such information would be evaluated by those who normally participate in the use of the code. The criterion is, of course, a prophylactic one. The scientist may and should be able to discern a great deal that would escape the layman, but he must first be sure of reading signs that are there, not signs imagined to be there because of ignorance of communicative conventions. Is someone's silence a sign of hostility, inattention, ignorance, or respect? Is the key information in a speech in the words, in the manner of delivery, in the fact that it is given at all, or here, or now, or in all of these? And so on. Cross-cultural examples are badly needed. A scholar needs only reflect how he evaluates political performance and response in his own society, and assume that matters are no less ramified elsewhere. Still, knowing that matters are complex is not the same as knowing how the complexities work. We broach here the more general subject of communication, as a perspective within which to assess the use of language. Whatever the instrument or approach, the investigator is coming from a background that makes one set of assumptions, implicit as well as explicit, about the patterning of communication into a community that may well make quite another set of assumptions. There arises the problem of what may be called *communicative interference*—misinterpretation of the import of features of communication by reading another system in terms of one's own. Obviously the interference can be mutual, investigator and respondent misreading each other. It seems unlikely that all communicative interference can be avoided, but it seems quite possible that its effect can be controlled and allowed for. Control and allowance call for *political ethnography* as the prerequisite of other modes of research.

I am conscious that my anthropological background may bias my standpoint, but I can see no alternative to this strategy. Whatever else one wants, presumably one wants validity. And validity depends upon one's ability to assess a hierarchy of factors that enter into statements of opinion and attitude that in turn depend upon the underlying communicative patterns of a community. I know no way to obtain the necessary knowledge of communicative patterns (with special reference to political life) other than by the type of intensive investigation of cultural milieux for which ethnography is the technical name.

It is my impression that many social scientists approach cross-cultural research from the other end. Concern with stimulus equivalence and particular instruments takes primacy. The main focus of attention becomes one in which the realities of cultural diversity are not interesting and revealing, but obstacles to be wished away, so that certain canons can be observed, certain instruments used. It is my impression that two factors tend to reinforce such an approach. One is a belief that to be scientific the investigator must follow certain models of measurement and design, coupled with the conviction that he must be scientific in the sense in question; from this tends to follow a strategy in which the instrument determines the problem, rather than the reverse. A second factor is the availability of large sums of money for research that can purport to provide "scientific" results as to matters on which policy-makers must decide or be informed. The prospect that American-sponsored opinion research could obtain the true views of much of the world's population at the present time may strike one as ludicrous; but the needs and purses of policy-makers, and the needs and careers of aspiring investigators, have combined to deny the ludicrous before. One can only hope that the dominant trend in American social science will be to place the accuracy and adequacy of what this country knows about the rest of the world ahead of misguided expertise in superficial instruments and specious results.

The nature of the control that the comparative researcher must exercise can be shown in terms of a set of interrelated questions that can be conflated as follows:

Whether (in what degree, on what terms) something is possible (acceptable, appropriate) in the local situation.

Given material originating in a speech code that is not a local one, the questions ask:

(a) whether it is possible to find equivalents in the local code, that is, to translate at all;

(b) given possible equivalents, in what degree these equivalents are acceptable in local discourse—by local criteria of acceptability, how do the equivalents scale as to oddity, normality, difficulty or ease with which grasped, and so on;

(c) given acceptable equivalents, on what terms are these equivalents judged appropriate or inappropriate to the circumstances of their intended use. At this point three factors of context and rules of speaking must be considered: (a) some material may not be presently translatable into a local speech code without changing the code itself through loanwords, new formations from native morphemes, altered syntactic patterns and distributions; (b) some possible translations may be harmfully odd or awkward; (c) some acceptable translations may be inappropriate to the circumstances of one's work in ways that color results.

The general assumption to be made is that exact equivalence cannot be obtained, and that validity is to be achieved through control of the factors that affect equivalence.

It is useful to distinguish three levels of equivalence (the levels could, of course, be subdivided):

1. message-form;
2. conceptual content;
3. communicative context

That is, message as form; message as content; message as act.

(1) *Message-Form.* Here we are concerned with words and sentence patterns purely as forms that may or may not be equated as between two speech codes. Some sort of equivalence of message-form is obviously indispensable to the use of any verbal instrument or material comparatively, and an exact and stable equivalence looms large for those for whom stimulus equivalence is a major consideration.

Cross-cultural researches have generally employed the technique of "back translation." The original material is translated into the local code. The translated version is then translated back into the original code. The original and the retranslated versions of the material are compared. This comparison reveals sources of difficulty and inaccuracy.

In its conscious attention to problems of translation, this technique certainly is superior to what Anderson calls "the naive approach" of those who pass over the subject with a reference to having a native speaker translate and a second bilingual perhaps check the first.[50] But back translation must be considered more a detector of difficulties than a solution to them.

There would seem to be four types of response to the difficulties and discrepancies detected by back translation. One is to abandon the technique, judging some features of one's questionnaire or whatever simply as untranslatable in equivalent scope.[51]

Now it is important to emphasize this matter of equivalent scope. The common history of some parts of the world has given rise over time to a high degree of intertranslatability among languages, with regard to both semantic content and its expression in conventional elements of similar size (words, phrases, sentences). Even in Europe, of course, serious difficulties may arise.[52] As between European languages and the rest of the world, difficulties are even greater. The many oversimplifications of cognitive differences between speakers of different languages should not lead to obliviousness of their real existence. It remains true, however, that very much is ultimately translatable "had we world enough and time." The greatest obstacles arise when one is attempting to attain precision in small compass. Then the absence of a way of rendering plainly the difference between *many* and *too many*, *much* and *too much* in Arabic, or of an equivalent for *may or may not* as a check-list response in French, may prove painful.[53] Although it has been argued that comparative data on Poles and Americans would be difficult to obtain in terms of questions about reading, because English has one verb, read, Polish some twelve (to read habitually, completely, aloud, to a group, the same thing, a meaning into a text, burying oneself, and so on), notice that by enlarging the scope from one word to a verbal phrase in English, one can utilize the very glosses just given above to explain the Polish verbs ("to read habitually," " . . . completely," and so on) and also exploit such English expressions as "to finish reading," "to give a reading," "to reread," "to read into," "to pore over," and so on. With a paragraph with which to work and sufficient comparative cultural knowledge, one could hope to specify rather precisely just the matching of senses desired. With no constraints of time and cost, one could hope to enable most Polish and English speaking respondents to understand perhaps most questions that could be phrased in either language, although not all. But constraints of time and cost, and the related constraint of scope—a single question or set of alternative phrases—may make such validity impractical.

A second response in the use of back translation is to seek to eliminate differences among versions. Let me introduce here two abbreviations, *SL* for the language from which something is translated (source language), and *TL* for the language into which something is translated (translation language, or "target-language"—the term used by C. F. Voegelin in articles on translation in the early 1950s in the *International Journal of American Linguistics*). A given item in an *SL* may give rise to more than one version in a *TL*; conversely, retranslation may give rise to multiple *SL* versions. Schachter sought to eliminate differences among back translations (*SL* versions), for example.[54] The goal presumably is to attain an invariant relationship between *SL* and *TL* in message-form, in words and sentence structure.

The difficulty is that invariant equivalence in form is no guarantee whatever of the conceptual relationship. In Nigeria, Ashanti are reported regularly to translate a native term in English as *lie*, yet the standard situation to which the term applies is one of telling something that is true. What would seem to have happened is that the Ashanti and English speakers use their respective terms of utterances that contain a common feature having to do with social action rather than truth value. In English we do not apply *lie* to all utterances that lack correspondence with truth; consider "an official denial," "putting a good face of things," "whitewash," "polite excuse," and even "little white lies." Plain *lie* seems to imply a statement told to harm or deceive (and notice that *falsehood* and *untruth*, referring literally to the relation between statement and fact, lack the force of *lie*). A *lie* is or may be an injury; not only truth value but also social consequences are part of its import. Among the Ashanti, one is obligated to inform one's mother's brother of any act or word to his harm, and that positive responsibility is designated with a distinct term; one is obligated *not* to inform others, especially nonrelatives, of whatever is said or done within the family, and to do so is designated by the term that Ashanti translate in English as *lie*. Ashanti interpreters seem to have struck an equivalence between what is the major breach of verbal responsibility in their society and what they take to be the major breach among English speakers—to tell what is so to those who should not be informed in one case, to tell what is not so to those who should be informed in the other. One can imagine the spurious reliability with which Ashanti would agree that it was a most serious thing to *lie* (as well as the odds against finding out about intrapersonal family affairs by direct questioning).

A third response to the versions produced in back translation is to consider them as "alternative forms which approach measurement of the same conceptual realm with somewhat different linguistic irrelevancies." Back translation would be used actually to generate added versions of the original material:

> Back translation, when used as an iterative procedure with a new translation for each iteration, will produce a population of items in each language with heterogeneous and random errors. A random sample of items in each language, or use of different versions with randomly selected subsamples of subjects, should provide equivalence save for random error.[55]

Under some circumstances this procedure might work, for example, where the alternate versions were regarded by respondents as stylistic choices without referential or social implication. Such circumstances, however, can be known to obtain only when positively investigated, and never can be guaranteed in advance. Thus the proposal takes for granted precisely what is in question, what must be treated as problematic: the semantic and social import of changes in message-form.

A fourth response is to regard the versions produced by back translation as providing evidence of stylistic, semantic, and social factors operative in responses to the original material, and to analyze the evidence so as to control for differences. It is this response which I consider to be the only adequate one. It may be, indeed, that the instrument with which back translation began should be itself abandoned (when Phillips ceased translating his questionnaire, he did not cease field work and translation in the generic sense of finding ways of making sense of Thai conceptions in English academese), or radically modified. Mitchell states:

> Agencies in the field which are aware of this [need for considerable knowledge of local culture and language to attain conceptual equivalence] are becoming increasingly opposed to what some of them refer to as "canned questionnaires sent from the United States." They feel that a client's attempt to preserve the exact form of his questions, especially precoded ones, can only lead to major errors. One agency now insists that clients attach a paragraph of explanation or a *rationale* to each question submitted. Once the agency discovers the intention behind a question—that is, the kind of answer which is desired and how the question will be used—it formulates its own version.[56]

Thus, there would seem to be widespread realization that back-translation, insofar as it achieves equivalence, must aim beyond equivalence of message-form to conceptual equivalence, and that conceptual equivalence entails both ethnographic knowledge of the local milieu and a willingness to abandon or to constantly control for the effects of fixed message-form. Such is the import of the discussion by Blanc of interviewing in Israel, by Hudson of his interviewing in the Arab Middle East, of Schachter in his "random probe" technique, and the general conclusion reached in his review by Deutscher.[57]

Once one reaches this conclusion, the possibility of a variety of techniques for probing equivalence becomes more salient. Back translation tends to focus attention on the most superficial aspect of the work, the equivalence of overt form. When one seeks to understand underlying conceptual structures and behavioral rules, techniques that deliberately seek to violate expectations in order to disclose their boundaries and character, for example, become possible. The total behavior of respondents becomes, not mostly a distraction, but a source of potential insight into the semantic and social dimensions of the activity in which respondents and oneself are mutually engaged in constructing and maintaining. (On this score I have in mind the sociological work of Erving Goffman, Harold Garfinkel, and Aaron Cicourel.)[58]

(2) *Conceptual equivalence.* Much of the problem of conceptual equivalence has emerged in the discussion of equivalence of message-form, and much is too technical for elaboration here. Certain points should be made, however, as to the implications of some current work.

First of all, it should be clear that bilinguals as such offer no magic solution. Our discussion of Ashanti *lie* has indicated this. Some have thought to have bilinguals respond to both language versions (*SL, TL*) as an indication of equivalence. This approach may work, and it is a useful source of evidence. The fact, however, is that bilingualism is not a unitary phenomenon. There are different types of relationship among the semantic systems of bilinguals, such that the two semantic systems sometimes are kept independent and sometimes merged. The degree of merging can vary. Also, the two languages are often not affectively neutral, but evaluated in ways that affect perception of and response to materials and persons associated with each.[59] Bilinguals must be used (preferably beginning with the investigator himself), but it must be possible to assess and control for the type of bilingualism and for its adequacy.

An instrument that is widely employed is the semantic differential. In its original use by Osgood and his associates, the semantic differential taps connotational, rather than referential, meaning, and is intended primarily to reach universal dimensions, rather than to reveal cultural peculiarities. Useful understanding of cultural peculiarities may still emerge.[60] Osgood has had success in getting varied respondents to make the forced choices of often arbitrary nature that the method requires. Although the factor-analytic technique originally has been questioned, it seems entirely likely that useful indications of the movement of opinion along broad lines can be obtained. Osgood once reported, for example, that during the Soviet-American alliance of World War II responses placed the Soviet Union as more positive on all good counts, including being perceived as more Christian.

The original device consists of seven-interval scales and a set of words ("concepts"). Each scale is intended as a polar contrast: good-bad, strong-weak, active-passive, sweet-sour, sharp-dull, clean-dirty, and so on. Respondents are asked to rate each concept on each scale, the concepts ranging across anything of interest: kinsmen, political figures, self, abstract concepts. The results are factor-analyzed. Major factors found have been evaluative (good-bad and those scales that cluster with it), activity (active-passive, and those scales that cluster with it). Sometimes the second and third scales seem to coalesce as a dynamic factor. Not all the same scales fall together in all cultures, and the placement on scales, of course, may vary. Clean-dirty is highly evaluative in our culture, but a Navaho may rate a grandmother as relatively dirty in a dispassionate descriptive sense. It can be seen that the semantic differential only indirectly discloses much of the actual cognitive structures of political life in a society, but that its limitation to connotative evaluations of a rather universal sort enables it to escape many of the difficulties confronting semantic understanding of detailed cognitive structure.[61]

The discussion of Whorfian and other topics in the first part of this chapter has suggested some of the pitfalls that may beset translation. There has developed in recent years an important ethnographic literature on methods for determining semantic categories, their dimensions, and relationships. Anyone interested in controlling the terminology of a sector of political behavior would do well to consult this literature.[62]

The fundamental principle of this semantic work is paradigmatic contrast within locally valid frames. It is in this respect that such semantics goes consciously beyond back translation. Back translation asks for utterances that are in some way paraphrases, or quasi-paraphrases, of the original material. The responses are likely to illuminate problems of homonymy, synonymy, superordinate vs. subordinate terms, and personal and social connotation, that is, problems centering around the original utterance as a sort of magnetic nucleus. Full semantic control also requires obtaining the set of terms or utterances that are linked with the original in the given frame of reference, not because of positive association, but because of negative contrast. One needs to know not only that respondents might in the circumstances consider *pale, clear, light* as possible alternatives for something originally intended as *white,* but also that in the given frame whatever is *white* and so on is precisely not *black (cloudy, dark).* In assessing responses, the investigator has inevitably in mind a set of alternatives from among which a given response is

328

implicitly or explicitly chosen. Research to that end employs the concept of what I have referred to as paradigmatic contrast, and is well illustrated in the work cited in footnote 62. One seeks to determine the set of contrasting responses that can occur within a given frame, the dimensions on which the responses contrast, and the principle or implicit question that defines the frame. In the course of such research one also discovers other aspects of the semantic organization of native terms.

One can readily see that stable equivalence of message-form may be quite misleading if the underlying set of possible contrasts and their dimensions of contrast are different as between the two languages. Exact matching between paradigmatic sets cannot be expected very often, but knowledge of their nature enables the investigator to control evaluation of responses made in terms of them. Often enough divergencies can be allowed for within the material itself, if qualifying phrases, "but not . . . ," "just the . . . ," can be added.

Conceptual equivalence is not a matter of semantics in the ordinary linguistic sense alone; that is, it is a matter not only of reference to objects, ideas, persons, but also of indication of attitude, intent, expected consequences, and the like. All this appears simply from consideration of what might be taken to be the simplest responses, "yes" and "no." The linguist and anthropologist Stanley Newman once gave orally a paper on the multiplicity of ways of uttering "yes" in English. These ways are tacitly known and utilized by members of the community, and hence must be explicitly known and controlled, or allowed for, by the investigator. (It can be observed in passing that the problems of comparing research apply within our own society, where the usual speech code of investigators cannot be taken as identical with that of their respondents, and where the communicative interference may be all the more damaging because it is overlooked.)

Edmund Glenn states (citing the Arab linguist E. Shouby as his source) that Arabs tend to interpret simple English "no" as "yes," and simple English "yes" as a polite "no".[63] A genuine "no" would have to be emphasized (and, by implication, so would a genuine "yes"). We have then a little paradigm of the interdependence of conceptual content and full message-form. Because an affirmative or negative response can itself be a sentence, let me illustrate the paradigm by labelling the words that occur as *Sentence-form*, and the additional features of message-form that determine the manner in which it is said as *Key*. We have, then,

| | | Sentence Form | |
		"yes"	"no"
Key	Polite	no	yes
	Emphatic	yes	no

Recall here the Egyptian Arabic village cited as an example in the first section of this essay. It is indeed a general principle that when the sentence form of a message is contradicted by its expressive form, it is the expressive form that is overriding in determining the true import. (I am using *expressive form* here as a shorthand label for whatever features of styles, voice, gesture, and the like that may be integrated into the marking of key as polite, emphatic, mocking, brusque, and the like.)

Within every speech code it is possible to indicate degrees of deference and demeanor, of intimacy and distance, of respect and authority. In some cases, such as the Japanese and Javanese, the very choice of sentence form must take into account the appropriate marking of such things in different personal relationships. Cases in which the marking intrudes into the overt grammatical form of what we normally write down must not blind us to the presence of the same functions in features that we do not normally write or attend to as linguistic.

The great linguist Ferdinand de Saussure stressed early in this century that a comparative standpoint in linguistics must comprehend both lexicon and grammar, because what was expressed by grammatical means in one language would be found expressed by lexical means in another. The principle must be generalized to communication as a whole. From a comparative standpoint, the conceptual import of an utterance, what is taken to have been said, always will depend on sentence-form, taken together with other signals; and just where particular imports are conveyed may vary from one group to another. The English sociologist Basil Bernstein has stressed the differences in this respect within the same society, depending on class, family, and situation.[64] We know too little systematically and comparatively, but techniques for the study of vocal signals, body idiom, and the handling of spatial relationship have been developed.[65]

These considerations bring me to the fact that an utterance is a matter not only of form and conceptual content, but of social action as well. In an interview, as in ordinary conversation, one operates in terms of a system of communicative acts as well as in terms of systems of communicative forms and contents. To this I now turn.

(3) *Communicative context.* Groups differ in their patterning of communication and in their use of verbal means within such patterning. So much is a truism. Anthropologists and linguists, unfortunately, have far too little to offer by way of basic knowledge as to such patterning. Their insights have tended to remain scattered and even unpublished. Even linguists directly engaged in communicative change, those of the Summer Institute of Linguistics whose goal is to introduce the Bible into more than 2,000 diverse speech communities, fail to take systematic account of the communicative matrices in which they work. Present formal models of communication are of little help, because they impose limited, a priori designs, concealing just what

is diverse and problematic cross-culturally, and offering no heuristic aid to the discovery of systems of communication that actually obtain. To illustrate: the formal models known to me all are satisfied to posit two participants, a speaker and a hearer (source and destination, and so on). The merest acquaintance with ethnographic fact shows the importance and diversity of ways in which *three* parties determine communicative rules: various patterns of addressor, addressee, and auditor; addressor, addressee, and spokesman; addressor, addressee, and interpreter; and the like.

As a heuristic device for discovering ethnographically the local rules of communication the following set of factors, keyed mnemonically to the word *speaking*, may be useful.[66] (The approach is developed in somewhat more detail in other papers).

S: Setting, Situation, Scene. Both temporal and spatial setting may be determinative; psychological setting, or scene, must be considered as well.

P: Participants, Persons. From one to many. A particular rule may specify the presence of just one person of a certain type, of two, of three.

E: Ends. Two senses of *end* are coupled here: end in view (intent, purpose), and end as outcome. Communicative acts are often to be distinguished in terms of the purpose and/or expected outcome. Of course, one distinguishes conventional purposes, actual motives, latent and manifest functional outcomes, and so on.

A: Act Sequence. Two aspects of communicative acts are coupled here: the form, as the overt signals that occur (or are to occur), and the content the signals manifest. Two field activities that roughly correspond are transcription (form) and translation (content). The distinction answers to the notion of "saying the same thing (content) in different ways (forms)"; conversely, the Song of Songs read with and without reference to Christ's church. With regard to status as an act, "Is that (form) a threat (act) or a promise (act)?"

K: Key. The manner in which done: seriously or in jest; perfunctorily or with commitment; with eloquence or awkwardness; impetuously or with hesitation; willingly or reluctantly. Although this factor is closely linked to purpose, being commonly taken as evidence of intent, there are conventional ways of displaying manner, so that manner and intent can differ as in the relation between acting and naive expression, or Michael Flanders' line, "Always be sincere, my boy, whether you mean it or not."

I: Instrumentalities. Here are coupled two main aspects of communicative means: channels (auditory, visual) and codes.

N: Norms of interaction and of interpretation. By norms of interaction are meant such things as a requirement that participants not interrupt each other (as opposed to communicative norms by which interruption is per-

331

missible): that speaking time be allotted approximately equally (in contrast with norms that some have no claim on speaking time); that none present should leave before a certain point (as in church services); that speech not part of the scheduled focus of an event can occur if whispered (as often in our society, vs. Maori practice, where no attention to scheduled speechmaking need be paid at all); that the asker of a question has a right to speak again; and so on. By norms of interpretation are meant shared understandings not otherwise expressly provided for, things under the heading of "what everybody knows"; the use of background information, "common sense," the rationality of everyday life. Obviously this category comprises things referable to others singled out here, and beyond that is something of a promissory wastebasket. The work in progress of the sociologists Harold Garfinkel, Harvey Sacks, Emmanuel Schegloff, and others, however, is rapidly giving it content and developing it as a perspective on the whole.

G: *Genres.* Here are intended the varieties of communicative event and act: oratory, poetry, conversation, announcing; interviewing; a joke, a request, insult, promise, threat; and so on. Communicative behavior is entirely accountable for in terms of a series of communicative acts. Acts are independent of events in that the same type of act may be imbedded in different types of larger-scale act or event; for example, a joke may occur in a conversation, a poem, a speech, a sermon.

Whereas no heuristic scheme can provide in detail for a local situation, experience with ethnographic materials has shown that the scheme just given provides for all types of factors noted so far. It is not that every local rule will depend on all the factors, but rather that one needs a comprehensive scheme so that he will not overlook factors that may be relevant. [One needs also the understanding that there is a system of rules to be discovered. In my experience, some cross-cultural investigators (missionaries and anthropologists) remain ethnocentric when it comes to communicative patterns, failing to grasp rules that their own anecdotes show to have been staring them in the face. To cite two examples that have recently come to my attention: in some New Guinea groups it is not accident or "gossip" when, getting nowhere directly in one's problems with a local leader, one finds discussion with the leader's associates to clear the way for understanding, but going through the local proper channels; or in an Indian university it is not an affront when a head official sends an intermediary to discuss directly behavior that has upset him, but a kindness, because to come himself would mean dismissal.]

Most local rules will be specified in terms of a few factors. Sometimes just two components will be involved, as when politics is discussed in a particular code (content/code); sometimes three, as when politics is discussed in one code in an office or other public place, and in another code at home (content/scene/code), or in a different code as between officials and friends (content/participant/code), or only by certain persons (content/participant/code). More complex relationships, of course, may obtain, as when in a certain setting before certain persons only certain other persons can discuss politics, and then only in a specific code to a particular purpose.

Although the general wisdom and knowledge of social science in the study of interpersonal behavior is relevant here, a useful rule-of-thumb for communicative rules is a formula analogous to that in terms of which this section is organized: form/content/context (corresponding somewhat to the semiotic formula of Charles Morris, syntactics, semantics, pragmatics). A feature of concern, such as a code, a topic of statement, a setting, is to be considered a form, contrasting with others of a set of such forms (other codes, other topics, other types of statement, other settings, and so on). Some sort of meaning or import will be attached to the choice of one rather another of the set, just as in virtue of contrast within the set, some standard or conventional contrast is being implied. Further import will be attached to the choice of a given form and its associated meaning, in the light of the context in which the choice occurs, and special "marked" meanings can be conveyed by manipulating the relationship between form-meaning composite and contexts. Thus in many communities, if not all, there is a choice among a set of styles or modes of address and speech (forms), each considered proper, observing usual social norms (meanings) in contexts defined by one or more other factors of speaking (participants, setting, topic, and so on) (contexts). When these modes are arranged in a hierarchy as to respect, one can mark flattery, compliment, derogation, and insult by manipulating the relationship between the styles and their usual meanings, on the one hand, and contexts on the other. Of course, humor, mockery, and so on may also be thus expressed and they will vary with other factors, and with the community as a whole, as to whether manipulation of such relationships is taken as directed at an auditor (say, an interviewer), and when simply expressive of the speaker, when a comment on the topic, and the like.

From a linguistic standpoint, one is speaking here of *context-sensitive rules,* rules that specify the character of an element in dependence on contexts in the form $x \rightarrow y/z$ (e.g., Code is to be taken as Bahasa Indonesian in the district administrator's office), or, where alternates are concerned,

Code	[Indonesian]	[District administrator's office]
	[Minangkabau]	[District administrator's home].

Or, one can be thought of as describing a "communicative lexicon," specifying the features of form, of meaning, and of contextual selection of communicative elements just as a dictionary specifies the shapes, meanings, and contextual restrictions of words [e.g., *love*: /ləv/, "zero score" (tennis)].

333

The concern of the comparative student of political life will be with the rules that most directly affect discussion of politics and the asking of questions about it. Given that the behavior will be assessed in terms of the local system of communicative acts, the investigator will be particularly concerned with rules governing what may be generically called *interrogative behavior*. The sort of scheme and rules just discussed point toward discovery of just who can ask whom, in what way, by what means, when and where, about political attitudes and activities, and with what intents and what likely effects. The general set of questions posed earlier in this section applies: What is possible? What acceptable? What appropriate?

The local system may be such that certain communicative acts and genres are excluded from the outset. Various scholars have pointed out that the questionnaire and the formal interview are far from universal, and as types of acts may either be unintelligible or interpreted in ways injurious to results. High proportions of no answers, don't knows, undifferentiated responses, and self-contradicting results may reflect deficiencies in message-form and conceptual equivalence, but also, very likely, may reflect problems of the nature of acts by which information was obtained. One must know how members of the community obtain information from each other—obtaining information from others is surely universal—and be guided accordingly.

An anthropologist working in Chiapas, Mexico, found the Mayan residents to respond to direct questioning with a simple "nothing." Clearly it is not that they are unable to obtain information from one another. The likely explanation is that direct questions, as a form of statement, carry the meaning of rudeness. [It is common enough in American Indian, as in other languages, to have two forms of request or command, one polite (say, a future) and one not (say, an imperative).] Similar distinctions extend to ways of mentioning topics in many communities (in Bihar, India, a wife is expected to complain in general terms about the food her husband's family provides, but to mention a particular food is an insult to them), and generally to ways of conducting communication.

Often enough the interpretation of an investigator's acts in terms of the local system will not be so helpfully revealing of failure as "nothing." An answer will be given. Although one scholar finds justification for doubting that research methods elaborated in the West are suitable at all for Southeast Asia, another believes that the standard techniques of the West are applicable, if the interviewer overcomes the distorting effects of the pervasive courtesy bias by not asking questions for which there is any obviously pleasing answer. Having entered into the interview situation, a respondent from these societies feels obligated not to distress the interviewer; moreover, an interviewer from the same society is under the same obligation with respect to the respondent. Obviously, results of such research cannot be taken at face value, but once the local norm is understood, materials can be designed and can be interpreted so as to allow and account for the effects of the norm.

A complementary bias often likely to result from the use of interviewers from the same society as the respondents is that the interviewers will be just those newly educated, upwardly mobile young persons most concerned to show their distance from those they interview.

Among the many ways in which local rules can affect investigation of political life, I shall single out only one more specific to interviewing, that of what may be called *communicative routines*. Just as there are rules for sentences, so also there are rules for longer stretches of discourse, either by one person or between persons—rules for interchanges of welcome and farewell, narration, prayer, speech-making, petitioning, and the like. Extended information-seeking thus involves not only rules governing a single act, but patterns extending over a string of such acts. Sometimes there may be a local pattern that might be put to advantage; Tibetan nomads, for example, have a well-worked-out system of question and answer for obtaining information about the location of other groups. There may be a strong feeling about the observance of norms for extended discourse: among the Ngoni of Africa, someone who violates the norms for reporting experiences may be told to go back and begin again. Certain underlying assumptions may rule out types of sequential behavior employed in our own society, as when the Araucanians of Chile value accuracy of speech and memory in such a way that to ask a person to repeat orally is to imply inaccuracy and thus insult him. Among the Toba of Argentina, an initial direct answer indicates that the potential respondent is busy and has no time for questions; if he has time, he will not give a direct answer right off. (Expectations as to the structure and direction of verbal sequences may, of course, conflict within our own society, as in the study by Strauss and Schatzmann mentioned earlier.)[57]

In view of the importance of sequential organization of discourse, it is striking that there are almost no descriptions of it. One suggestive account has been given by Frake as to "how to ask for a drink in Subanun"; a pioneering essay that permits one to see a set of such routines in the context of cultural values is that by Albert on the Burundi.[68] Sociologists such as Sacks, Schegloff, and others are analyzing conversational routines and their assumptions in our own society. Cross-culturally, however, an anthropologist or linguist has typically referred to the importance of a sequentially structured activity, such as gossip, in such a way as to make it clear that there are rules as to how one does it in the society in question, but leave us none the wiser as to what the rules are. It seems likely that knowledge of local patterns for reporting experience will help researchers seek information in locally meaningful sequences, and help interpret responses to other instruments. (A "no response," for example, may reflect a local sense of *nonsequitur*.) Knowledge of such local patterns may guide research strategy by indicating what sorts of information might be expected to emerge spontaneously from unguided discourse, and what types of information, being omitted from normal discourse style, would have to be sought in other ways.

The possibility always remains, of course, that certain topics—perhaps politics—are neither spontaneously elaborated nor acceptably questioned about in direct form. This fact brings us to a brief consideration of the notion of *communicative type*.

So far our discussion of communicative context has dealt mostly with particular rules and patterns, especially those that would affect the planning and managing of an interview or other immediate situation for obtaining information. I believe it likely that communities can be characterized at a more general level as to patterning of communication, so that eventually a comparative typology will be possible. Such a typology would include two features of special importance to political research focused on verbal means and verbal data: the place of verbal communication about political life in the community, and the general relation of verbal communication to the rest of behavior.

With regard to the place of verbal communication about political life:

(a) it has been proposed that verbal investigation of political opinion is in fact inappropriate as an act to most of the populations of many countries. In Southeast Asia, the formation and expression of opinion is found to be restricted to relatively small portions of the population.[69] It would seem that armed struggle, hunger strikes, refusal to pay taxes, and so on, are expressions of opinion, but, of course, what is meant is verbal response of a certain type. In my view, opinion is universal. What varies should be stated as to who has the right (or obligation) to express opinion, to whom, under what circumstances, (for example, the rules of political communication). Not long ago in our own society, women did not have legitimate public political opinions, and national polls today do not usually consult school children, although the children sometimes poll themselves. What is at stake presumably is the nature of the opinion present in different sectors of the society, in relation to the communicative structure of the society: how informed (detailed) is the opinion, and what are the outcomes, consequences, of the persons in question having opinions?

In the mutual management of the situation between investigator and respondent, the respondent may well have good reason to calculate the consequences of disclosing opinion, or even of having opinion (cf., Negroes in the American South in the presence of local whites). The matter is also sensitive when an answer implies a commitment, not just of the respondent, but also of some larger group for which or to which one is responsible.

Insofar as comparative political research is concerned with opinion, then, it is mandatory to analyze the communicative structure of the society in question with respect to the handling of opinion before proceeding to the design and use of materials.

To cite briefly the Maori as an illustration: white officials sometimes call public meetings of Maori to consider matters affecting them; often, the Maori express no opinion at the meeting, the officials conclude that the Maori lack interest in the matter, and they proceed to decide it themselves. The Maori then react with annoyance at not having been consulted.

In point of fact, expression of opinion among the Maori is governed by a variety of rules, consistent and understandable in themselves, but different from official expectations in ways that produce communicative interference. For the Maori, expression of opinion is governed by a concern to avoid hasty decision, a concern for consensus among those affected by a matter, and a respect for elders and the self-respect of others generally. Thus, arrangements for a marriage must be discussed at great length just to show proper respect for the couple. Someone who comes to a quick judgment on a matter is suspected. Matters that affect a group as a whole are discussed at length, but while still under discussion the issue probably would not be talked about with outsiders; certainly individuals would not feel free to express individual opinions that might seem to represent the group as a whole. Once consensus has been reached, an elder person would normally voice it, just as a man does not normally express an opinion in the presence of an elder brother. Notice also that one does not indicate disapproval of a proferred idea in so many words, but by failing to talk about the idea at all.

Thus at a public gathering one will not find free and general discussion of opinion before others. There may very well be no discussion at all, possibly indicating disapproval, and often indicating, not lack of interest, but as yet lack of consensus. Only if a public meeting happened to occur after the lengthy, independent processes of the Maori community had themselves resulted in consensus would it (the meeting) evoke the expression of opinion expected by officials. Commonly Maori come to such meetings, are silent, resume afterwards their own discussions at length, and are frustrated when there is no way for the eventual result to reach the officials. An interviewer or survey-taker among the Maori would presumably find himself in much the same relation to them as the white official.

(b) the relation of verbal statement to beliefs and action varies as between cultures. Running through our discussion has been the implicit question of what it means to say something to an outsider. Among the Navaho it is a cardinal sin to lie to a fellow Navaho, and practically an obligation to deceive a Zuni. Among the Lue of Thailand, deceptive eloquence is an admired accomplishment and has no simple relationship to what we consider lying. Beyond this are more general valuations of the use of language. Among the Wishram Chinook (an American Indian group), statements about the future were not willingly made in unqualified form unless the matter referred to was assured of happening. There was a general orientation toward the use of language as something not casually done, toward formal discourse as requiring certainty and as enacting, confirming that which is stated. Such general reticence in the use of speech is characteristic of a number of societies, contrasting with a loquacity in others that suggests that most speech is considered cheap.

A test for matters crucial to political research would be to discover if verbal acts can be withdrawn, and if so, which, how, and to what extent. Are responses to an interviewer under the heading of verbal acts that imply commitment in local terms, or acts that can be disowned, perhaps as soon as uttered?

A concept of importance is that of *performative* utterances. Some verbal statements themselves do what they say; for example to say "I promise" can be to do the act of promising itself. Communities and contexts differ as to the performative status of particular statements, and as to the general pervasiveness of performative status.

We have only the bare beginnings of a comparative typology of societies as to the organization and valuation of speech. A pioneering anthropological treatment is Margaret Mead's account of three Pacific Island groups. Two of the groups represent a cross-cultural extension of the Bernstein contrast between personal and positional social control mentioned in the first section, in that in the one public opinion is a matter of gatherings in which reasoning and merit of argument tend to prevail in open discussion; in the other the fate of an opinion is determined by the social status of the holder. The Keesings have treated elite communication in Samoa, and Barth has analyzed maintenance and loss of authority associated with contrasting communicative patterns among the Pashto and Baluchi.[70] The work of Edward Hall[71] is especially valuable in calling attention to nonverbal dimensions of cross-cultural communication. A variety of cultural factors that can play a part in communicative modes are surveyed by Doob from the standpoint of persuasion, but systems are not analyzed.

It seems likely that there are areal patterns in communicative type (cf., the Southeast Asia courtesy bias mentioned earlier). Alan Lomax has discerned areal patterns in musical communication that are suggestive for communication generally. An areal classification on a world scale would certainly be desirable, but requires much more sociolinguistic, folkloristic, and communicative ethnography than as yet exists.

Conclusion

My task has been to consider what linguistics can offer to the political scientist as a basis for assessing the role of language in political life and for conducting research. It would be pleasant to be able to say that one could expect to obtain the services of linguists specialized in the problems we have considered. Given an initial sophistication with regard to linguistic problems, the political scientist could turn the technical applications over to an expert. Our discussion has indicated that this ideal situation is far from being the case. The linguistic aspects of comparative political research entail the application of a basic science that does not yet exist, one that is only slowly coming into being under the rubrics of sociolinguistics, ethnography of communication, and the like.

This situation is partly the fault of the linguist. There continue to be many linguists who would not regard the problems discussed in this essay as part of linguistics at all. For them, the science of linguistics is not the science of language, but of some formal partial model of language as an essence virginally detached from existence. Indeed, linguistics has always tended to be a somewhat separate, alienated discipline. It began in the history of Western civilization with the study of forms of language put forward as the norms of an elite, justifying ideologically a political rule. In modern terms it has striven for independence in terms of assumptions that single out a normatively ideal form for study, abstracted from context and use, and the attractiveness of the patterning of linguistic form has helped justify attention to structure at the expense of function. This state of affairs is beginning to change, as increasing attention is being paid to function. One wonders if the corresponding attention to verbal detail and language will come to be paid by the political scientist, and the social scientist generally, in ways informed by modern linguistic knowledge. The social scientist has typically not had the linguistic skills to deal with verbal data in technically adequate ways, and has tended to regard language as something linguists describe in grammars, or as an immaterial medium of more serious matters, such as politics, economics, religion, or as all three at once. Just as the linguist has tended to concentrate on content, abstracted from use and form, so the social scientist has tended to concentrate on content, abstracted from use and form. In the process, what has been neglected has been the patterning intrinsic to speaking, to the use of language—the materials of a comparative rhetoric, logic, poetics, sociolinguistics, and, incidentally, a basis for an applied comparative political science (in other words, a general theory of the role of language in society based on adequate empirical studies). The social scientist has been intent upon seeing through language to other things, the linguist upon stopping at grammar's edge.[72]

Yet it remains the case, in political life as in other aspects of life, that:

> ... the language we use to enquire into and negotiate our actions, is no secondary factor, but a practical and radical element in itself. To take a meaning from experience, and to try to make it active, is in fact our process of growth. Some of these meanings we receive and recreate. Others we must make for ourselves, and try to communicate.[73]

Given the fact that one cannot speak glibly of the one language of a society but must specify the particular speech codes in use among a group of people and the relation of these linguistic means to other communicative means, it remains that once such specification has been made, it becomes possible to trace ways in which the means available shape thought and action. One may even try to explicate the insights of those who have commented on the quality of the language of political life—Orwell in "Politics and the English Language"; various writers on the consequences for German of Nazism; the linguistic crisis of confidence in the time of Thucydides, discussed as *paracharaxein* (defacement of the coinage) by Gilbert Murray; and what one reviewer has dubbed the political philology of Sukarno's Indonesia. Or one may attempt to evaluate the adequacy and honesty of language from the standpoint of what the historian of the functional view of language, Verburg, has seen as language's chief function, delosis (clarity).[74] Nonetheless, such tasks are beyond the linguist as pure linguist and also beyond the social scientist who has no linguistic control of the society he studies. Perhaps the interest of political scientists in language as a means for comparative research will lead them to an interest in language as a means of political life, and "political philology," or whatever one wishes to call it, will take a vital place in the new understanding of the role of language in human experience now promising to emerge.

Even if the interest of the political scientist remains limited to linguistics as a means, let me hope that this will result in an effective interest in the linking of linguistic training and social science training, for only through such linking can the necessary personnel and basic resources be produced.

For the foreseeable future it seems all too likely that a point will come in most pieces of comparative research at which some of the practical linguistics required must be supplied by political scientists themselves. Control of the meanings in the data in hand, the concrete particulars of the communicative situation itself, will require personal sophistication in linguistics and linguistic (communicative) ethnography. In many cases, perhaps one can obtain the advice of persons with experience in the area. Because such persons will have accumulated more information than one needs, one must expect to have to grapple with the adjustment of investigative means and ends oneself.

As a concept for the linguistic portion of this process, Robert Holt has suggested the notion of a *linguistic pretest*. A linguistic pretest would undertake an assessment of the local situation as to choice of speech code—the repertoire of local codes, their scope, and symbolic connotations; and patterns of the use of the codes and of communication generally—who can communicate what to whom, in what way, and so on, and to what extent, and with what degree of acceptability and appropriateness. A number of suggestions that might find a place in such a pretest have been made in the course of this

340

essay and there are others in the literature on translation and cross-cultural research. No general model for such a pretest now exists, and it is important to keep in mind that the work the political scientist may need to do for his practical ends may contribute to the building of basic theory at the same time.

As ideal guidelines, summarizing the viewpoint of this chapter, I would stress the following:

(1) general knowledge of the cultural setting and local speech codes;

(2) open-ended exploration of the local communicative behavior, especially with regard to the kinds of materials and events by means of which one expects to obtain information;[75]

(3) a view of discrepancies, difficulties, variations, spontaneous comments, and the like as evidence for the local system that governs respondents' statements and other conduct, and their assessment of the investigator's;

(4) emphasis on validity rather than on stimulus-equivalence or reliability, such that one does not expect to find exact equivalence in codes, message-forms, contents, and acts as between the local community and that which is the source of one's inquiry, but does expect to be able to calibrate the two interacting systems so as to control and allow for lack of equivalence;

(5) controlled covariation as the principal strategy for discovering local rules and their effects on validity of responses (what difference does it make if code X is used rather than code Y, and what underlies the difference? if word X, rather than word Y? if intonation X, rather than intonation Y? if routine X, rather than routine Y? if setting X, rather than setting Y? and so on).

Let me close by observing that if sophistication in linguistics and ethnography can help the political scientist to do a better job, the job he does may contribute in turn to a general social science of language. Work done for practical ends can contribute to the building of basic theory at the same time and to the closing of the gap between linguistics and social science which makes difficult a true understanding of language itself.

CHAPTER 8

Diachronic Methods in Comparative Politics

SYLVIA L. THRUPP
University of Michigan

Many specialists in comparative politics are developing a new interest in history, which for a long time has been neglected by political scientists who engaged in the behavioral revolution. This regenerated interest in historical materials can be seen in the development of historical data archives and in the efforts of some scholars to examine the happenings of the past in terms of new concepts and with contemporary research techniques. Most behavioralists now recognize that their studies of contemporary phenomena can be enriched by adding a historical dimension.

This historical dimension is especially important for comparativists who study political development. After all, the concept development necessarily implies change over a period of time. Historical materials thus assume a position of great importance in studies of this type. The complementarity of scholarly interests between political scientists and historians is treated in Chapter 8 by Professor Sylvia L. Thrupp of the Department of History at the University of Michigan.

Professor Thrupp's published works include The Merchant Class

343

of Medieval London; Change in Medieval Society *(ed.);* Early Medieval Society *(ed.); and numerous articles on medieval social and economic history in various periodicals. She was also the Founding Editor and is now co-editor with Eric R. Wolf of the international quarterly,* Comparative Studies in Society and History.

THE MOST CHALLENGING innovation that comparative politics has produced is the idea of extending its cross-cultural comparisons backwards in time. True, the idea is not wholly new—it occurred to Herodotus. But it found no firm place in Greek political science, because its implications for theory were not realized. For the same reason, the comparative study of societies through time has never had any secure footing in any of the American social sciences. Nor has the behavioral movement, of which comparative politics in this country is an offshoot, paid any particular attention to time-dimensions. On the contrary, its chief effect has been to heighten the fascination and widen the scope of that already wide problem-territory in which the gifted observer of a living scene commands so rich a universe. In consequence the behavioral sciences are overwhelmed by a torrent of findings which they are frantically trying to channel conceptually and to control by generalization. It is a tribute to the vigor and ingenuity of comparative politics that in its global extension of contemporary research it is trying to tie this, in a way that has never been systematically attempted before, to studies through time, and to direct both, together, to the testing of theory and to the generating of new theory.

A child of the age of jet-travel to international conferences, the idea has been rushed into action in large-scale projects with minimal waste of time in preliminary argument over the methods to be employed. Discussion has been diverted to choices among statistical techniques because these have been developing so rapidly, but seems now to be returning to the question of choice among methods.[1] This paper rejects as a red herring the notion that the choice is between quantitative and nonquantitative methods. Rather, methodological choice is seen as turning on one's degree of sensitivity to the uses of differences for the purpose of generalization, as well as of similarities.

The argument draws on earlier as well as recent experience with comparative methods. Assessment of the advantages of a method is in terms of its chances, in the light of experience, of overcoming three main difficulties that have hitherto hampered all efforts to apply comparative methods to human affairs. The essay concludes that comparative politics will in general stand a better chance of overcoming the more insidious of these difficulties if at least some of its studies cut much further back in time than is at present contemplated. Among some of the older social scientists a stock response to any such proposal is one of alarm. But the younger generation appears to be less fearful, and to have more curiosity. At the suggestion of students studying survey research methods at the University of Minnesota who read an earlier draft of this work, some illustrations have been added of kinds of historical

345

material that survive in quantity yet have not been fully exploited, and of how an historian goes about comparative work.

The Meaning of Diachronic Analysis

The term *diachronic* is borrowed from anthropology. Synchronic comparison being there taken for granted (if only by way of the paradoxical fiction that the simpler societies have existed in a kind of timeless contemporaneity), any method that relies on successive synchronic comparisons within a chronological framework is called *diachronic*. This reliance is the one feature common to all of the methods of comparative politics to be reviewed here. It excludes only such survey research procedures as at the start necessarily have no precedent. However, to the extent that survey research procedures similar in nature are repeatedly applied in the same regions, they will become diachronic, as has happened to American sociological research on some parts of the home front.

The term could help comparative politics avoid clumsy circumlocutions. It is neat and neutral, free of the mixed associations that attach to the adjective *historical*. Unfamiliar to historians, most of whom would doubtless denounce it as jargon, it is no Trojan horse through which the techniques of purely narrative and descriptive historical writing could subvert the citadel of social science. It trails no ambiguous imagery: current talk of longitudinal and cross-sectional data unwarily evokes the image of a surgeon or of a planner confident that he is operating on a homogeneous body or on one to be made so. It puts one on guard against the vagueness of contrasting research as dealing either with the present or with the past. *The present* is a euphemism for the reach of people's active memories and of their hopes for the future, which in both directions is elastic. When the flow of events is fast and exciting, the reach of memory may shrink while hope runs farther into the future; in times of stagnation the reverse may occur. Research will be described here as "present-minded" if it is conducted within a time-perspective no longer than a life-span of some sixty years. Few diachronic studies that run up to the 1950s or 1960s have been systematically diachronic over a period even half this long, but whereas some have drawn extensively on knowledge of conditions prior to the twentieth century, others have done so only cursorily or not at all.

It is axiomatic that in order to generalize, diachronic methods, like any others, have to look first for similarities; the attention paid to individual differences has to be controlled by classification and by attempts at measurement, so that they will come up for analysis only as kinds and ranges of difference. A capacity to observe similarities and differences with equal care, while still selecting only those that will be relevant to generalization in terms

346

of the concepts and hypotheses employed, is rare. Aesthetic sensibilities favoring similarity or difference seem to be among the many principles of prior selection at the stage of observation that escape conscious control. Again, the degree of flexibility that one can exercise in modifying received hypotheses, or in devising new ones, at the dictates of the evidence, depends probably on temperament as well as on training. In principle, all methods profess to embody some degree of impartiality at the stage of observation and of flexibility at the stage of analysis, yet their procedures may impose severe limitations on the latter, and since the two stages are in practice never really separable, sensitivity to relevant differences may also be reduced. Comparative politics offers a fascinating example of how in a new field encouraging experiment, methods continue to display the same range of variation in these respects as has been customary.

The four methods so far adapted to diachronic use may be ranked as follows, according to the degree of sensitivity to relevant differences that is built into them: (1) the method of selecting closely related groups of societies or political systems, with emphasis on the study of concomitant variations; (2) the method of comparing two or more societies exhibiting sharp contrasts as well as similarities; (3) the method of working from polar typologies of traditionality and modernity; (4) the method of interpretive model-building out of quantitative aggregate data. The first two demand a high sensitivity to cultural nuances and to changes in these through time, although the first puts a higher premium on it. The second method can never in any respect be as thorough as the first, and its value is indeed mainly exploratory, in suggesting hypotheses rather than in firmly testing them. The third imposes a rigid economy on sensitivity to cultural nuances as likely at the start to be a mere distraction. The fourth eliminates it altogether.

The last two are brave attempts to seize what is common in the social and political transformations that accompany industrialization. Endeavoring to simplify without distorting, they implicitly incorporate the idea of direction derived from Western experience, and work from models consisting of inventories of items selected as measures or indicators of the extent and pace of change in that direction. Daniel Lerner, perhaps the outstanding protagonist of the third method, defends basing these inventories on as few as four processes which he regards as core characteristics of the take-off into modernization: as a report of the UNESCO Paris conference of April 1965 summarizes his views, "models should be kept simple and abstract until it was quite clear that there was no parsimonious way of accounting for well-established differences among empirical cases."[2] In admitting the need, at some point, of elaborating the models, this defense invites the question of what degree of care will be taken, along the way, to establish empirical differences. If data-gathering proceeds only by reference to very simple models, it could turn out, when these come to be elaborated, that much evidence of kinds of difference having a significant bearing on the conclusions has been ignored or thrown out as garbage. This garbage is retrievable only to the extent of the reliance on written records. To the extent of the reliance on oral informants, it will be irretrievable. The method in its diachronic aspect is therefore weak and will remain weak even if the process of elaboration of models leads it towards the greater rigor of the first method.

The fourth, the only wholly original method that has appeared, being tethered to the oddities of bureaucratic policy in the compilation of statistics, has little leeway to expand or vary its inventories. It is really an anti-method, filled with paradox. Instead of starting with a set of questions, it has to look around for questions that might be answered by the ranked correlations among aggregate data, the regional comparisons, and the indices of co-variancy that are its products. Of necessity most of these questions have a qualitative side to them; but the method itself has to stay austerely quantitative, trying to quantify the evolutionary idea that is implicit in its working model. It measures differences with maximum precision, but to the extent that its products are only a refined form of description and not self-explanatory, it is fair to say that it neglects differences that might qualify the similarities it presents, differences that escape official statistics and may be unquantifiable. This hardly matters if its role is mainly to help other methods cope with many problems that are in part quantitative. But its secure diachronic reach, because reliable statistics come only from the more advanced industrial nations, is very limited. Like a heavy truck flown to a planet where road-building has been sketchy, all it can do is career up and down one short highway, at present barely thirty years long. To explore this quantitative planet more thoroughly, jeeps are needed.

These last two methods embody only specific reasons for becoming diachronic. They aim at empirical generalization over a time-depth that is comfortably short, no longer than social science has often handled before. Their justification has certainly no bearing on the timeless propositions that guide the top-level ordering of general theory. The concepts of process with which they work—urbanization, industrialization, the spread of literacy, and so on—come from everyday talk rather than out of theoretical discussion. The concept of social mobilization is just academic shorthand, at a low level of abstraction, for topics of everyday discussion. The spread of these environmental changes is so entangled with new political phenomena that a political scientist can hardly retain authority as an expert on the world scene without some comparative study of them.,

Yet experience with descriptive generalization about these processes of change, even if it has to huddle at first under the rather floppy umbrella of "modernization," and feels safe only by barricading off the farthest past by crude typology, leads on, simply through comparison of its conclusions, to higher generalization. The historical sociologists, who roam more freely, are helping to catalyze this. S. N. Eisenstadt has lately drawn together a number of signs that the concept of an institution, which has so often lent itself to static and mechanical uses, is being transformed under our eyes into the concept of institutionalization.[3] Reinhard Bendix takes a middle ground in advocating that a distinction be drawn between bureaucracy and bureaucratization.[4] If Eisenstadt reads the signs correctly, even theorists who have withdrawn from empirical research will have to take note of them.

These and other straws in the wind are still of no help to the student who wants to know if there is any general justification for diachronic methods.

The theoretical arguments for diachronic method appear in discussion of the first method listed earlier. They have been presented very concisely in a recent contribution to debate over the future of social and political anthropology, by Aidan Southall.[5] Southall takes it for granted that the health of a discipline is to be measured by the interplay between research and general theory, the latter being of little use as a guide unless it is responsive to correction or modification from the procedures of generalization from research. He attributes many of the weaknesses of structural-functional theory to the failure of research to provide the kinds of data and generalization which could correct ambiguities in the theory. This failure, he contends, has arisen from two errors of method. In the first place, the particular societies and political systems that have been confronted for comparison have been selected quite arbitrarily, because someone had happened to study them, or on the unproven assumption that they were genuinely representative of different types. With a few exceptions, such as Marshall Sahlins' work on Polynesia,[6] careful study and analysis of the range of differences among the several examples of any types have been neglected. The second error, especially noticeable in some of the early work on African political systems, has been to assume that they were static, or to handle sequences of change only casually. The primeval systems were seen as "set in amber."

Southall urges that comparative study concentrate on cognate societies, that is, on societies known to be similar in structure, traditions, and environment. As he insists, "The point is that *differences arising from similarities* are the most fruitful field from which to generalize."[7] The study should be diachronic in order to examine the variables at work both in conditions of stability and in conditions of stress, the temporal pattern or phasing of these being important. The period of time covered should be as long as possible in order that models, tried out on each society in turn, may be tested for explanatory power throughout a sequence of changes.

Southall's arguments echo and reinforce the reasoning behind the project now in progress for study of eleven of the small European democracies.[8] Much the same kinds of error have been made by political scientists in Europe as by social anthropologists in Africa. Generalization has been often

349

from cases that were in obvious respects exceptional, and despite Europe's "past-mindedness," with indifference to gaps and anomalies in historical evidence used. Indeed, scholars in all our disciplines have displayed a truly bizarre individualism in their readiness to generalize from scattered cases or from pet examples arbitrarily described as typical. Such work can be correct only by accident or by brilliance of intuition. All types of theory, not only functional analysis, have suffered accordingly, and it is not the fault of the theorists.

The advantages of diachronic analysis, and the argument for running its more rigorous applications as far back in time as may be feasible, may be wrongly interpreted in either of two ways. It would be an error to greet the method as a means only to better control of variables in a greater quantity of situations from which analysis could then wash out the time element altogether. On the other hand, it would be even more foolish to suppose that what is intended is a futile attempt to present the exact length of time sequences involved in the interaction of variables as matter for generalization.

The bearing of rigorous diachronic method is on the tentative overtures that all existing theory, except the tightest of systems analysis, is ready to offer temporal relationships in the interplay of variables. For the most part these have been limited to intergenerational relationships. The use of these and other such overtures, and their extension through empirical generalization working with concepts of process, may result in stretching their temporal range. Far from being grounds for pessimism, the diagnosis of past errors in the bases of empirical generalization, now that we have methods for correcting them, is exhilarating.

Cross-Cultural Research

One way in which diachronic method could be of use to comparative politics is through fresh analysis of sources of difficulty in cross-cultural work. As is well known, comparative methods were adopted in a number of the human sciences in the nineteenth century, under the stimulus of evolutionary thought, only to suffer a blight of discouragement in the 1890s.[9] Enthusiasm survived only in the young science of anthropology, where research soon outran the generalizing capacity derived originally from the idea of classifying and describing stages of evolution. In sociology, to the extent that it became cross-cultural, the reverse occurred. In political science there was a better balance, but here, as in history, comparative study long remained peripheral to the main professional interests. These four disciplines are the most closely related of those that have experimented with comparative methods: they have a common ancestry in ancient Greek thought, and all have both influenced and drawn on modern social philosophy. In short, they are cognate societies, and could be studied as such—with attention to internal intellectual and social structure, to the borrowing of ideas, and to what the public expected of them—by the rigorous method which Southall advocates. The study could start at least as far back as the mid-nineteenth century and run, picking up the professionalization of anthropology and sociology along the way, to the present. For better control of social variables, it could be conducted with the same research design in several different countries.

Such work would arrive at different conclusions according as the investigator inclined to one or other of two premises: (1) that interest in cross-cultural work self-evidently demonstrates the triumph of rationality over ethnocentrism; or (2) that irrationalities may still be disguised through rationalization. On the first premise, the obstacles to scientific fruition would be located quite simply in traditional imprecisions of method, in professional inertia, in lack of public support, in political circumstances that make for imbalances in the data obtainable. On the second premise, the range of difficulties is widened. The general impressions to which it gives rise may be summarized in sketches of different patterns of interplay between intellectual and social variables.

In one model, though the intellectual effort thrown into mastery of the natural environment may be very impressive,[10] intellect acquires more or less specialized roles in a society only in devising for it, and maintaining, a unique relation with supernatural powers.[11] Whether the religious specialists do their thinking in isolation or are influenced by knowledge of the religious thinking of other peoples is immaterial; in the model, the efficacy of myth or theology, and of ritual, for the solidarity of the group and for personal comfort, depends on avoidance of any involvement with the religious ideas and practices of other groups. The religious specialists can retain their function only as they discourage this by associating it with danger to the individual and by setting an example of incuriosity. But ethnocentrism towards contemporary groups is absolute only where it enforces spatial isolation, as in the case of religious sects withdrawing to a wilderness. It cannot rule out curiosity arising from intelligent interest in techniques and products, possibilities of trade, and modes of warfare. In a primitive setting, contacts with outsiders in friendly intercourse through chance or trade are a means of adding to the body of pragmatically useful knowledge.

In another direction, however, the dependence on religious specialists, and their control over curiosity, is absolute. Working from fear of death and of the dead, they merge the past into the relationships with the supernatural that are the basis of the group's solidarity. No motive for enquiry into past experience can then arise. Beyond the reach of the memory of the living, this perpetually is lost. The dead who are encountered in vision and dream speak in the terms dictated by myth. Since the latter will also shape whatever expectations of the future may exist, present-mindedness is water-tight, literally encircled by myth.

It is easy, almost too easy, to explain all this by Durkheimian theory: consciousness is developed through myth within the containing bounds of ethnocentrism and present-mindedness, which are seemingly as necessary, as comforting to it, as the womb to the foetus. But one is then focusing on the aspect of consciousness that is most obviously social and value-charged, to the neglect of the logical powers that are being directed to mastery of the physical environment, are making the economic life of the group possible, and are improving it through invention and the borrowing of outsiders' techniques. This aspect of the myth-controlled society is harder to investigate because it lacks structured roles. Structure emerges in the role of the smith, but here a technical skill has taken on the mantle of awe, as though its value for the survival of the group could be given recognition only indirectly.

The erosion of myth by philosophy, in the educated Greek world of the fifth and fourth centuries B.C., failed to erode the old containing walls of ethnocentrism and present-mindedness. Like a religion just beginning to assert a claim to universalism but still rooted in localized experience, rationality fed on rough impressions of the latter, on intuitive reflection, and on a desire to replan society. It replaced the mythical relation with the past by typologies condensing recent Greek experience, with incurious side-glances at the barbarian world. This casual device for coping with the empirical past and present and with other cultures, and the habit of drawing moral generalizations supposedly applicable to all men and all ages out of one's philosophical hat, formed the tradition that Plato bequeathed to political science. As Averroës came close to admitting when he likened Plato's science to twelfth-century medicine because it had a practical branch and a theoretical branch, the two had little bearing on each other except normatively.[12] The possibility of carrying inventiveness further, of inventing the idea of a more equal partnership between intuition and observation, was impeded by the narrow base of the philosopher's role. As this was structured through the Academy, it leaned both in speculation and in political ambition towards open imitation of the role of the all-powerful myth-makers of old. Empirical curiosity had a freer rein in the Greek world than in a primitive society in conditions of cultural contact, but was still no better structured; it had no roles that could compete or be allied with that of the philosopher (save the allied role of physician). Ethnographic and even historical information about the barbarian world was acceptable but only on terms of pragmatic usefulness, political or economic. The labor that Herodotus devoted to inventing and implementing the idea of historical enquiry into a problem—the problem of moral justification of Athenian leadership—was by this criterion pointless.[13] The Academy's orientation towards the future, its satisfaction with controlling the past by typology, and its conviction that philosophy was the only road to moral truth preserved its present-mindness intact.

Ultimately it became possible for the political scientist and the historian to borrow from each other and even to be united in one person, as in the case of Machiavelli, Montesquieu, and other persons of their times. Preconditions for this were some chastening of the claims of political science through being transplanted to a milieu dominated by a time-conscious religion, and public recognition of historical enquiry as having political and moral value. But the conditions of meaningful alliance appear to rest in some similar experience of error on both sides, in the discovery of hitherto unrecognized discontinuities which call for reinterpretation of the relationship of one's own time to the farther past. J. G. A. Pocock has explored this problem on a comparative basis, with special reference to a number of early modern European countries where diverse legal traditions had to be faced.[14] The consequence, where the problem was acute, was to give historians greater analytical ability, to force them to work out explanations, to acquire the power to compare one period with another instead of dwelling always on continuities. Political science, in turn, gained more comparative power than traditional typologies had provided. In Montesquieu's time, it began at last to respond to the age-old popular curiosity about Asia.[15]

Reformulation of the idea of progress, just when industrialization was gathering speed and stringing the nations out along a scale of measurement that had not obtruded before, rudely shoved everyone into problems of explanation. Resistance to explanations of past progress in terms that would allow of future narrowing of the gaps between the nations gave ethnocentrism, in its more blatant forms, a field day. Ethnocentrism was no less strong in the liberal views that looked for the improvement of backward nations through the spread of representative government, French education, or other products of Western history. It lurked in the assumption that Europe had already set the standards of progress.

Yet evolutionary thought, in stirring up ethnocentrism, at the same time made more of a fight against it possible. Comparative study became the arena of the fight. Two brief examples from English historical thought will illustrate the point. Thomas Arnold, who drew his sustenance from Vico and from more recent European philosophy of history, was hardly typical of early nineteenth-century English historians. Although he did not live long enough to carry out any comparative work, he was moving towards comparative study of the evolution of social structures as the only means he could see, to make historical knowledge coherent. He generalized happily about "natural periods" in the history of nations.[16] But coming to the present (1840) he found himself wrestling with a bias towards the theory of inequalities in racial genius. This theory, one of the many ways of evading problems of explanation in history, could compliantly allow the genius of a nation that showed any unexpected advance to have been latent. But Arnold, hazarding the suggestion that the powers of the Slavonic nations "may be as yet only partially developed," added a geopolitical argument.[17]

One of the men Arnold influenced, E. A. Freeman, moved out of national history into the comparative study of past and contemporary political systems, including federalism. When the Oxford School of Modern History was founded in the middle of the century, he tried to get this activity built into its program, but failed because the idea ran against the policy of training specialists in ancient and modern history respectively.[18] In 1873 he proposed that his own generalizing interests be recognized as a new science to be called *Comparative Politics*. It was his hope that E. B. Tylor, with whom he was acquainted, would welcome this as a twin to his own newborn science, soon to become known as *anthropology*.[19] The hope was naive, because to Freeman the superiority of the "Aryan" races was a part of the divine order, daily fortifying his animus against Irishmen and Turks. But he was sufficiently shaken, on realizing that Tylor made "all man-folk one lot," to drop his scheme.[20]

The hardening of professional structures and standards in history at this time, around archival research, was a main factor in the lack of sympathy among historians for Freeman's proposals. A gentleman-scholar of the old style who would work only in his own library in the country, Freeman, when he finally became Regius Professor at Oxford, was out of touch with students. He had neither new facts nor new theory. But none of the professional structures proved capable of generating the dynamic theory that was needed. The elements were there, but it took Marx to fuse them; it was he who created the comparative politics of the nineteenth century.

There are similarities between all these situations and our own. But the changing conditions of life in the areas of cross-cultural research and the nature of professional training have made the differences more significant. Like the primitive trader on his rounds, the political researcher gets information of a practical character and avoids putting his nose in religious matters. If the conditions of life are changing, however, some of the fact will block out spheres of change in values. Again, the Greek philosophers' sense of superiority is well diffused among us, as regards the "non-West"; the stupidest freshman takes credit for Einstein. The sense of superiority in having been progressive is perhaps all we have in mind in speaking of a common Western ethnocentrism. But in so far as it used to rest on the notion that primeval African life, for example, or Chinese civilization, was static, it betrays ignorance of research in these fields.[21] Nor do we look for new extensions of industrialization to duplicate the early Western patterns, as Marx did.[22] We cannot hope entirely to eliminate ethnocentrism or present-mindedness, but we are learning to manage them better.

Common Problems of History and Social Science[23]

To guard against taking an ethnocentric view of "developing" nations, one is told repeatedly not to impose on them "the model of Western development." But what is this model? Historians are partly to blame for the vagueness of answers. Perhaps a first point of rapprochement between history and comparative politics should be to consider the kinds of error that have been common to work in history and in social science.

In the first place, the kinds of generalization that have been demanded of historians, and have consequently by feed-back dominated the interaction between historical and theoretical knowledge, have referred to long-run trends derived from conspicuous cases, to the neglect of tested generalization about possible reasons for nonconformity with these trends. Despite historians' love of exploring byways, they have left unexplored many that now seem important, such as the small European democracies, areas and sectors stagnating or regressing within a "developing" country, and many others. Cases of nonconformity to a trend, and patently divergent short-run trends, have alike been dismissed as unimportant or "erratic."

Historians have also often over-stretched the uses of typology to simplify their impression of the period just preceding the point of time at which they choose to dive into research. Ideally, they try to overhaul these impressions at intervals, in order to avoid taking all the movements they encounter as new. This problem is never wholly soluble, for the social environment regarded as a whole is always new, tradition is always being reconstituted, and tricks of perspective inevitably distort "transformations" earlier than the one being studied in detail. But there are certain recurrent areas of recognizable error—for example, those relating to problems of spatial and social mobility,[24] and the restructuring of social groups—in which historians are becoming more sophisticated. Discussion of their experience in such areas might be of help to social scientists adopting diachronic methods.

A third area of common danger is that of generalization about values. In abstract theory, in historical sociology, and in the ordering of research, values have been a wild card, with too little attention to opposition and conflict.[25]

One of the difficulties of communication via reading each other's work is that of differences in style of presentation. In playing down explicit statement of theory historians irritate social scientists by seeming to assume a deprecatory attitude to it: they seem to be saying, I arrived at my conclusions without any help from theory but simply from long and patient study of my empirical materials. What they are most aware of in each other's work is differences in point of view, a notion that includes a penumbra of presuppositions about the weighting of hypotheses which is not necessarily conveyed by the drill-ground parade of concepts that is mandatory in the open-

355

ing paragraphs of a work in social science. Quantification is not an issue; as Carl Friedrich has remarked, " . . . how quality and quantity are combined depends on the nature of the problem."[26]

The use of cross-national or cross-regional comparison in historical work has been haphazard. Outside economic history there has really been little experience with the diachronic methods that have been discussed here. Marc Bloch's work on social structures has been a stimulus to further work on medieval aristocracies and peasantries, which by adding new techniques has radically revised some of his conclusions. Similarly, Pirenne's work has led on to much more systematic comparative studies of urbanization than are yet available for post-medieval Europe.[27] The trend towards comparative study, wherever it can lead to better formulation of a problem, is now strong. But even cooperative work has in many fields got no further than the preliminary stage of assembling parallel ranks of basic materials. At a later stage, it always turns out that fresh research in the primary sources is needed, all round.

Colossal labor has been devoted to organizing national archives in Europe, and in printing selections of their materials, and guides to them, but provincial archives and their acquisitions of private records have grown so continuously in this century that the demand now for guides to the total amount of historical material available, in order that selections may be made for processing in data banks, cannot be met very rapidly. Preliminary guides to the survival of the governmental records will obviously come first, and will themselves be an eye-opener into the long history of bureaucratization. Ecclesiastical archives are enormous, and private records relating to families, business firms, and associations flow continuously into provincial archives as their owners become aware that they are of value for research. Historians are accustomed to working slowly because they have to use literary sources, including newspapers, as well as explore archival materials. Where skilled content analysis can usefully save labor, they are open to its extension.

The techniques that historians have so far applied to bulky series of records are in many ways analogous to those of field research. Some of their sources are actually replies to governmental questionnaires—for example, Domesday Book—or judicial questionnaires, in the records of courts employing inquisitorial procedures. It is also a useful technique of historical "reconstruction" to regard many other sources as though they were answers to questions from contemporaries, some of which would have been answered evasively in order to conceal the truth of the matter, some unreliably, and some honestly because at the time a check on the answer would have been possible or because no motive for concealment can be detected. Some historical sources give evidence that a live interview could not have elicited, for example, wills, of which there are vast series running back in Europe to the thirteenth century, records of property transactions, of poor relief administration, and business accounts. Conventional rules that limit access to certain classes of recent records betray the fact that they may contain sensitive material.

Though the historian is inconsolably envious of the field researcher's opportunities to observe and question, he has the compensation of chronological depth. As survey research accumulates its own archives, it will be able to combine both advantages. Demographic work offers the simplest examples of how they may be combined, because the age and sex structure of a community in a given year will reveal, when chronological patterning for that community is available, where that year stands in a repetitive cycle or in relation to crises of unemployment or sickness.[28]

European historical work has long tended, as comparative politics tends, to concentrate on central policy-making structures and on the mechanics of administration. It has gone also into the recruiting of officials and the personal composition of representative bodies, and into the more obvious aspects of venality, and is beginning to move into use of records of litigation and of criminal justice for evidence of the limits of tolerance of conflict and malaise. Montesquieu generalized freely about the latter, but comparative material to set beside today's problems of political alienation in weak new states will take time to work up. But the fact that work on both fronts can proceed at the same time, if there are channels of communication, can be helpful to both.

A channel for communication of this kind now exists, in the form of an international quarterly conducted jointly by historians and social scientists, *Comparative Studies in Society and History*, and a brief report on its first seven years of operation is available.[29] The experiment continues to explore avenues of cooperation through bringing critical theoretical discussion to bear on fresh research in a variety of processes of change.

Some of this research is of the kind that will benefit from the large-scale processing of quantifiable and verbal data that new technology is making possible. But the nature both of the historical and contemporary materials and of the kinds of perceptiveness that are required for grasp of the new aspirations and new forms of action, which every age worth living in has engendered and our own so desperately needs, impose imbalances on much of the most important kinds of evidence, making it recalcitrant to the new technology. Like ethnocentrism and present-mindedness, imbalances in the evidence constitute difficulties, but they are also inescapable conditions of cross-cultural research. They can be wholly bypassed only at the cost of dullness and futility. Diachronic methods in free experimentation are a means of cross-checking on futilities before we go too far with them.

Harold Lasswell's picture of the ideal political science center of the future makes no mention of diachronic method. It invites the use of historical information, as though this could be produced by any pick-and-shovel man, in lumps for later processing. It assigns prehistorians, historians, and social anthropologists the task of providing "a map of the succession of human cultures."[30] This is a modest role. Like learned men of old invited to a princely court, the visitors would be allowed to answer such questions as the prince chose to put to them. Let us, in the map of the future of our professional culture, instead put a federal center.

General Bibliography

1. Aberle, D. F., A. K. Cohen, A. K. Davis, Marion J. Levy, Jr., and F. X. Sutton. "The Functional Prerequisites of a Society," *Ethics*, Vol. 60, No. 2 (January, 1950), pp. 100–111.

2. Adams, Richard N., and Jack J. Preiss. *Human Organization Research: Field Relations and Techniques*. Homewood, Ill.: Dorsey Press, 1960.

3. Almond, Gabriel, A. "A Comparative Study of Interest Groups and the Political Process," *The American Political Science Review*, Vol. 52, No. 1, (March, 1958), pp. 270–282.

4. ———. "A Developmental Approach to Political Systems," *World Politics*, Vol. 17 (January, 1965), pp. 183–214.

5. ———. "Comparative Political Systems," *The Journal of Politics*, Vol. 18 (August, 1956), pp. 391–409.

6. Almond, Gabriel A., and G. Bingham Powell, Jr. *Comparative Politics: A Developmental Approach*. Boston: Little, Brown, 1966.

7. Almond, Gabriel A., and James S. Coleman (eds.). *The Politics of the Developing Areas*. Princeton, N.J.: Princeton University Press, 1960.

8. Almond, Gabriel A., and Sidney Verba. *The Civic Culture: Political Attitudes and Democracy in Five Nations*. Princeton, N.J.: Princeton University Press, 1963.

9. Anscombe, F. J. "The Validity of Comparative Experiments," *Journal of the Royal Statistical Society*, Series A (General), Vol. 111, Part III (1948), pp. 181–211.

10. Apter, David E. "A Comparative Method for the Study of Politics," *American Journal of Sociology*, Vol. 64 (November, 1958), pp. 221–237.

11. ——— (ed.). *Ideology and Discontent*. New York: The Free Press, 1964.

12. Bauer, Raymond A. (ed.). *Social Indicators*. Cambridge, Mass.: The M.I.T. Press, 1966.

13. Becker, Howard, and Alvin Boskoff (eds.). *Modern Sociological Theory in Continuity and Change*. New York: The Dryden Press, 1957.

14. Bendix, Reinhard. "Concepts and Generalizations in Comparative Sociological Studies," *American Sociological Review*, Vol. 28, No. 4 (August, 1963), pp. 532–539.

15. Bock, Kenneth Elliott. *The Acceptance of Histories: Toward a Perspective for Social Science*. Berkeley: University of California Press, 1956.

16. Bredemeier, Harry Charles, and Richard M. Stephenson. *The Analysis of Social Systems*. New York: Holt, Rinehart, and Winston, 1962.

17. Cicourel, Aaron V. *Method and Measurement in Sociology*. New York: The Free Press, 1964.

18. Cohen, Ronald, and John Middleton (eds.). *Comparative Political Systems: Studies in the Politics of Pre-Industrial Societies.* Garden City, N.Y.: The Natural History Press, 1967.

19. "Comparative Cross-National Research," *International Social Science Bulletin,* Vol. 7, No. 4 (1955), pp. 553–641.

20. Converse, Philip E. "A Network of Data Archives for the Behavioral Sciences," *Public Opinion Quarterly,* Vol. 28 (Summer, 1964), pp. 273–286.

21. Deutsch, Karl W. "Toward an Inventory of Basic Trends and Patterns in Comparative and International Politics," *The American Political Science Review,* Vol. 54 (March, 1960). pp. 34–57.

22. Doob, Leonard W. "Scales for Assaying Psychological Modernization in Africa," *Public Opinion Quarterly,* Vol. 31, No. 3 (Fall, 1967), pp. 414–421.

23. Easton, David. *A Framework for Political Analysis.* Englewood Cliffs, N.J.: Prentice-Hall, 1965.

24. ———. "An Approach to the Analysis of Political Systems," *World Politics,* Vol. 9 (April, 1957), pp. 383–400.

25. Eckstein, Harry, and David E. Apter (eds.). *Comparative Politics: A Reader.* New York: The Free Press, 1963.

26. Edinger, Lewis J., and Donald D. Searing. "Social Background in Elite Analysis: A Methodological Inquiry," *American Political Science Review,* Vol. 61, No. 2 (June, 1967), pp. 428–445.

27. Eggan, Fred. "Social Anthropology and the Method of Controlled Comparison," *American Anthropologist,* Vol. 56, No. 5 (October, 1954), pp. 743–763.

28. Eisenstadt, S. N. "Communications Systems and Social Structure: A Preliminary Comparative Analysis," *Public Opinion Quarterly,* Vol. 19 (Summer, 1955), pp. 153–167.

29. ———. *Essays on Comparative Institutions.* New York: John Wiley and Sons, 1965.

30. ———. *The Political Systems of Empires.* New York: The Free Press, 1963.

31. ———. "Primitive Political Systems: A Preliminary Comparative Analysis," *American Anthropologist,* Vol. 61 (April, 1955), pp. 200–220.

32. Etzioni, Amitai. *The Active Society: A Theory of Societal and Political Processes.* New York: The Free Press, 1968.

33. Festinger, Leon, and Daniel Katz (eds.). *Research Methods in the Behavioral Sciences.* New York: Dryden Press, 1953.

34. Ford, Clellan S. (ed.). *Cross-Cultural Approaches: Readings in Comparative Research.* New York: Taplinger Press, 1967.

35. Gardiner, Patrick. *The Nature of Historical Explanation.* London: Oxford University Press, 1952.

36. Goode, William J., and Paul K. Hatt. *Methods in Social Research.* New York: McGraw-Hill Book Co., 1952.

37. Gross, Llewellyn (ed.). *Symposium on Sociological Theory.* Evanston: Row, Peterson, 1959.

38. Heckscher, Gunnar. *Comparative Government and Politics.* London: George Allen and Unwin, 1957.

39. Holt, Robert T., and John E. Turner. *The Political Basis of Economic Development: An Exploration in Comparative Political Analysis.* Princeton, N.J.: D. Van Nostrand Co., 1966.

40. Inkeles, Alex, and Peter H. Rossi. "National Comparisons of Occupational Prestige," *American Journal of Sociology,* Vol. 61 (January, 1956), pp. 329–339.

41. Jacobson, Eugene. "Methods Used for Producing Comparable Data in the OCSR Seven-Nation Attitude Study," *The Journal of Social Issues,* Vol. 10, No. 4 (1954), pp. 40–51.

42. Janowitz, Morris. "Social Stratification and the Comparative Analysis of Elites," *Social Forces,* Vol. 35, No. 1 (October, 1956), pp. 81–85.

43. Johnson, Chalmers. *Revolutionary Change.* Boston: Little, Brown, 1966.

44. Kahin, George M., Guy J. Pauker, and Lucien W. Pye. "Comparative Politics of Non-Western Countries," *The American Political Science Review,* Vol. 49 (December 1955), pp. 1022–1041.

45. Kim, Young C. "The Concept of Political Culture in Comparative Politics," *The Journal of Politics,* Vol. 26 (May, 1964), pp. 313–336.

46. Klauser, Samuel Z. *The Study of Total Societies.* Garden City, N.Y.: Doubleday, 1967.

47. Köbben, André J. "New Ways of Presenting an Old Idea: The Statistical Method in Social Anthropology," *The Journal of the Royal Anthropological Institute of Great Britain and Ireland,* Vol. 82, Part II (1952), pp. 129–146.

48. Kuhn, Thomas S. *The Structure of Scientific Revolutions.* Chicago: The University of Chicago Press, 1962.

49. LaPalombara, Joseph. "The Utility and Limitations of Interest Group Theory in Non-American Field Situations," *The Journal of Politics,* Vol. 22 (February, 1960), pp. 29–49.

50. Lerner, Daniel, Ithiel Pool, and Harold D. Lasswell. "Comparative Analysis of Political Systems: A Preliminary Statement," *Public Opinion Quarterly,* Vol. 15 (Winter, 1951-1952), pp. 715–733.

51. Levy, Marion J., Jr. *Modernization and the Structure of Societies.* Princeton, N.J.: Princeton University Press, 1966.

52. ———. *The Structure of Society.* Princeton, N.J.: Princeton University Press, 1952.

53. Levy, Marion J., Jr., and Lloyd A. Fallers. "The Family: Some Comparative Considerations," *American Anthropologist,* Vol. 61 (August, 1959), pp. 647–651.

54. Lijphart, Arend. "Typologies of Democratic Systems," *Comparative Political Studies,* Vol. 1 (April, 1968), pp 3–44.

55. Loomis, Charles P. *Social Systems: Essays on Their Persistence and Change.* Princeton, N.J.: D. Van Nostrand Co., 1960.

56. Macrides, Roy C. *The Comparative Study of Politics.* New York: Random House, 1955.

57. Macrides, Roy C., and Bernard E. Brown. *Comparative Politics: Notes and Readings.* Homewood, Ill: Dorsey Press, 1968.

58. Marsh, Robert M., "The Bearing of Comparative Analysis on Sociological Theory," *Social Forces*, Vol. 43, No. 2 (December, 1964), pp. 188–196.

59. Merritt, Richard L., and Stein Rokkan (eds.). *Comparing Nations: The Use of Quantitative Data in Cross-National Research.* New Haven: Yale University Press, 1966.

60. Merton, Robert K. *Social Theory and Social Structure.* Glencoe, Ill: The Free Press, 1957.

61. Miller, S. M. "Comparative Social Mobility," *Current Sociology*, Vol. 9, No. 1 (1960), pp. 1–89.

62. Moore, Frank W. (ed.). *Readings in Cross-Cultural Methodology.* New Haven: HRAF Press, 1961.

63. Moore, Wilbert E. *Order and Change: Essays in Comparative Sociology.* New York: John Wiley and Sons, 1967.

64. Nadel, S. F. *The Theory of Social Structure.* Glencoe, Ill.: The Free Press, 1957.

65. ———. *The Foundations of Social Anthropology.* Glencoe, Ill.: The Free Press, 1951.

66. Osgood, Charles E., George J. Suci, and Percy H. Tannenbaum. *The Measurement of Meaning.* Urbana: University of Illinois Press, 1957.

67. Parsons, Talcott. *The Social System.* Glencoe, Ill.: The Free Press, 1951.

68. ———. *Essays in Sociological Theory: Pure and Applied.* Glencoe, Ill.: The Free Press, 1954.

69. Parsons, Talcott, Kasper D. Naegele, and Jesse R. Pitts. *Theories of Society: Foundations of Modern Sociological Theory* (2 vol.) New York: The Free Press, 1961.

70. Parsons, Talcott, and Edward A. Shils (eds.). *Toward a General Theory of Action: Theoretical Foundations for the Social Sciences.* Cambridge, Mass.: Harvard University Press, 1951.

71. Payne, Stanley L. "The Ideal Model for Controlled Experiments," *Public Opinion Quarterly*, Vol. 15 (Fall, 1951), pp. 557–562.

72. Przeworski, Adam, and Henry Teune. "Equivalence in Cross-National Research," *Public Opinion Quarterly*, Vol. 30, No. 4 (Winter, 1967), pp. 551–568.

73. Radcliffe-Brown, A. R. "The Comparative Method in Social Anthropology," *The Journal of the Royal Anthropological Institute of Great Britain and Ireland*, Vol. 81, Parts I and II (1952), pp. 15–22.

74. ———. *Structure and Function in Primitive Society*, New York: The Free Press, 1952.

75. Rapoport, Anatol. "Comments on 'The Comparative Method in the Social Sciences," *Philosophy of Science*, Vol. 22, No. 1 (January, 1955), pp. 118–122.

76. Rommetveit, Ragnar, and Joachim Israel. "Notes on the Standardization of Experimental Manipulations and Measurements in Cross-National Research," *Journal of Social Issues*, Vol. 10, No. 4 (1954), pp. 61–68.

77. Rose, Arnold M. *Theory and Method in the Social Sciences.* Minneapolis: University of Minnesota Press, 1954.

78. Rustow, Dankwart A. "New Horizons for Comparative Politics," *World Politics*, Vol. 9 (July, 1957), pp. 530–549.

79. Schachter, Stanley. "Interpretative and Methodological Problems in Replicated Research," *The Journal of Social Issues*, Vol. 10, No. 4 (1954), pp. 52–60.

80. Schapera, I. "Some Comments on the Comparative Method in Social Anthropology," *American Anthropologist*, Vol. 55, No. 3 (August, 1953), pp. 353–362.

81. Searing, Donald C. "The Comparative Study of Elite Socialization," *Comparative Political Studies*, Vol. 1, No. 4 (January, 1969), pp. 471–500.

82. Selltiz, Claire, Marie Jahoda, Morton Deutsch, and Stuart W. Cook. *Research Methods in Social Relations*. New York: Henry Holt and Company, 1960.

83. Siffin, William J. (ed.). *Towards the Comparative Study of Public Administration*. Bloomington, Ind.: Indiana University Press, 1959.

84. Sjoberg, Gideon. "The Comparative Method in the Social Sciences," *Philosophy of Science*, Vol. 22, No. 2 (April, 1955), pp. 106–117.

85. Spencer, Robert F. (ed.). *Method and Perspective in Anthropology*. Minneapolis: University of Minnesota Press, 1954.

86. Suchman, Edward A. "The Comparative Method in Social Research," *Rural Sociology*, Vol. 29, No. 2 (June, 1954), pp. 123–137.

87. Sutton, Francis X. "Representation and the Nature of Political Systems," *Comparative Studies in Society and History*, Vol. 2 (October, 1959), pp. 1–10.

88. Szalai, Alexander, *et al.* Multinational Comparative Social Research. *The American Behavioral Scientist*, Vol. 10, No. 4 (December, 1966), entire issue.

89. Teune, Henry. "Measurement in Comparative Research," *Comparative Political Studies*, Vol. 1 (April, 1968), pp. 123–138.

90. Thompson, James D., *et al.* (eds.). *Comparative Studies in Administration*. Pittsburgh: University of Pittsburgh Press, 1959.

91. Thompson, Laura. *Toward a Science of Mankind*. New York: McGraw-Hill Book Co., 1961.

92. Tucker, Robert C. "Towards a Comparative Politics of Movement-Regimes," *American Political Science Review* (June, 1961), pp. 281–289.

93. Verba, Sidney. "Some Dilemmas in Comparative Research," *World Politics*, Vol. 20, No. 1, October, 1967, pp. 111–127.

94. Wildavsky, Aaron B. "A Methodological Critique of Duverger's Political Parties," *The Journal of Politics*, Vol. 21, No. 2 (May, 1959), pp. 303–318.

95. Wiseman, H. C. *Political Systems: Some Sociological Approaches*. London: Routledge and Kegan Paul, 1966.

96. Zollschan, George K., and Walter Hirsch (eds.). *Explorations in Social Change*, Boston: Houghton Mifflin Co., 1964.

Notes to the Text

1. The Methodology of Comparative Research *(1–20)*

ROBERT T. HOLT AND JOHN E. TURNER

1. John G. Kemeny, *A Philosopher Looks at Science* (Princeton, N.J.: D. Van Nostrand, 1959), p. 96.

2. *Ibid.*, p. 135.

3. Herbert A. Simon, "Political Research: The Decision-Making Framework," in David Easton (ed.), *Varieties of Political Theory* (Englewood Cliffs, N.J.: Prentice-Hall, 1966), p. 16.

4. Thomas S. Kuhn, *The Structure of Scientific Revolutions* (Chicago: University of Chicago Press, Pheonix Edition, 1964), pp. 10 ff.

5. Emile Durkheim, *The Rules of Sociological Method* (Glencoe: The Free Press, 1950), pp. 125–140; S. F. Nadel, *The Foundations of Social Anthropology* (London: Cohen & West, Ltd., 1951), pp. 222–227; George P. Murdock, "Anthropology as Comparative Science," *Behavioral Science*, Vol. 2, No. 4 (October, 1957), pp. 249–254. Permission to quote granted by the Mental Health Research Institute and by the author.

6. Murdock, *op. cit.*, p. 249. Emphasis added.

7. Nadel, *op. cit.*, pp. 229–230.

8. R. A. Fisher, *The Design of Experiments* (London: Oliver and Boyd, 1960, Seventh Edition), pp. 18 ff.

9. William L. Hays, *Statistics for Psychologists* (New York: Holt, Rinehart, and Winston, 1963), pp. 216–217. Emphasis added.

10. See pp. 11–13.

11. Max Weber, *Gesammelte Aufsatze zur Religionssoziologie* (three volumes, Tubingen, 1922). Most of the first volume has been translated by Talcott Parsons under the title, *The Protestant Ethic and the Spirit of Capitalism* (New York: Scribner, 1958).

12. Talcott Parsons, *Essays in Sociological Theory* (Glencoe: The Free Press, 1954, Second Edition), p. 27.

13. The impossibility of controlling directly for all factors is precisely the reason why Fisher argues so cogently for the "simple" device of randomization.

14. S. F. Nadel, "Witchcraft in Four African Societies: An Essay in Comparison," *American Anthropologist*, Vol. 54, No. 1 (January–March, 1952), p. 18. Permission to quote granted by the American Anthropological Association.

15. *Ibid.*, pp. 21–22.

16. Clyde Kluckhohn, "Universal Categories of Culture," in A. L. Kroeber (ed.), *Anthropology Today* (Chicago: University of Chicago Press, 1962), pp. 304–320; Marion Levy, "Structural-Functional Requisite Analysis," [See *The Structure of Society* (Princeton, N.J.: Princeton University Press, 1952), pp. 27–110]; G. Sjoberg, "The Comparative Method in the Social Sciences," *Philosophy of Science*, Vol. 22, No. 2 (April, 1955), pp. 106–117.

17. On this point, see Lucian W. Pye, "Introduction: Political Culture and Political Development," in Lucian W. Pye and Sidney Verba (eds.), *Political Culture and Political Development* (Princeton, N.J.: Princeton University Press, 1965), pp. 11–13.

18. Samuel H. Beer, *British Politics in the Collectivist Age* (New York: Alfred A. Knopf, 1965), p. 350. Emphasis added. See also, pp. 122, 184–185, 257, 262–263.

19. Obviously, an abstention on important votes has different nuances in Congress, when contrasted with the House of Commons. Congressmen may refuse to record the votes because of conflict between their personal views and those of their constituents, and occasionally they may abstain so that the other side can win—a concession that will enable them to get something they want on another issue. But most abstainers in Congressional voting are simply absent from the House or Senate when the roll-calls are taken.

We wish to acknowledge fruitful conversations about Congressional roll-calls with two of our colleagues, Professors Charles H. Backstrom and David E. RePass.

20. Beer, *op. cit.*, p. 185.

21. *Ibid.*, pp. 184–185.

22. See William G. Cochrane, *Sampling Techniques* (New York: John Wiley and Sons, 1953), pp. 160–188.

We are indebted to Professor Raymond O. Collier of the Department of Educational Psychology, University of Minnesota, for discussing the problem with us and for calling this reference to our attention.

2. Competing Paradigms in Comparative Politics *(21–71)*

ROBERT T. HOLT AND JOHN M. RICHARDSON, JR.

1. See, for example, Roy C. Macridis, *The Study of Comparative Government* (Garden City: Doubleday & Co., 1955); David Easton, *The Political System* (New York: Alfred A. Knopf, 1953); Howard A. Scarrow, "The Scope of Comparative Analysis," *The Journal of Politics*, Vol. 25, No. 3 (August, 1963); Sigmund Neumann, "Comparative Politics: A Half-Century Appraisal," *Journal of Politics*, Vol. 19, No. 3 (August, 1957), pp. 369–390; and Harry Eckstein, "A Perspective on Comparative Politics, Past and Present," in Harry Eckstein and David Apter, (eds.), *Comparative Politics* (New York: Free Press, 1963), pp. 3–32.

2. See Thomas S. Kuhn, *The Structure of Scientific Revolutions* (Chicago: University of Chicago Press, Phoenix Edition, 1964).

3. *Ibid.*, pp. 11–13. See also chapter 1, pp. 2–4.

4. *Ibid.*, p. 41. Permission to quote granted by the University of Chicago Press.

5. John G. Kemeny, *A Philosopher Looks at Science* (Princeton: Van Nostrand, 1959), p. 138.

6. *Ibid.*

7. May Brodbeck, "Models, Meaning and Theories," in *Decisions, Values and Groups*, Vol. 1 (London: Pergamon Press, 1960), pp. 3 ff.

8. Kemeny, *op. cit.*, p. 96.

9. See Kuhn, *op. cit.*, p. 26 and L. I. Schiff, "A Report on the NASA Conference on Experimental Tests of Theories of Relativity," *Physics Today*, Vol. XIV (1961), pp. 42–48. Permission to quote granted by the University of Chicago Press.

10. Kuhn, *op. cit.*, p. 30.

11. Kemeny, *op. cit.*, p. 133.

12. Kuhn, *op. cit.*, p. 40.

13. *Ibid.*, p. 51.

14. *Ibid.*, p. 23. Kuhn observes that " . . . a paradigm is rarely an object for replication. Instead, like an accepted judicial decision in the common law, it is an object for further articulation and specification under new or more stringent conditions."

15. *Ibid.*, p. 37.

16. We should make it clear that we are not using the term *admissibility* in the general way that it is used by philosophers of science. See, for example, Morris R. Cohen, "Reason in Social Science," in Herbert Feigl and May Brodbeck, (eds.), *Readings in the Philosophy of Science* (New York: Appleton-Century-Crofts, 1953), pp. 663–673.

17. On these more general criteria, see Herbert Feigl, "The Scientific Outlook: Naturalism and Humanism," in Feigl and Brodbeck (eds.), pp. 8–18, and Kemeny, *op. cit.*, parts I and II.

18. Kuhn, *op. cit.*, p. 20.

19. *Ibid.*, p. 17.

20. See Robert T. Holt, "A Proposed Structural-Functional Framework," in James C. Charlesworth (ed.), *Contemporary Political Analysis* (Glencoe, The Free Press, 1967), pp. 86–107; and Robert T. Holt and John E. Turner, *The Political Basis of Economic Development* (Princeton: Van Nostrand, 1966), Chapter 3.

21. "A Proposed Structural-Functional Framework," pp. 86–87. Two of these concepts, *mechanism* and *process*, are very ill defined.

22. *Ibid.*, p. 92. A more general statement for the image of a fully developed theory is contained on pp. 95–99.

23. *Ibid.*, pp. 91–92.

24. Holt and Turner, *op. cit.*, p. 307. The hypothesis has been rewritten so that it fits in better with the argument of this essay. Its original form was "a government . . . that does not contribute significantly to the satisfaction of the adaptive functional requisite is a prerequisite for take off." The two statements are equivalent.

25. *Ibid.*, p. 318. Again the proposition has been restated to better fit the format of this essay.

26. *Ibid.*, pp. 318–319.

27. See "A Functional Approach to Comparative Politics," in Gabriel A. Almond and James S. Coleman (eds.), *The Politics of the Developing Areas* (Princeton: Princeton University Press, 1960); and Gabriel A. Almond and G. Bingham Powell, Jr., *Comparative Politics: A Development Approach* (Boston: Little, Brown, 1966).

28. "A Functional Approach to Comparative Politics," p. 59.

29. Almond and Powell, *op. cit.*, pp. 30–31.

30. Holt, "A Proposed Structural-Functional Framework," pp. 90–92.

31. Almond and Powell, *op. cit.*, p. 21.

32. *Ibid.*, p. 22.

33. *Ibid.*, p. 73.

34. *Ibid.*, p. 64.

35. *Ibid.*, p. 300.

36. See, for example, *Cybernetics; or, Control and Communication in the Animal and the Machine* (New York: John Wiley & Sons, 1948) and *The Human Use of Human Beings* (Boston: Houghton Mifflin, 1951), especially Chapter 1.

37. The approach has been developed and elaborated in the Yearbook of the Society, *General Systems*. For a useful introductory discussion, see Hall and Fagem, "Definition of a System," *General Systems*, Vol. I (1956), and O. R. Young, "The Impact of General Systems Theory on Political Science," *General Systems*, Vol. IX (1964), especially pp. 239–241.

38. A recent article dealing with "The Impact of General Systems Theory on Political Science" (Young, *op. cit.*) listed fifteen political scientists "who had used some of the concepts of general systems theory." Those who had made significant contributions to comparative politics included Karl Deutsch, J. David Singer, Richard Snyder, *et al.*, Quincy Wright, Harold Lasswell, David Easton, Seymour Lipset, and Dwight Waldo.

39. See *The Political System* (New York: Alfred A. Knopf, 1953); "An Approach to the Analysis of Political Systems," *World Politics*, Vol. IX (1956–57), pp. 383–400, reprinted in S. Sidney Ulmer, *Introductory Readings in Political Behavior* (Chicago: Rand McNally, 1961), pp. 136–147; *A Framework for Political Analysis* (Englewood Cliffs, N.J.: Prentice Hall, 1965); *A Systems Analysis of Political Life* (New York: John Wiley & Sons, 1965) and *Varieties of Political Theory* (Englewood Cliffs, N.J.: Prentice Hall, 1966), introduction and Chapter 7.

40. *Nationalism and Social Communication* (New York: John Wiley & Sons, 1953); *The Nerves of Government: Models of Communication and Control* (Glencoe: The Free Press, 1963).

41. Weiner, *Human Use of Human Beings*, p. 3 ff; see also W. Ross Ashby, *Introduction to Cybernetics* (New York: John Wiley Science Editions, 1956) pp. 2–6 and Chapters 2 and 10.

42. Young, *op. cit.*

43. For a relatively readable example of such an exercise, see W. Ross Ashby, *Design for a Brain* (New York: John Wiley & Sons, 1960, Second Edition).

44. *Introduction to Cybernetics*, p. 1. For similar statements, see Weiner, *Human Use of Human Beings*, Chapter 1, and Young, *op. cit.* pp. 239–240.

45. It should be emphasized that this view is explicitly Weinerian. For a somewhat different explication of cybernetics, see Ashby, *Introduction to Cybernetics*, and Viktor M. Glushkov, *Introduction to Cybernetics*, translated by Scripta Technica, Inc. (New York and London: Academic Press, 1966).

46. In order to truncate our discussion, we are not making the usual distinction between regulation, processes related to system maintenance and control, processes related to system goal attainment.

47. Deutsch, *The Nerves of Government*, pp. 217 ff.

48. *Ibid*, pp. 234 ff.

49. See, for example, Weiner, *Cybernetics;* Glushkov, *Introduction to Cybernetics;* or for a more formal, textbook approach, Michael Harrison, *Introduction to Switching and Automata Theory* (New York: McGraw Hill, 1965), Chapters 1 and 2.

50. See especially, *A Systems Analysis of Political Life* and *A Framework for Political Analysis*. In many respects, including the definition of a political system, Easton is much closer to structural-functional analysis.

51. *The Political System*, p. 319.

52. *Varieties of Political Theory*, p. 144. Our discussion will be based primarily on Chapter 7 in *Varieties of Political Theory* [Chapter 2 in *A Systems Analysis of Political Life*], in which the basic elements of Easton's framework are summarized. Permission to quote granted by Prentice Hall, Inc. and by John Wiley & Sons.

53. *Varieties of Political Theory.* p. 146.

54. *Ibid.*, p. 147.

55. *Ibid.*, p. 153.

56. *Ibid.*, p. 137.

57. *Ibid.*, p. 152.

58. *Ibid.*, p. 151.

59. *A Systems Analysis of Political Life*, p. 344.

60. *Varieties of Political Theory*, p. 151

61. *Ibid.*

62. *Ibid.*, p. 147.

63. *Ibid.*

64. *Ibid.*

65. *Ibid.*, p. 148.

66. For a discussion of emergent and reductive explanations, see May Brodbeck, "Methodological Individualisms: Definitions and Reduction," *Philosophy of Science*, Vol. 25, No. 1 (January, 1958), pp. 1–22. The treatment of psychological approaches in this essay closely parallels that found in Holt and Turner, *op. cit.*, pp. 19–34.

67. Harold Lasswell, *Psychopathology and Politics* (Chicago: The University of Chicago Press, 1931).

68. Everett E. Hagen, *On the Theory of Social Change* (Homewood, Ill.: Dorsey Press, 1962). David C. McClelland, *The Achieving Society* (Princeton, N.J.: Van Nostrand, 1961).

69. Lucian Pye, *Politics, Personality and Nation-Building: Burma's Search for Identity* (New Haven: Yale University Press, 1963), p. 228. Permission to quote granted by Yale University Press.

70. This propositional statement of Pye's thesis is taken from Holt and Turner, *op. cit.*, pp. 24–25.

71. See Norman Cameron and Ann Magaret, *Behavior Pathology* (Boston: Houghton Mifflin, 1951), pp. 217–245 and 337 for a further discussion of these points.

72. In Chapter I of *Politics, Personality and Nation Building,* Pye draws attention to the importance of socialization process in his framework.

73. Vera V. French, "The Structure of Sentiments: Part III—A Study of Philosophicoreligious Sentiments," *Journal of Personality*, Vol. 16, No. 2 (December, 1947), pp. 209–244.

74. James Shields, "Twins Brought Up Apart," *The Eugenics Review*, Vol. 50 (July, 1958), pp. 115–123.

75. Anthony F. C. Wallace, *Culture and Personality* (New York: Random House, 1961), pp. 42–43. Permission to quote granted by Random House,Inc.

76. John Maynard Keynes, *The General Theory of Employment, Interest, and Money* (New York: Harcourt, Brace and Co., 1935).

77. John Von Neumann and Oscar Morganstern, *Theory of Games and Economic Behavior* (Princeton: Princeton University Press, 1947, Second Edition).

78. See p. 58 and footnote 122.

79. See, for example, Anthony Downs, *An Economic Theory of Democracy* (New York: Harper and Row, 1957). A more recent work that draws upon Downs' formulation but also criticizes it is William H. Riker and Peter C. Ordeshook, "A Theory of the Calculus of Voting," *American Political Science Review*, Vol. LXII, No. 1 (March, 1968), pp. 25–42.

80. See Mancur Olson, *The Logic of Collective Action: Public Goods and the Theory of Groups* (Cambridge: Harvard University Press, 1965); Duncan Black, *The Theory of Committees and Elections* (Cambridge: Cambridge University Press, 1958); and Michael J. Leiserson, "Factions and Coalitions in One Party Japan: An Explanation Based on the Theory of Games," *American Political Science Review*, Vol. LXII, No. 3 (September, 1968), pp. 770–777.

81. See Thomas C. Schelling, *The Strategy of Conflict* (Cambridge: Harvard University Press, 1960) and Kenneth E. Boulding, *Conflict and Defense: A General Theory* (New York: Harper and Row, 1962).

82. See Kenneth Arrow, *Social Choice and Individual Values* (New York: John Wiley & Sons, 1951), and Gordon Tullock and James M. Buchannan, *The Calculus of Consent: Logical Foundations of Constitutional Democracy* (Ann Arbor: University of Michigan Press, Ann Arbor Paperback Edition, 1965).

83. In *The Scope and Method of Political Economy* (London: Macmillan & Co., 1891), pp. 34–35, John Neville Keynes defines a *positive science* as "a body of systematized knowledge concerning what is . . . ." See also Milton Friedman, "The Methodology of Positive Economics," in May Brodbeck (ed.), *Readings in the Philosophy of the Social Sciences* (New York: Macmillan, 1968), pp. 508–527, and James M. Buchannan, "Marginal Notes on Reading Political Philosophy," in Buchannan and Tullock, *The Calculus of Consent*, pp. 307–322.

84. William H. Riker, *The Theory of Political Coalitions* (New Haven and London: Yale University Press, 1962).

85. *Ibid.*, pp. 3–31.

86. *Ibid.*

87. *Ibid.*, p. 7. Permission to quote granted by Yale University Press.

88. See David Easton, *The Political System*, pp. 90–232.

89. *The Theory of Political Coalitions*, p. 10. Permission to quote granted by Yale University Press.

90. *Ibid.*, pp. 10–11.

91. *Ibid.*, p. 12.

92. *Ibid.*

93. In this discussion. Riker is obviously concerned with the problem of persuading skeptical members of his own discipline that this approach is meaningful in *their terms* as well as his own.

94. Riker cites Von Neumann and Morganstern's approach as an example: "We shall assume," they emphasize, "that the aim of all participants in the economic system . . . is money, or equivalently, a single monetary commodity. This is supposed to be unrestrictedly divisible and substitutable, freely transferable and identical, even in the quantitative sense, with whatever 'satisfaction' or 'utility' is desired by each participant . . . The individual who attempts to obtain these respective maxima is also said to act 'rationally.' " (See *The Theory of Games and Economic Behavior*, pp. 8–9 and *The Theory of Political Coalitions*, pp. 16–18.)

95. Riker cites Luce and Raiffa's definition of rationality as an example of this approach: "Given a social situation in which exist two alternative courses of action leading to different outcomes and assuming that participants can order these outcomes on a subjective scale of preference, each participant will choose the alternative leading to the more preferred outcome." (See *The Theory of Political Coalitions*, pp. 18–19, and R. Ducan Luce and Howard Raiffa, *Games and Decisions*, New York: John Wiley and Sons, 1957, Chapter 2.)

96. See the very interesting discussion of "experimental determinations of utility" in *Games and Decisions*, pp. 34–37.

97. *The Theory of Political Coalitions*, p. 20.

98. *Ibid.*, p. 22.

99. *Ibid.*

100. *Ibid.*, p. 23.

101. *Ibid.*

102. But we must emphasize again that this "revised form of the rationality condition" is a revision of the *rules of interpretation* of the Von Neumann-Morganstern approach. It is not a revision of the theoretical element.

103. See *The Theory of Political Coalitions*, p. 28.

104. *Ibid.*, p. 31.

105. It would seem from Riker's introduction that an even stronger argument is being made, namely, that no phenomena which cannot be perceived as zero sum are of concern to political scientists; however, this is not clear. For alternative approaches that do not impose the zero sum restriction, see Tullock and Buchannan, *The Calculus of Consent* and Boulding, *Conflict and Defense*, Chapter 3.

106. Riker summarizes his propositions on p. 211. However, for two out of the three propositions, we have used the more precise statements in earlier chapters.

107. *The Theory of Political Coalitions*, p. 32.

108. *Ibid.*, p. 211. For further elaboration and supporting evidence, see Chapters 5, 6, and 7. Riker identifies different types of side payments that can be made in the process of coalition formation and different situations in which strategic advantages (or disadvantages) exist for particular types of coalitions.

109. *Ibid.*, p. 211. For further elaboration and supporting evidence, see Chapters 8 and 9.

110. A detailed discussion of the derivation of the size principle and the strategic principle is presented in *The Theory of Political Coalitions*, Appendices I and II.

111. *Ibid.*, p. 47. It should be noted, however, that this "analogous proposition" is actually somewhat different than (1), because the descriptive term *believe* is introduced. Riker does not address himself to the problem of determining the perceptions (beliefs) of participants with regard to the size of winning coalitions. Nor does he consider the situation where the belief of participants differ. However, these would both be important points if the paradigm was more fully elaborated.

112. *Ibid.*, p. 66 ff.

113. *Ibid.*, pp. 67 and 68.

114. *Ibid.*

115. *Ibid.*

116. *Ibid.*, pp. 70–71.

117. *Ibid.*, p. 71.

118. Herbert A. Simon, *Administrative Behavior*, (New York: The Free Press, 1957), pp. 80–81.

119. This argument has been developed in greater detail in J. M. Richardson, Jr., *Partners in Development* (East Lansing: Michigan State University Press, 1969), Appendix II.

120. Anthony Downs, *Inside Bureaucracy* (Boston: Little, Brown, 1967).

121. Gordon Tullock, *The Politics of Bureaucracy* (Washington: Public Affairs Press, 1965).

122. See, for example, Gerald M. Meir, *Leading Issues in Development Economics* (New York: Oxford University Press, 1964); Edward Ames, *The Soviet Economic Processes* (Homewood, Ill.: R. D. Erwin, 1965) and P. J. D. Wiles, *The Political Economy of Communism* (Cambridge: Harvard University Press, 1962).

123. See especially, *Models of Man: Social and Rational; Mathematical Essays on Rational Human Behavior in a Social Setting* (New York: John Wiley and Sons, 1957), pp. 241–273. See also Richardson, *Partners in Development*, Chapter 9 and Appendix II.

124. Arthur S. Banks and Robert Textor, *A Cross-Polity Survey* (Cambridge: Massachusetts Institute of Technology Press, 1963) and Bruce M. Russett, Hayward R. Alker, Jr., Karl W. Deutsch, Harold D. Lasswell, *World Handbook of Political and Social Indicators* (New Haven: Yale University Press, 1965).

125. See, "The Theoretical Basis of Data Programs," in Richard L. Merritt and Stein Rokkan, *Comparing Nations* (New Haven and London: Yale University Press, 1966), p. 37.

126. Russett, *et al.*, p. v. Permission to quote granted by Yale University Press.

127. *Ibid.*, p. 111.

128. *Ibid.*, pp. 261–262.

129. *Ibid.*, pp. 221 and 88.

130. It is sometimes not recognized that the regression of one variable on another may be linear even if the distribution of the two variables is not bivariate normal. Consider the following table:

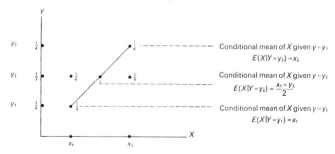

The joint probability distribution for the Y marginal is U-shaped and the X

373

marginal distribution is unimodal and symmetric. The regression of X on Y is linear.

131. Russett, *et al., op. cit.*, p. 315.

132. This point is discussed in Chapter 1 on pp. 2–4.

133. Paul E. Meehl, "Theory Testing in Psychology and Physics: A Methodological Paradox," *Philosophy of Science* (June, 1967), p. 112.

134. *Ibid.*, p. 114.

135. The claims of psychologists and statisticians who use this technique tend to be more modest. See, for example, Harry H. Harman, *Modern Factor Analysis* (Chicago: University of Chicago Press, 1964), especially Chapter 6; D. N. Lawley and A. E. Maxwell, *Factor Analysis as a Statistical Method* (London: Butterworths, 1963), especially Chapter 1; and Sir Cyril Burt, "The Appropriate Uses of Factor Analysis and Analysis of Variance," in Raymond B. Cattel (ed.), *Handbook of Multivariate Experimental Psychology* (Chicago: Rand McNally, 1966), Chapter 8.

136. R. J. Rummel, "Understanding Factor Analysis," *Journal of Conflict Resolution*, Vol. XI, No. 4 (December, 1967), p. 448. Permission to quote granted by the *Journal of Conflict Resolution*.

137. *Ibid.*, p. 455.

138. *Ibid.*, p. 444. The complete passage from which this quotation is taken is the following: "Confronted with entangled behavior, unknown interdependencies, masses of qualitative and quantatitive variables, and bad data, many social scientists are turning toward factor analysis to uncover major social and international patterns. Factor analysis can simultaneously manage over a hundred variables, compensate for random error and invalidity, and disentangle complex interrelationships into their major and distinct regularities."

139. Regarding the use of factor analysis in theory construction, Rummel observes: "A confusion between the empirical and analytic parts of a theory may have militated against a more theoretical use of factor analysis in the literature. The geometric or algebraic nature of the factor model can structure the analytic framework of theory. The factors themselves can be postulated. From then, operational deductions with empirical content can be derived and tested." (See *ibid.*, p. 454.)

140. A relatively complete "Bibliography of Factor Analysis in Conflict and International Relations" is presented in Rummel, "Understanding Factor Analysis," pp. 478–480.

141. Raymond B. Cattel, "The Dimensions of Culture Patterns by Factorization of National Characters," *Journal of Abnormal and Social Psychology*, Vol. 44 (1949), pp. 443–469. For later refinements, see "The Culture Patterns Discoverable in the Syntal Dimensions of Existing Nations," *Journal of Social Psychology*, Vol. 32 (1950), pp. 215–253 and Cattell, *et al.*, "An Attempt at More Refined Definitions of the Culture Dimensions of Syntality of Modern Nations." *American Sociological Review*, Vol. 17 (1952), pp. 408–421.

142. Phillip M. Gregg and Arthur S. Banks, "Dimensions of Political Systems: Factor Analysis of a Cross-Polity Survey," *American Political Science Review*, Vol. 59, No. 3 (1965), pp. 602–614.

143. R. J. Rummel, "Dimensions of Conflict Behavior Within Nations, 1946–1959," *Journal of Conflict Resolution*, 10 (1966), pp. 65–73. Raymond Tanter, "Dimensions of Conflict Behavior Within and Between Nations, 1958–1960," *Journal of Conflict Resolution*, 10 (1966), pp. 41–64.

144. Arthur S. Banks and Phillip M. Gregg, "Grouping Political Systems: Q Factor Analysis of a Cross Polity Survey," *American Behavioral Scientist*, Vol. IX, No. 3 (November, 1965), pp. 3–6.

145. *Ibid.*, p. 6. Permission to quote granted by Sage Publications, Inc.

146. See Irma Adelman and Cynthia Taft Morris, "A Factor Analysis of the Interrelationship Between Social and Political Variables and Per-Capita Gross National Product," *Quarterly Journal of Economics*, Vol. LXXIX (1965), pp. 555–578; and "A Quantitative Study of Social and Political Determinants of Fertility," *Economic Development and Cultural Change*, Vol. 14, No. 2 (January, 1966), pp. 129–158; also *Society, Politics and Economic Development: A Quantitative Approach* (Baltimore: John Hopkins Press, 1967).

147. See also, Rummel, "Understanding Factor Analysis."

148. For an example of this approach, see Adelman and Morris, "A Factor Analysis of the Interrelationship Between Social and Political Variables and Per-Capita Gross National Product," pp. 558–561.

149. See Rummel, "Dimensions of Conflict Behavior Between and Within Nations," p. 10. Rummel mentions this issue briefly and apparently opts for the product moment/point bi-serial approach. However, a more detailed discussion with examples would be most helpful.

150. For a discussion of this point, see Harry H. Harmon, *Modern Factor Analysis* (Chicago: University of Chicago Press, 1964), Chapter 6, especially p. 115.

151. Thurstone's criteria of "simple structure" are, of course, the most common. For a discussion, see Harman, *op. cit.*, Chapters 6 and 12. For a detailed discussion of the "simple structure criteria," see L. L. Thurstone, *Multiple Factor Analysis* (Chicago: University of Chicago Press, 1957), pp. 32 ff.

152. Thurstone, *Multiple Factor Analysis*, p. 61.

153. For example, in "Understanding Factor Analysis," Rummel observes, "The approach to the interpretation of factor patterns is a matter of personal taste, communication, and research strategy. The scientist may wish to use concepts that are congenial to the interests of the reader, to facilitate communication, encourage thought about the findings and make their use easier. There is always the danger, however, of the fallacy of misplaced concreteness. The interpretations of the findings within the research and lay community may be as much a result of the tag itself as of what the tag denotes." (P. 471.)

154. "Dimensions of Conflict Behavior Within and Between Nations," p. 1. Permission to quote granted by *The Journal of Conflict Resolution*.

155. *Ibid.*, p. 21.

156. *Ibid.*, p. 5.

157. *Ibid.*, p. 9.

158. Harman, *op. cit.* pp. 114–115.

159. Rummel, "Dimensions of Conflict Behavior Within and Between Nations," p. 11; see also Harman, *op. cit.*, Chapter 14, and Henry F. Kaiser, "Computer Program for Varimax Rotation in Factor Analysis," *Educational and Psychological Measurement*, Vol. 19 (1959), pp. 413–420.

160. Harman, *op. cit.*, p. 113; Thurstone, p. 58.

161. J. Scott Armstrong, "Derivation of Theory by Means of Factor Analysis or Tom Swift and His Electric Factor Analysis Machine," *The American Statistician*, Vol. 21, No. 5 (December, 1967), pp. 17–21.

162. *Ibid.*, pp. 20–21. Permission to quote granted by the American Statistical Association and the author.

3. The Comparison of Whole Political Systems *(73-121)*

FRED W. RIGGS

1. I base my use of the word *organization* in this sense on the definitions offered by Theodore Caplow in *Principles of Organization* (New York: Harcourt, Brace & World, 1964), p. 1.

2. Elsewhere I have tried to adapt and restructure theories of organization to the situations found in traditional and transitional societies. See my "Organization Theory and Political Development," (Bloomington, Ind.: Department of Political Science, Indiana University, Carnegie Seminar, 1969). (Mimeo.)

3. See, for example, Arthur Banks and Robert Textor, *Cross-Polity Survey* (Cambridge, Mass.: MIT Press, 1963), B. M. Russett *et al.*, *World Handbook of Political and Social Indicators* (Yale, 1964); and R. Merritt and S. Rokkan (eds.), *Comparing Nations* (Yale, 1966).

4. Kenneth Organski, *Stages of Political Development* (New York: A. A. Knopf, 1965).

5. In subsequent papers I have substituted the term "elected assembly" for "legislature" not only to emphasize that elected membership is crucial for the concept but also to avoid the functional implication of the word "legislature," namely, that it "legislates," i.e., makes laws. Elected assemblies may or may not make laws, although they typically do. In later writings I have treated the elected assembly, party system, and the electoral system as components of a larger political sub-system called the "constitutive system." See, for example, "Bureaucratic Politics in Comparative Perspective," *Journal of Comparative Administration*, Vol. I, No. 1 (May, 1969), pp. 16–17.

6. For empirical studies that show the impact of bureaucratic patterns of organization in feudalistic societies, see Rushton Coulborn, *Feudalism in History* (Princeton: Princeton University Press, 1956); James Fesler, "French field administration: The beginnings," *Comparative Studies in Society and History*, V (October, 1962); and John W. Hall, "Feudalism in Japan—A Reassessment," *Comparative Studies in Society and History*, V (October, 1962).

7. See, for example, Lucian W. Pye, *Aspects of Political Development* (Boston: Little, Brown, 1966), pp. 45–47.

8. These ideas have been expanded upon in another essay of mine, "The Theory of Political Development," James C. Charlesworth (ed.), *Contemporary Political Analysis* (New York: Free Press, 1967), pp. 317–349.

9. The classic description of bureaucratic power is given by Karl A. Wittfogel, *Oriental Despotism: A Comparative Study of Total Power* (New Haven: Yale University Press, 1957). A major analysis of bureaucratic transformations is contained in S. N. Eisenstadt, *The Political Systems of Empires* (New York: Free Press of Glencoe, 1963).

10. For an examination of some historic evidence to substantiate the cyclical alteration of hierocephalic and paracephalic polities, see my essay, "The Ambivalence of Feudalism and Bureaucracy in Traditional Societies," prepared for the 1964 conference of the American Political Science Association, Chicago, Ill., September, 1964 (mimeo).

11. Both the terminology proposed here and the definitional criteria have been revised and elaborated in my subsequent essay, "The Structures of Government and Administrative Reform," Ralph Braibanti and Associates, *Political and Administrative Development* (Durham, North Carolina: Duke University Press, in press).

12. See my book, *Administration in Developing Countries: The Theory of Prismatic Societies* (Boston: Houghton Mifflin, 1964).

13. Karl Deutsch, *Nationalism and Social Communication* (New York: John Wiley & Sons, 1953).

4. Parsimony and Empiricism in Comparative Politics: An Anti-Scholastic View *(123-149)* JOSEPH LAPALOMBARA

* In the revision of this essay I have had the helpful suggestions of Robert Holt, my colleagues, Roger Masters and Sidney Tarrow, and graduate students in the Minnesota Seminar on Comparative Methods. In acknowledging their assistance, I do not mean to associate them with my point of view or conclusions. Work on this chapter was made possible in part by financial assistance from the Stimson Fund of Yale University.

I wish also to note that a somewhat revised version of this chapter appeared in *Comparative Politics*, Vol. 1, No. 1 (October, 1968), pp. 52–78.

1. The usual procedure followed by writers reflecting on the behavioral revolution is to cite George Catlin's *The Science and Method of Politics* (New York: Alfred A. Knopf, 1927) and Charles Merriam's *New Aspects of Politics* (Chicago: University of Chicago Press, 1925). A. F. Bentley's *The Process of Government* (Chicago: University of Chicago Press, 1949) was originally published in 1908 and attention to it was regenerated by David Truman's justly admired *The Governmental Process* (New York, Alfred A. Knopf, 1951). Although the work of Harold Lasswell extends back approximately four decades, the most relevant volume would be his *The Analysis of Political Behavior: An Empirical Approach* (London: K. Paul, Trench, Trubner, and Co., 1948).

Other important works associated with the ferment for change would include R. A. Dahl and C. E. Lindblom, *Politics, Economics and Welfare* (New York: Harper & Brothers, 1953) and, some years later, R. A. Dahl, *A Preface to*

Democratic Theory (Chicago: University of Chicago Press, 1956); R. C. Snyder, H. Bruck, and B. Sapin, *Foreign Policy Decision Making* (New York: The Free Press, 1962); David Easton, *The Political System* (New York: Alfred A. Knopf, 1953); B. Berelson, P. F. Lazarsfeld, and W. McPhee, *Voting: A Study of Opinion Formation in a Presidential Campaign* (Chicago: University of Chicago Press, 1954); Glendon Schubert, *Quantitative Analysis of Judicial Behavior* (New York: The Free Press, 1959); Herbert Simon, *Administrative Behavior*, 2nd ed. (New York: The Macmillan Company, 1957).

2. Ray C. Macridis, *The Study of Comparative Government* (Garden City, N.Y.: Doubleday, 1954). The Northwestern Seminar is reported in "Research in Comparative Government," *American Political Science Review*, Vol. 47 (September, 1953), pp. 641–675. Other important landmarks include S. Neumann, "Comparative Politics: A Half-Century Appraisal," *Journal of Politics* (August, 1957); George McT. Kahin, *et al.*, "Comparative Politics of Non-Western Countries," *American Political Science Review* (December, 1955), pp. 1022–1041; G. A. Almond, *et al.*, "A Suggested Research Strategy in Western European Government and Politics," *American Political Science Review, ibid.*, pp. 1042–1049; G. A. Almond, "A Comparative Study of Interest Groups and the Political Process," *American Political Science Review* (March, 1958), pp. 270–282. Much of the flavor of the changes effected since the 1950s can be gleaned from H. Eckstein and D. E. Apter (eds.), *Comparative Politics: A Reader* (New York: The Free Press, 1963).

3. See, for example, E. M. Kirkpatrick, "The Political Behavior Approach," *PROD*, Vol. 2 (November, 1958), pp. 9–13; Roland Young (ed.), *Approaches to the Study of Political Science* (Evanston: Northwestern University Press, 1959); H. Eulau, *The Behavioral Persuasion in Politics* (New York: Random House, 1963). Robert Dahl's summary and analysis of the behavioral movement is worth reading: "The Behavioral Approach in Political Science: Epitaph for a Monument to a Successful Protest," *American Political Science Review*, Vol. 55 (December, 1961), pp. 763–772.

4. The antibehavioral views of Leo Strauss and his followers are contained in H. Storing (ed.), *Essays on the Scientific Study of Politics* (New York: Holt, Rinehart and Winston, 1962). A typically European criticism is Bernard Crick's *The American Science of Politics* (Berkeley: University of California Press, 1959). In sociology, some of this protest is contained in Maurice Stein and Arthur Vidich, *Sociology on Trial* (Englewood Cliffs, N.J.: Prentice-Hall, 1963). See particularly the brilliant critical essay by Alvin Gouldner. My observations about some of the consequences of these developments are contained in my "Decline of Ideology: A Dissent and an Interpretation," *American Political Science Review*, Vol. 60 (March, 1966), pp. 5–18. See also, J. C. Charlesworth (ed.), *The Limits of Behavioralism in Political Science* (The American Academy of Political and Social Science, October, 1962).

5. Much of what I would score as the New Scholasticism emanates from the prolific pen of Talcott Parsons and especially from T. Parsons and E. Shils, *Toward a General Theory of Action* (Cambridge: Harvard University Press, 1959). The best overall criticism of Parsons' theories is contained in Max Black (ed.), *The Social Theories of Talcott Parsons* (Englewood Cliffs, N.J.: Prentice-Hall, 1962). Black's essay is a brilliant critique and his rendering of Parsons' central postulates in plain English is both amusing and sobering. The difficulties created by Parsons (not all of them intended, to be sure)

378

are evident in the work of Fred Riggs, such as his *Administration in Developing Countries: The Theory of Prismatic Society* (Boston: Houghton Mifflin, 1964), and in his "Agraria and Industria; Toward a Typology of Public Administration," in W. J. Siffin, *Toward the Comparative Study of Public Administration* (Bloomington, Ind.: Indiana University Press, 1957). Other works that contain one or more of the characteristics and problems I am alluding to here would include (but are not limited to) the following: Edward Shils, *Political Development in the New States* (Gravenhage: Mouton, 1962); G. A. Almond (ed.), *The Politics of the Developing Areas* (Princeton: Princeton University Press, 1960); S. N. Eisenstadt, *The Political Systems of Empires* (New York: The Free Press, 1963); D. E. Apter, *The Gold Coast in Transition* (Princeton: Princeton University Press, 1955); and in a number of the volumes on political development sponsored by the SSRC Committee on Comparative Politics, including my own *Bureaucracy and Political Development* (Princeton, N.J.: Princeton University Press, 1963).

6. See R. T. Holt and J. E. Turner, *The Political Basis of Economic Development* (Princeton, N.J.: D. Van Nostrand Co., 1966).

7. D. E. Apter, *The Political Kingdom in Uganda* (Princeton: Princeton University Press, 1961). For Apter's more recent theoretical formulations, see *The Politics of Modernization* (Chicago: University of Chicago Press, 1965).

8. S. M. Lipset, *The First New Nation* (New York: Basic Books, 1963).

9. *Ibid.*, p. 344.

10. I refer here not so much to Deutsch's *The Nerves of Government* (New York: The Free Press, 1963), which I consider an imperfect and overly zealous application of cybernetics concepts and theory to political systems, but, rather, to his *Nationalism and Social Communication* (Cambridge: M.I.T. Press, 1953) and, of course, the many contributions he has made, alone or with colleagues at Yale, in the matter of rendering his concept of "social mobilization" susceptible to rigorous, empirical comparative analysis. Deutsch is the only social scientist I know who represents the Aristotelian mean between Plato and, say, a census enumerator.

11. Morroe Berger, *Bureaucracy and Society in Modern Egypt* (Princeton: Princeton University Press, 1957).

12. See, for example, Riggs, *Administration in Developing Countries, op. cit.*, Parts 2 and 3.

13. G. A. Almond and J. S. Coleman (eds.), *The Politics of the Developing Areas* (Princeton: Princeton University Press, 1960), pp. 3–64, esp. pp. 9–25 on "The Common Properties of Political Systems."

14. H. V. Wiseman, *Political Systems: Some Sociological Approaches* (London: Routledge & Kegan Paul, 1966), pp. 101–117, *passim*.

15. Wiseman derives these generalizations from H. Johnson, *Sociology: A Systematic Introduction* (London: Routledge & Kegan Paul, 1961). I find it almost impossible to believe that a British scholar, trained at Balliol College, would let such intellectual pretentiousness pass with only the mildest reproach.

16. One of the most rigorous attacks on structure-functionalism is Carl G. Hempel, "The Logic of Functional Analysis," in Llewellan Gross (ed.), *Symposium on Sociological Theory* (New York: Harper & Row, 1959), pp. 271–307. The Hempel critique is of functionalism as a logical system and as such it

is not immediately relevant here. Nevertheless, I do not think that anyone has provided a satisfactory reply to Hempel. See, for example, D. M. Martindale (ed.), *Functionalism in the Social Sciences*, Monograph 5, American Academy of Political and Social Science, February, 1965.

17. Wiseman, *op. cit.*, p. 216.

18. Although I cannot develop this point here, I wish to stress it for consideration. Whether by means of cultural diffusion—or by endogenous development—it does seem to me that the range of concrete structural alternatives for managing politics and government is not only finite but limited to many of the very institutions we have come to identify as culturally natural to the West. After more than a decade of talking with colleagues who are non-Western scholars, reading their published output, and travelling in a number of non-Western areas, I am no longer easily convinced of the exotic character of such political systems.

A good case in point would be the political party that appears to be ubiquitous, even if one may concede a variation in function, as well as the designation of political party for groups and organizations that would not meet a reasonable definition of the concept. On this point see the introductory and concluding chapters of J. LaPalombara and M. Weiner (eds.), *Political Parties and Political Development* (Princeton: Princeton University Press, 1966).

19. See Giovanni Sartori, *Parties and Party Systems*, forthcoming.

20. The literature on political development is too vast to cite. The interested reader should consult the bibliography in Holt and Turner, *op. cit.*, and the excellent bibliographical essay in C. E. Black, *The Dynamics of Modernization* (New York: Harper & Row, 1966).

21. One important result of postwar political research in Africa, Asia, and Latin America is the recognition by many scholars of those areas that it is now necessary to return to Western political systems, both for testing propositions about contemporary political institutions and behavior and for historical data to analyze in more systematic ways the evolution of political systems there. In this regard, C. E. Black, *The Dynamics of Modernization, op. cit.*, is very instructive reading indeed.

22. I cannot overstress the problem of the information gap. In a field where I have done considerable field work—interest group organization and behavior—I can testify that the amount of even straight descriptive information about the so-called developed societies of the West is extremely limited. No one in Italy has yet produced a full-scale study of one or more interest groups; German scholars have published a few articles and a book or two; for France, the work of Jean Meynaud remains striking for its lack of intellectual company; only in England have there been more than a few books published, and these tend to treat interest groups morphologically and as pathological phenomena. Some items that the reader may want to consult for illustrative purposes in this field are Jean Meynaud, *Les Groupes de Pression en France* (Paris: Armond Colin, 1958); J. LaPalombara, *Interest Groups in Italian Politics* (Princeton: Princeton University Press, 1964); J. D. Stewart, *British Pressure Groups* (Oxford: Oxford University Press, 1958); Henry Ehrmann, *Organized Business in France* (Princeton: Princeton University Press, 1957); S. E. Finer, *Anonymous Empire: A Study of the Lobby in Great Britain* (London: Pall Mall Press, 1959); H. Eckstein, *Pressure Group Politics* (Stanford: Stanford University Press, 1960); Myron

Weiner, *The Politics of Scarcity: Public Pressure and Political Response in India* (Chicago: University of Chicago Press, 1960). Most of these scholars are American. Compare these studies with the literature on American interest groups cited in Harmon Zeigler, *Interest Groups in American Society* (Englewood Cliffs, N.J.: Prentice-Hall, 1964).

23. For England and the United States there are many traditional works, some of them of the highest quality, on the national legislature. The works of Walter Bagehot, S. K. Bailey, Lord Campion, A. V. Dicey, H. Finer, and Sir Ivor Jennings come quickly to mind for England. Herman Finer, C. J. Friedrich, and others have also served the U.S. well, as have more recent studies by scholars like Donald Mathews, Gordon Baker, Dwaine Marvick, and James D. Barber. But once we leave these two countries, we are confronted once more with an enormous information gap. G. Sartori's *Il Parlamento Italiano* (Naples 1963) is an important exception, as is G. P. Gooch's now classic *The French Parliamentary System* (1935). Article-length studies on the French legislature have been published by P. Campbell, "The French Parliament," *Public Administration* (1953); M. Debré, "Trois Characteristiques du System Parlementaire," *Revue Française de Science Politique* (March, 1955); and by Mattei Dogan whose prolific works are too numerous to cite but can be found in the *Revue Française de Science Politique* (1953, 1957), the *Revue Française de Sociologie* (1961, 1965), and other journals. An excellent monograph on aspects of French legislative behavior is Duncan MacRae, *Parliament, Parties, and Society in France, 1946–1958*, (New York: St. Martin's Press, 1967). Lewis Edinger, "Continuity and Change in the Background of German Decision-Makers," *Western Political Quarterly* (March, 1961); "Post-Totalitarian Leadership: Elites in the German Federal Republic," *American Political Science Review* (March, 1960); Otto Kirchheimer, "The Composition of the German Bundestag, 1950," *Western Political Quarterly* (1950); G. Lowenberg "Parliamentarism in West Germany: The Functioning of the Bundestag," *American Political Science Review* (March, 1961), and a few others have treated Germany. But except for these and a few other countries we have a dearth of data, and almost none of what exists was *designed* as comparative study. We need therefore at both the national and local levels of many countries the kind of sophisticated, rigorously ordered and executed comparative work represented by J. Walke, *et al., The Legislative System* (New York: John Wiley & Sons, 1962). This volume clearly indicates how much that is useful we can in fact derive from comparative studies of segments of political systems.

24. For a detailed treatment of this problem, see my "Social Science in Developing Countries: A Problem in Acculturation." Paper presented at the Annual Meetings of the American Political Science Association, Washington, D.C., September, 1965 (mimeo).

25. The most organized effort to reexplore what it is political scientists should do, and how, is James C. Charlesworth (ed.), *A Design for Political Science: Scope, Objectives, and Methods*, Monograph 6 of the American Academy of Political and Social Science, December, 1966. Regarding the specific matter of "proper scope," Vernon Van Dyke in his "The Optimum Scope of Political Science," *ibid.*, pp. 1–17, makes a balanced case for greater attention to policy content. My colleague, Frederick M. Watkins, presents a telling case for emphasis on process, all the more striking in my view in that as a distinguished scholar of political thought Watkins might have been expected to

381

emphasize the content side in that much of the literature of Western political thought is encompassed by the *livres de circonstances* umbrella. See *ibid*, pp. 28–33, for Watkins' statement, as well as the lively conference discussion which follows.

26. Pioneers in the effort to transform the field of public administration would certainly include Fritz Morstein-Marx, whose *The Administrative State* (Chicago: University of Chicago Press, 1957) reveals a debt to Max Weber unmarred by complex abstractions and excessive neologisms; and Fred W. Riggs, whose voluminous contributions have been instructive, even in those instances where readers such as myself have found some of his concepts and formulations unnecessarily complex. Riggs, however, has also been the prime mover in the development of the Comparative Administration Group, whose "Occasional Papers" series now includes a number of theoretical contributions, of a less-than-cosmic ambition, that are certain to have a favorable impact on the comparative analysis of public administrative systems. The first batch of the better "Occasional Papers" appears in J. Montgomery and W. Siffin (eds.), *Approaches to Development: Politics, Administration and Change* (New York: McGraw-Hill, 1966). I have attempted to provide an assessment both of theoretical models in comparative administration and of theories of political development in my "Public Administration and Political Change: A Theoretical Overview," in Charles Press and Alan Arian (eds.), *Empathy and Ideology* (Chicago: University of Chicago Press, 1967).

27. Gabriel Almond, whose earlier work profoundly influenced important shifts in theoretical and empirical focus in comparative politics, is one political scientist who has led the movement toward greater attention to the output side of the polity. See, for example, his "Political Systems and Political Change," *American Behavioral Scientist*, Vol. 6 (June, 1963), pp. 3–10, an early formulation that emerged from discussion and a summer seminar held by the SSRC Committee on Comparative Politics; and his more recent "A Developmental Approach to Political Systems," *World Politics*, Vol. 17 (January, 1965), pp. 183–214. Other political scientists could be named here as well, and an interesting overview of their writings and the approaches they represent to the study of public administration comparatively is included in Ferrel Heady, *Public Administration: A Comparative Perspective* (Englewood Cliffs, N.J.: Prentice-Hall, 1966).

Nevertheless, it is significant that much of both the theoretical and the empirical leadership in public administration during the last fifteen or twenty years has been provided by such sociologists as S. N. Eisenstadt, *op. cit.*, Morroe Berger, *op. cit.*; Robert K. Merton, *et al.*, *Reader in Bureaucracy* (Glencoe, Ill.: The Free Press, 1952); Reinhard Bendix, *Nation-Building and Citizenship* (New York: John Wiley & Sons, 1964); Philip Selznik, *TVA and the Grass Roots* (Berkeley: University of California Press, 1949); Michel Crozier, *The Bureaucratic Phenomenon* (Chicago: University of Chicago Press, 1964); and such economists as Joseph J. Spengler, in his jointly edited *Administrative and Economic Development in India* (Durham: Duke University Press, 1963); A. H. Hanson, *Public Enterprise and Economic Development* (London: Routledge & Kegan Paul, 1959); and Bert F. Hoselitz, "Levels of Economic Performance and Bureaucratic Structures," in J. LaPalombara (ed.), *Bureaucracy and Political Development* (Princeton: Princeton University Press, 1963).

28. Volumes thus far published in the Gross series include: B. Akzin and Y.

Dror, *Israel: High Pressure Planning* (1966); H. J. Arndt, *West Germany: Politics of Non-Planning* (1966); D. E. Ashford, *Morocco-Tunisia: Politics and Planning* (1965); F. G. Burke, *Tanganyika: Preplanning* (1965); J. Friedman, *Venezuela: From Doctrine to Dialogue* (1965); E. E. Hagen and S. F. T. White, *Great Britain: Quiet Revolution in Planning* (1966); J. LaPalombara, *Italy: The Politics of Planning* (1966); and R. J. Shaper, *Mexico: Mutual Adjustment Planning* (1966).

29. See J. LaPalombara, "Alternative Strategies for Developing Administrative Capabilities in Emerging Nations," *CAG Occasional Papers* (Bloomington, Ind., 1966).

30. Charlesworth, *A Design for Political Science, op. cit.*, p. 202.

31. *Ibid.*, p. 207.

32. See J. LaPalombara, *Interest Groups in Italian Politics, op. cit.*, pp. 15–17.

33. David Easton, "The Current Meaning of Behavioralism in Political Science," in J. C. Charlesworth (ed.), *The Limits of Behavioralism . . . " op. cit.*, p. 17.

34. The studies of Michigan's Survey Research Center have been notoriously methodologically rich and theory poor. The last volume published by this group, however, represents a first and welcome step toward correcting this deficiency. See Angus Campbell, Philip Converse, Warren E. Miller, and Donald E. Stokes, *The American Voter* (New York: John Wiley & Sons, 1960).

35. See LaPalombara and Weiner, *op. cit.*, Ch. 1. Cf. the chapter by Rupert Emerson in the same volume.

36. On this point, see Karl W. Deutsch, "Recent Trends in Research Methods in Political Science," in Charlesworth, *A Design for Political Science, op. cit.*, pp. 149–178, whose enthusiasm about future data collections I do not share. In any event. I must confess that, until I am assured that some of the questions of comparability I have raised in this paper have been more adequately resolved, Deutsch's surmise that by 1975 we may have some fifty million IBM cards of "data" to draw upon is much more disquieting than it is reassuring. See *ibid.*, pp. 152–157.

37. *Ibid.*, p. 158.

5. Political Systems and Developmental Change *(151-171)*

DAVID E. APTER

1. See David E. Apter, *The Politics of Modernization* (Chicago: The University of Chicago Press, 1965).

2. Robert M. Marsh, *Comparative Sociology* (New York: Harcourt, Brace, and World, 1967), pp. 33–37 and 155–186.

3. In collaboration with several colleagues from the Politics of Modernization Project at Berkeley and in the practical context of comparing four West African and three Latin American cases, I have attempted to clarify the conceptual bases originally employed.

4. David E. Apter, "Political Analysis and the Boundary Question" (forthcoming).

5. David E. Apter, "Notes on a Theory of Non-democratic Representation," *Nomos*, X (New York: Atherton Press, forthcoming).

6. We need theoretical categories which, although less general than those offered by Marx, Durkheim, Weber, or Parsons, are more analytically refined than those employed by Russet, *et al.*, who use primarily available indicator data.

7. Several efforts have been made, both in the Politics of Modernization Project and elsewhere, to test the logical coherence of the general models employed. In particular, Mr. Mario Barrera has attempted to incorporate the variables using a wide sample of countries and computer techniques; while Professor Donald W. Katzner of the Department of Economics, University of Pennsylvania, has made a logical test of a somewhat simplified version of the earlier models. (See his "Political Structure and System and the Notion of Logical Completeness" [unpublished manuscript].)

8. Indeed, if at early stages of the development process it is possible to "manage" through some kind of bureaucratic political system—whether an army, a single party, or a civil service—at later stages of development, as a country moves toward major industrialization, political systems are likely to succeed one another more and more rapidly unless a powerful and highly centralized type of political system is established to control the process. Only after the shift to industrialization does such a highly centralized type of political system rapidly outlive its usefulness.

9. As a concept, it originated in the sociological literature of the late nineteenth century concerned with the growing differences between agricultural and industrial societies. The work of Durkheim is the simplest and clearest of these formulations, whereas Weber's is the most complex and interesting. Toennies's, although commonly used, was the most superficial. From these and other sociological thinkers (Sombart, for example), modern structural analysis arose, of which Parsons' is the most recent example.

10. This imposes very special problems, including the meritocracy problem posed by Michael Young in which talent, ability, and informational creativity form the new basis for ordering society. Accordingly, a functional elite is produced, while, on the other hand, society casts out "superfluous men." See Harold L. Wilensky, *Organizational Intelligence* (New York: Basic Books, 1967), *passim*.

11. I prefer the present formulation to the technological notion of modernization used by Levy and others, although I would be more inclined to accept the latter as appropriate to a definition of industrialization. See Marion J. Levy, Jr., *Modernization and the Structure of Societies* (Princeton: Princeton University Press, 1966), pp. 9–15.

12. By a *ceiling*, I mean the limits imposed by the political system-type on the deployment of natural and human resources for development purposes. To take an extreme example, if we compare India with China, both high population-increase countries, in terms of per capita income rises during the 1950s, we can see that Chinese per capita income between 1950 and 1958 grew at an annual rate of 11.5 percent; while Indian per capita income growth during the same period was about 1.5 percent. Although the differences are obviously not entirely the result of the fact that the former represents a mobilization

system-type and the latter a reconciliation system-type, the political system ceiling for each is a critical factor. See the discussion by S. K. Nath, "Indian Economic Development," *Planning and Growth in Rich and Poor Countries,* W. Birmingham and A. G. Ford eds., (London: George Allen and Unwin, 1966), pp. 144–145.

13. In addition, we need to add a more interesting possibility; namely, that each type is increasingly vulnerable to the other acts as a potential "with-input" for the other.

14. The situation would be different for highly industrialized societies, where, I would argue, the greater the degree of industrialization, the greater the need for information; hence, the long-term tendency is toward the reconciliation system.

6. Cross-Cultural Survey Research in Political Science
(173–294)   FREDERICK W. FREY

* I should like to express my gratitude to David A. Booth for many helpful comments and to Robert Holt and John Turner for their patience and encouragement. Part of the research on which this essay is based was supported by the Advanced Research Projects Agency (ARPA) of the Department of Defense under order No. 736, monitored by the Office of Naval Research (ONR) under contract No. N00014–66–CO163–AO1.

1. One of the foremost contributors to survey research, Herbert Hyman, once offered an unpublished definition of survey research on which I have built. He saw it as "a large scale systematic inquiry in a natural setting based on the procedure of questioning." "Primary Collection of Data," *Ankara University Political Sciences Faculty Lecture Notes,* Chapter VIII, p. 7. Cf., also Fred N. Kerlinger, *Foundations of Behavioral Research* (New York: Holt, Rinehart and Winston, 1967), pp. 393–395.

2. Myron Weiner, "Political Interviewing," in Robert E. Ward (ed.), *Studying Politics Abroad: Field Research in the Developing Areas* (Boston: Little, Brown and Company, 1964), pp. 115–116.

3. *Ibid.,* p. 116. In one sense, Weiner is quite correct. A "uniform questionnaire" would, of course, be inappropriate. The problem is that he tacitly limits surveys to completely "uniform questionnaires."

4. Marion J. Levy, Jr., *The Structure of Society* (Princeton, N.J.: Princeton University Press, 1965), p. 144.

5. *Ibid.,* p. 146.

6. Clyde Kluckhohn and William Kelly, "The Concept of Culture," in Ralph Linton (ed.), *The Science of Man in the World Crisis* (New York: Columbia University Press, 1945), p. 97.

7. Margaret Mead, "National Character," in A. L. Kroeber (ed.), *Anthropology Today* (Chicago: University of Chicago Press, 1953), p. 647.

8. Gabriel A. Almond and Sidney Verba, *The Civic Culture* (Princeton, N.J.: Princeton University Press, 1963), pp. 13–15.

9. Cf., Stein Rokkan and H. C. J. Duijker, "Organizational Aspects of Cross-National Social Research," *Journal of Social Issues*, Vol. X, No. 4 (1954), p. 8 (Permission to quote granted by the Society for the Study of Social Issues); R. Boguslaw, "Sociometric Methodology and Valid Cross-National Research," *International Social Science Bulletin*, Vol. 7 (1955), p. 570.

10. For information on the history of survey research, see, for example, Wilson Gee, *Social Science Research Methods* (New York: Appleton-Century-Crofts, 1950), p. 300 ff.; Frederick F. Stephan, "History of the Uses of Modern Sampling Procedures," *Journal of the American Statistical Association*, Vol. 43 (1948), pp. 12–39. Charles Y. Clock (ed.), *Survey Research in the Social Sciences* (New York: Russell Sage Foundation, 1967), pp. xiv-xvii; and Nathan Glazer, "The Rise of Social Research in Europe," in Daniel Lerner (ed.), *The Human Meaning of the Social Sciences* (New York: Meridian Books, 1959). The dates refer to the classic failures of the Literary Digest Poll in 1936 and most Presidential polls in 1948.

11. Almond and Verba, *op. cit.*, p. 43.

12. Robert K. Merton, "Notes on Problem-Finding in Sociology," in Robert K. Merton, Leonard Broom, and Leonard S. Cottrell, Jr. (eds.), *Sociology Today* (New York: Basic Books, 1959), p. xiii.

13. Angus Campbell, "Recent Developments in Survey Studies of Political Behavior," in Austin Ranney (ed.), *Essays on the Behavioral Study of Politics* (Urbana, Ill.: University of Illinois Press, 1962), p. 45.

14. Talcott Parsons, *The Structure of Social Action* (New York: McGraw-Hill Book Company, 1937), p. 743.

15. Robert R. Sears, "Transcultural Variables and Conceptual Equivalence," in Bert Kaplan (ed.), *Studying Personality Cross-Culturally* (Evanston, Ill.: Row, Peterson and Co., 1961), pp. 445–446.

16. Herbert H. Hyman, "Strategies in Comparative Survey Research," unpublished lectures delivered at the Inter-University Consortium for Political Research, Ann Arbor, Michigan, July, 1963, p. 61. I am most grateful to Professor Hyman for permission to refer to these lectures.

17. Cf., Jacob Goldstein, "The Relative Advantages and Limitations of the Panel and Successive-Sample Techniques in the Analysis of Opinion Change," *Journal of Social Psychology*, Vol. 50 (1959), p. 306. An interesting example of a methodologically focused cross-cultural survey project is the Cornell Cross-Cultural Methodology Project described in several papers by Suchman and others. Cf., for example, Max Ralis, Edward A. Suchman, and Rose K. Goldsen, "Applicability of Survey Techniques in Northern India," *Public Opinion Quarterly*, Vol. XXII (1958), pp. 245–250. There are numerous examples of cross-cultural trials of specific tests, instruments, and techniques.

18. Howard Maclay and Edward E. Ware, "Cross-Cultural Use of the Differential," *Behavioral Science*, Vol. 6 (1961), p. 185. Permission to quote granted by the Mental Health Research Institute and the authors.

19. Bradford B. Hudson, Mohamed K. Barakat, and Rolfe LaForge, "Introduction to Problems and Methods of Cross-Cultural Research," *Journal of Social Issues*, Vol. 15 (1959), p. 6. Permission to quote granted by the Society for the Psychological Study of Social Issues.

20. Joachim Israel and Ragnar Rommetveit, "Notes on the Standardization of Experimental Manipulations and Measurements in Cross-National Research," *Journal of Social Issues*, Vol. 10, No. 4 (1954), p. 61. Permission to quote granted by the Society for the Psychological Study of Social Issues.

21. See the well-known work by Kenneth Eells, *et al.*, *Intelligence and Cultural Differences* (Chicago: University of Chicago Press, 1951). On the specific linguistic differences between social classes (in England), see, for example, Basil Bernstein, "Social Class and Linguistic Development: A Theory of Social Learning," in A. H. Halsey, Jean Floud, and C. Arnold Anderson, *Education, Economy and Society* (Glencoe, Ill.: The Free Press, 1961), pp. 288–314. An excellent illustration of similar problems within Nigeria is furnished by William J. Hanna and Judith L. Hanna, "The Problem of Ethnicity and Factionalism in African Survey Research." *Public Opinion Quarterly*, Vol. 30 (1966), pp. 290–294.

22. Almond and Verba, *op. cit.*, p. 57.

23. *Ibid.*, p. 56.

24. Daniel Lerner, with Lucille W. Pevsner, *The Passing of Traditional Society* (Glencoe, Ill.: The Free Press, 1958).

25. *Journal of Social Issues*, Vol. 10 (1954).

26. William Buchanan and Hadley Cantril, *How Nations See Each Other* (Urbana, Ill.: University of Illinois Press, 1953).

27. Lloyd A. Free, *Six Allies and a Neutral* (Glencoe, Ill.: The Free Press, 1959).

28. James Gillespie and Gordon W. Allport, *Youth's Outlook on the Future*, (Garden City: Doubleday, 1955).

29. K. H. Silvert and Frank Bonilla, *Education and the Social Meaning of Development: A Preliminary Statement* (New York: American Universities Field Staff, 1961).

30. *Journal of Social Issues*, Vol. 15 (1959).

31. Almond and Verba, *op. cit.*

32. One comprehensive published bibliography on cross-cultural and cross-national survey research, although now quite out-of-date, is Stein Rokkan, "Comparative Cross-National Research: II Bibliography," *International Social Science Bulletin*, Vol. VII (1955), pp. 622–641. A fuller and newer bibliography is urgently needed. One covering English language periodicals has been prepared as part of the Human Factors in Modernization Project at M.I.T.: Frederick W. Frey (ed.), *Survey Research on Comparative Social Change: A Bibliography* (Cambridge, Mass.: M.I.T. Press, 1969). Much useful bibliographic material has been assembled by the Midwest Universities Institute for Cross-Cultural Research and Training in Sociology, directed by Allen D. Grimshaw at Indiana University. See Allen D. Grimshaw, *Preliminary Bibliography of Abstracts of Theoretical and Technical Publications on Cross-Cultural Research in Sociology (1955–July, 1966)*, Department of Sociology, Indiana University, Bloomington, Indiana, August 15, 1966 (mimeo.). Everett Rogers and his associates at Michigan State University have also compiled valuable bibliographies on survey problems in developing societies. See Alfred Wilson,

387

Survey Research Methods in Developing Nations, An Annotated Bibliography, Department of Communication, Michigan State University, East Lansing, Michigan, First revision, March, 1967 (mimeo.); A. D. Steeves, *Problems in Cross-Cultural Comparative Research: Primarily Focusing on the Problems of Validating Sociological and Social Psychological Instruments Cross-Culturally: An Annotated Bibliography*, Department of Sociology, Michigan State University, East Lansing, Michigan, 1965 (mimeo.); and Gordon Whiting, *Annotated Bibliography on Methodological Problems in Comparative Cross-Cultural Survey Research*, Department of Communication, Michigan State University, East Lansing, Michigan, 1964 (mimeo.). Robert T. Holt and John E. Turner of the University of Minnesota have published *A Bibliography on Planned Social Change*, Center for Comparative Political Analysis, Department of Political Science, University of Minnesota, Minneapolis, Minnesota, 3 vols., January 1, 1967, which contains many useful entries related to cross-cultural survey research.

33. David Aberle, *et al.*, "The Functional Prerequisites of a Society," *Ethics*, Vol. LX (1950), p. 100. Permission to quote granted by the University of Chicago Press. For similar comments see, for example, Sears, *loc. cit.*, p. 445; Almond and Verba, *op. cit.*, p. 55; or Wilbert E. Moore, *Social Change* (Englewood Cliffs, N.J.: Prentice-Hall, 1963), pp. 114–115.

34. Clyde Kluckhohn, "Universal Categories of Culture," in Kroeber (ed.), *Anthropology Today, op. cit.*, p. 508.

35. This situation is revealed, for example, by scrutiny of the categories used to describe polities in Arthur S. Banks' and Robert B. Textor's pioneering *A Cross-Polity Survey* (Cambridge, Mass.: M.I.T. Press, 1963). Cf., Phillips Cutright, "National Political Development," *American Sociological Review*, Vol. 28 (1963), p. 254.

36. Campbell, *loc. cit.*, p. 45.

37. Herbert H. Hyman, "Research Design," in Ward (ed.), *op. cit.*, pp. 155–156.

38. Hyman, *loc. cit.*, pp. 162–163; Almond and Verba, *op. cit.*, p. 52.

39. Cf., for example, Rokkan and Duijker, *loc. cit.*, p. 12; Hyman, *loc. cit.*, p. 170 ff. and "Strategies . . .," pp. 32–54;; Hudson, *loc. cit.*, pp. 6–7.

40. Hudson, *ibid.*, has commented that ". . . research has a way of yielding information on questions that may be unanticipated. Therefore, even though the studies are focused upon issues that may represent relatively stable characteristics, . . . it may yield information upon some that are [not]. Therefore, correspondence in time may be more important than is initially apparent."

41. Erwin K. Scheuch, "The Cross-Cultural Use of Sample Surveys: Problems of Comparability," in Stein Rokkan (ed.), *Comparative Research across Cultures and Nations* (The Hague: Mouton, 1968), p. 198.

42. Rokkan and Duijker, *loc. cit.* A roughly similar set of distinctions is suggested by Arrigo L. Angelini in "Perspectives and Problems in Cross-Cultural Research," *Proceedings of the Ninth Congress of the Interamerican Society of Psychology*, December, 1964, pp. 17–22. Angelini discerns four types of cross-cultural research: (1) the researcher analyzes a behavior known in his own culture in another culture, (2) the researcher replicates in his own culture studies performed earlier in another culture, (3) a researcher from one culture

invites colleagues from other cultures to form a team to do research in their various cultures according to a plan developed by the original researcher, and (4) cooperative research plans are developed by a group of investigators from different cultures for work in their respective cultures.

43. Frederick W. Frey, "Surveying Peasant Attitudes in Turkey," *Public Opinion Quarterly*, Vol. XXVII (1963), pp. 335–355.

44. Hyman, "Strategies . . . ," *op. cit.*, pp. 81–82; Herbert Hyman and Paul B. Sheatsley, "The Dynamics of American Attitudes toward Communism and Civil Liberties," National Opinion Research Center, University of Chicago, August, 1956. (Mimeo.)

45. "Secondary Analysis in the Developing Areas," *Public Opinion Quarterly*, Vol. 31 (1967), pp. 272–278. Another form of this tactic was used in *The Civic Culture*, for which a subsample of respondents, representing important "citizen-types," was reinterviewed in each nation. However, the thrust of the re-interviewing was more to obtain additional depth of information rather than to perform an intensive panel analysis of changes from one interview to another. Almond and Verba, *op. cit.*, pp. 46–47. Yet another, different example of transforming an earlier survey into a panel study, along with some interesting comments on the difficulties of designating a theoretically appropriate and feasible population of interest, is furnished by Richard D. Lambert, "Some Problems of Cross-Cultural Research: The Poona Factory Studies," un-published paper presented to the 1966 Summer Seminar, Midwest Universities Institute for Cross-Cultural Research and Training in Sociology, Bloomington, Indiana.

46. For a useful discussion, see Frank Bonilla, "Survey Techniques," in Ward (ed.), *op. cit.*, pp. 142–145.

47. O. H. Mowrer, "Emerging Conceptions of Neurosis and Normality," in Francis L. K. Hsu (ed.), *Aspects of Culture and Personality* (New York: Abelard-Schuman, 1954), p. 130.

48. Stein Rokkan, "The Comparative Study of Political Participation: Notes Toward a Perspective on Current Research," in Ranney (ed.), *op. cit.*, pp. 58–59.

49. Vilhelm Aubert, Burton R. Fisher, and Stein Rokkan, "A Comparative Study of Teachers' Attitudes to International Problems and Policies: Pre-liminary Review of Relationships in Interview Data from Seven Western European Countries," *Journal of Social Issues*, Vol. 10, No. 4 (1954), p. 29. Permission to quote granted by the Society for Psychological Study of Social Issues.

50. James S. Coleman, *The Adolescent Society* (Glencoe, Ill.: The Free Press, 1961).

51. Thus, the diversity may be more apparent than real. One can easily assemble a group of nations that includes rich and poor, big and little, hot and cold, democratic and authoritarian, ancient and recent, modern and traditional, rural and urban, flat and mountainous, and so on, through a long list of characteristics. Here, apparently, is maximal diversity, unless one looks at combinations of characteristics. Then he may find that only two or three *types* of nations are represented. The hot, rural, traditional, poor, authoritarian, and recent, and the cold, urban, modern, rich, democratic, and ancient may

cluster markedly. One really has represented a much smaller set of nation-types (of combinations or characteristics) than the gross enumeration suggests. The specialist will perceive that this point is analogous to the distinction between alternative versus simultaneous application of quota controls.

52. Excerpts from "The Multinational Comparative Research Corporation" by Alexander Szalai are reprinted from the *American Behavioral Scientist*, Vol. X, No. 4 (December, 1966), by permission of the publisher, Sage Publications, Inc.

53. Some useful recent treatments are: American Political Science Association, Interim Report, Committee on Professional Standards and Responsibilities, "Ethical Problems of Political Scientists," September 1, 1967, (mimeo.); Ralph L. Beals and the Executive Board of the American Anthropological Association, "Background Information on Problems of Anthropological Research and Ethics," *American Anthropological Association Fellow Newsletter*, Vol. 8, No. 1, January, 1967; "Testimony Presented to U.S. Senate Sub-Committee on Government Operations, Senator Fred R. Harris, Chairman, by Alex Inkeles, Professor of Sociology, Harvard University, July 19, 1966," *Congressional Record—Appendix*, July 19, 1966, pp. A3811–A3814; Paul Miller, "Comments on a Proposal to Establish a National Foundation for the Social Sciences," *The American Sociologist*, Vol. 2, No. 3, August, 1967, pp. 160–161; Luther J. Carter, "Social Sciences: Where Do They Fit in the Politics of Science?" *Science*, Vol. 154, October 28, 1966; Edward A. Shils, "Social Inquiry and the Autonomy of the Individual," in Daniel Lerner (ed.), *The Human Meaning of the Social Sciences* (New York: Meridian Books, 1959), pp. 114–157; J. A. Barnes, "Some Ethical Problems in Modern Fieldwork," *British Journal of Sociology*, Vol. XIV, No. 2, June, 1963, pp. 118–134; and Irving L. Horowitz (ed.), *The Rise and Fall of Project Camelot* (Cambridge, Massachusetts: M.I.T. Press, 1967). See, Gideon Sjoberg (ed.), *Ethics, Politics and Social Research* (Cambridge, Mass.: Schenkman Publishing Co., 1967).

54. American Political Science Association, "Ethical Problems of Political Scientists," *op. cit.*, p. 6.

55. Szalai, *loc. cit.*, p. 2.

56. *Ibid.*

57. *Ibid.*, p. 3.

58. Excerpts from "Image-Making in Field Research: Some Tactical and Ethical Problems of Research in Tropical Africa" by William John Hanna are reprinted from the *American Behavioral Scientist*, Vol. VIII, No. 5 (January, 1965), by permission of the publisher, Sage Publications, Inc. For an interesting viewpoint see also Lewis Anthony Dexter, "Role Relationships and Conceptions of Neutrality in Interviewing," *American Journal of Sociology*, Vol. LXII (1956), pp. 153–157.

59. *Loc. cit.*, p. 16.

60. "The large scale survey on political themes is among the most sensitive and vulnerable research that can be undertaken overseas." Frank Bonilla, "Survey Techniques," in Ward (ed.), *Studying Politics Abroad, op. cit.*, p. 150.

61. Leo Crespi, "The Influence of Military Government Sponsorship in German Opinion Polling," *International Journal of Opinion and Attitude Research*, Vol. IV (1950), pp. 151–178.

62. For example, S. Biesheuvel found in his African surveys that sometimes ". . . the attitude enquiry was seized upon as a likely channel through which objections could be voiced and possibly brought to the attention of the right quarter." "Methodology in the Study of Attitudes of Africans," *Journal of Social Psychology*, Vol. 47 (1958), p. 172. Fearfulness of governmentally sponsored surveys as compared to privately sponsored was empirically demonstrated, for example, in Japan after World War II. See Herbert Hyman, "World Surveys: The Japanese Angle," *International Journal of Opinion and Attitude Research*, Vol. I (1947), pp. 18–29, esp. 23. The courtesy bias is discussed further in Emily L. Jones, "The Courtesy Bias in South-East Asian Surveys," *International Social Science Journal*, Vol. XV (1963), pp. 70–76.

63. Herbert H. Hyman *et al.*, *Interviewing in Social Research* (Chicago: The University of Chicago Press, 1954), p. 185.

64. *Ibid.*, pp. 185–190. See also Hyman's *Survey Design and Analysis* (Glencoe, Ill.: The Free Press, 1955), pp. 40–56.

65. See Prodipto Roy and Frederick C. Fliegel, "Sponsorship, Personnel, Institutional Affiliation and Institution Building," in Gerald D. Hursh (ed.), *Survey Research in Developing Societies* (forthcoming). I am most grateful to Drs. Roy and Fliegel for making available to me an advance copy of their chapter.

66. Stein Rokkan, "Archives for Secondary Analysis of Sample Survey Data: An Early Inquiry into the Prospects for Western Europe, "*International Social Science Journal*, Vol. XVI (1964), p. 50.

67. Lloyd and Susanne H. Rudolph, "Surveys in India: Field Experience in Madras State," *Public Opinion Quarterly*, Vol. XXII (1958), p. 241. Permission to quote granted by the copyright holder.

68. *Ibid.*, p. 239.

69. See, for example, Alex Bavelas, "Communication Patterns in Task-Oriented Groups," in Daniel Lerner and Harold D. Lasswell (eds.), *The Policy Sciences* (Stanford: Stanford University Press, 1951), pp. 193–202; Harold J. Leavitt, "Some Effects of Certain Communication Patterns on Group Performance," *Journal of Abnormal and Social Psychology*, Vol. XLVI (1951), pp. 327–336.

70. Rokkan and Duijker, *loc. cit.*, p. 19.

71. Roy and Fliegel, *loc. cit.*

72. Alain Girard summed up the relevant discussion of a recent conference on survey problems in developing societies as follows:

> A few basic principles emerge . . . The first of these principles admits of no exception: the interviewers must belong to the same racial groups as the persons amongst whom the survey is conducted.
>
> Further limitations follow in so far as it is desirable that the social status of the interviewers should be as close as possible to that of the persons interviewed so as to prevent the development of too marked a feeling of inferiority on the part of the latter.

"Introduction," *International Social Science Journal*, Vol. XV (1963), p. 16.

73. Lincoln Armstrong, "Technical Surveying Difficulties in India" (mimeo., n.d.), p. 11. Cf., Elmo C. Wilson and Lincoln Armstrong, "Inter-

viewers and Interviewing in India," *International Social Science Journal*, Vol. XV (1963), p. 51. A valuable discussion of "Interviewers and Interviewing," in developing societies is presented by Allan F. Hershfield, Niel G. Roling, and Graham B. Kerr, in Chapter 12 of *Survey Research Methods in Developing Societies*, *op. cit.*, forthcoming.

74. Armstrong, *loc. cit.*, pp. 11–23.

75. See Frey, "Surveying Peasant Attitudes in Turkey," *loc. cit.*, pp. 348–351.

76. See, for example, Lloyd E. Borg, "Interviewing School," *International Journal of Opinion and Attitude Research*, Vol. II (1948), pp. 396–397. Some years ago Hyman observed that "lists of the qualifications required for good interviewers have been made to sound like a catalogue of all the virtues— . . . ," *Interviewing in Social Research* (Glencoe, Ill.: The Free Press, 1954), p. 306. I should also call attention to the obvious fact that there are many different kinds of interviewing and that the qualities and skills most desirable in the candidate would seem to depend on the type of interviewing contemplated.

77. Eleanor P. Clarkson, "The Problem of Honesty," *International Journal of Opinion and Attitude Research*, Vol. IV (1950), p. 85.

78. Jorge M. Mendez, remarks at the Third International Conference on Public Opinion Research, WAPOR, September, 1948, in *International Journal of Opinion and Attitude Research*, Vol. III (1949), p. 317. Michel Hoffman, "Research on Opinions and Attitudes in West Africa," *International Social Science Journal*, Vol. XV (1963), p. 68. See also Paul B. Sheatsley, "An Analysis of Interviewer Characteristics and Their Relationship to Performance: Part I and II," *International Journal of Opinion and Attitude Research*, Vol. IV (1950), pp. 473–498, and Vol. V (1951), pp. 79–94.

79. See, for example, Hyman, *op. cit.*, Interviewing and Social Research, pp. 304–309, 361–370 (by Sheatsley); Frederick Mosteller, *et al.*, *The Pre-Election Polls of 1948* (New York: Social Science Research Council, 1949), pp. 143–147 (by Hyman); *Interviewing for NORC* (Denver: National Opinion Research Center, revised ed., 1947). More recent discussions of interviewer training are Charles H. Backstrom and Gerald D. Hursh, *Survey Research* (Evanston, Ill.: Northwestern University Press, 1963), pp. 134–147; Robert L. Kahn and Charles F. Cannell, *The Dynamics of Interviewing* (New York: John Wiley & Sons, 1957), pp. 233–252; Stephen A. Richardson, Barbara S. Dohrenwend, and David Klein, *Interviewing: Its Forms and Functions* (New York: Basic Books, 1965), pp. 288–291. For a suggestion that refusal rates at least could be markedly reduced over those obtained by "typical or average interviewers" through longer and more intensive interviewer training, see Herbert G. Heneman Jr. and Donald G. Paterson, "Refusal Rates and Interviewer Quality," *International Journal of Opinion and Attitude Research*, Vol. III (1949), pp. 393–398.

80. Remarks of John Maloney, "Problems of Opinion Polls in the Different Countries," WAPOP Proceedings, *International Journal of Opinion and Attitude Research*, Vol. III (1949), p. 318.

81. *Loc. cit.*, p. 57. On the need to match respondents and interviewers, see, e.g., William John Hanna and Judith Lynne Hanna, "The Problem of Ethnicity and Factionalism in Africa Survey Research," *Public Opinion Quarterly*, Vol. XXX (1966), pp. 290–294.

82. Elmo C. Wilson, "Problems of Survey Research in Modernizing Areas," *Public Opinion Quarterly*, Vol. XXII (1958), p. 230.

83. *Ibid.*, p. 231.

84. A related technique involves developing "random walk routes" from randomly selected starting points in the urban quarter.

85. Erwin K. Scheuch, "The Cross-Cultural Use of Sample Surveys . . . ," *loc. cit.*, p. 194. Scheuch's article and that by Hursh cited in footnote 65, both of which I encountered after this paper had been prepared in first draft, provide many useful examples of most of the points made in this section— examples which space precludes inserting here.

86. Stein Rokkan, "Party Preferences and Opinion Patterns in Western Europe: A Comparative Analysis," *International Social Science Bulletin*, Vol. VII (1955), pp. 579 ff., and Eugene Jacobsen, "Methods for Producing Comparable Data in the OCSR Seven-Nation Attitude Study," *Journal of Social Issues*, Vol. 10 (1954), pp. 43–44.

87. Cf., for example, Duijker, *loc cit.*, pp. 562–563. He also notes that some of the sample controls used by Radvanyi in Mexico included eating habits, footwear, sleeping habits, and dress.

88. Eric Stern and R. Lalive d'Epinay, "Some Polling Experiences in Switzerland," *Public Opinion Quarterly*, Vol. XI (1947–1948), pp. 553–557. See also Hyman, "Strategies in Comparative Survey Research," *op. cit.*, p. 50; Almond and Verba, *op. cit.*, pp. 65–66; Bradford Hudson, *et al.*, *loc. cit.*, p. 6; Buchanan and Cantril, *op. cit.*, p. 108, for similar observations on the easy assumption of cross-cultural equivalence of demographic or social background variables.

89. Scheuch, again, points out the marked differences in the number and kinds of sampling units employed in *The Civic Culture* study, and on this basis objects to the global standard error formula they employed. The primary sampling unit frames ranged from 30,000 communities in Germany from which 100 were selected to 92 provinces in Italy from which 13 were selected. Intermediate stage clustering effects also differed conspicuously across the five nations. Such variation, however, seems to have been essential simply because the administrative structures of the five societies differed in fundamental ways. Scheuch's quarrel is with the failure to provide separate error estimates for each country, not with the variations in multi-stage procedures used. *Loc. cit.*, pp. 192–194.

90. For a recent field comparison of quota and random samplings in Warsaw, for example, see Andrzej Sicinski, "Public Opinion Surveys in Poland," *International Social Science Journal*, Vol. XV (1963), pp. 91–110, esp. p. 100.

91. See, for example, Morris H. Hansen, William N. Hurwitz, and William G. Madow, *Sample Survey Methods and Theory* (New York: Wiley, 2 vols. 1953); Frederick J. Stephan and Philip J. McCarthy, *Sampling Opinions* (New York: Wiley, 1958); Leslie Kish, *Survey Sampling* (New York: Wiley, 1965); William G. Cochran, *Sampling Techniques* (New York: Wiley, 1953); W. Edwards Deming, *Some Theory of Sampling* (New York: Wiley, 1950). An excellent elementary introduction to sampling techniques and conceptualization, together with discussion of many points mentioned in this section, is the chapter

on "Sampling" by Hursh in Gerald D. Hursh (ed.), *Survey Research Methods in Developing Nations: The Criterion of Variance* (forthcoming).

92. Frank Bonilla, "Survey Techniques," in Robert A. Ward (ed.), *op. cit.*, p. 144.

93. See, for example, Lloyd and Suzanne H. Rudolph, "Surveys in India: . . . ," *loc. cit.*, pp. 235, 237–239.

94. Stanley L. Payne, *The Art of Asking Questions* (Princeton, N.J.: Princeton University Press, 1951).

95. Similar (or should I say "equivalent"?) considerations are found in other areas of science. For example, the use of models in social and natural science involves analogous concerns. The scientist must develop an understanding of the dimensions along which his model faithfully represents its object and those in which it does not. In experimental research, the scientist wants to "match" his treatment and control groups (i.e., show that they are equivalent) prior to the experimental treatment. To do this he must either specify the dimensions along which the matching is to be done and argue that these are the critical dimensions for his experiment, or else use random assignments to groups to achieve this result. Such randomization, however, is always of persons from some limited population, so that when he thinks about generalizing his results, the experimentalist still encounters problems of equivalence (i.e., what other populations are equivalent to the one on which he experimented.)

96. Recent research on national stereotypes, for example, indicates that the stereotypes revealed by respondents in the interview depend significantly on the number and kind of national groups presented for comparison. See, for example, Lufty N. Diab, "Factors Affecting Studies of National Stereotypes," *Journal of Social Psychology*. Vol. 59 (1963), pp. 29–40.

97. Almond and Verba, *op. cit.*, p. 58.

98. The interrelatedness of all survey operations again becomes evident here. If the sample is to be used to generate norms or standards for expressing equivalence, then this consideration must enter into the sample design. The fact that one type of respondent is more media exposed than most others in some accidental or special sample, while another type of respondent is also more media exposed than respondents in another different accidental or special sample really means nothing unless the two samples can be shown to have interesting parallel characteristics. If one needs to use his samples to generate norms as well as to furnish direct information concerning a specific group, he must plan for this from the start. This is especially true for highly purposive samples.

Further elaboration of the distinction between absolute and relative types of data, (but not equivalence) can be found in Paul F. Lazarsfeld and Herbert Menzel, "On the Relation Between Individual and Collective Properties," in Amitai Etzioni, (ed.) *Complex Organizations: A Sociological Reader* (New York: Holt, Rinehart and Winston, 1961), pp. 422–440.

99. *Op. cit.*, pp. 64, 63.

100. R. Boguslaw, *loc. cit.*, p. 567.

101. "New Dimensions of Meaning for Cross-section Sample Surveys in Politics," *International Social Science Journal*, Vol. XVI (1964), p. 31, n.1.

102. See, David C. McClelland, *The Achieving Society* (Princeton, N.J.: Van Nostrand, 1961), pp. 24–25.

103. See, for example, Henry A. Landsberger and Antonio Saavedra, "Response Set in Developing Countries," *Public Opinion Quarterly*, Vol. XXXI (1967), pp. 214–229; Richard Christie, Joan Havel, and Bernard Seidenburg, "Is the F-Scale Reversible?" *Journal of Abnormal and Social Psychology*, Vol. 56 (1958), pp. 143–159; Arthur Couch and Kenneth Keniston, "Yeasayers and Naysayers: Agreeing Response Set as a Personality Variable," *Journal of Abnormal and Social Psychology*, Vol. 60 (1960), pp. 151–174; Dean Peabody, "Attitude Content and Agreement Set in Scales of Authoritarianism, Dogmatism and Economic Conservatism," *Journal of Abnormal and Social Psychology*, Vol. 63 (1961), pp. 1–11; J. E. Milholland, "Theory and Techniques of Assessment," *Annual Review of Psychology*, Vol. 15 (1964), pp. 311–346; Thomas S. Cohn, "The Relation of the F-Scale to a Response Set to Answer Positively," *Journal of Social Psychology*, Vol. 44 (1956), pp. 129–133; and Martha T. Mednick and Sarnoff A. Mednick, *Research in Personality* (New York: Holt, Rinehart and Winston, 1963), Chapter 6.

104. C. James Klett and David W. Yaukey discuss such research in their article, "A Cross-Cultural Comparison of Judgments of Social Desirability," *Journal of Social Psychology*, Vol. 44 (1959), pp. 19–26, and offer evidence for cross-national variations in social desirability judgments. See also Douglas P. Crowne and David Marlowe, "A New Scale of Social Desirability Independent of Psychopathology," *Journal of Consulting Psychology*, Vol. 24 (1960), pp. 349–354; Marvin R. Goldfried, "A Cross-validation of the Marlowe-Crowne Social Desirability Scale Items," *Journal of Social Psychology*, Vol. 64 (1964), pp. 137–145; Le Roy H. Ford, Jr., "A Forced-choice, Acquiescence-Free Social Desirability (Defensiveness) Scale," *Journal of Consulting Psychology*, Vol. 28 (1964), p. 475; Allen L. Edwards, *The Social Desirability Variable in Personality Assessment and Research* (New York: Dryden, 1957); Bernard M. Bass, "Development and Evaluation of a Scale for Measuring Social Acquiescence," *Journal of Abnormal and Social Psychology*, Vol. 53 (1956), pp. 296–299.

105. Eric Stern, Comments from "Proceedings of the Third International Conference on Public Opinion Research, WAPOR," *International Journal of Opinion and Attitude Research*, Vol. III (1949), p. 332.

106. William H. Hunt, Wilder W. Crane, and John C. Wahlke, "Interviewing Political Elites in Cross-cultural Comparative Research," *American Journal of Sociology*, Vol. LXX (1964), p. 67.

107. See, for example, Converse, *loc. cit.*

108. An interesting further check on the impact of closed items is the use of "random probes" of such items during the final administration of the instrument, as suggested by Howard Schuman, "The Random Probe: A Technique for Evaluating the Validity of Closed Questions," *American Sociological Review*, Vol. 31 (1966), pp. 218–222.

109. George Murdock, *Social Structure* (New York: Macmillan, 1949), p. 2. The fact that an activity or institution can be found, to some extent, in every known society does not mean, of course, that all or even most people in every society are familiar with it! In general, for cross-cultural *survey* research, the more interesting uniformities would be those which were universal for *individuals* rather than only for larger social units but not for all individuals.

Cf., also, Kluckhohn, "Universal Categories of Culture," *loc. cit.* and John C. Smith-Jones, *Problems of Methodology in Comparative Research.* On Cattell's influence, for example, see William G. Rodd, "A Cross-Cultural Study of Taiwan's Schools," *Journal of Social Psychology*, Vol. 50 (1959). pp. 3–36, esp. p. 7.

110. See, for example, Richard H. Solomon, "Communication Patterns and the Chinese Revolution," *The China Quarterly*, No. 32 (1967), pp. 88–110; James Guyot's work in Burma; and, although it is not extra-cultural, Rufus P. Browning and Herbert Jacob, "Power Motivation and the Political Personality," *Public Opinion Quarterly*, Vol. XXVIII (1964), pp. 75–90.

111. For example, see Jules Henry and Melford Spiro, "Psychological Techniques: Projective Tests in Field Work," in *Anthropology Today, op. cit.*, pp. 418–419, and A. I. Hallowell, *Culture and Experience* (Philadelphia: University of Pennsylvania Press, 1955), pp. 45ff. An excellent critical survey of the application (essentially anthropological) of projective devices in cross-cultural research is Gardner Lindzey, *Projective Techniques and Cross-Cultural Research* (New York: Appleton-Century-Crofts, 1961).

112. *Ibid.*, p. 45.

113. E. T. Sherwood, "On the Designing of TAT Pictures with Special Reference to a Set for an African People Assimilating Western Culture," *Journal of Social Psychology*, Vol. 45 (1957), pp. 161–190. S. Biesheuvel, "Methodology in the Study of Attitudes of Africans," *loc. cit.*, p. 176. A detailed interpretive commentary on each of the original pictures can be found in Morris I. Stein, *The Thematic Apperception Test* (Cambridge, Mass.: Addison-Wesley, 1955). See, also, for example, P. Verhaegen and J. L. Laroche, "Some Methodological Considerations Concerning the Study of Aptitudes and the Elaboration of Psychological Tests for African Natives," *Journal of Social Psychology*, Vol. 47 (1958), pp. 249–256. Harold H. Anderson and Gladys L. Anderson, *An Introduction to Projective Techniques* (Englewood Cliffs, N.J.: Prentice-Hall, 1951), pp. 258–271, shows several modifications of TAT pictures for Mexican Indian, Southwest African native, and South Pacific-Micronesian cultures. Lindzey, *op. cit.*, also refers to a number of instances where researchers felt important modifications in the TAT were necessary to employ it effectively in other cultures (pp. 73, 164, 241, 270, 277).

114. Ephraim Rosen, "A Cross-Cultural Study of Semantic Profiles and Attitude Differences," *Journal of Social Psychology*, Vol. 49 (1959), p. 137. Note also the late Paul Deutschmann's judgment that ". . . the differential is an ideal instrument for studying attitude in cross-cultural situations"; "The Semantic Differential and Public Opinion Research," *Public Opinion Quarterly*, Vol. XXIII (1959), p. 436.

115. Charles E. Osgood, George J. Suci, and Percy H. Tannenbaum, *The Measurement of Meaning* (Urbana, Ill.: University of Illinois Press, 1957).

116. C. Scott Moss, "Current and Projected Status of Semantic Differential Research," *Psychological Record*, Vol. 10 (1960), p. 50.

117. *Loc. cit.*, p. 143.

118. George J. Suci, "A Comparison of Semantic Structures in American Southwest Culture Groups," *Journal of Abnormal and Social Psychology*, Vol. 61 (1960), pp. 25–30.

119. Howard Maclay and Edward E. Ware, "Cross-Cultural Use of the Semantic Differential," *Behavioral Science*, Vol. 6 (1961), p. 189.

120. Osgood, Suci, and Tannenbaum, *The Measurement of Meaning, op. cit.*, pp. 77–78.

121. For example, the findings for the Navaho from the Southwestern Study: see, Charles E. Osgood, "The Cross-Cultural Generality of Visual-Verbal Synesthetic Tendencies," *Behavioral Science*, Vol. 5 (1960), pp. 154–155, 167.

122. Hideya Kumata and Wilbur Schramm, "A Pilot Study of Cross-Cultural Methodology," *Public Opinion Quarterly*, Vol. XX (1956), p. 231.

123. Osgood, *loc. cit.*, p. 148, n.1.

124. This total extractable variance, however, as Osgood and his associates point out, is far from overwhelming. It seems generally to have been about 50 percent of all variance in the studies which used more limited sets of scale and was "much less" in the *Thesaurus* study with its greater diversity of scales. Cf., *The Measurement of Meaning*, pp. 38, 47, 64.

I should also note that the arithmetic of the discussion of variance extracted in *The Measurement of Meaning* is confusing. Under almost any plausible construction the percentages add up to more than 100 percent of extractable variance. See *ibid.*, pp. 72–73. However, I do not think that this apparent confusion significantly alters the stated conclusions.

125. Percy Tannenbaum, "Selected Applications of the Semantic Differential," *Public Opinion Quarterly*, Vol. XXIII (1959), p. 436.

126. Hadley Cantril and Lloyd A. Free, "Hopes and Fears for Self and Country," *The American Behavioral Scientist*, Vol. VI Supplement (1962), p. 8. The present discussion relies primarily on the Cantril and Free article just cited along with F. P. Kilpatrick and Hadley Cantril, "Self-Anchoring Scaling, a Measure of Individuals' Unique Reality Worlds," *Journal of Individual Psychology*, Vol. 16 (1960), pp. 158–173, and Hadley Cantril, "A Study of Aspirations," *Scientific American*, Vol. 208, No. 2 (February, 1963), pp. 41–45.

127. See Donald R. Matthews and James W. Prothro, *Negroes and the New Southern Politics* (New York: Harcourt, Brace and World, 1966), pp. 286–294.

128. See Lloyd A. Free, *Six Allies and a Neutral* (Glencoe, Ill.: The Free Press, 1959) and several subsequent reports from the Institute for International Social Research, Princeton, N.J.

129. Cantril and Free, *loc. cit.*, pp. 19–30.

130. Bruce W. Anderson, "On the Comparability of Meaningful Stimuli in Cross-Cultural Research," *Sociometry*, Vol. 30 (1967), p. 126.

131. Joseph B. Casagrande, "The Ends of Translation," *International Journal of American Linguistics*, Vol. 20 (1954), pp. 339–340.

132. Indeed, Moss ". . . can envision the theoretical and practical usefulness of a 'world semantic atlas', with semantic factors determined for each language/culture group . . ." *Loc. cit.*, p. 48.

133. If the second language is learned in school *through the medium of the first language*, the resulting bilingualism would be compound—context would be the same. But if the second language were learned in school directly, say in another country, without recourse to translation into the first language, then the

bilingualism is said to be coordinate. Obviously, intermediate gradations are also possible. For useful brief discussions, see John B. Carroll, "Research on Teaching Foreign Languages," in N. L. Gage, *Handbook of Research on Teaching* (Chicago: Rand McNally, 1963). pp. 1085–1087; Susan Ervin and Robert T. Bower, "Translation Problems in International Surveys," *Public Opinion Quarterly*, Vol. 16 (1952), pp. 595–604; and Anderson, *loc. cit.*

134. Carroll, *loc. cit.*, p. 1085.

135. Robert M. Marsh, *Comparative Sociology: A Codification of Cross-Societal Analysis* (New York: Harcourt, Brace and World, 1967), p. 274.

136. Charles E. Osgood and T. A. Sebeok, "Psycholinguistics: A Survey of Theory and Research," *Journal of Abnormal and Social Psychology*, Supplement, Vol. 49 (1954).

137. Casagrande, *loc. cit.*, p. 338.

138. William E. Lambert, J. Havelka, and C. Crosby, "The Influence of Language-acquisition Contexts on Bilingualism," *Journal of Abnormal and Social Psychology*, Vol. 56 (1958), pp. 239–244, and William E. Lambert, J. Havelka, and R. C. Gardner, "Linguistic Manifestations of Bilingualism," *American Journal of Psychology*, Vol. 72 (1959), pp. 77–82.

139. See Ervin and Bower, *loc. cit.*, pp. 600–601.

140. For example, Stanley Schacter, "Interpretation and Methodological Problems of Replicated Research," *Journal of Social Issues*, Vol. 10 (1954), pp. 52–60, esp. p. 59.

141. P. Verhaegen and J. L. Laroche, *loc. cit.*, p. 252. Classic studies making the same point for within-cultural research are Leonard Schatzman and Anselm Strauss, "Social Class and Modes of Communication," *American Journal of Sociology*, Vol. LX (1955), pp. 329–338, and Basil Bernstein, "Some Sociological Determinants of Perception," *British Journal of Sociology*, Vol. IX (1958), pp. 159–174.

142. See, for example, Eugene A. Nida, *Toward a Science of Translating* (Leiden: E. J. Brill, 1964) and Reuben A. Brower (ed.), *On Translation* (Cambridge, Mass.: Harvard University Press, 1959). Although only devoting a few pages to translation per se, Joyce O. Hertzler, *A Sociology of Language* (New York: Random House, 1965), also contains a number of useful comments, as do Herbert P. Phillips, "Problems of Translation and Meaning in Field Work," *Human Organization*, Vol. 18 (1959), pp. 184–192; Haim Blanc, "Multilingual Interviewing in Israel," *American Journal of Sociology*, Vol. 62 (1956), pp. 205–209; and Dell Hymes (ed.), *Language in Culture and Society* (New York: Harper and Row, 1964).

143. Nida, *op. cit.*, p. 51.

144. A third aspect of the basic interrogative strategy of a cross-cultural survey involves equivalence in the conditions of interrogation, apart from the survey instrument. The conditions of administration of the questionnaire or of the interview must be examined for their comparability.

145. At this point, the possibility of significant respondent or interviewer fatigue is estimated through a search for deterioration in the quality or quantity of response to later items. Such deterioration might be manifested in a higher incidence of "Don't Know" replies and item refusals, in more laconic answers

to open questions, in a reduced selection of responses which are likely to be probed, and so on. Actually, the major sections of the instrument should each be examined in this fashion since, for example, there is a counterpart of fatigue that might be labeled "coldness" which can afflict the initial stages of an interview. Performance is below par because either the respondent or the interviewer or both have not yet "warmed up" to the task. See Robert E. Mitchell, "Survey Materials Collected in the Developing Countries: Obstacles to Comparisons," in Stein Rokkan (ed.), *Comparative Research Across Cultures and Nations, op. cit.,* p. 224.

146. Adam Przeworski and Henry Teune, "Equivalence in Cross-National Research," *Public Opinion Quarterly,* Vol. 30 (1966–1967), pp. 551–568; William A. Scott, "Attitude Measurement," in Gardner Lindzey and Elliot Aronson (eds.), *Handbook of Social Psychology* (Cambridge, Mass.: Addison-Wesley, rev. ed. 1968), Chapter 11, pp. 204–272.

147. For example, Przeworski and Teune present the following hypothetical scheme for measuring "political activity" in Poland and the United States.

A. *Formally identical items:* Does the respondent
  1. Follow political news,
  2. Vote in elections,
  3. Attend political meetings,
  4. Talk with friends about politics,
  5. Try to be acquainted with political issues?
B. *System-specific items—U.S.:* Does the respondent
  6. Contribute money to parties or candidates,
  7. Place sticker on car,
  8. Volunteer help in campaigns,
  9. Testify at hearings,
  10. Write letters to Congressmen in support of or against policies or programs?
C. *System-specific items—Poland:* Does the respondent
  11. Fight for execution of economic plans,
  12. Attempt to influence economic decisions,
  13. Join a party,
  14. Participate in voluntary social works,
  15. Develop ideological consciousness?

Thus, from a total set of 15 items, 5 identical and 10 system-specific, 10 items would be asked in each country. Items 1, 2 and 5 might be the subset of the formally identical items which scale for the pooled samples, and items 6 and 10 from the U.S. sample and items 11, 12, and 13 from the Polish sample might display sufficiently high correlations with the three identity items to warrant their being considered "equivalent" to them. See, Przeworski and Teune, *loc. cit.,* p. 558.

148. *Ibid.,* p. 558.

149. Matthews and Prothro, *op. cit.,* pp. 525, 516, and John P. Robinson, Jerrold G. Rusk, and Kendra B. Head, *Measures of Political Attitudes* (Ann Arbor, Mich.: Survey Research Center, Institute for Social Research, University of Michigan, 1968), pp. 413–414.

150. Galtung, *op. cit.,* pp. 40–41. Paul F. Lazarsfeld and Herbert Menzel, "On the Relation Between Individual and Collective Properties," in Amitai

Etzioni (ed.), *Complex Organizations, A Sociological Reader* (New York: Holt, 1961), pp. 422–440.

151. Henry Teune, "Intra-System Comparisons in Cross-Systems Analysis," unpublished paper presented to the 1968 Annual Meeting of the American Political Science Association, Washington, D.C., September 3–7, 1968, pp. 19–20.

152. See Przeworski and Teune, *loc. cit.*

153. See Norman H. Nie, G. Bingham Powell, Jr., and C. Kenneth Prewitt, "Social Structure and Political Participation: Developmental Relationships," *American Political Science Review*, Vol. LXIII (1969), forthcoming. I am grateful to my colleague, Professor Hayward Alker, Jr., for bringing this article to my attention.

154. Kenneth W. Terhune, "An Examination of Some Contributing Demographic Variables in a Cross-National Study," *Journal of Social Psychology*, Vol. 59 (1963), pp. 209–219.

155. Galtung uses the phrase "fallacy of the wrong level." *Op. cit.*, p. 45.

156. See Erwin Scheuch, "Cross-National Comparisons Using Aggregate Data . . . ," *loc. cit.*, pp. 148–164; Hayward R. Alker, Jr., *Mathematics and Politics* (New York: Macmillan, 1965), pp. 101–105; Mathilda W. Riley, *Sociological Research, A Case Approach* (New York: Harcourt, Brace and World, 1963), pp. 707–709; Raymond Boudon, "Propriétés Individuelles et Propriétés Collectives: Un Probleme d'Analyse Écologique," *Revue Française de Sociologie*, Vol. IV (1963), pp. 275–299; Otis D. Duncan, R. P. Cuzzort, and B. Duncan, *Statistical Geography* (New York: Free Press of Glencoe, 1961), pp. 68–80; Leo A. Goodman, "Some Alternatives to Ecological Correlation," *American Journal of Sociology*, Vol. 64 (1959), pp. 610–625; and "Ecological Regressions and the Behavior of Individuals," *American Sociological Review*, Vol. 18 (1953), pp. 663–664; Otis D. Duncan and Beverly Davis, "An Alternative to Ecological Correlation," *American Sociological Review*, Vol. 18 (1953), pp. 665–666; William S. Robinson, "Ecological Correlations and the Behavior of Individuals," *American Sociological Review*, Vol. 15 (1950), pp. 351–357; Herbert Menzel, "Comment on Robinson's Ecological Correlations and the Behavior of Individuals," *American Sociological Review*, Vol. 15 (1950), p. 674; and E. L. Thorndike, "On the Fallacy of Imputing the Correlations Found for Groups to the Individuals or Smaller Groups Composing Them," *American Journal of Psychology*, Vol. 3 (1939), pp. 122–124. Alker distinguishes several other "fallacies," using a covariance model, including the "universal fallacy," "selective fallacy," "contextual fallacy," "historical fallacy," and "cross-sectional fallacy." Only the "ecological" and "individualistic" fallacies relate to misplaced level; the others involve faulty inference across distributions, "contexts" or settings, and time. They do not seem more likely in cross-systemic research than in any other type of research so they are not discussed here.

157. Some major references are: Peter M. Blau, "Structural Effects," *American Sociological Review*, Vol. 25 (1960), pp. 178–193; James A. Davis, Joe L. Spaeth, and Carolyn Huson, "Analyzing Effects of Group Composition," *American Sociological Review*, Vol. 26 (1961), pp. 215–225; David L. Sills, "Three 'Climate of Opinion' Studies," *Public Opinion Quarterly*, Vol. XXV (1961), pp. 571–573; James A. Davis, "Compositional Effects, Role Systems and the

Survival of Small Discussion Groups," *Public Opinion Quarterly*, Vol. XXV (1961), pp. 574–584; John A. Michael, "High School Climates and Plans for Entering College," *Public Opinion Quarterly*, Vol. XXV (1961), pp. 585–595; Martin L. Levin, "Social Climates and Political Socialization," *Public Opinion Quarterly*, Vol. XXV (1961), pp. 596–606; James S. Coleman, "Comment on Three 'Climate of Opinion' Studies," *Public Opinion Quarterly*, Vol. XXV (1961), pp. 607–610; Arnold S. Tannenbaum and Jerald G. Bachman, "Structural Versus Individual Effects," *American Journal of Sociology*, Vol. 69 (1964), pp. 585–595; Ernest Q. Campbell and C. Norman Alexander, "Structural Effects and Interpersonal Relationships," *American Journal of Sociology*, Vol. 71 (1965), pp. 284–289; Tapani Valkonen, "Individual and Structural Effects in Ecological Research," Paper prepared for the Symposium on Quantitative, Ecological Analysis in the Social Sciences, Evian, France, September 12–16, 1966; and David Nasatir, "A Note on Contextual Effects and the Political Orientation of University Students," *American Sociological Review*, Vol. 33 (1968), pp. 210–219. I am indebted to Professor Everett M. Rogers for bringing Valkonen's useful paper to my attention.

158. Factor analysis has sometimes been used to reduce a large set of control properties to a more manageable number. See, for example, Nasatir, *loc. cit.*

159. I refer particularly to sociometric approaches producing data which can be treated as directed graphs, large matrices, flow networks, paths, lists to be processed, etc. The relevant literature is too extensive to cite, but a useful introduction can be obtained from Chapter 14, "Measures of Structural Characteristics," in James S. Coleman, *Introduction to Mathematical Sociology* (New York: The Free Press of Glencoe, 1964), pp. 430–468 and J. L. Moreno, *et al.* (eds.), *The Sociometry Reader* (Glencoe, Illinois: The Free Press, 1960).

7. Linguistic Aspects of Comparative Political Research (295-341)
DELL HYMES

1. I should like to thank Robert Holt for inviting me to participate in the seminar at the University of Minnesota, and those who took part in the seminar for their comments, especially James Jenkins and Pertti Pelto. In revising this paper, I have had the benefit of a draft of a long, thoughtful report by Irwin Deutscher on his inquiry into the relevance of language and linguistics for sociology. The title shows its relevance here: "Notes on language and human conduct. Some problems of comparability in cross-cultural and interpersonal contexts" (Part I treats "Asking questions cross-culturally;" Part II develops the thesis that the same problems obtain in research within our own society). [1968, In Howard S. Becker, David Reisman, Robert S. Weiss, and Blanche Geer (eds.), *Institutions and the Person: Essays presented to Everett C. Hughes.* Chicago: Aldine]. I am happy that our perspectives are quite similar, and am grateful to Deutscher for references to the sociological literature otherwise unknown to me. In the preface to his report, Deutscher writes: "From my perusal of relevant research and polemics, I can only assume that political scientists are all but oblivious to the role of language in behavior—both from a methodological and a substantive perspective . . . ." The statement encourages me to think that the present paper is useful, while the present volume yet shows the

401

statement to be already in need of qualification. In this effort to present for students of political science a line of thinking that has originated in a quite different enterprise, Professor Holt has been especially stimulating, and any success is partly because of him.

2. F. M. Barnard, *Herder's Social and Political Thought, From Enlightenment to Nationalism* (Oxford: Clarendon Press, 1965), pp. 117, 118, 142.

3. For survey of the development, see especially Harry Hoijer (ed.), *Language in Culture* (Chicago: University of Chicago Press, 1954); Joshua Fishman, "A Systematization of the Whorfian Hypothesis," *Behavioral Science*, 5: 232–239 (1960); and references in Dell Hymes (ed.), *Language in Culture and Society* (New York: Harper and Row, 1964), pp. 150–153. (*This collection is cited hereafter as LCS.*)

4. G. Matore, *Le vocabulaire et la société sous Louis-Philippe* (Geneva-Lille: Droz, 1951); *La Méthode en Lexicologie* (Paris, 1953).

5. Raymond Williams, *Culture and Society, 1780–1950* (Garden City, N.Y.: Anchor Books, 1960), p. xi.

6. Ward H. Goodenough, "Property and Language on Truk: Some Methodological Considerations," in *LCS*, pp. 185–188.

7. Roger Brown, *Words and Things* (Glencoe: The Free Press, 1958), Chapter 8, considers "concrete": "abstract" in terms of subordination—superordination, and I have adopted the basic point from him. Brown's discussion of "Linguistic relativity and determinism," Chapter 7, remains probably the best cautious introduction to the subject.

8. For studies exploring the methodology and content of such relationships, see A. Kimball Romney and Roy G. D'Andrade (eds.), *Transcultural Studies in Cognition* [Special publication, *American Anthropologist*, 66 (3), Part II, June 1964]; Eugene A. Hammel (ed.), *Formal Semantic Analysis* [Special publication, *American Anthropologist*, 67 (5), Part II, October, 1965]; and Mary Black and Duane Metzger, "Ethnographic Description and the Study of Law," in Laura Nader (ed.), *The Ethnography of Law* [Special publication, *American Anthropologist*, 67 (6), Part 2, December, 1965], pp. 141–165.

9. See, for example, a point made by George Orwell in his well-known essay, "Politics and the English Language," first published in the late English journal *Horizon*, and cited here from Denys Val Baker (ed.), *New English Writing* (New York: Vanguard Press, 1947), pp. 189–205.

10. See Uriel Weinreich, "On the Semantic Structure of Language," in Joseph Greenberg (ed.), *Universals of Language* (Cambridge: M. I. T. Press, 1963).

11. Pierre Alexandre, "Sur les Possibilités Expressives des Langues Africaines en Matière de Terminologie Politique" ("The Expressive Possibilities of African Languages in the Matter of Political Terminology"), *Sociological Abstracts*, 12 (1), 17941 (1964), p. 14. For the original article, see *Afrique et Asie*, 56 (4): 23–29 (1967).

12. Elman R. Service, "Kinship Terminology and Evolution," *American Anthropologist*, 62: 747–763.

13. Max Gluckman, "The Technical Vocabulary of Barotse Jurisprudence," *American Anthropologist*, 61: 743–759.

14. See Brown, *Words and Things*, pp. 255–256.

15. Ward H. Goodenough, Review of Felix and Marie M. Keesing, Elite Communication in Samoa, *Language*, 33: 424–429 (1957).

16. Eric H. Lenneberg, "Cognition in Ethnolinguistics," *Language,* 29: 463–471 (1953), pp. 464–465; Brown, *Words and Things*, p. 231.

17. Goodenough, "Property and Language on Truk."

18. See A. Meillet, "The Feminine Gender in the Indo-European Languages," translated in *LCS*, p. 124; notice also the discussion by Marcel Mauss, "On Language and Primitive Forms of Classification," *LCS*, pp. 125–127, elaborating significantly on the social origin of categories.

19. Susan M. Ervin, "The Connotations of Gender," *Word,* 18: 248–261 (1962).

20. A. Irving Hallowell, "Ojibwa Ontology, Behavior, and World View," in Stanley A. Diamond (ed.), *Primitive Views of the World* (New York: Columbia University Press, 1964), p. 56.

21. See discussion in Hymes, "On Typology of Cognitive Styles in Language (with examples from Chinookan)," *Anthropological Linguistics*, 3(1): 22–54 (1961).

22. See Howard MacLay, "An Experimental Study of Language and Non-Linguistic Behavior," *Southwestern Journal of Anthropology*, 14: 220–229 (1956); John B. Carroll and Joseph B. Casagrande, "The Function of Language Classifications in Behavior," in Eleanor Maccoby, T. H. Newcomb, E. L. Hartley (eds.), *Readings in Social Psychology* (3rd edition), (New York: Henry Holt, 1958), pp. 18–31; and discussion in Hymes, "Linguistic Aspects of Cross-Cultural Personality Study," in Bert Kaplan (ed.), *Studying Personality Cross-culturally* (Evanston: Row, Peterson, 1961), pp. 313–359.

23. Roger W. Brown and Eric H. Lenneberg, "A Study in Language and Cognition," *Journal of Abnormal and Social Psychology*, 49: 454–462 (1954); "Studies in Linguistic Relativity," in Maccoby, Newcomb, Hartley, *op. cit.*, pp. 9–18.

24. See Hymes, "Two Types of Linguistic Relativity," in William Bright (ed.), *Sociolinguistics* (The Hague: Mouton, 1966), pp. 114–167.

25. Joyce O. Hertzler, *A Sociology of Language* (New York: Random House, 1965).

26. A point I have discussed in several contexts, e.g., "A Perspective for Linguistic Anthropology," in Sol Tax (ed.), *Horizons of Anthropology* (Chicago: Aldine Press, 1964), pp. 92–107; and the article cited in n. 21. Systematic cross-cultural study of such differences is now being launched by Susan Ervin-Tripp, John Gumperz, and Dan Slobin of the University of California, Berkeley, and a preliminary manual has been prepared; a related guide, drawing on ethnographic illustrations, has been prepared at the University of Pennsylvania by myself and others.

27. For an interesting contrast, see J. L. Fischer, "The Stylistic Significance of Consonantal Sandhi in Trukese and Ponapean," *American Anthropologist*, 67: 1495–1502 (1965).

403

28. See the account of verbal and nonverbal channels for ideologies and the general analysis in James Peacock, *Rites of Modernization: Symbolic Action in Indonesian Proletarian Drama* (Chicago: University of Chicago Press, 1968). On expressivity in Indonesian political language, note Denzel Carr, "Homorganicity in Malay and Indonesian in Expressives and Quasi-Expressives," *Language*, 42: 370–7 (1966), esp. pp. 375–6. A recurrent phenomenon, long stretches of political speech in which no new referential content occurs, has given rise to a stock story about translation. An apparently true instance of the story is reported as follows: Owing to the mixed composition of the Hawaiian legislature, it is necessary to employ continually two languages. All speeches in English are immediately translated into Kanaka, and vice versa. On this occasion the interpreter innocently exposed a fundamental characteristic of the native tongue in replying to a member. A Hawaiian had spoken possibly ten minutes since his last words were translated. A friend, anxious that nothing of importance should be lost, asked why the interpreter did not perform his duty and give the English-speaking members the benefit of the words just uttered. The reply was: "He has said nothing fresh yet." The speaker had simply repeated in new phraseology the substance of his previous remarks and so skillfully was it done that the friend, although somewhat conversant with the tongue, was misled by Kanaka volubility. [Erasmus Darwin Preston, "The Language of Hawaii," Philosophical Society of Washington, *Bulletin*, 14: 37–64 (1900), pp. 56–57.]

29. See reference in n. 11, and generally, Joshua Fishman, Charles A. Ferguson, and Jyotirindra das Gupta (eds.), *Language Problems of Developing Nations* [Englewood Cliffs, N.J.: Prentice-Hall, 1969.) (Papers from a conference sponsored by the Social Science Research Council Committee on Sociolinguistics at Airlie House, November, 1966).

30. See Susan M. Ervin, "Semantic Shift in Bilingualism," *American Journal of Psychology*, 74: 233–241 (1961); and "Navaho Connotative Judgements: The Metaphor of Person Description," in Hymes (ed.), *Studies in Southwestern Ethnolinguistics* (The Hague: Mouton, 1967). See also Joshua Fishman, "Language Maintenance and Language Shift as a Field of Inquiry," in his *Language Loyalty in the United States* (The Hague: Mouton, 1965), pp. 424–454.

31. Anselm Strauss and Leonard Schatzmann, "Cross-Class Interviewing: An Analysis of Interaction and Communicative Styles," *Human Organization*, 14: 28–31 (1955); Leonard Schatzmann and Anselm Strauss, "Social Class and Modes of Communication," *American Journal of Sociology*, 60: 329–38 (1955). The first article is reprinted in R. N. Adams and J. J. Preiss (eds.), *Human Organization Research* (Homewood, Ill.: The Dorsey Press, 1960) pp. 205–213; the second is reprinted in Alfred G. Smith (ed.), *Communication and Culture* (New York: Holt, Rinehart, Winston, 1966), pp. 442–455.

32. Basil Bernstein, "Elaborated and Restricted Codes: Their Social Origins and Some Consequences," in John J. Gumperz and Dell Hymes (eds.), *The Ethnography of Communication* [Special Publication, *American Anthropologist* 66 (6), Part 2, December, 1964], pp. 55–69; reprinted in Smith, *Communication and Culture*, pp. 427–441.

33. John Boman Adams, "Culture and Conflict in an Egyptian Village," *American Anthropologist*, 59: 225–235 (1957); I am indebted to David French for calling this case to my attention. The immediately relevant portion is re-

printed in *LCS*, pp. 272–273, as "On Expressive Communication in an Egyptian Village."

34. Michael Moermann, "Ethnic Identification in a Complex Civilization: Who Are the Lue?", *American Anthropologist*, 67: 1213–1230 (1965). The relation of language boundaries to communication boundaries in cross-cultural research, as practiced by anthropologists, is analyzed in my "Linguistic Aspects of the Concept of 'Tribe'," in June Helm (ed.), *Proceedings of the 1967 Spring Meeting of the American Ethnological Society* (Seattle: University of Washington Press, 1968), pp. 23–48.

35. S. F. Nadel, *The Nuba* (London: Oxford University Press, 1947), p. 13; see also Nadel, *A Black Byzantium* (London: Oxford University Press), regarding ethnolinguistic mosaics.

36. Einar Haugen, "Dialect, Language, Nation," *American Anthropologist*, 68: 922–935 (1966). Permission to quote granted by the American Anthropological Association.

37. Hans Wolff, "Intelligibility, and Inter-ethnic Attitudes," *Anthropological Linguistics*, 1 (3): 34–41 (1959); reprinted in *LCS*, pp. 440–445.

38. An illustration of interaction between linguistic traits and cultural attitudes is given by Moermann:

Although speakers of a Northern (Thai) dialect often seem to understand speakers of another Northern dialect more easily than they can understand Siamese (Central Thai), the genetic significance of this relative intelligibility is difficult to evaluate since Northern speakers react to and discuss dialects solely in terms of lexicon. The comparative unintelligibility of Siamese results from its Cambodian and Sanskrit borrowings rather than from differences of tonal structure which might be of greater genetic significance. Differences of tone among the Northern dialects are ignored or automatically compensated for by the native listeners. (*Op. cit.*, p. 1226, n. 6.) Permission to quote granted by the American Anthropological Association.

39. Cf. Einar Haugen, "Semicommunication: The Language Gap in Scandinavia," *Sociological Inquiry*, 36: 280–297 (1966). On these problems generally, see also Charles A. Ferguson and John J. Gumperz (eds.), *Linguistic Diversity in South Asia: Studies in Regional, Social, and Functional Variation* (Bloomington, Ind.: Research Center in Anthropology, Folklore and Linguistics, Publication 13, 1960).

40. Laura Nader, "A Note on Attitudes and the Use of Language," *Anthropological Linguistics*, 4 (6): 24–29 (1962).

41. Charles A. Ferguson, "Diglossia," *Word*, 15: 325–340 (1959); reprinted in *LCS*, pp. 429–437. See also Mervyn Alleyne, "Communication and Politics in Jamaica," *Caribbean Studies*, 3 (2), 22–61 (1963).

42. Susan Ervin-Tripp, "An Analysis of the Interaction of Language, Topic, and Listener"; John J. Gumperz, "Linguistic and Social Interaction in Two Communities," in Gumperz and Hymes, *The Ethnography of Communication*, pp. 86–102, 137–153, respectively. Gumperz develops the notion of verbal repertoire in this article.

43. For examples in this paragraph, see John L. Fischer, "Social Influences in the Choice of a Linguistic Variant," *Word*, 14: 47–56 (1958) (reprinted in

LCS, pp. 483–488); work of Henry Kucera on Czech; William Labov, *The Social Stratification of English in New York City* (Washington, D.C.: Center for Applied Linguistics, 1966); Joan Rubin, "Bilingualism in Paraguay," *Anthropological Linguistics*, 4 (1): 52–58 (1962); work of John Gumperz on Indian bilingualism.

44. Alexandre, *op. cit.* Permission to quote granted by Sociological Abstracts, Inc.

45. Charles A. Ferguson, "National Sociolinguistic Profile Formulas," in William Bright (ed.), *Sociolinguistics* (The Hague: Mouton, 1966). On theoretical considerations, see also W. A. Stewart, "An Outline of Linguistic Typology for Describing Multilingualism," in Rice (cited n. 47), where some of the criteria for profile formulas are developed; and John J. Gumperz, "Speech Variation and the Study of Indian Civilization," *American Anthropologist*, 63: 976–988 (1961) (reprinted in *LCS*, pp. 413–423), for a discussion from the standpoint of dialectology. Sociolinguistic surveys of East African nations are now underway, and should have important results both empirically and conceptually.

46. Joseph H. Greenberg, "The Measurement of Linguistic Diversity," *Language*, 32: 109–115 (1956); Stanley Lieberson, "An Extension of Greenberg's Measures of Linguistic Diversity," *Language*, 40: 526–531 (1964); see also Uriel Weinreich, "Functional Aspects of Indian Bilingualism," *Word*, 13: 203–33 (1957).

47. Frank A. Rice (ed.). *Study of the Role of Second Languages in Asia, Africa and Latin America* (Washington, D.C.: Center for Applied Linguistics, 1962). Gumperz' paper (n. 45) on India is the best concise overview of one major area. See also [John Macnamara (ed.), Problems of Bilingualism], *Journal of Social Issues*, 23 (2) (1967) and *Proceedings of the June 1967 Moncton (Canada) Conference on Bilingualism*.

48. Uriel Weinreich, *Languages in Contact* (New York: Linguistic Circle of New York, 1953).

49. Marcel Cohen, *Pour un sociologie du language* (Paris: Albin Michel, 1956); see also *LCS*, *passim*.

50. R. Bruce W. Anderson, "Equivalence and Variance in Cross-Cultural Research: A Quest for Data Relating to the Impact of Translation on Comparability," paper read at the second session on sociolinguistics, annual meeting, American Sociological Association, Miami Beach, Florida, August, 1956. Revised as "On the Comparability of Meaningful Stimuli in Cross-Cultural Research," *Sociometry*, 30 (2) (1967), pp. 124–236. Anderson cites Norman D. Sundberg, "The Use of the MMPI [Minnesota Multi-Phasic Personality Inventory] for Cross-Cultural Personality Study: A Preliminary Report on the German Translation," *Journal of Abnormal and Social Psychology*, 57: 124–5 (1958); Harrison G. Gough and Harjit S. Sandhu, "Validation of the CPI [California Psychological Inventory] Socialization Scale in India," *Journal of Abnormal and Social Psychology*, 32: 544–547 (1964).

51. Among those who have discussed problems of translation of social science instruments are the following (listed chronologically): Susan Ervin and Robert T. Bower, "Translation Problems in International Surveys," *Public Opinion Quarterly*, 16: 595–604 (1953); Joseph B. Casagrande, "The Ends of Trans-

lation," *International Journal of American Linguistics*, 20: 335–340 (1954); Eugene Jacobsen, "Methods Used for Producing Comparable Data in the O.C.S.R. Seven-Nation Attitude Studies," *Journal of Social Issues*, 10: 40–51 (1954); Stanley Schacter, "Interpretive and Methodological Problems of Replicated Research," *Journal of Social Issues*, 10: 52–60 (1954); Haim Blanc, "Multilingual Interviewing in Israel," *American Journal of Sociology*, 62 (2): 205–209 (1956); Bradford Hudson, *et al.*, "Introduction: Problems and Methods of Cross-Cultural Research," [Bradford Hudson (ed.), Cross-cultural Studies in the Arab Middle East and United States: studies of young adults], *Journal of Social Issues*, 15 (3): 1–4 (1959); Herbert P. Phillips, "Problems of Translation and Meaning in Fieldwork," *Human Organization*, 18: 184-192 (1959–60), reprinted in R. H. Adams and J. Preiss (eds.), *Human Organization Research, Field Relations and Techniques* (Homewood, Ill.: Dorsey Press, 1961), pp. 290–307; Florence R. Kluckhohn, "A Method for Eliciting Value Orientations," *Anthropological Linguistics*, 2 (2) 1–23 (1960); Raymond Fink, "Interviewer Training and Supervision in a Survey of Laos," [Alain Girard (ed.), Opinion Surveys in Developing Countries], *International Social Science Journal*, 15 (1): 21–34 (1963); Emily L. Jones, "The Courtesy Bias in South-East Asian Surveys," *International Social Science Journal*, 15 (1): 70–76 (1963); Gabrielle Wuelker, "Questionnaires in Asia," *International Social Science Journal*, 15 (1): 35–47 (1963); William H. Hunt, Wilder W. Crane, and John C. Wahlke, "Interviewing Political Elites in Cross-Cultural Comparative Research," *American Journal of Sociology*, 70 (1): 59–68 (1964); Robert E. Mitchell, "Survey Materials Collected in the Developing Countries: Sampling, Measurement, and Obstacles to Intra- and International Comparisons," *International Social Science Journal*, 17 (4): 665–685 (1965); Howard Schuman, "The Random Probe: a Technique for Evaluating the Validity of Closed Questions," *American Sociological Review*, 31 (2): 218–222 (1966). Phillips' article contains a useful survey of the literature on translation. A bibliography of work on translation is given in my *Language in Culture and Society* (New York: Harper and Row, 1964), pp. 98–100. See also C. F. and F. M. Voegelin, "Anthropological Linguistics and Translation," *To Honor Roman Jakobson*, 2159–2190 (The Hague: Mouton, 1967).

52. Cf., the discussion by Deutscher in Becker, Reisman, Weiss, and Geer (eds.), *op. cit.*, of "friend" *Freund: Bekannte, ami; connaissance, amigo:* "know" vs. *connaitre: savoir, kennen: wissen.*

53. These examples are from Blanc, *American Journal of Sociology*, 62: 208 and Hunt, *et al.*, *American Journal of Sociology*, 70: 66 by way of Deutscher.

54. Schacter, *Journal of Social Issues*, 10.

55. Anderson, *Sociometry*, 30.

56. Mitchell, *International Social Science Journal*, 17, 677–78, as quoted in Deutscher. Permission to quote granted by UNESCO.

57. Blanc, *American Journal of Sociology*, 62; Hudson, *et al.*, *Journal of Social Issues*, 15; Schacter, *Journal of Social Issues*, 10.

58. Aaron V. Cicourel, *Method and Measurement in Sociology* (New York: Free Press of Glencoe, 1964); "Fertility, Family Planning, and the Social Organization of Family Life: Some Methodological Issues," *Journal of Social Issues*, 23 (1967); Erving Goffman, "The Neglected Situation," in Gumperz and

Hymes, *The Ethnography of Communication* (Washington, D.C.: American Anthropological Association, 1964), pp. 133–136; Harold Garfinkel, "The Routine Grounds of Everyday Activities," *Social Problems*, 11: 225–250 (1964); *Studies in Ethnomethodology* (Englewood Cliffs, N.J.: Prentice-Hall, 1968). The article by Cicourel and some of the studies by Garfinkel are especially relevant as analyses of the methodological problems of survey research.

59. See n. 22, and articles in [John Macnamara (ed.), Problems of Bilingualism], *Journal of Social Issues*, 23 (2) (1967), especially Wallace E. Lambert, "The Social Psychology of Bilingualism," 91–109; and John Macnamara, "The Bilingual's Linguistic Performance: A Psychological Overview," 58–77. See also John B. Carroll, "Quelques Mesures Subjectives en Psychologie: Frequence des Mots, Significativité et Qualité de Traduction," *Bulletin de Pschologie*, 19: 580–92 (1966), discussed by Macnamara.

60. Cf. Ervin-Tripp on Navaho connotative judgments, in Hymes, *Studies in Southwestern Ethnolinguistics*.

61. See the article on Navaho connotative judgments by Ervin-Tripp (n, 30), and generally, Charles E. Osgood, "Semantic Differential Technique in the Comparative Study of Cultures," [A. Kimball Romney and Roy G. D'Andrade (eds.), Transcultural studies in cognition], *American Anthropologist*, 66 (3), Part 2 (1964).

62. As an introduction to the perspective underlying it, three articles may be especially recommended:
Ward H. Goodenough, "Cultural Anthropology and Linguistics," in Paul L. Garvin (ed.), *Report of the Seventh Annual Round Table Meeting on Linguistics and Language Study* (Washington, D.C.: Georgetown University Press, 1957), pp. 167–173 (reprinted in *LCS*, pp. 36–39); Charles O. Frake, "The Ethnographic Study of Cognitive Systems," in [Thomas Gladwin and W. C. Sturtevant (eds.)], *Anthropology and Human Behavior*, pp. 72–85; and W. C. Sturtevant, "Studies in Ethnoscience," [A. Kimball Romney and Roy G. D'Andrade (eds.), Transcultural Studies in Cognition], *American Anthropologist*, 66 (3), Part 2, pp. 99–131. More technical indications of what is done can be found in the following articles: Harold C. Conklin, "Lexicographical Treatment of Folk Taxonomies," in F. W. Householder, Jr. and Sol Saporta (eds.), *Problems in Lexicography* (Bloomington, Ind.: Research Center in Anthropology, Folklore and Linguistics, Publication 21, 1962): 119–141; "Ethnogenealogical Method," in W. Goodenough (ed.), *Explorations in Cultural Anthropology* (New York: McGraw-Hill, 1964), pp. 25–55; Frake, "The Diagnosis of Disease among the Subanun of Mindanao," *American Anthropologist*, 63: 113–132 (1961), reprinted in *LCS*, pp. 193–206. Additional information may be examined in contributions to a volume on formal semantic analysis edited by Hammel, including the essays by Leonard Pospisil, "A Formal Analysis of Substantive Law: Kapauka Papuan Laws of Land Tenure"; Roy G. D'Andrade, "Trait Psychology and Componential Analysis"; and Anthony F. C. Wallace, "The Problem of the Psychological Validity of Componential Analysis." Eugene A. Hammel (ed.), Formal Semantic Analysis, *American Anthropologist*, 67 (5), Part 2, (1965), pp. 186–214; 214–228, 229–248, respectively. Of special interest for the study of political behavior may be a methodological article by Black and Metzger on "Ethnographic Description and the Study of Law," in Laura Nader (ed.), *The Ethnography of Law*.

408

63. Edmund Glenn, "Semantic Differences in International Communication," *Etc.: A Review of General Semantics*, 11: 163–180 (1954).

64. See the work of Bernstein (cited in n. 30). See also my article, "On Communicative Competence," Report of the Planning Conference on Research Problems in the Study of the Language of Disadvantaged Children (New York: Yeshiva University, Ferkauf Graduate School, Department of Educational Psychology, 1967); this will appear in revised and expanded form as a volume published by the University of Pennsylvania Press.

65. George L. Trager, "Paralinguistics: A First Approximation," *Studies in Linguistics*, 13: 1–12 (1958), reprinted in *LCS*, pp. 274–279; Charles F. Hockett, "Ethnolinguistic Implications of Studies in Linguistics and Psychiatry," in W. Austin (ed.), *Report of the Ninth Annual Round Table Meeting of Linguistics and Language Study* (Washington, D.C.: Georgetown University Press, 1960), pp. 175–193; R. E. Pittenger and H. L. Smith, Jr., "A Basis for Some Contributions of Linguistics to Psychiatry," *Psychiatry*, 20: 61–78 (1957); Ray L. Birdwhistell, "Some Relations Between American Kinesics and Spoken English," in Alfred G. Smith (ed.), *Culture and Communication* (New York: Holt, Rinehart, and Winston, 1966), pp. 182–189; Edward T. Hall, *The Silent Language* (New York: Doubleday, 1964); *The Hidden Dimension* (New York: Doubleday, 1966); Adumbration as a Feature of Intercultural Communication, in Gumperz and Hymes, *The Ethnography of Communication*, pp. 154-163; Hall and William Foote Whyte, "Intercultural Communication: A Guide to Men of Action," *Human Organization*, 19: 5–12 (1960), reprinted in Smith, *Culture and Communication*, pp. 567–576.

66. "Models of the Interaction of Language and Social Setting," [John Macnamara (ed.), Problems of Bilingualism], *Journal of Social Issues*, 23 (2): 8–28 (1967); and cf. "The Ethnography of Speaking," in [T. Gladwin and W. C. Sturtevant (eds.)] *Anthropology and Human Behavior* (Washington, D.C.: Anthropological Society of Washington, 1962), pp. 13–53; "Directions in Ethno-linguistic Theory," [Romney and D'Andrade, Transcultural Studies of Cognition], *American Anthropologist*, 66 (3), Part 2 (1964), pp. 6–56; Introduction: Toward Ethnographies of Communication," [Gumperz and Hymes, The Ethnography of Communication] *American Anthropologist*, 66(6), Part 2 (1964) pp. 1–34.

67. Strauss and Schatzmann, *Human Organization*, 14.

68. Charles O. Frake, "How to Ask for a Drink in Subanum," [Gumperz and Hymes, The Ethnography of Communication] *American Anthropologist*, 66 (6), Part 2 (1964), pp. 127–132; Ethel Albert, " 'Rhetoric,' 'Logic,' and 'Poetics' in Burundi: Culture Patterning of Speech Behavior," [Gumperz and Hymes (eds.), The Ethnography of Communication], *American Anthropologist*, 66 (6), Part 2 (1964), pp. 35–54. See also papers by James Fernandez and James Peacock in June Helm (ed.), *Proceedings of the 1966 Spring Meeting of the American Ethnological Society* (Seattle: University of Washington Press, 1966).

69. Wuelker, *International Social Science Journal*, 15.

70. Margaret Mead, "Public Opinion Mechanisms Among Some Primitive Peoples," *Public Opinion Quarterly*, 1: 5–16 (1937); "Some Cultural Approaches to Communication Problems," in Lyman Bryson (ed.), *The Communication of Ideas* (New York: Harper, 1948), pp. 9–26; both discussed by F. M. Keesing

409

and Marie M. Keesing, *Elite Communication in Samoa: A Study in Leadership* (Stanford: Stanford University Press, 1956), pp. 276–279; Frederick Barth, "Ethnic Processes in the Pathan-Baluchi Boundary," in Indo-Iranica: *Mélanges présenté à George Morgenstiern à l'occasion de son soixante dixième anniversaire* (Weisbaden: Otto Harrassowitz, 1964), pp. 13–20; Leonard Doob, *Communication in Africa, A Search for Boundaries* (New Haven: Yale University Press, 1961).

71. Hall, *The Silent Language*.

72. This argument is developed in the articles cited in n. 52 and n. 54.

73. Williams, *Culture and Society*, p. 357 (cited in n. 5).

74. Orwell, as cited in n. 9; references to German and the Greeks are mentioned in my "Directions in Ethno-Linguistic Theory" (n. 66), p. 37; cf. Herbert Luthy, "In Search of Indonesia," *New York Review of Books*, 6 (9): 4–6 (May 26, 1966); on function and clarity, cf. Pieter A. Verburg, *Taal et Functionaliteit* (Wegeningen, The Netherlands: Veenan and Sons, 1952), and "Delosis and Clarity," *Philosophy and Christianity* (Kampen, The Netherlands: J. H. Kok, 1966), pp. 1–22.

75. Note here the critical analysis of survey research by Cicourel, *Method and Measurement in Sociology*.

8. Diachronic Methods in Comparative Politics *(343-358)*

SYLVIA L. THRUPP

1. Stein Rokkan, "Trends and Possibilities in Comparative Social Science," *Social Sciences Information*, IV (December, 1965), offprinted as Publication no. 226 of the Chr. Michelsen Institute.

2. *Ibid.*, p. 17.

3. S. N. Eisenstadt, "The Study of Processes of Institutionalization, Institutional Change, and Comparative Institutions," in his *Essays on Comparative Institutions* (New York: Wiley & Sons, 1965), pp. 3–68.

4. Stein Rokkan, *op. cit.*, p. 11.

5. Aidan Southall, "A Critique of the Typology of States and Political Systems," in *Political Systems and the Distribution of Power*, A.S.A. Monographs 12 (1965), pp. 113–137.

6. Marshall D. Sahlins, *Social Stratification in Polynesia* (Seattle: University of Washington Press, 1958), and "Poor Man, Rich Man, Big-Man, Chief: Political Types in Melanesia and Polynesia," *Comparative Studies in Society and History*, V (April, 1963), 285–304.

7. Southall, *op. cit.*, p. 131.

8. Rokkan, *op. cit.*, p. 12.

9. See Fritz Redlich, "Toward Comparative Historiography," *Kyklos*, 11 (1958), pp. 361–389, and Erich Hrothacker, *Logik und Systematik der Geisteswissenschaften* (Bonn, 1948), ch. 3.

10. See Claude Lévi-Strauss, *La Pensée Sauvage* (Paris: Plon, 1962), Ch. 1.

410

11. The reference is also to those especially responsive to myth, who would be among the "intellectuals" as defined in Edward Shils, "The Intellectuals and the Powers: Some Perspectives for Comparative Analysis," *Comparative Studies in Society and History*, I (1958-1959), 5–22.

12. *Averroës' Commentary on Plato's Republic*, tr. and ed. by E. I. J. Rosenthal (Cambridge University Press, 1950), pp. 111–112.

13. For a recent assessment of Herodotus, see M. I. Finley (ed.), *The Greek Historians* (New York: Viking Press, 1959), pp. 1–7.

14. J. G. A. Pocock, "The Origins of Study of the Past: A Comparative Approach," in *Comparative Studies in Society and History*, IV (1962), 209–246.

15. See Donald F. Lach, *Asia in the Making of the West*, Vol. I, Books I and II, *Century of Discovery* (University of Chicago Press), 1964.

16. Thomas Arnold, edition of *Thucydides*, Vol. I, 2nd ed. (Oxford, 1840), appendix I, pp. 503 ff.

17. Thomas Arnold, *Lectures in Modern History*, edited from the 2nd London edition by H. Reed (New York: Appleton, 1845), pp. 47–48.

18. W. R. W. Stephens, *The Life and Letters of Edward A. Freeman* (1895), I, 121–124.

19. Edward A. Freeman, *Comparative Politics* (New York, 1874), Ch. 1.

20. Stephens, *op. cit.*, II, 231 (letter to Tylor); two earlier letters to Tylor, *ibid.*, pp. 57, 77. Freeman, who in 1881 lectured in the United States, was uneasy in the presence of Negroes; he wrote to a friend, "This would be a grand land if only every Irishman would kill a negro and be hanged for it." *Ibid.*, p. 242.

21. Joseph Needham, *Time and Eastern Man* (London: Royal Anthropological Institute, 1965), p. 44; for a review of work now in progress on African history, see A. D. Low, "Studying the Transformation of Africa," *Comparative Studies in Society and History*, VII (1964), 21–36.

22. For elaboration of this point, Reinhard Bendix, "Modernization and Inequality," *Comparative Studies in Society and History*, IX, no. 3 (April, 1967).

23. Bibliography relevant to this section is obtainable in mimeographed form as "Bibliography on problems and examples of comparative study in history," from the secretary of the Department of History, University of Michigan, Ann Arbor.

24. See S. N. Eisenstaft, *op. cit.*, pp. 275–304, for sociological comment.

25. For some examples, see Julian Pitt-Rivers, "Honour and Social Status," in J. G. Peristiany (ed.), *Honour and Shame: The Values of Mediterranean Society* (1966), pp. 19–78.

26. Carl J. Friedrich, "Some General Theoretical Reflections on the Problems of Political Data," at p. 58 in Richard L. Merritt and Stein Rokkan (eds.), *Comparing Nations: The Use of Quantitative Data in Cross-National Research*, 1966. For one political historian's reflections, William O. Aydelotte, "Quantification in History," *American Historical Review*, LXXI (April, 1966), 803–825.

27. Evidenced in Oscar Handlin and John Burchard (eds.), *The Historian and the City* (Cambridge: M.I.T. and Harvard University Press, 1963).

28. For historical evidence of this kind from Venice, Daniele Beltrame, *Storia della popolazione di Venezia dalla caduta della republica* (Padua, 1954).

29. Sylvia L. Thrupp, "A Working Alliance among Specialists: Comparative Studies in Society and History," *International Journal of Social Science*, XVII (1965), 696–709.

30. Harold D. Lasswell, *The Future of Political Science* (New York, Atherton Press, 1963), pp. 231–233.

Author Index

413

Author Index

414

Subject Index